Learning Through Language in Early Childhood

# Open Linguistics Series

*Series Editor*
Robin Fawcett, University of Wales, Cardiff

This series is 'open' in two senses. First, it provides a forum for works associated with any school of linguistics or with none. Most practising linguists have long since outgrown the unhealthy assumption that theorizing about language should be left to those working in the generativist-formalist paradigm. Today large and increasing numbers of scholars are seeking to understand the nature of language by exploring one or other of various cognitive models of language, or in terms of the communicative use of language, or both. This series is playing a valuable part in re-establishing the traditional 'openness' of the study of language. The series includes many studies that are in, or on the borders of, various functional theories of language, and especially, (because it has been the most widely used of these) Systemic Functional Linguistics. The general trend of the series has been towards a functional view of language, but this simply reflects the works that have been offered to date. The series continues to be open to all approaches, including works in the generativist-formalist tradition.

The second way in which the series is 'open' is that it encourages studies that open out 'core' linguistics in various ways: to encompass discourse and the description of natural texts; to explore the relationships between linguistics and its neighbouring disciplines – psychology, sociology, philosophy, cultural and literary studies – and to apply it in fields such as education, language pathology and law.

Relations between linguistics and artificial intelligence are covered in a sister series, Communication in Artificial Intelligence. Studies that are primarily descriptive are published in a new series, Functional Descriptions of Language.

*Recently published titles in the series:*

*Thematic Development in English Texts*, ed. Mohsen Ghadessy

*Ways of Saying: Ways of Meaning: Selected Papers of Ruqaiya Hasan*, eds Carmel Cloran, David Butt and Geoffrey Williams

*Language Policy in Britain and France: The Processes of Policy*, Dennis Ager

*Genre and Institutions: Social Processes in the Workplace and School*, eds Frances Christie and J.R. Martin

*Educating Eve: The 'Language Instinct' Debate*, Geoffrey Sampson

*Summary Justice: Judges Address Juries*, Paul Robertshaw

*Pedagogy and the Shaping of Consciousness: Linguistic and Social Processes*, ed. Frances Christie

# Learning Through Language in Early Childhood

Clare Painter

**CONTINUUM**
London ◆ New York

**Continuum**
The Tower Building
11 York Road
London SE1 7NX

370 Lexington Avenue
New York
NY 10017-6550

First published 1999
Reprinted 2001

**British Library Cataloguing-in-Publication Data**
A catalogue record for this book is available from the British Library
ISBN 0-304-70056-8 HB
ISBN 0-8264-5450-X PB

Typeset by Textype Typesetters, Cambridge
Printed and bound in Great Britain by Bookcraft (Bath) Ltd,
Midsomer Norton, Somerset

# Contents

# Preface

For children of many different literate societies, all over the world, the age of 5 to 7 years heralds the beginning of their formal education. At this point in their lives they are deemed ready to undertake learning within an institutional setting, in line with a common intuition that some kind of developmental watershed has been reached. While there are doubtless a number of factors which could be proposed as relevant to our feeling that a 5-year-old is 'ready' for schooling, a significant one must relate to our perceptions of the child's stage of cognitive development. The theme of this book is that this cognitive readiness can be explained in terms of crucial linguistic developments and experiences, particularly in the years between the ages of 3 and 5.

In reflecting on children's readiness for school, we cannot but recognize that the key characteristic of learning within the setting of the institution is that it will be dominated by language. At the outset, it will involve learning to use language in a new (i.e. written) medium, but quite apart from the achievement of initial literacy itself, everything else the child is learning will be accessed through language: from the construal of new symbol systems (mathematics, music) to the construal of the various bodies of 'knowledge' formalized within the culture. In addition, all the evidence for the child's success or failure in acquiring new knowledge is provided by his or her spoken and written discourse. Given all this, there are strong grounds for arguing that learning cannot fruitfully be considered apart from languaging, and that developments in learning, whether conceived of in terms of cognitive skills or knowledge acquisition, will also constitute developments in language.

These thoughts prompted the longitudinal case study of informal learning through language presented in this book. It is an account of one child's development and use of language between the ages of 30 months and 5 years, in which the enterprise of making sense of the world is seen to provide the impetus for linguistic developments, which in turn enable further conceptual development. The case study suggests strongly that in this pre-school period there are a number of key developments in the language which, taken together, constitute changes in conceptual resources which are highly relevant to the child's pending move into school education.

The case study itself forms Chapters 3 to 6 of the book, each taking a different facet of the experiential world that the child is coming to understand and exploring how language is used in its construal. Chapter 3 takes the world of things, Chapter 4 the world of events, Chapter 5 the interior realm of thinking and its external face as saying, while Chapter 6 looks at relations of cause and effect. The case study is oriented to describing how the developing language functioned for the child in the service of interpreting these facets of experience.

The linguistic descriptions provided are underpinned by the theoretical framework of systemic-functional linguistics (SFL), as developed by M.A.K. Halliday (e.g. 1978a, 1994) and J.R. Martin (1992a). SFL is chosen as a linguistic theory whose particular orientations allow it to be seen simultaneously as the basis for a theory of learning. This is a position which will be argued in Chapter 2, following a consideration of various alternative and/or complementary theoretical approaches with which the book opens. By the final chapter, the findings of the case study can be summarized in terms of both the linguistic developments which have taken place up to 5 years of age and how they prepare the child cognitively for school learning.

The goals of the research reported here are both descriptive and theoretical. On the one hand, the account of language development, based on a rich, naturalistic, longitudinal data set, collected during the third, fourth and fifth years of the child's life, adds to the picture of children's language provided in the literature, including earlier SFL case studies of younger children (e.g. Halliday 1975, Painter 1984, Oldenburg 1987, Torr 1998). On the other hand, the account is framed in terms of the non-linguistic understandings being construed so as to argue the thesis that learning is a linguistic enterprise and that 'cognitive' processes, such as classifying, generalizing, inferring and reasoning, can most usefully be considered as semiotic processes observable on occasions of language in use.

# 1 The ontogenesis of language and learning: a survey of approaches

This book will examine one child's language development from the perspective of how the language grows in response to being used as a tool for learning about the world. Since a dialectical relation is proposed between the learning of language and the learning of other things, the study needs to be located with respect to both language acquisition research and strands of research in developmental psychology. This chapter will therefore outline a variety of approaches to the development of language and/or thought, as a background against which the theoretical perspective informing this research – that of systemic-functional linguistics – can be presented and understood. The literature to be discussed here has been grouped into two main sections, those approaches which focus on the individual in relation to the universal character of language and thought and those which focus on the social-interactive character of language and learning.

## 1 Universalist/individualist approaches to the development of language and thought

There is a wealth of literature which addresses the ontogenesis of language and thought within essentially universalist frameworks. These concern themselves with unchanging, common properties of the human mind and of language, construing the latter 'monologically' in terms of the individual's knowledge rather than 'dialogically' as an interpersonal system. Three main approaches will be considered here: first that of mainstream American linguistic theory; then a less theoretically cohesive body of psycholinguistic research that has investigated early language development and its relation to conceptual development; and finally the developmental psychological theory of Jean Piaget.

### 1.1 Linguistics and language acquisition

Within twentieth-century linguistics, the area of 'language acquisition' was made a central concern by Chomsky in the 1960s when he postulated that every child possesses an innate language faculty, as an autonomous component of the mind. This component was said to specify a 'Universal Grammar' (Chomsky 1976: 36) – a kind of innate universal blueprint to which the syntax of any particular language would conform. On the basis of this Universal Grammar (UG), the language faculty constructs the grammar of the particular language found in the child's environment, such a grammar taking the form of 'a finite algebraic system that can "generate" an infinite range of expressions' (Lightfoot 1991: 4).

One characteristic of this approach is that it draws a sharp distinction between 'competence' and 'performance', that is, between knowing a language and using it:

> The language faculty creates a grammar that generates sentences . . . We say that a person knows the language generated by this grammar. Employing other related faculties of mind . . . he can then proceed to use the language that he now knows. (Chomsky 1976: 36)

The knowledge/use duality authorizes linguists to concern themselves solely with the former, also called 'internalized language' (Chomsky 1986: 22), and to ignore all aspects of language as a phenomenon of human social life. In this way it becomes unremarkable to describe a grammar as 'usable for such purposes as speech production and comprehension' (Lightfoot 1991: 3), as though these were optional and somewhat incidental and marginal aspects of the phenomenon. The idealization of the object of study as 'internalized language' reflects Chomsky's motivation for concerning himself with language at all, which is to 'discover abstract principles that govern [the mind's] structure and use, principles that are universal by biological necessity' (1976: 4). For him, the commonality of human thought is assumed and poses the following question for science:

> How comes it that human beings with such limited and personal experience achieve such convergence in rich and highly structured systems of belief . . . ? (Chomsky 1976: 5)

His answer to this question is to look to the universal structure of the human mind including the 'component' that is human language, though it should be noted that these are construed without reference to their neurophysiological embodiment.

In the thirty years or so since Chomsky presented his 'innateness hypothesis', many linguistic theories have come and gone, including his own theory of the time, transformational-generative grammar. But neither the kind of formalist linguistics espoused by him, nor the centrality of innateness (nativism) as an issue within such theories, has lost favour. As with Chomsky, the current interest in language acquisition by American linguists is unrelated to any more general interest in child development. The goal rather is that theorizing about language acquisition should provide criteria by which to evaluate competing models of abstract representations of English syntax, or to identify what the form of the proposed innate UG might be. An 'idealized' child is simply equated with a 'language acquisition device' (Williams 1987: ix), having the task of applying hypotheses and principles to sample utterances as a means of generalizing to 'the correct infinite set [of sentences] that defines the adult language' (Pinker 1986: 54). Questions of interest within this paradigm concern the innate 'principles' (Wexler 1982), 'parameters' (Lightfoot 1991) or 'constraints' (Behrend 1990) which will enable a child to form correct hypotheses about the mother tongue.

To construct the appropriate grammar in line with UG principles, the child needs some exposure to speech, but it is assumed that only a minimal kind of 'triggering' input is sufficient:

> We may persist with the idea that the trigger consists of nothing more than a haphazard set of utterances in an appropriate context. (Lightfoot 1991: 13–14)

In the terms of this theory, language used in the child's social environment is haphazard and 'degenerate' (Lightfoot 1991: 3) because it lacks any overt information on disallowed forms, and without this no learner could correctly hypothesize the kind of abstract formal grammar proposed.

Given all this, the key issue for language acquisition research has become that of 'learnability', of solving the 'logical problem' of language acquisition in the face of inadequate input data, as discussed in Baker and McCarthy 1991, Saleemi 1992, Crain 1993 and elsewhere. A frequently cited example of a linguistic generalization unavailable to the child from speech data concerns the relationship between certain English declaratives and corresponding interrogatives (see e.g. Cook and Newson 1996: 8–10, Gleitman 1986: 11, Lightfoot 1991: 3–4). Gleitman, for example, explains that an English interrogative sentence made up of two clauses involves 'fronting' of the auxiliary verb of the *main* clause. For example, *Is the man who is a fool amusing?* and not * *Is the man is a fool who amusing?* She argues:

> The important point here is that it is hard to conceive how the environment literally gives the required information to the learner. Surely only the correct sentences, not the incorrect ones, appear in the input data. But the generalization required for producing new correct sentences is not directly presented, for no hierarchy of clauses appears in real utterances – only a string of words is directly observable to the listener. And certainly there is no instruction about clauses. Even if mothers knew something explicit about these matters, which they do not, it would not do much good for them to tell the aspiring learners that 'It's the *is* in the higher clause that moves'.

In a similar way, Lightfoot (1991: 4) notes:

> Children are not systematically informed that certain forms do not exist, or that they are 'ungrammatical', and so the crucial evidence – the nonoccurrence of

forms like [*is the book which on the shelf is dull?] – is not contained in normal childhood experience.

On this reasoning, it becomes necessary to account for the above examples by positing an innate principle of 'structure-dependence' which guides children to perform formal operations in a way that respects grammatical structures. The formalist view of language as an abstract algebra and the accompanying conception of the learning task as one of working out just what is permissible among the myriad of formal possibilities inevitably make the whole business of language acquisition appear mysterious and impossible unless one grants that the individual possesses an innate grammar.

However, exploring this particular example in the light of child language data makes matters less mysterious. There is no question that children are able to assemble and reassemble items into structures long before using multi-clause questions. The understanding of the hierarchical nature of the constituent structure of language is after all the achievement of the 'two-word period'. This understanding is not one that the child has to come to when beginning to use questions containing embedded clauses. On the contrary, any child will have spent months or years interpreting and using language on the basis of gradually accumulated understandings about its constituent structure, before any such interrogatives are essayed (see Chapter 3 for some accounts of one child's use of embeddings). Moreover, the language development literature abounds in descriptions of children who plainly shift from treating 'pieces' of input as unanalysed chunks initially, to disassembling and reassembling the parts into structures (e.g. Brown 1973: 399, Peters 1983). Given the data available, the assertion that by the time the child is considering the more complex sentence types, s/he has available only an input accessible in terms of 'a string of words' cannot be accepted as a compelling argument for assuming an *innate* cognitive principle that language is configurational.

Attending to empirical data on children's changing speech patterns, however, has not been a feature of linguistic work on language acquisition. This is because 'the issue of learnability, as formulated and used in Language Acquisition, does not require looking at acquisition data' (Ingram 1989: 29). As argued in one of the standard texts:

> We are . . . under no obligation to pay special attention to child grammars . . .
> Idealizing to 'instantaneous' acquisition, i.e. ignoring data about developmental stages for the moment, does not seem to us to introduce significant distortions.
> (Hornstein and Lightfoot 1981: 30, note 8)

Thus, while some linguists working within the UG framework do see the relevance of investigating 'intermediate grammars' based on child language data (e.g. Hyams 1986), the principle of idealizing to instantaneous acquisition has led many to support their arguments with constructed example sentences, sometimes accompanied by intuitions about their plausibility in an input corpus.

Lack of concern with child language data is often matched by an equal lack of interest in research which has addressed itself to investigating such data. This is evident from the way problems in language learning are conceived and discussed. One example given by Gleitman concerns the problem a child will have at the beginning of the language acquisition process. She suggests a situation where a mother says *rabbit jumps* on observing a rabbit jumping, and argues that if the child believes that things are nouns, then that child

> can suppose English is a noun or subject-first language, in which case *rabbit* is the required noun; or he can suppose English is a verb or predicate-first language, in which case *rabbit* is the required verb. Given all this, it's hard to know how the child gets started. (Gleitman 1986: 20)

This view of the problems of getting started in language learning appears to be uninformed by the wealth of work in developmental psychology and functional linguistics of the 1970s, such as Newson's (1978), Brazelton and Tronick's (1980), and Trevarthen and Hubley's (1978, Trevarthen 1980) work on intersubjectivity, Ninio and Bruner's (1978) work on early naming, the research of Dore (1975) and Bates (1976) on early speech acts, Bloom's (1973) study of the one-word stage and Halliday's (1975, 1979a) account of the protolanguage phase and subsequent transition into language. Familiarity with such work (to be discussed below in Section 2.1) would make it clear that interpreting a phrase like *rabbit jumps* should not be seen as where the child gets started at all.

An even more thoroughgoing version of the theory that language structure itself is innate comes from Bickerton (1982, 1984) who has argued that some children have no input data at all. Bickerton (1982) claims that research into adult-infant linguistic interaction as a means of understanding language learning is necessarily irrelevant, because there are particular generations of children in history who could not have learned language in such a way. These are 'the first generation' of human language users, and the first generation of speakers of a creole. His argument is that these speakers must have relied upon an innate 'bioprogram' which determined the form of language which emerged. Given the fact that we have no recorded text data available in either case, Bickerton's argument has rested heavily on other sources of evidence. These are the alleged syntactic similarity between different creoles with different parentages and the alleged dissimilarity between creoles and their parent languages.

The validity of one or both of these claims has been contested by other creolists (e.g. Foley 1984, Goodman 1984, Samarin 1984, Seuren 1984), but whatever the facts of the creole situations Bickerton refers to, there is no logical necessity to assume that language could only have arisen in the first place through an innate bioprogram which specifies particular abstract syntactic structures. Foley (1984) argues that because the genetic encoding of adaptive change lags very far behind the actual implementation of the changes (Bateson 1978), any genetic encoding of language must anyway have happened much later than the first acquisition. Thus, he concludes, 'hundreds of generations must have acquired language without a genetic program' (Foley 1984: 343). And a plausible account of how those early generations may have done so is offered by Halliday on the basis of an analogy with the observed evolution of symbolizing in the individual.

According to Halliday's (1989: 8–9) account,

> language would have begun in the form of a small number of signs for expressing general meanings relating to the needs of human beings in their relations with others: meanings such as 'give me' (some object), 'do (some service) for me', 'behave (in a certain way) for me', and also 'be together with me', 'come and look (at this) with me', 'I like (that)', 'I'm curious (about that)', 'I don't like (that)', and so on. The essential function of the symbol is that of sharing: shared action, or shared reflection.

He then goes on to argue that these signs could have evolved into names:

> Then (following the model of the child), particular (individual) persons and particular (classes of) objects come to be associated in regular, repetitive contexts with general meanings of this kind. So a particular sign evolves as 'I want to be together **with you**' and that becomes a name of a person or a kin relationship; another evolves as 'give me (a particular kind of) food', and so becomes the word for food, or some class of edible things; another as 'I'm curious about (the animal that's making) **that noise**', and so becomes the name of the animal species; and so on.

The development of language described here, where general vocal symbols (with general meanings of demanding and expressing curiosity or reaction and the like) evolve into names, matches Halliday's (1975) description of the ontogenetic development of language, which will be discussed further in Chapter 2. It has recently been echoed in Aitchison's contention that ontogeny correlates with phylogeny in the gradual development of the 'naming insight' following earlier simple communicative signs (Aitchison 1996). More importantly it is also compatible with recent biological theory on the evolution of mind and language, which finds the view of language as hard-wired into the brain to be 'not in accord with the known facts of human biology and brain science' (Edelman 1992: 211, 228).

Halliday's suggestions on phylogenetic human symbol development stand in stark contrast to Bickerton's more recent account, which also draws on child language data to hypothesize about phylogenesis – in his case to argue that language is a universal inbuilt cognitive structure. Bickerton (1990) insists that language did not evolve initially as a communicative system but as a 'system of representation' of the properties of the world. He thus looks no earlier than the one-word stage of children's speech as exemplifying the evolutionary transition between no language and language, arguing that since the shift to true language in the child is abrupt and without intermediate stages, so the evolutionary transition must have been sudden – the result of a single mutation. Quite apart from the fact that the evidence he provides – a few dozen utterances from two separate points in the child's development – can hardly prove his point, Bickerton's *a priori* privileging of the representational function of language ignores longstanding criticism of this position from child language researchers (e.g. Bruner 1975, Bates and MacWhinney 1979, Painter 1984). Adopting the stance he does means that he is never led to explore the ontogenesis of the symbols used in the single-word stage and thus to address evidence for the communicative beginnings of linguistic development.

Ultimately, the claims about language acquisition made by linguists arguing for innate universal grammar derive from their premises about language. While specific pieces of evidence in favour of UG can be challenged piecemeal, the claims for it are in the end unconvincing to the extent that the basic conceptions about language are not accepted. If language is not construed in terms of the specified properties of an infinite array of sentences, if the primary function is not construed as that of mirroring the observed world, if it is not seen as desirable to dichotomize between knowledge of language and its use and to ignore the latter, then the case for UG will not appear a strong one. It will appear even less compelling if adult speech to children is not considered to be a deficient and degenerate sample and if human belief and knowledge are not seen as strikingly similar across different cultures.

So while Chomskyan linguists apparently believe that 'We must all be nativists of some sort by now; the arguments developed by Chomsky and his associates . . . and by Fodor in philosophy of language have carried the day' (Atkinson 1992:2), their arguments in fact 'carry the day' only among those who are prepared to accept all their questionable premises, premises which one philosopher of language has recently characterized as 'initial missteps . . . so destructive and far reaching that, once taken, they make it impossible to achieve a coherent theory of language' (Ellis 1993: 15).

Because the nativists characterize language as an abstract representation of syntactic structures, universal to humankind and inborn, requiring only minimal or no triggering data in order for the mature form of a specific language to emerge, they are not led to explore questions relating to the role language plays in the life of the developing child. And clearly theories building upon these premises are ill-suited to address questions of interest to educators, such as the way language might develop or fail to develop as a response to educational praxis, or how it might be implicated in children's varying success in acquiring knowledge in school, or how children's early experience of language at home constitutes a preparation for formal instruction.

Indeed, the way language is frequently characterized in terms of a set of sentence structures has encouraged the idea that language acquisition is complete before children reach school age:

> By about 4 years of age the speaker sounds essentially adult, though his sentences tend to be quite short because the use of embeddings is limited . . .
> (Gleitman 1986: 6)

Such a view, which regards discourse from a pre-schooler as 'essentially' indistinguishable from adult discourse, clearly removes entirely from the educational agenda any issue of language development as a responsibility of the school during the period when literacy is developed and the knowledge of specialized disciplines is confronted through language.

Thus, it can be seen that the major approaches to language acquisition from within mainstream linguistic theory are premised upon certain axioms about language (and learning) which preclude them from raising, let alone answering, any questions related to the way language is developed in the processes of learning.

## 1.2 Language and thinking: psycholinguistic approaches

Although, as discussed above, most linguists who write about language acquisition have given no priority to investigating the speech of young children, this is by no means a neglected area of research. On the contrary, children's early talk has been of particular interest to developmental psychologists as a means of examining the relationship between the acquisition of language and the acquisition of concepts. The researchers being grouped here do not share any single theoretical position in relation to either psychology or linguistics, but have tended to agree on the general nature of that relationship. Whereas Chomskyan linguists stress that some kind of universal grammar is a quite distinct cognitive structure, the psycholinguists have generally preferred the position that language (or a language) develops in order to encode cognitive categories. The question of whether the cognitive categories are innate or learned is then a separate matter for debate, on which different stands are taken. The position can be seen as similar to the linguists' in that linguistic and non-linguistic aspects of cognition are distinguished, but it is fundamentally different in that the two are seen as related, with conceptual development most commonly regarded as a necessary precursor of language development.

This view has been articulated, for example, in Bloom's (1993) study of initial word learning, in which she defines language as 'a system of expression', designed 'for taking the internal, personal, private mental meanings of individuals and making them external and public' (Bloom 1993:19). Here, meaning is unequivocally located in the mental realm external to language and language is viewed as an expression form for non-linguistic thoughts. This is a position which has been pervasive in the language acquisition literature coming from developmental cognitive psychology, as can be seen in the metaphors used for discussing language acquisition, particularly that of 'mapping' language onto a non-linguistic representation of knowledge:

> It could be the case that words map directly onto the child's cognitive representations. (Barrett 1986: 65)

> It is often argued that words must map onto concepts that have already been worked out nonlinguistically. (Markman 1989: 36)

> Children could begin by mapping words onto preestablished conceptual categories. (Clark 1991: 60)

A variation on this is the image of elements of language as material capable of 'attachment' to concepts:

> Conceptual theories assume that the child attaches a language term to one of his concepts. (Nelson and Lucariello 1985: 69)

> . . . the traditional child language 'mapping problem': how children attach the forms of language to what they know about objects, events and relations in the world. (Bloom 1993: 21-2)

> [Words] are attached to either object concepts or to actions and relations. (Dromi 1993b: 57)

Particularly with respect to the literature on lexical development, there has been variation and sometimes ambiguity as to whether the extralinguistic meaning to which language is 'attached' consists of material reality (Greenfield and Smith 1976, Waxman 1990: 143), perceptual constructs (Clark 1973), or concepts (e.g. Slobin 1973, Johnston 1985, Nelson and Lucariello 1985), as well as considerable debate about the way concepts are formed and stored. (See Merriman 1986, Dromi 1987, 1993a for reviews of approaches here.) But until recently a uniform trend has been to see language as mirroring some prior reality, concept or meaning outside of itself and for that reality or meaning to be viewed either as given or as formulated before language arises. There is a compatibility here with formalist linguistic theories in the exclusive focus on the representational function of language, in the assumption that what is to be represented is universal in character and in the view of language as form rather than meaning.

Twenty years ago Bruner could claim this to be the consensus view, citing researchers working within various psychological paradigms:

> The work of Sinclair de Zwart (1967), of Roger Brown (1977) of Katherine Nelson (1978), and more recently of Rosch (1973) and of Anglin (1977) argues overwhelmingly that the child sorts out his universe conceptually into categories and classes, is able to make distinctions about actions and agents and objects before he has the language for making those distinctions in speech. 'The concept is . . . there beforehand, waiting for the word to come along that names it' (Brown 1977). It still remains a mystery how the child penetrates the communicative system and learns how to represent in language what he already knows in the real world – i.e. conceptually. (Bruner 1978: 245)

However, even then, the consensus was not total and there have always been arguments from among the ranks of cognitive psychologists themselves (e.g. Schlesinger 1977, Gopnik and Meltzoff 1986, Nelson 1991b) that in fact language may have a role to play in shaping, rather than just expressing, cognition, and that what is to be cognized is not simply available ready-structured for the child to perceive. Schlesinger (1977), for example, mounts a case against 'cognitive determinism' on the grounds that categories such as the case roles of 'agent' or 'affected' could not be inferred from extralinguistic experience. He exemplifies this by suggesting that the experiences of Mummy giving a bottle, Mummy holding a bottle and a bottle holding milk are events with various interpretations of agency possible, while those of the child bumping a wall or sitting on a bed will not reveal whether or not bed and wall should be understood, and therefore expressed linguistically, as 'affected'. He also points out that the way these roles are construed by different languages is in any case too varied for it to be reasonable to assume that they are cognitively sorted out before language is used. (See Painter 1984: 7–8 for a similar argument.)

More recently qualifications to a strict cognitive determinism have been expressed more frequently by psycholinguists (e.g. Gelman and Coley 1991, Bowerman 1993). However, their reservations tend to be based on doubts as to whether empirical data on children's speech and comprehension can be said to confirm the position, rather than from theoretical misgivings about the conception of language implied. Consequently the view of language as a form of expression for some non-semiotic order of reality still prevails in work such as that of Bloom (1993), or Johnston (1985), who asserts that 'unless language is viewed as potential nonsense, conceptual notions must be acquired prior to their verbal expression' (p. 963). Yet this view of language fundamentally contradicts the principles of the most widely known theory of the linguistic sign – that put forward by Saussure at the beginning of the century.

Saussure argued that a sign has two components – a 'signifier' and a 'signified' – which are generally glossed as 'sound image' and 'concept image' respectively. While these glosses offer a duality that can be readily appropriated by the view that signifiers (read as words) stand for signifieds (read as non-linguistic concepts), this would be a misunderstanding. It is the conjunction of the signifier and the signified which constitutes the sign, and it is the sign, comprising both the signifier and signified, which may 'stand for' or denote something external to itself. Saussure's point is precisely that a linguistic sign such as a name is two-faced – the expression in sound, such as /haʊs/, and the concept 'house' being mutually delimiting. Saussure (1978: 112) describes a linguistic sign as serving 'as a link between the uncharted morass of thought and sound so that there is necessarily a reciprocal delimitation of units'. And since the expression image and the conceptual image are mutually constitutive, there is no distinction implied between constructing a lexical class and a conceptual one – it must amount to the same thing.

Moreover, conceptual meaning in semiotic theory involves at least two aspects: that of value (sense) and signification (denotation). The value of a signified lies in its meaning as defined by its relation to other signs in the system. Thus at the simplest level, the meaning of *cottage* has to be understood in relation to *terrace, townhouse, semi, villa, mansion*, etc. The signification of a name, on the other hand, concerns its referential or denotational function: what counts as examples of objects, qualities or actions belonging to the class represented by the name. This is the aspect of meaning most transparent to us in general, but a key point of Saussure's argument is that this denotational or signifying relation is itself determined by the value relations between names. (That is to say, without knowing the 'house' paradigm we cannot be sure of the signification of any name belonging to it such as *cottage* or *villa*.)

Without a perspective on value relations, language acquisition theorists will not be led to explore meaning in terms of oppositions inhering within the child's language at any point. Instead they will speak of 'correct mapping' of linguistic forms and will require adult language forms as evidence that meanings are being encoded. For example, Slobin (1973), in a classic paper, looks for evidence that his Hungarian subject is encoding locational meaning in the child's production of the prepositions of the adult language. However, when children's linguistic systems are analysed in terms of their own value relations, the speakers can be seen to realize some semantic distinctions in formally different ways from the adult language. For example, the child subject described in Painter 1984 at first constructed locational meanings using nouns such as *garden, chair, drawer* rather than prepositional phrases such as *to the garden, on the chair, in the drawer*. Evidence that these locational nominals constituted a distinct class lay not only in their exclusive use in contexts implying a locational meaning (and never for example in naming contexts), but also in the grammatical fact that they were never modified with adjectives in the way that other nouns were (p. 189). It is also possible for children to construe quite different semantic distinctions from those found in the adult language, as evidenced by Halliday's (1975) child subject, who used different grammatical mood structures to signal whether or not information given to the addressee concerned previously shared experience. These examples illustrate that it is only by exploring value relations (oppositions) obtaining within the language that the child's meaning system can be understood.

The consequence of appreciating that meaning depends on value relations is that concepts like 'location', 'possession', 'causality' or 'temporality' (cf. Slobin 1973, 1982) cannot be seen as freestanding *a priori* givens that we somehow cognize and then subsequently find a way to express in our particular language. This is not to decry the usefulness of speaking in terms of ideational domains such as these. What is important is to recognize that these domains represent an abstraction of general meaning areas common across languages, which should not be reified into categories with some language-external existence.

By contrast, the removal of meaning to a location outside the language system, in the way that many researchers have done, results in language development being readily viewed solely in terms of whether or not the child has 'acquired' the lexical, morphological, syntactic or phonological forms of the adult language. As Bowerman (1985:1313) notes in reflecting on the child language field, 'In general, the way in which languages organize meaning has not been regarded as an integral part of their structure, equivalent in status to syntactic or morphological structure.' When this happens, linguistic structure is reduced to superficial formal features seen as having no real bearing on the universal and unvarying character of conceptual life – a position fundamentally compatible with the linguists' divorcing of language and other aspects of cognition. With respect to learning, dichotomizing between meaning and form means that the development of language need not be viewed as implying any corresponding development at the conceptual level since conceptual organization precedes linguistic expression.

Ironically, one reason for the appeal of 'cognitive determinism' may lie in the unconscious influence of the language system on our patterns of thinking. The argument that the speaker's task is to convey his or her concepts in the appropriate linguistic forms and the hearer's task is to 'attach' the intended meanings to these forms, makes use of a version of what Reddy (1979) has termed the 'conduit metaphor'. By this term Reddy refers to a bias inherent in the semantics of English which predisposes its speakers to see the elements of language as containers or channels which allow non-linguistic meaning to be transferred from one mind to another. This predisposition is evident in expressions such as *It's difficult to put my idea into words*; *The speech was full of difficult concepts*; *That remark was completely impenetrable* (where language forms are containers) or *He needs to get his thoughts across better*; *That paragraph conveys the right idea* (where non-linguistic thought is the cargo). Reddy suggests that it is this metaphor which encourages the reification of ideas and concepts as external to any speaker or any communicative act, although this is fundamentally illogical.

Reddy's basic contention, also elaborated by Martin (1987) and Ellis (1993), is that arguments couched in terms of the conduit metaphor sound persuasive, indeed simple common sense, precisely because the grammar of English has naturalized this way of talking about thinking and language. In other words it has rendered commonsensical and self-evident a dichotomy between meaning and form which allows the two to be related in terms of words conveying 'underlying' meanings, ideas or concepts.

This position, which emerges in much of the psycholinguistic literature, does not necessarily foreground innateness as an issue, but it nonetheless has much in common with the orientations of mainstream American linguistics. In particular, the dualizing of meaning and form, with only the latter assigned to language, the privileging of referential and denotational meaning over value relations and the concern for the universal and unchanging aspects of the human mind are all tendencies compatible with formal linguistics. And where the linguists focus on the universal character of linguistic structure at the 'deepest' and most abstract level, the developmental psychologists focus on the universal character of concepts which come to the surface when mapped on to linguistic forms.

### 1.3 Jean Piaget: stages of cognitive development

Some consideration has now been given to the issue of conceptual development as discussed by psycholinguists particularly interested in its relation to language acquisition. However, any summary consideration of research into cognitive development needs also to take particular account of the work of Jean Piaget, the century's major figure in the field of developmental psychology. His importance relates not only to his stature within the field of developmental psychology, but also to his enormous influence on educational theory and practice.

Where the linguists have focused on 'universal grammar' as an attribute of the human mind, and the psycholinguists have explored the relation between this (or a more local form of language) and the universal conceptual terrain it maps on to, Piaget has focused on the universal stages of development between birth and adolescence. Although not greatly concerned with the development of language, he was a strong critic of Chomsky's innatist views (see Piatelli-Palmerini 1980). In his writings, Piaget emphasizes the difference between the child's cognitive structures and those of the adult, and stresses the crucial importance of experience in enabling changes to those cognitive structures over time – a position incompatible with Chomsky's more strongly nativist stance.

In general terms, Piaget argues that children gradually develop cognitive structures and strategies for thinking logically, and this is done primarily through their engagement with the material environment. He has proposed four universal stages in cognitive development with ordered substages within each main stage. The first, or sensori-motor, period, which obtains until about 2 years of age, is characterized by 'egocentrism', arising from an initial state 'when no distinction is made between the self and nonself' (Piaget 1977: 277), and in which 'the baby is submerged in a chaos of interesting impressions without there being any distinction between his internal state and things outside' (Piaget 1977: 207). It can be seen that Piaget, writing in the 1920s, was influenced by the work of Freud in developing these ideas, but more recent studies of infant behaviour give them little support (see Section 2.1 below).

One alleged manifestation of egocentrism in young children is that they are unable to conceive of any perspective other than their own, and/or are unable to adapt to another's perspective. In addition they are regarded as having an undeveloped symbolic sense – being, for example, unable to distinguish between fantasy and truth – and in general are misled by their immediate perceptions into illogical thinking. Cognitive development within Piagetian theory involves a gradual 'decentring' until at adolescence the individual reaches the full flowering of objective, logical scientific modes of thought (Piaget 1976).

Evidence for the validity of these stages comes largely from experiments in which children are given tasks to carry out. Their different responses to the tasks at different ages are interpreted in terms of their use of cognitive strategies characteristic of a particular stage. If a child cannot manage some particular task it is because she or he is not yet at the appropriate stage of cognitive development. Individuals might develop at different rates, but it is argued that no child will succeed in any task requiring the cognitive abilities of a particular stage or substage until he or she has passed through all preceding (sub-)stages.

Piaget's theory of cognitive stages, articulated in his publications over half a century, has been widely influential, but has nonetheless been subjected to a barrage of criticism from within the discipline of psychology itself. One line of attack, mounted by Sugarman (1987, 1993) has been that Piaget has been quite inconsistent, and indeed incoherent or circular, in his interpretations of his own empirical findings. At the same time, other writers have addressed the validity of the empirical data on which those interpretations are based, questioning the conduct of the experiments which provide evidence for the cognitive stage theory. These critiques have shown that children's cognitive abilities were consistently underestimated by Piaget, because he did not necessarily design tasks to which young children could relate (McGarrigle and Donaldson 1974, Borke 1975, Donaldson 1978, Samuel and Bryant 1984), he did not take into account the interaction between the amount and kind of information to be processed by the child subject (Smedslund 1964, Bryant and Trabasso 1971, Halford 1982) and he did not design experiments to test his own conclusions (Cohen 1983).

In addition there is a body of criticism which relates to the lack of attention paid by Piaget to the language which mediates the experimental task. For example, Inhelder and Piaget (1964) claim that children cannot form 'true concepts' and thus cannot construe classes or the taxonomic relations between classes. Macnamara (1982) critiques two main experiments designed to support this argument. One experiment is an object-sorting task in which children are requested to place together things that 'are alike', or that 'go together'. However, as Macnamara points out, these are instructions susceptible of reasonable interpretations other than that of grouping things together in a taxonomic hierarchy. In the other task, children are shown pictures of objects, such as flowers, some of which belong to a subclass of that object, such as primulas. They are then judged on their ability to respond 'correctly' to the enquiry *Are there more primulas or flowers?* Piaget interprets the younger children's 'incorrect' responses as demonstrating that children cannot handle the logic of class inclusion until the age of 6 or 7 years, but it could more sensibly be argued that such a question cannot reasonably be given a 'literal' interpretation by anyone who *does* have control of the logic of class inclusion, and that the way the children make sense of the question demonstrates the opposite of what Piaget and Inhelder assert. Macnamara does not go this far but argues that a range of more careful experimental work demonstrates that both these experiments 'were vitiated by ambiguous or misleading instructions' (1982: 60).

In a similar way, many others have argued that the language which mediates experimental tasks may be ambiguous (Donaldson 1978; Macnamara 1982) or misunderstood (Siegel 1978; Wood 1988) or may guide children's interpretations in ways not appreciated by the adult monitoring the child's behaviour (Rommetveit 1978, 1985; Butterworth 1992). In sum, these critiques, and the new experiments which form part of them, have demonstrated that much of Piaget's experimental work is flawed by a failure to construe the experiment as a context with interpersonal and semiotic dimensions.

These more social dimensions, which are disregarded in the experiments, in fact get little attention in the theory generally. In explaining the nature of development, the emphasis is always on the importance of the individual child's interactions with the material environment rather than with other communicating persons. As one of Piaget's interpreters explains,

> The subject himself is the mainspring of his development, in that it is his own activity on the environment or his own active reactions to environmental action that can make progress. (Sinclair 1974: 58)

It is the need to cope with information from the environment that cannot be interpreted by means of the current cognitive structures which is held to move the child to the next cognitive stage, but language is not seen as significant in either constituting or interpreting this information. Piaget's view on the relation between cognitive and linguistic development is entirely compatible with much of the psycholinguistic literature:

> Linguistic progress is not responsible for logical or operational progress. It is rather the other way around. (Piaget 1972: 14)

With this belief that language development is the result rather than the cause of cognitive development, Piaget was interested in children's spontaneous speech as a way of gaining insight into their cognitive abilities. He took this approach in two ways. First there is the functional taxonomy of young children's utterances which he proposed (Piaget 1955). He based this on naturalistic observations of children in a nursery school and proposed that the proportions of particular kinds of utterances would change over time. This approach is echoed in that developed in the 1970s, when speech-act theory was used to theorize about language development (e.g. Dore 1975). Piaget's goal, however, was to use child language data to support his view of cognitive development, and his claim was that his six-and-a-half-year-old subjects had a high proportion of egocentric utterances (non-addressed, or addressed but failing to adapt to another's perspective). He proposed that the proportion of egocentric utterances would decrease as a child progressed from the sensori-motor stage towards the stage of concrete operations (Piaget 1976). Thus Piaget used evidence of children's speech-act types as a way of assessing or illustrating cognitive level.

The second way in which Piaget linked speech and cognitive strategy was with respect to the representation in speech of logical relations such as causality. In this case, he used evidence of the use or lack of use of particular linguistic forms to infer and assess the child's cognitive stage. For example, he reports data suggesting that younger children do not code causal relations in speech:

> In the three lists of complete vocabularies given by Mlle. Descoeudres [(1922)] 'because' is used by the 7-year-old but not by the 5-year-old child. (Piaget 1977: 78)

This is interpreted by Piaget as evidence for the particular cognitive stage of the younger children who he believes cannot express causal inferences. At this point therefore Piaget seems again to see language use as reflecting thinking strategies.

When considering Piaget's language data, it is necessary to recognize a particular problem arising from a lack of awareness of the relation between text and context (this will be further discussed in Chapter 2). While Piaget need not be criticized for being insensitive to this in the 1920s, the effect of ignoring it has surely affected the collection and interpretation of the data. One point made forcefully by Cohen (1983: 129) is that Piaget did not recognize that by closely tracking a single speaker in a multiparty speech event, he was distorting the conversational structure and therefore probably misrepresenting the function of utterances.

Another problem is that Piaget did not realize that the context of situation in which he was observing language was not the most appropriate for the kind of 'reflective' language he was interested in. When following children at play in a kindergarten, he was observing language used largely with only one kind of tenor relation (peer–peer) and in a mode where language accompanies some other behaviour, rather than constituting the activity going on. With regard to the children's language, Piaget (1977: 84) observed that

> Nothing could be harder to understand than the notebooks which we have filled with the conversation of Pie and Lev. Without full commentaries, taken down at the same time as the children's remarks, they would be incomprehensible. Everything is indicated by allusion, by pronouns and demonstrative articles – 'he, she, the, mine, him, etc.' – which can mean anything in turn.

Because he did not appreciate that these are characteristic features of anyone's language in such a context of situation, Piaget was bound to underestimate the linguistic, and hence the cognitive, potential of the children he was observing.

Whether evidence of greater linguistic facility would have affected his views is, however, doubtful. When discussing Pie's speech, or the absence of *because* clauses in kindergarten talk, he appears to see language use as reflecting cognitive ability. But he does not hesitate to insist that when a child uses language in ways which imply greater cognitive understanding than the theory has proposed, we must be wary of this apparent facility with language. For example, the fact that 'pre-operational' children are well able to use common nouns in speech would seem to challenge the notion that they have not developed conceptual categories for classes of objects. But in this case Piaget argues that the linguistic evidence is misleading:

> The generality of a word may be very weak for a child so that symbolically the word is closer to an image than a concept . . . In other words the fact that a child calls a cat a cat does not prove that he understands the 'class' of cats. (Piaget and Inhelder 1964: 3)

Overall, despite his occasional recourse to language data, as well as his use of interviews to illustrate or support his theories on cognitive development, Piaget largely dissociates language and thought, and in this respect he can be placed within a much wider group of scholars, including many who give a much more central place to language in their research.

Piaget takes issue with innatist linguistic theory because he views language as resulting from cognitive development (which in turn results from interaction with the environment), whereas the linguists argue for language as an autonomous cognitive structure (Piatelli-Palmerini 1980). However, the similarities between the two camps are as striking as their differences. Both theorize the individual as a biological being with universal characteristics, unsituated with respect to any social, communicative or cultural context. Both agree that language plays no part in developing cognition, and both stress the universal course of development, whether it be the maturation of an innate faculty or the treading of an undeviating path of cognitive stages.

Despite having been challenged in so many ways, Piaget's work remains highly influential within the educational sphere, where his ideas carry certain implications. If one views cognitive development as unfolding in a universal pattern according to an individually programmed developmental time scale, with general interaction between the individual and the material environment as the key determining factor, then a particular view of the educational process is implied. For one thing the assumption of the universality of the cognitive stages leaves no place for considering cultural differences in learning patterns. Secondly, the privileging of the material over the interpersonal (to say nothing of the semiotic) environment in the theory leads to the valuing of a learning environment which is materially rich and in which the individual child is seen as best able to direct his/her own learning by engaging with that environment.

> [T]he foundation for development of mental activity in a young child is the recognition of the importance of his potential as an active doer rather than a passive recipient of the wisdom of others. (Schwebel and Raph 1974: 24)

The theory therefore suggests that the role of teachers is not likely to be crucial (except as a possible hindrance to the child's learning explorations) since the child cannot be 'taught' what she or he is not cognitively ready to learn, and since language, through which teaching is typically conducted, does not play a part in the development of cognition. The theory 'de-emphasizes the role of the teacher as an explainer, director, or imparter of information' (Schwebel and Raph 1974: 24). This position is echoed by Piaget's editors, Gruber and Voneche, in their discussion of the ideal Piagetian educational environment. They contrast a 'Socratic' teacher-directed verbal mode of education with the 'Eldorado' hope of a materially rich school where the adult 'participates with the child in the processes of discovery and learning' and in which 'the main idea is that the teacher shares her knowledge with the child by living it' (Piaget 1977: 692).

The result of these ideas in the education system has been the valuing of a 'child-centred' pedagogy which leaves children free to pursue their path at their own pace along the universal road of cognitive development. This is done by promoting individual activity over knowledge and talk. As Walkerdine observes,

> The polarization of passive remembering and active learning produced the most important theoretical tenet in the recent history of the primary school. (Walkerdine 1984: 155)

In this way, Piagetian theory has disconnected learning from languaging and construed verbal interaction as promoting mental inaction.

### 1.4 Overview: the monologist orientation

Several bodies of literature which address the issue of language and mind have now been referred to – the linguistic view of innate linguistic structure, the psycholinguistic work on lexical and syntactic development and its relation to concept development, and Piaget's work on the development of cognition – and it has been argued that there is little reason to accept these formulations, which are flawed in a number of ways. The linguists and psycholinguists dichotomize between meaning and form, pay insufficient attention to value relations within the symbolic system, take as unproblematically given what it is that is encoded by language and adopt a monologist view which addresses only its representational function. Piaget's theory similarly dichotomizes between language and thought and similarly fails to theorize the situations in which language is being enacted. Unlike the linguists he does attend to language in use, but interprets its significance in inconsistent ways. Moreover his exploration of the communicative intent of children's speech is only used to show that any interpersonal function is insignificant, that the natural starting place in development is monologue rather than dialogue and that the natural mode of learning is a solitary one.

None of these approaches would suggest that a theory of learning need concern itself very deeply with a theory of language. All tend to downplay the role of language in the construal of experience: if language simply maps on to or names our thoughts, or if language is a cognitive structure quite separate from others, which has reached maturity by the time the child is of school age, then it can hardly have a central place in learning; and if the mind develops through the individual's solitary and self-motivated interaction with the environment, by doing and not by listening, as Piaget suggests, then again language does not come into the picture.

## 2 Social-interactional approaches to the development of language and thinking

While research using the kinds of theoretical frameworks from linguistics and psychology so far discussed continues strongly, other lines of developmental research have also been flourishing over the past fifteen or twenty years. These alternative approaches, from within psychology, child language research, anthropology and sociology, are all oriented towards a view of language as social or interactional in character and they provide more appealing frameworks for addressing the role of language in learning.

## 2.1 Studies of neonatal behaviour

One body of research – much of it initiated in the 1960s by Jerome Bruner and his associates – was inspired by a search for 'signs of what innate structure of intelligence lay dormant or weakly expressed in [neonates]' (Trevarthen 1974: 230). Unlike Chomsky's purely hypothetical account of innateness, the theoretical positions which have emerged from this work are based on numerous painstaking observational studies of infant behaviour, both naturalistic and experimental. (See e.g. Schaffer 1977, Lock 1978, Bullowa 1979, Messer 1994.) And in contrast to Piaget's empirical work, the research is premised on the recognition that infants develop within a rich interpersonal and semiotic environment. Consequently, it is not the baby alone but the mother–infant dyad which is the unit under investigation. The conclusion reached is that 'human intelligence develops from the start as an interpersonal process' (Trevarthen 1974: 230), with 'activities of the cognitive and rational system . . . open from the start to selective influences from the feelings, preferences and abilities of the infant's caretaking companions' (Trevarthen 1987: 178).

Trevarthen argues that, far from being unable to distinguish between self and other or self and world, as Piaget suggests, 'The infant is inherently capable, first, of differentiating himself from the world, and, second, of distinguishing things from persons' (Trevarthen 1980: 324). Some evidence for this is provided by research showing that within the first weeks or months of life, infants display a preference for attending to people over other stimuli (Field and Fox 1985; Messer 1994). Moreover, experimental manipulations of social interaction with babies aged from 6 weeks to 3 months show that infants recognize the contingencies of normal communicative interaction (Murray and Trevarthen 1985, K. Bloom et al. 1987). Both the facial gesturing and the vocalizing of infants will vary depending on the interactive behaviour of the communicating partner. These early sensitivities and behaviours are further developed by the end of the first year when children habitually follow another's line of regard (Scaife and Bruner 1975) and address others to draw their attention to objects in the environment (Bates 1976; Trevarthen and Hubley 1978). They may do this either to 'request' things or to share attention – the latter particularly being associated with displays of positive affect (Mundy et al. 1992).

The difference from the Piagetian orientation is exemplified by Trevarthen's (1980: 336) claim that 'The only reasonable psychological theory of education is that children possess an intrinsic and growing motivation to gain knowledge from others'. Thus the Piagetian image of the egocentric baby, initially unable to distinguish itself from others, unable to engage in communicative behaviour and unable to adapt its communicative behaviour to the addressee to take account of the other's different knowledge or perspective, has been replaced by a fundamentally different picture. Trevarthen, like Piaget, is concerned with the universal characteristics of the child, but sees the most important of these as being that the infant is above all oriented to, responsive to and adaptive to other persons and to learning which is mediated through others.

The ramifications of this perspective are profound. It provides first of all a basis for recognizing the mutuality of teaching and learning, in opposition to the Piagetian view that children cannot be taught but learn through a process of private discovery. Most importantly, therefore, this perspective provides for the centrality of language in the learning process. While the studies cited are themselves concerned with development before the emergence of language, the premise that learning is mediated through significant others allows for continuity between the pre-linguistic and linguistic phases of life, since learning which is mediated through others is necessarily semiotic in nature.

The further implication of this, argued by Butt (1989: 106), is that neither the objects that present themselves for exploration, nor the nature of those objects, nor the contexts in which they arise can now be seen as universal 'givens' of experience available to the child as an autonomous individual. Instead of a developmental move from the private formulation of meaning or concepts to their public expression through language (as in the cognitive determinism models), there is now seen to be a movement from a cooperative exchange of attention with others to a harnessing of this to enhance exploration of and action on the world of objects. From this perspective, there may be individual experience, but there can be no question of private meanings being translated into public language, as in the orthodox model of language and thinking. Meaning is always construed in interaction with others.

## 2.2 Studies of 'motherese'

Another body of research focusing more directly on the development of language was also under way in the 1970s. Rather than being motivated by any interest in the innate characteristics of children, this work arose as a challenge to the innatist arguments of formal linguists (Snow 1979). The goal was to show that the language young children hear is neither fragmented nor impoverished but might actually be well designed to facilitate language learning. Thus the study of the speech of adult caregivers became the object of attention and so again the interpersonal environment of the child was foregrounded.

The characteristics of caretaker speech, also known as 'baby talk (BT)' (Ferguson 1977) 'motherese' (Newport *et al.* 1977) or 'child directed speech' (Gallaway and Richards 1994), are summarized by Snow (1977) and by Wells and Robinson, who suggest it involves 'systematic modifications . . . at all linguistic levels' (1982: 16). For example, a greater use of pitch range with more rising tones is attested (Garnica 1977), which may be assumed to alert the infant to the speaker's communicative intent, while a slower rate of delivery (Sachs *et al.* 1976), a more restricted range of sounds and sound-sequences and more careful pronunciation (Ferguson 1977) serve to aid the child in processing the stream of speech. Syntactic simplicity is accompanied by considerable repetition of utterances and parts of utterances (Snow 1972, Ferguson 1977), while the speech is also concerned on the whole with aspects of the immediately observable situation and thus 'tends to be highly redundant in context' (Wells and Robinson 1982: 16). Such features of adult speech to young children can be readily interpreted as simplifying and clarifying processes which function to facilitate communication. If they also facilitate language learning, then it implies that language is learned as a communicative tool for the exchange of meaning, rather than to provide a nomenclature for preformed concepts.

From this work, it has not been difficult to demonstrate that the language addressed to young children, or used in their hearing, is no random, poorly structured sample of speech. However, a lack of suitable tools for dialogic discourse analysis, as discussed by Blank *et al.* (1978), Brown (1980) and Wells and Gutfreund (1987), has been recognized as a problem for researchers wishing to demonstrate the efficacy of caretaker speech. This, together with a lack of well-articulated theories about the way the ongoing exchange of meaning might assist language learning, meant that many early attempts to demonstrate the importance of caretaker speech in facilitating language acquisition were somewhat limited. Some attempted to correlate discrete and sometimes disparate grammatical and semantic aspects of parents' speech 'input' either with specific aspects or with the general rate of their children's language development (e.g. Newport *et al.* 1977, Cross 1978, Furrow *et al.* 1979). Others, hypothesizing the importance of timely adult models, such as observed by Brown and Bellugi (1964), evaluated the linguistic development of children who had participated in experimental sessions where adults were self-consciously 'expanding' or recasting all their immature utterances (Cazden 1965, Nelson *et al.* 1973). While there were many interesting findings, no clear consensus emerged from the results of these kinds of studies. In a recent review, Pine argues that formulating the issue 'in terms of how facilitative child directed speech might turn out to be is ultimately unlikely to be very productive' (1994: 37).

Some interactionally oriented language acquisition research draws on post-Chomskyan strands in linguistic theory, which foreground the communicative status of utterances rather than their formal syntactic characteristics. Searle's (1969) development of speech act theory, which focuses on the illocutionary intent of utterances, has been influential, together with work within linguistics on the level of 'pragmatics', which is similarly concerned with the context-dependent meaning of utterances in use (Bates 1976, Levinson 1983). Ideas from these approaches have helped extend the view of language learning to encompass the acquisition of communicative skills. This has meant looking at the child's increasing repertoire of speech acts (Dore 1975, 1978, Bates 1976, McTear 1985), at turntaking skills (Kaye and Charney 1980, McTear 1985), at control of topic (Brown 1980, Ochs and Schieffelin 1983) and so on, as aspects of the child's growing linguistic abilities. These approaches have been important in providing ways of considering linguistic development apart from the traditional 'mean length of utterance' or inventory of morphemes acquired (Brown 1973).

However, while these approaches do foreground the fact that language is used to act in the world, they may be hampered by building on a model which sees language in terms of the individual's knowledge. As discussed earlier, in those models of language which have developed from a Chomskyan generative model, the linguistic system itself is conceived of as a set of rules which define structural descriptions of sentences. These may be rules of syntax, defining sentences in terms of combinations of classes of units, such as NP, VP; or more semantically oriented rules, defining allowable configurations of such structural functions as agent, instrument, affected, etc. These rules constitute the (basis of the) speaker's knowledge of his/her language system. With the recognition of the communicative function of the system, the model is extended by positing another set of rules which constitute the individual's pragmatic or communicative, as against grammatical, competence – that is, knowledge of when it is appropriate or obligatory to use particular forms (see e.g. Hymes 1971).

Attempts to formalize rules of use are in terms of conditions upon the use of particular speech acts, which are based on the formalization of speaker beliefs and intentions (Levinson 1983). In all this, the individual speaker and the individual speech act are central. This has the weakness of avoiding a truly interpersonal approach, and it continues to draw Chomsky's sharp distinction between 'knowing' a linguistic form and being able to use it. Thus the framework of pragmatics maintains the dichotomy between form and meaning that has been shown to be problematic in the psycholinguistic tradition, rather than reconceptualizing language more radically to develop the insight that language is learned to exchange meaning.

In addition to problems with the linguistic underpinnings of some interactionally oriented research, there have been reservations expressed about some of the practical or political results of the changed conceptions of language learning. Once the communicative partner is brought into the picture so that the development of language can be viewed not as the maturation of an innate structure or the attachment of names to privately acquired concepts, but as something susceptible to interpersonal experience, then there is likely to be an interest in the quality of that experience. One result of this has been a concern with the characteristics of the 'mother talk' of rapid learners (Cross 1977, 1978), and with comparisons between different maternal 'styles' and how these correlate with differences in the language development of their offspring (Lieven 1978, Schachter et al. 1979, Howe 1981). There is a danger in this, especially since middle-class

English-speaking mothers are the most extensively studied group and their children the most successful in formal education. As Urwin (1984: 271) notes, 'This work is itself contributing to a normalization of what mother–child interaction consists of, and a new orthodoxy in what constitutes the role of the mother.'

This construction of a new version of the ideal mother occurs because the mother–child dyads are studied as though existing outside any broader social context, as if their interactions are simply those of two socially unsituated individuals. Where there is no social theory in terms of which the behaviours studied can be interpreted, they will tend to be read as 'natural' and universal. Alternatively, where variations in behaviour of different dyads are observed, these will be seen as a matter of more or less felicitous interpersonal adjustment between the two individuals involved, or else in terms of what produces 'best' or most rapid 'acquisition' of the target commodity. This then leads to a valuing of a particular style, as can be observed, for example, in the work of Schachter and colleagues in America, who note that, in contrast with the verbal behaviour of disadvantaged mothers, 'advantaged mothers appear to support and facilitate the actions of their toddlers' (1979: 156). They then propose an early intervention programme to teach disadvantaged mothers the middle-class styles of interaction as a means of improving the children's cognitive development. Walkerdine and Lucey have also argued that Tizard and Hughes' (1984) study of British middle-class and working-class mother–child dialogues similarly normalizes the middle-class style and even 'pathologises . . . the meanings produced by some of the working-class mothers' (1989: 99).

To sum up the discussion so far, it can be argued that a focus on caregiver talk provides a fruitful perspective on language development in its recognition that language is essentially dialogic in character and that language learning is therefore an interpersonal and not an individual negotiation with the world. Three interrelated weaknesses have, however, been identified in the work so far discussed. One is the lack of a theory that would inform the analysis of adult–child interactions as pedagogic events so as to delineate more clearly the role that the adult plays as teacher. A second problem is the lack of a linguistic theory that construes language as essentially dialogic without either losing sight of its cognitive function or dichotomizing knowledge and use. And a final problem is the lack of a social, as opposed to an interpersonal, perspective, which would allow mother–child interactions to be theorized as realizing patterns of meaning with significance beyond the individual dyad.

Within the literature on parent–child interaction itself can be found attempts to address all these problems, drawing on theoretical work from psychology, anthropology and sociology, as well as from systemic linguistics, which theory will be discussed separately in Chapter 2.

### 2.3 Vygotsky: a social approach to cognitive development

The most interesting aspect of work on caregiver–child conversations relates to their analysis as pedagogic interactions, on the assumption that it is not just the syntactic form of an individual utterance that may provide appropriate 'input' for language learning, but the interactive relationship of one partner's utterance to the other. While the earliest debates were influenced by the innatist challenge to behaviourism (Skinner 1957) and focused on the importance of the child's imitation of adult speech (Ervin 1964, Whitehurst and Vasta 1975), more recent work pays greater attention to the adult's role and has either used, or can be interpreted within, the framework of Vygotsky's developmental theory.

Although Vygotsky was a contemporary of Piaget, working in Russia, his influence on Western education has been negligible compared with that of Piaget. His major work *Thought and Language* was suppressed in 1936, two years after its publication (which followed Vygotsky's early death), and was not translated into English until 1962. Nonetheless, in recent years renewed attention has been given to his ideas, which are notable for the explicit role given to language in mediating learning of all kinds (see e.g. Wertsch 1984, 1991, Bruner 1986, Hickmann 1987, Hasan 1995). Vygotsky's position is summarized by Butt (1989: 106) as 'the idea that social interaction is the central source of structure in the mind of the individual'. This is clearly a position compatible with that arrived at by Trevarthen and his colleagues, whether or not they were directly influenced by Vygotsky's writings.

With respect to ontogenesis, Vygotsky was concerned with the development of what he called the 'higher psychological functions', those uniquely human qualities of mental life such as 'voluntary attention' or 'logical memory'. In the theory, a key characteristic of these higher mental functions is that they are mediated by the use of signs. So, for example, even the use of a simple sign, such as a knot in a handkerchief, transforms remembering from being a process solely determined by direct stimulation from the environment into a process that can be voluntarily regulated and can eventually become the object of conscious reflection (Vygotsky 1978).

A second and related characteristic of higher psychological functions is that they derive from social interaction. According to Vygotsky, all higher mental functions appear twice in ontogenetic development: first as inter-mental functions, during interactions with others mediated by speech, and later as intra-mental functions mediated by internalized semiotic processes. The development of cognition within the individual thus depends on prior social-linguistic inter-mental activity: 'The internalization of cultural forms of behavior involves the reconstruction of psychological activity on the basis of sign operations' (Vygotsky 1978: 57). As Wertsch explains, 'By coming to master the mediational means of social interaction, the child masters the very means needed for later independent cognitive processing' (Vygotsky 1981a:190–1). Clearly, the most important such mediational means is the semiotic system of language, and thus it is in the mastery of language that the child learns the means of higher mental functioning.

This can be illustrated by the way perception develops from its 'natural' biological basis. Infants are confronted with sensory data from birth onwards and processes of perception must precede the use of language to categorize and construe experience. But soon language-mediated social interactions with others will begin to mediate and shape the child's perceptions until eventually the linguistic categorizations become part of the child's own internal psychological apparatus, at which point the child's perceptual experience is irrevocably changed. As Lee (1987: 91) puts it,

> This representation of the perceptual field gives the child's operations a greater freedom from the concrete, visual aspects of the situation. Speech mediates and supplants the immediacy of natural perception – the child perceives the world through his speech as well as through sensory perception.

In this way, Vygotsky provides a more sophisticated account than that of cognitive determinism. It is one which recognizes that infants, as biological beings, have a mental life from the first but that with the advent of speech, mental functioning comes to be shaped by language. Language, however, can only function in this way as a feature of the individual's (intra-mental) cognition on the basis of having been initially experienced (inter-mentally) in communicative exchanges with others.

One limitation in Vygotsky's theory is that, although it is language in use which is at the heart of his ideas, his writings did not satisfactorily theorize a linguistic unit of use – such as utterance (Bakhtin 1986), exchange (Berry 1981), text (Halliday and Hasan 1976, 1989) or genre (Bakhtin 1986, Martin 1992a) – but simply proposed the word as the key unit for analysis, focusing particularly on the generalization inherent in worded categories and on their intersubjective nature:

> The word plays a central role not in the isolated functions but the whole of consciousness. In consciousness, the word is that which, in Feuerbach's words, is absolutely impossible for one person but possible for two. The word is the most direct manifestation of the [socio-]historical nature of human consciousness. (Vygotsky 1987: 298)

Whatever the limitations of taking the word as the central unit of linguistic exchange, Vygotsky was careful to distinguish referential meaning from other aspects of word meaning, pointing out that in contexts of use, an adult and child can arrive at intersubjective agreement about a word's reference without sharing the same complex system of sense relations. In this way the communicative purposes of each party can be achieved, even though the interactants are not on an equal footing intra-mentally.

In his discussion of conceptual development, Vygotsky distinguished between 'everyday', or 'spontaneous', concepts and 'scientific' ones. Everyday concepts are learned through use in 'situationally meaningful, concrete applications' (Vygotsky 1987: 216), and the exercise of conscious awareness and volition with respect to them would be a relatively late development. A scientific concept deriving from a theoretical discipline, on the other hand, can only be understood in terms of its place in a system of relations established through conscious awareness and control, by such means as formal definitions (Lee 1987: 201).

The development of scientific concepts depends on the metasemiotic potential of language – its ability to represent itself – and is the result of formal instruction in school, where voluntary control and reflectiveness will be called upon. Lee (1987: 99) interprets Vygotsky as arguing that this mode of thinking using scientific concepts depends on a cultural context, which

> will not be actualised until social institutions evolve which are dependent on regimenting language in certain ways so as to make such definitional equivalences a presupposition of their existence. In addition, thinking in concepts depends on social institutions which instruct children in the types of voluntary control necessary for such thinking.

And in a similar way, the development of writing abilities, the acquiring of foreign languages or of mathematics are analogous examples of the learning of a semiotic whose mastery requires that it become an object of conscious attention and reflection.

In the context of discussing effective instruction, as well as that of assessing children's cognitive abilities, Vygotsky proposed that it was important to ascertain what the child could achieve jointly with an adult or more capable peer, as well as what the child could achieve unaided. The difference between the two levels of achievement constitutes the child's 'zone of proximal development'. It is in this zone, a little beyond the child's 'actual developmental level as determined by independent problem solving' (Vygotsky 1978: 86), that effective instruction could take place. This is because it is the skills that children can only demonstrate in collaboration with more expert partners – inter-mental skills – that are in the very process of being learned, becoming intra-mental.

Vygotsky did not specify the exact nature of the more capable partner's contribution to the child's learning in any detail. When discussing tutorial situations, he suggested that different teachers

> might employ different modes of demonstration in different cases: some might run through an entire demonstration and ask the children to repeat it, others might initiate the solution and ask the child to finish it, or offer leading questions. (Vygotsky 1978: 86)

Thus, observation of a solution, sharing the workload or indirect guidance through talk were all suggested as possible collaborative means, with the understanding that successful achievement by the child (including by imitation of observed solutions) will only be possible if the task is within his or her potential developmental level.

Another important aspect of Vygotsky's notion of development was his insistence that each new stage depends on and reconstitutes the achievements of the previous stage, so that development proceeds not as a unilinear sequence, but 'in a spiral, passing through the same point at each new revolution while advancing to a higher level' (1978: 56). For example, memory is initially unmediated, simply a direct response to the environment. Then, external signs (whether a knotted handkerchief or a linguistic utterance) begin to control the function of memory. But at a later point still, the mediated activity of memorizing takes place as an entirely internal process. This latest stage may appear most similar to the very initial stage – as if the child has abandoned the need for mediating signs – but what has happened is that the sign use has become internalized, so that a point where memory functions without external forms of mediation has been arrived at again, but at a higher level, as in Figure 1.1.

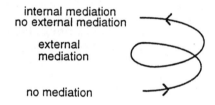

internal mediation
no external mediation

external
mediation

no mediation

**Figure 1.1** Vygotsky's view of the spiral nature of the development of mental functions

In general terms, Vygotsky's writings offer a theoretical position which foregrounds the nature of language as a communicative tool and argues that the mind is shaped by language in use. He thus recognizes that language is a means both of acting in the world and of interpreting it. His emphasis on the dialogic nature of language and on the zone of proximal development provides a role for the teacher in the learning process which is quite at odds with the Piagetian model of the child's natural course of development. And rather than a developmental model of linear stages, he sees learning as a dialectical, spiralling process, where achievements at one 'level' provide a stepping stone for the next, which, having been attained, transforms the earlier level. Another contrast with the Piagetian view of education is that, within a Vygotskyan framework, the effective teacher's role must necessarily be a verbal one. This follows from the argument that it is the internalization of forms of semiotic mediation that enables the higher mental functioning of attention, memory, abstraction and so on. Here, Vygotsky emphasized the importance for learning of the self-reflexive, metasemiotic characteristic of language and suggested that the disciplinary studies of formal education capitalize on this potential for making linguistic meaning an object of reflection. Thus, while he recognized the mediating potential of various semiotic modes, language was given priority in the shaping of thought.

Although Vygotsky's theory provides little in the way of a model of a linguistic system, in terms of syntactic or other forms and relationships, it has provided a fertile set of ideas for theorizing the significance of language in use and of culture in the individual's development. Most importantly, this is achieved without creating the usual and unhelpful dichotomies between language and thought on the one hand and nature and culture on the other. Because of this, his ideas have had some influence on recent reconceptualizations of the discipline of psychology which also stress the cultural construction of mind (see Section 2.6 below).

One of Vygotsky's ideas in particular – the concept of the zone of proximal development – has proved to be particularly attractive in language acquisition research, despite the fact that it was developed in the context of considering the place of formal school learning with older children. The notion that 'that which the child is able to do in collaboration today, he will be able to do independently tomorrow' (Vygotsky 1987: 216-17) can in fact be linked to a number of the interactionist studies of early language learning. For example, Bruner (1978: 253, Ninio and Bruner 1978) is one of several researchers to discuss the role of the parent in stretching the child's linguistic achievement by continually 'upping the ante'. That is to say, children are not allowed to rest on their laurels, rehearsing the meanings and forms familiar to them, but are constantly pushed to achieve just beyond their current limits by the adults with whom they interact.

Bruner's later writings (e.g.1986) explicitly acknowledge his intellectual debt to Vygotsky in the discussion of what he calls conversational and situational 'formats' which are managed by the adult to 'scaffold' the child's language learning. These scaffolds provide stable and predictable contexts for the child's contribution to the discourse, and in such contexts, the adult

> reduces the degrees of freedom with which the child has to cope, concentrates his attention into a manageable domain, and provides models of the expected dialogue from which he can extract selectively what he needs for filling his role in discourse. (Bruner 1978: 254)

In addition, the parent must vary the format so as to extend the contexts and functions of the child's linguistic repertoire and act as a 'communicative ratchet', preventing the child from slipping back from the currently attained level of performance. One important aspect of this work is that by focusing on a format such as that provided by the reading of a picture book as a context for learning names, Ninio and Bruner (1978) are better able to analyse the interaction as a text, looking at the relationship of one dialogic move to another, rather than simply summing utterance types used by either party.

Other examples of parental scaffolding can be found in longitudinal case studies from Scollon (1979) and Painter (1986, 1989). The children studied are shown achieving jointly with adults syntactic or narrative constructions that they are unable to achieve monologically until a later date. Educationists have drawn on these kinds of studies to advocate an analogous provision of scaffolding in classrooms where children are learning to write (as discussed in Applebee and Langer 1983, Lehr 1985, Painter 1986).

Of course these accounts of the particular scaffolding techniques of English-speaking, white, middle-class parents can still be appropriated to naturalize one particular interactional style. Gray (1986) warns against this in pointing out the futility of engaging Australian Aboriginal children in the kinds of questioning and commentary that constitute verbal scaffolding of book reading for a white middle-class child when that kind of discourse is quite unfamiliar to the Aboriginal learner. Michaels (1981) makes a similar point with respect to American teachers and their 'guiding' responses to children's morning news stories in the classroom. Confronting children in school with a quite unfamiliar form of linguistic interaction may be far from providing them with a 'scaffolding' experience. In fact, Vygotsky's argument that social semiotic activity shapes mental functioning should alert us to this by leading us to expect that children from different cultures and subcultures will have different interactional experience leading to different intra-mental cognitive styles (revealed in different discursive styles).

## 2.4 Ethnographic studies: cultural variation in language use

One way of countering the normalization of the interactional patterns of a single cultural group is provided by the ethnographic descriptions of social life in different cultures and subcultures, such as those reported in Schieffelin and Ochs (1986). In a study directly influenced by Vygotskyan theory, Rogoff (1990), for example, surveys infant development in a range of different cultures, exemplifying a variety of manifestations of the principle of learning through guided participation, with caregivers gradually relinquishing more control of an activity over time. Other ethnographic work, however, shows that, whatever the merits of scaffolding techniques in formal instructional contexts, it is not a cultural universal for parents to view themselves as teachers and take on a tutorial role. Heath's (1983) celebrated study, for example, documents patterns of language use over a ten-year period within two small, poor, neighbouring rural communities in the south-eastern United States, one white and one black. She describes how the patterns of talk – the 'ways with words' – are guided by and create different social practices and values in the two communities. She also stresses that children in the black community had to learn language, as well as other things, by observation and trial and error, rather than through collaboration and with support from more capable partners. However, while cooperative scaffolding of the kind described in the language development literature for middle-class households was noticeably absent, the children did clearly learn from closely observing more capable speakers and actors. The latter in turn provided – through such means as teasing – repeated situations in which the learners could participate in inter-mental activity and learn through language in use.

Other important work, describing parent–child talk in different cultural contexts, is provided by Ochs and Schieffelin (1984). They describe the types of interpersonal interaction in which children of two different cultures – the Western Samoans and the Kaluli of Papua New Guinea – engage, showing how they are different from each other and from the 'white middle-class developmental story'. They argue that language acquisition is an aspect of socialization, and propose that

> Caregivers' speech behavior expresses and reflects values and beliefs held by members of a social group. In this sense, caregivers' speech is part of a larger set of behaviors that are culturally organized. (p. 310)

Ochs (1990) discusses the notion of 'language socialization' – socialization both through and into language – and finds it compatible with Vygotskyan theory, among others (p. 304). Noting the role of language in the shaping of mind, she says:

> A basic tenet of language socialization is that language must be studied not only as a symbolic system that encodes local social and cultural structures, but also as a tool for establishing (i.e. maintaining, creating) social and psychological realities. (Ochs 1990: 287–8)

Ochs discusses the need to make principled links between contextual dimensions and linguistic forms in order to investigate language socialization, recognizing that this will not be a simple matter of one-to-one correspondences between contextual feature and linguistic structure. In fact because she is adding a pragmatic dimension (here termed 'discourse') on to a traditional Chomskyan view of grammar, she cannot readily theorize a relation between culture and grammar and regards Sapir's having done so as a key weakness of his hypothesis that the language habits of the community predispose speakers to interpret experience in particular ways (Sapir 1949). She herself argues that discourse – i.e. knowledge of 'norms, preferences, and expectations relating language to context' – constitutes the key aspect of linguistic competence that should be focused on (Ochs 1990: 301).

Within a similar anthropological tradition is the work of Scollon and Scollon (1981), which compares aspects of their young daughter's language development and use with features of the language of the Athabaskan community of Alaska. They distinguish between the literate orientation of their daughter's cognitive development and the Athabaskan orientation, which they refer to as 'bush consciousness', arguing that these different forms of consciousness result from the different linguistic habits of the communities which display them. Although their work is not framed in terms of Vygotskyan psychology, they too in effect present a Vygotskyan case for the role of social-semiotic practices in developing particular intramental cognitive orientations.

### 2.5  Bernstein: cultural reproduction through language

Perhaps the most thoroughgoing account of the role of language in the socialization process is offered by the British sociologist, Basil Bernstein (1971, 1973, 1975, 1987, 1990), who went further than Vygotsky in addressing the question of how the higher mental functions might develop differently depending on the nature of the semiotic mediation provided by language, and who, in comparison with many ethnographic studies, was less concerned to describe patterns of social interaction than to account for why particular practices, norms and beliefs should arise at a particular time and place.

In Bernstein's work, the different interactional and linguistic practices within the family, and the cultural discontinuity faced by working-class children upon entering formal education, are interpreted within a comprehensive theory of cultural production and reproduction, in which the role of language is seen as central. In outline, one aspect of this theory concerns the argument that the organization of social relations in the family leads to particular forms of social interaction between the members, mediated by particular fashions of speaking. The familial role structure relates to social class and the patterns of interacting and speaking construct a particular social positioning.

Bernstein (1971) argues that, in urban Britain, working-class families are more likely to favour a strongly 'positional' family role system, where the status, rights and duties of members depend largely on ascribed characteristics of gender, age and generation, whereas middle-class families tend towards a 'personal' role system, based on achieved status and individual personalities. This results in correspondingly different interactional patterns within the family group, which are particularly significant with respect to four critical 'socializing contexts' – the 'regulative', 'instructional', 'imaginative' and 'interpersonal'. These four situation types constitute contexts for interaction between mother and child which relate to control, instruction, innovation/imagination and interpersonal relationships respectively (Adlam 1977).

There are two key points in this theory as described here. One is that the most significant expression of different interactional patterns in the family is constituted by language in use. The other is that the different linguistic patterns can be explained as symbolizing particular kinds of social structure. This then provides a way of linking observable micro encounters of the home with the macroscopic relations of society. The linguistic ways of meaning characteristic of the positional family Bernstein terms the 'restricted code' and those characteristic of the personal family are the 'elaborated code'. In writing of the codes in the 1960s, Bernstein described the restricted code as being more predictable, making use of a narrower range of syntactic and/or lexical forms and with less explicit elaboration of semantic relationships. It was said to be more fluent, involving less planning and fewer modal expressions of uncertainty. Elaborated code, by contrast, was described as less grammatically predictable, less fluent, with a greater tendency to modalize meaning, foreground the first person singular pronoun and elaborate semantic relationships explicitly (see e.g. Bernstein 1962a, 1962b, 1965).

In relating the two codes to the hierarchical organization of society, the restricted code is argued to be associated with a simple social division of labour: with a common set of shared identifications and experiences, such that the subjective intent of the participants can be left implicit and taken for granted. Elaborated code is associated with a more complex social division of labour: with conditions where not everything is shared, where the intent of the speakers who are interacting cannot be taken for granted. This code, later termed 'coding orientation', is thus explicit and expresses meanings which are 'universalistic' in being interpretable across different contexts:

> The simpler the social division of labour and the more *specific and local the relation between an agent and its material base*, then . . . the more restricted the coding orientation. The more complex the social division of labour, the less specific and local the relation between an agent and its material base, then . . . the more elaborated the coding orientation. (Bernstein 1982: 310)

Bernstein posited the family as only one site of socialization, paying attention also to the peer group and particularly the school. He suggested that the universalistic, context-independent meanings of the elaborated code are also those characteristic of what he calls 'uncommonsense' or 'educational' knowledge as opposed to 'commonsense . . . everyday community knowledge' (1975: 99). This distinction resonates with that made by Vygotsky between spontaneous and scientific concepts, in that commonsense knowledge arises in domestic contexts and constructs concrete non-technical meanings, as do spontaneous concepts, whereas educational knowledge involves the more abstract and technical meanings of school disciplines. In interpreting Bernstein, Halliday (1988a:11) describes the distinction as follows:

> Commonsense knowledge is typically transmitted in the home; it tends to be spoken, non-technical, informal, without boundaries, and with room for discretion on the part of the child learner, who can take it or leave it.

Educational knowledge usually comes packaged by the school; and it differs in these five ways: it is written, technical, formal, with strong boundaries and with much less discretion on the part of the learner. These two last points are covered in Bernstein's notion of classification and framing. So there is a difference in the typical forms in which these two kinds of knowledge are presented to us.

While it is Halliday who highlights particularly the association between educational knowledge and written language, Bernstein's point is that educational knowledge privileges the universalistic, explicit meanings associated with the elaborated coding orientation.

Bernstein's theory has been criticized as 'overly deterministic' (Urwin 1984:271), something which arises partly from the metaphors of 'transmission' (of culture) and 'socialization' (of the child) which he employed in his writings of the 1970s. Language 'acquisition', as Ochs (1990: 302) points out, is similarly problematic. As Halliday (1988a: 7) explains,

> Like acquisition, socialisation is a flawed metaphor. Both these terms tell us that there is something 'out there' that pre-exists, called society or language: by implication an unchanging something to which children are gradually moulded until they conform. But society and language are not unchanging . . . Now since Bernstein's early work there has tended to be a change, a change in which he himself has participated, in the metaphors used for exploring all these issues.

Another problem with Bernstein's theory of codes when first proposed was that it lacked the kind of empirical support that could be provided by naturalistic descriptions of mother–child discourse from different social classes. Instead, interview and questionnaire data provided much of the evidence for the two meaning styles. Since that time, ethnographic studies, such as those already described, of Heath (1983), Ochs and Schieffelin (1984) and Scollon and Scollon (1981), have all demonstrated the validity of the general claim that different social groups construct and construe social relations through language in their own characteristic ways, while Hasan and Cloran (Hasan 1988, 1989, 1991, 1992, 1999, Hasan and Cloran 1990, Cloran 1989, 1999) have used naturalistic data to investigate explicitly the linguistic variation posited by Bernstein, exploring its relevance with respect to gender as well as social class.

The account given here of Bernstein's theory is essentially that articulated in the 1970s, and although there has been considerable elaboration since, particularly in the articulation of macroscopic relations, the key insights of the earlier work are still being built on. As with all the approaches discussed here, Bernstein's is not a theory of language structure but focuses on the role of language in use. In its focus on speech in different situational contexts, such as the regulative or instructional, it calls for a view of language which can theorize variation according to use and relate texts to contexts. And in its focus on the way different social groups engage in different habitual ways of speaking it calls for a way of theorizing linguistic variation according to user. Without a way of modelling the relation between the language system and the use of the system, such variation is likely to be assumed to be variation in the size or potential of the system itself. For example, a claim that fewer explicit conjunctive links are made by a speaker from one group compared with another would be interpreted as a presumption that one speaker 'has' fewer conjunctions than another. Thus Labov (1969: 204), construing things from the perspective of American linguistic theory, misinterprets Bernstein as follows:

> The most extreme view which proceeds from this orientation – and one that is now being widely accepted – is that lower class black children have no language at all.

It can hardly be supposed that Bernstein was suggesting that restricted code users have no 'I' pronoun or 'because' conjunction, or that they could not form complex nominal groups, and so on. His claim was that in their habitual forms of discourse such forms were used much less frequently than by elaborated code users. That his ideas should have been reconstrued as a theory of linguistic deficit points to the crucial importance of underpinning social theories of language use with a linguistic model which is not universalistic, not exclusively oriented to language as system and which does not construe that system as knowledge possessed by an ideal speaker/hearer, in the way done by the Chomskyan model Labov was trying to adapt.

## 2.6 Language and social life

There are common threads to the various different theoretical approaches outlined in this section, from Trevarthen's work on newborn infants, Vygotsky's psychological theory, the various studies of language socialization and Bernstein's theory of cultural transmission. All are based on the general principle that consciousness is formed through semiotic practice, although this idea will be expressed very differently in terms of different problems posed by different theories and the different metalanguages which arise from particular disciplines.

Moreover, while the discussion here has been limited to approaches with an ontogenetic focus and a foregrounding of parent–child interaction, this principle finds sympathetic echoes in a number of current theoretical formations within the social sciences. Bernstein's insight that different ways of saying are indirectly related to the distribution of power in the wider society relates to European social theory as developed by Bourdieu (1991), who shows how symbolic production defines and constitutes relations of dominance and hierarchy, and by Foucault (1972, 1978), who discusses the relationship between our ways of talking about

the world and the way we act and are acted upon in it. This focus on the
semiotic constitution of reality achieved through social practice is found
again in the emerging fields of 'discursive psychology' (Harre and Gillett
1994) and 'cultural psychology', the latter defined in the following way:

> Cultural psychology is the study of the way cultural traditions and social
> practices regulate, express, transform, and permute the human psyche.
> (Shweder 1990: 1)

Shweder presents this discipline as premised upon the assumption that
human beings are above all meaning-making and that their environment
is an 'intentional' world, the principle of which is 'that nothing real "just
is"' (1990: 4). This kind of understanding is also a basis for an alternative
theoretical synthesis, that of 'social semiotics', presented in Lemke
(1990). While eschewing such 'mentalist' terminology as 'intention' or
'psyche', together with the 'autonomous domain of phenomena between
the biological and the social' (p. 192) which it implies, Lemke is similarly
concerned with viewing a social community as 'a dynamic, open semiotic
system of meaningful actions and meaning-making practices' (p. 191).

The importance of language as a semiotic system deployed in the
creation and interpretation of experience is everywhere stressed in these
writings and it is the province of linguistic theory to explore the nature of
that system. From the examination of the various perspectives on language
use in the life of the child which have been discussed here, it can be seen
that a relevant theory of language must have certain emphases which are
quite different from those of the Chomskyan tradition. In particular,
language must be construed in some terms which enable linguistic forms
to be interpreted as meaningful. Moreover, linguistic meaning must
encompass both the interpersonal dialogic role of an utterance (such as
requesting) and its representational function (such as classifying an
object). Linguistic meaning must also be relatable to the situational
context and to the broader sociocultural context. Finally, in the modelling
of language, there must be no irreconcilable dichotomy made between
language as an internally coherent system and the use of the system as
forms of meaningful social practice.

It will be suggested in the next chapter that systemic-functional
linguistic theory (SFL) comes closest to meeting these requirements,
largely because it has evolved as a means of addressing just the kinds of
questions concerning the role of language in social life and learning that
have been under attention here.

# 2 Systemic-functional linguistics: language as social semiotic

All the social theories described in the previous chapter have been concerned with the role of language in the mental and social formation of the child, offering insights which can be drawn on by linguistic theory. The particular contribution of a social linguistic theory, such as systemic-functional linguistics (SFL), is to suggest a model of the system of language which can help to explain its potential for use in the ways which have been described. This chapter will lay out the central theoretical concepts of SFL, showing how language is conceived both as an abstract system of relations and as an instrument for achieving social life and manifesting the culture. The account will begin with a sketch of language development intended to serve as a way of introducing some key orientations and dimensions of the theory. Then the nature of the adult system, particularly its (lexico-) grammatical core, will be explained, followed by an account of how the theory situates language in relation to social contexts of use. Having mapped out the general topography of the SFL model of language in context in this way, the final section will return to focus specifically on developmental issues. Here the theory will be re-presented in terms of how it offers insights towards a theory of learning, and the nature of the present case study as a contribution to such a theory will be introduced.

## 1 Systemic linguistics and language development

Systemic-functional linguistics (SFL), as developed by M.A.K. Halliday, draws on insights from Firth's (1957) system-structure theory, from Prague school linguistics (Danes 1974), from the glossomatics theory of Hjelmslev (1961) and from British and American anthropological linguistic traditions (Malinowski 1923, 1935, Sapir 1949, Whorf 1956). On every fundamental point concerning the nature of language it adopts a radically different perspective from that taken by American linguists addressing the 'problem of language acquisition', though like them it sees the emergence of language in the young child as a crucial issue to be addressed by linguistic theory.

Halliday prefers the metaphor of 'development' of language to that of 'acquisition' for a number of reasons which bear on the different theoretical perspective being taken. To speak of language as a commodity that is 'acquired' conjures an image of language as a finite, unitary, monolithic, unchanging phenomenon that an individual either 'has' or 'lacks'. This image sits happily enough with a conception of language as being at some deep level 'the same' formal system for all human beings, as being acquired 'once and for all' in toddlerhood and as being the mental property of an individual speaker-hearer once acquired. However, the metaphor sits much less comfortably with Halliday's view, which is of language as an infinite, variable, dynamic resource for meaning, which can continue to develop indefinitely and which is 'constructed and maintained interactively' (Halliday forthcoming).

In the following section, a brief account will be given of the SFL interpretation of the ontogenesis of language, in order to illustrate these various aspects of Halliday's view of language.

### 1.1  Developing 'protolanguage'

The social-interactive origins of language are emphasized in Halliday's account of language development, which can be linked to the studies of neonatal behaviour discussed earlier. Halliday refers to the gradually elaborated cooperative exchange of attention between infant and caregiver during the first six months of life in the following way:

> This exchange of attention is the beginning of language. It has no 'content', in the adult sense; but it has meaning. For the child, the meaning is 'we are together, and in communication; there is a "you" – and a "me"'. 'You' and 'me' are, of course, mutually defining; neither can exist without the other. (Halliday 1991b: 418–19)

In the suggestion that this initial intersubjective formation of the child's subjectivity constitutes the foundation for language, Halliday is stressing two things: that language is a system for meaning and that meaning is created in the process of mutual exchange.

The communication of the first few months is not linguistic, but a simple kind of 'protolanguage' does evolve when the child uses the communicative exchange of attention as a means of engaging with the phenomenal world, so that something external to the interactants finds a place in the communication. A number of studies have now described the way children, in the second half of the first year, begin to address other persons with their own invented vocalizations or gestures in order to draw their attention to objects or happenings around them. These are simple 'signs' in the Saussurean sense, in having a meaning coupled with an expression. (See Halliday 1975, 1979a, Painter 1984, Qiu 1985, Oldenburg 1990, Torr 1998 for SFL case studies of this stage, and Dore 1975, Dore et al. 1976, Bates 1976, Carter 1978, 1979, Menn 1978, Lock 1980 for descriptions within other frameworks.)

Because there is a consistency in the gestural or vocal expression used by the child on successive occasions and a consistency in the nature of the occasions of use, the communicating partner is able to interpret a meaning for the sign, to share the experience being attended to and to respond. For example a particular vocalization such as /ma/, or a gesture such as opening and shutting the fingers, might be addressed to the caregiver consistently and urgently in the presence of favourite food or toys and repeated until the caregiver responds by giving the object to the child. Such a sign could be glossed as 'give me that' or 'I want that'. Another vocalization – say /da/ – might be repeated by the child when pointing at a picture or object, resulting in the partner also attending to the object and perhaps also talking to the child. This sign could be glossed as meaning 'that's interesting – don't you agree?'.

One point about the protolanguage sign that emerges immediately is its status as an 'interact'. A gloss such as 'give me that' or 'that's interesting, don't you agree?' is an approximation in English to the kind of meaning being negotiated between the interactants when the caregiver is addressed by a protolinguistic vocalization or gesture. The meanings cannot be seen as simply imposed by the caregiver nor as simply owned by the child, since the success of the sign depends on the caregiver being able to interpret the child's expression in a way which makes sense to her but which also leads to a response that will satisfy the infant. Thus, the construal of meaning is necessarily a joint concern.

The interactive nature of the protolinguistic sign is a point of continuity with the child's earlier communicative experience; what is new is the entry into the communication of the domain of experience beyond the 'I' and 'you' – the 'objective' domain as opposed to the 'intersubjective'. Up till this point, that objective domain has been attended to, but not in communicative contexts (Trevarthen 1980, Bates *et al.* 1979). Now, by means of the protolanguage, engagement with the environment beyond the speaking interactants can be mediated through other people. Now either the intersubjective or the objective domain can be focused on as part of the communication.

Moreover, these domains can be focused on in different ways. They can be explored (with other people) in order to understand them better, or they can be acted on (through other people) in order to effect some change. These two modes of engagement, or 'forms of consciousness', Halliday (1992a) refers to as the 'reflective' and 'active' respectively.

Because the development of protolanguage is founded upon these two domains of prelinguistic experience (the intersubjective, the objective) and these two social modes of consciousness (action, reflection), it emerges neither in the form of a single symbol nor even a simple inventory of signs, but rather as a paradigm of alternatives. As shown in Figure 2.1, the intersection of each mode of consciousness with each domain of experience creates a semantic space with four possible ways of meaning, which Halliday terms the 'regulatory', 'instrumental', 'interpersonal' and 'personal' 'microfunctions'.

| Domain of experience | Form of consciousness | |
|---|---|---|
| | Action | Reflection |
| Intersubjective (I/you) | regulatory: 'you do' | interactional: 'being together' |
| Objective (s/he / it / them) | instrumental: 'I want that' | personal: 'that's interesting' |

**Figure 2.1**  Protolanguage: a paradigm of meanings (after Halliday 1992a)

In systemic theory, any paradigm of alternatives is termed a 'system' and modelled formally in a 'system network', the simplest kind being a set of mutually exclusive alternatives which are available for a particular initial choice ('entry condition'). In Figure 2.2 this is illustrated with the entry condition 'protolinguistic move' allowing for four meaning choices, one for each microfunction.

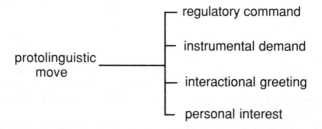

**Figure 2.2**  A simple system network illustrating microfunctional choices

The protolanguage system modelled above has just one meaning available for each microfunction. However, once there is a sign with both a signified (such as 'I want that') and a signifier, such as /ma/ – in other words, once there is an identifiable act of meaning within one of the four microfunctions – the possibility also immediately arises of a related alternative meaning within the same meaning area:

> An act of meaning implies a certain choice: if there is a meaning 'I want', then there can be a meaning 'I don't want', perhaps also 'I want very much', as alternatives. If there is a meaning 'I'm content', this can contrast with other states of being: 'I'm cross', 'I'm excited', and so on. (Halliday 1993b: 96)

Thus, taking Halliday's first example in this quotation, the instrumental meaning space might initially open up to a simple two-term opposition between [demand object] and [refuse object].[1] Then, at a later point, a finer, more 'delicate' contrast might be construed for the [demand object] option, as shown in Figure 2.3.

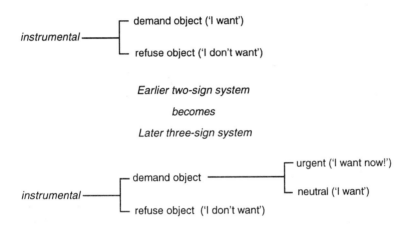

**Figure 2.3** Expansion of a system by the construal of more delicate options

It can be seen, then, that the semiotic system is being modelled as an expandable resource, a resource for making meaning, where meanings contrast with one another in sets of possibilities. Value relations are therefore at the heart of the description, and the meaning of 'I want' in the three-sign system is shown as different from that of the earlier system because it enters into a slightly different set of oppositions.

Of course, since it is the conjunction of meaning and sound which constitutes the protolinguistic sign, a description which elaborates all the meaning options is incomplete without an account of the realization of those meaning choices as sound or other expression forms. The meanings gain their actualization in vocal or gestural expression and conversely the expression forms actualize the meaning choices. In Figure 2.4, the realizations in expression form have been added to the simple system of three options within the instrumental function from Figure 2.3, using a small sloping arrow to indicate the realization.

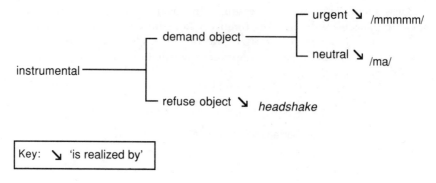

**Figure 2.4** A hypothetical instrumental protolanguage system

### *1.2  The nature of protolanguage*

In these three ways – in being a resource which engenders meaning which finds expression in sound, in being organized paradigmatically in terms of value relations and in being expandable – the infant's protolanguage shares characteristics of language proper. However, it differs from adult language in respects other than its size, and a consideration of these differences helps to foreground essential characteristics of the mature language system. These differences can be explored in terms of limitations in what protolanguage speakers can do with their sign system in actual contexts of use, and, more abstractly, in terms of the nature and organization of the paradigmatic resource itself. These in fact amount to the same thing viewed from different angles, since in systemic theory the use of the semiotic and its form are not two distinct phenomena.

With regard to the way the protolanguage system can be used, two related limitations are crucially important: its inability to categorize the phenomenal world and its inability to create dialogic roles where each speech (inter)act is responsive to the previous one, as in a sequence such as question, answer, acknowledgement. To illustrate the first point, we can imagine an expanded protolanguage system: the instrumental system described above and shown in Figure 2.4 might eventually be extended to include an option for a meaning interpretable as 'I want my dog', a meaning which would find expression in a unique vocalization (or gesture) which distinguished it from other signs. The system might also allow for a meaning within the personal function which could be glossed as 'look, there's a dog – that's interesting', having a different form of expression. Perhaps also there might even be a third sign, 'hello dog', with a different expression form again. But no matter how the system extends itself with new signs, it cannot construe the meaning of 'dog' as a separable, identifiable meaning element constant across these different contexts. By the same token, it does not allow for the various illocutionary meanings of 'I want', 'I observe' or 'I greet' to be factored out as separable meanings which could then be freely combined with different representational meanings like 'dog' or 'cat'.

The limitation of the protolanguage, then, lies in the nature of the sign as a meaning/expression complex which does not allow the teasing apart and separate notation of the representational and interpersonal aspects of meaning. It is inherent in the nature of the protolinguistic semiotic system that it does not allow a strand of representational choices, such as might be realized by lexical names, to be freely combined with interpersonal choices such as 'request', 'refuse', 'tell', 'ask', 'answer', 'challenge', and so on (which choices would also need a distinct realizational form). To achieve the separate notation and combined realization of two kinds of meaning, the semiotic needs to construe meanings as lexico-grammatical codings before they are recoded as sound.

## 1.3 The development of lexico-grammar

In the development towards the mother tongue, the lexico-grammatical expression of meaning is achieved when the action/reflection opposition at the heart of the protolanguage is reconstrued into a simultaneity. In other words instead of an act of meaning being *either* reflective (such as a personal utterance) *or* active (such as an instrumental one), it becomes possible for all utterances to construe representational meaning *and* simultaneously to construe a role for the speaker in relation to that meaning, with the two kinds of meaning freely combinable and recombinable. The change in the nature of the meaning system can be represented as in Figure 2.5 using a curly bracket ({) to indicate 'simultaneous' systems.

For different speech interacts to be freely combinable with different representations, it is of course necessary for there to be two strands to the realization. During a 'transition' phase, this is done by mapping one of two intonation contours onto a lexical name, allowing for a comment, such as *dog*, meaning 'that's a dog I see' to contrast with a demand, *dog*, meaning 'do something in relation to that dog' (see Halliday 1975, Painter 1984 for details). Figure 2.6 extends the earlier figure to include this example of how the two kinds of meaning are realized.

Eventually, as the possibilities for different speech roles expand, and as the representation of experience takes more complex forms than simple naming, the realization of the two kinds of meaning is achieved in the adult manner, whereby two strands of grammatical patterning are mapped onto one another. Semiotic action comes to be construed principally through the MOOD[2] system of adult lexico-grammar with options of [declarative], [interrogative], [imperative] and the like, while semiotic reflection is construed not just lexically, but through the TRANSITIVITY system, which classifies events into categories such as [material] and [mental] and construes them as configurations involving 'participant' roles, such as Actor and Goal. Example 2.1 exemplifies this dual grammatical patterning.

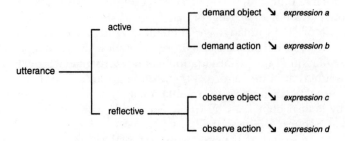

*Protolinguistic system of four alternative meanings construed by four distinct signs*

*becomes*

*Transitional language with two interpersonal meanings combinable with two representational meanings by means of simultaneous systems*

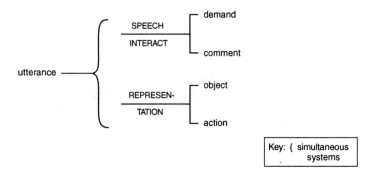

**Figure 2.5** The move from protolanguage to language

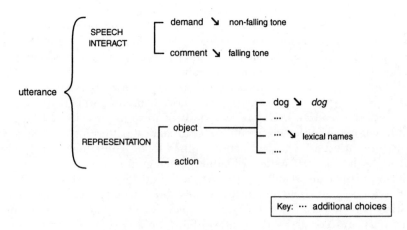

**Figure 2.6** 'Transition' phase realizations of two kinds of meaning

*Example 2.1*

| Can | dogs | catch | flies? |
|---|---|---|---|
| Finite | Subject | Predicator | Complement |
|  | Actor | Material Process | Goal |

*Structure realizing relevant MOOD choice*
*Structure realizing relevant TRANSITIVITY choice*

These parallel codings are the realizations of lexico-grammatical choices, and Figure 2.7 provides a highly simplified version of the choices which are being instantiated by this structure.

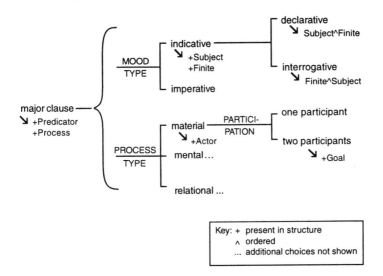

Key: +  present in structure
     ∧  ordered
     ...  additional choices not shown

**Figure 2.7** Simplified network illustrating options in MOOD and TRANSITIVITY systems

The move from protolanguage to language thus involves the development of a semiotic system with new characteristics. The meaning choices now have realizations in lexico-grammatical forms and these meaning choices evolve as two relatively independent strands – one concerned with interpersonal meaning and the other concerned with representation, or in Halliday's terms 'ideational' meaning. These strands Halliday refers to as 'metafunctions'. 'Functions' because they are fundamental uses of language – to interact with the addressee (interpersonal) and to make sense of experience (ideational) – and 'meta' because these extrinsic purposes have become the principle in terms of which the semiotic is organized.

In the process of evolving into this more complex kind of semiotic system, an additional metafunctional component develops. This one emerges not from any extrinsic function, but from the intrinsic function of organizing and relating the meanings construed by the other two metafunctions. In the process of participating in genuine dialogue, where speakers talk to each other about something over several turns, it becomes necessary to have ways of making it clear when the same thing is being referred to over successive utterances, of signalling when a change of direction or attitude is being made, of indicating what information is assumed to be shared between the speakers and what aspects of the message should be attended to as newsworthy, and so on. To enable the construction of coherent and relevant language in use, a third strand of options develops alongside the other two (Halliday 1979b). This is the 'textual metafunction', which includes the systems of REFERENCE, ELLIPSIS, CONJUNCTION and THEME.

To sum up, then, the systemic account of language development suggests that the lexico-grammar evolves to meet the twin requirements of the child: through the mediation of other persons both to act in the world and to reflect upon it. To enable both these functions to be fulfilled simultaneously in (virtually) any occasion of speech, the grammatical resources evolve as relatively distinct parallel sets of meaning options oriented to these different functions. Those functioning as a means of social action belong to the interpersonal metafunction, while those functioning to interpret experience belong to the ideational metafunction. A linguistic act of meaning involves simultaneous choices from both metafunctions. However, this development requires a third set of meaning choices – those of the textual metafunction, functioning to enable the other two by facilitating the ongoing coherence of the exchange of meaning in practice.

## 2  The nature of lexico-grammar

Two aspects of the lexico-grammar absent from a protolinguistic meaning system are the constituency organization of grammatical structures and the metafunctional organization of grammatical systems. These are characteristics common across languages, although their particular manifestations will vary from one language to another. In what follows, structures and systems are exemplified only from English, the language whose development will be illustrated in the following chapters.

The achievement of constituent structure has been generally recognized as a landmark in child language development. It follows the first moves into the mother tongue in which most children develop a language with only one kind of non-phonological unit – that of the word. But sooner or later the language expands to allow for the combination and recombination of words into grammatical structures, eventually providing the English speaker with systems of choices for four different sizes of unit: those of clause, group/phrase, word and morpheme, as shown in Table 2.1.

The most important classes of group are the nominal group, with a noun as Head word, and the verbal group, with a verb as Head word. Such groups have approximately the same status on the rank scale as prepositional phrases since all are intermediate in size and status between the clause and the word. However, 'whereas a group is an expansion of a word, a phrase is a contraction of a clause' (Halliday 1994:180), something which explains their different structural characteristics.

**Table 2.1**  The English rank scale exemplified

| Rank | Example |
| --- | --- |
| Clause | The Arabian mare was galloping round the racetrack |
| Group/phrase | The Arabian mare • was galloping • round the racetrack |
| Word | The • Arabian • mare • was • galloping • round • the • racetrack |
| Morpheme | The • Arab • ian • mare • was • gallop • ing • round • the • race • track |

The achievement of a rank scale of constituent structure is an important developmental step and one which greatly expands the meaning possibilities of the semiotic. The other key lexico-grammatical development, that of a metafunctionally organized system, similarly allows for rapid expansion of the meaning potential. In making the move from protolanguage to metafunctionally organized language, children develop a symbolic system with far greater potential for interpersonal communication and with a far greater potential for interpreting experience. It is true that protolinguistic symbols, which are tracked and interpreted by the child's interactive partners, enable infants to act in the world by requiring the addressee to give them goods and services, to repeat behaviours, to share affect and curiosity and so on. But with the development of interpersonal and ideational meanings, there arises the new possibility of sharing and exchanging a construal of experience. This in turn allows for the first time the sharing and exchanging of unshared experience – the creation of information as a substitute for shared experience.

*2.1 Interpersonal metafunction*

Actualizing the possibility of information exchange within the interpersonal metafunction brings about a development in the options for interaction through language, as new speaker roles of giving and demanding information are instantiated through the MOOD options of [declarative] and [interrogative]. Other interpersonal systems opened up by the possibility of exchanging information are those concerned with negotiating speaker and addressee judgements and attitudes towards the proposition. The interpersonal system of MODALITY is important here, opening up a semantic space between the positive and negative, the two poles construed by the system of POLARITY. The MODALITY system enables the expression of shades of PROBABILITY (*it might be; it could be; it must be*) or of USUALITY (*it sometimes is; it usually is; it always is*). Where language is mediating the exchange of goods and services, a 'proposal' rather than a proposition is negotiated and parallel systems of OBLIGATION *(you ought to; you have to; you're allowed to)* and INCLINATION *(I'm willing; I'm determined)* develop, as summarized in Table 2.2.

**Table 2.2** Modality systems in English

| OBLIGATION | INCLINATION | PROBABILITY | USUALITY |
|---|---|---|---|
| he must train | he's determined to train | he must train | he always trains |
| he should train | he's keen to train | he probably trains | he often trains |
| he may/can train | he's willing to train | he might train | he sometimes trains |

Modality options can be ranged, as in Table 2.2, according to a scale of high–median–low values, with various shades in between these also possible. In a similar way, English speakers can indicate their assessments through grading of qualities, quantities and so on *(very hot, hotter, too many, not enough)* (Martin 1992b). Through all these systems of the interpersonal metafunction, the speaker and hearer enact social relationships, as these various meanings are mapped onto ideational ones.

### 2.2 *Ideational metafunction*

The ideational metafunction provides the means of representing or construing phenomenal experience. The earlier example given concerned the construal of a class of things by the lexical name 'dog'. Such a meaning is one that the child arrives at through experience of communicating with other persons. As already discussed, the world is not accessible for understanding other than through the mediation of the significant others of the child's community, which means through the mediation of language. The mother tongue does not simply mirror what is 'out there' (or some mental representation of it), but provides an interpretation, in Halliday's words 'a theory of human experience' (Halliday, forthcoming).

Construing categories of phenomena is one aspect of theorizing experience, with different classes of word developing to do so: verbs for processes, nouns for entities, adjectives and adverbs for their qualities, and so on. But the ideational component is much more than a resource for naming, and the different word classes in English may in any case only be recognizable from the way they configure in larger constructions. The most central of these is the clause, since this is the unit most clearly carrying the three strands of metafunctional patterning. As an interpersonal construct the clause is a move in the exchange of goods and services (a proposal) or of information (a proposition). As an ideational construct it is an interpretation of experience as a process, some change from one state to another, involving participants and circumstances.

Halliday (1994) argues that the grammar makes a distinction between events experienced as outside ourselves and those which are inside our own consciousness, such as thinking, feeling and perceiving. These are construed as two different classes of process: 'material' and 'mental', each with its own configurations of participant roles and its own grammatical characteristics, as shown in Table 2.3.

**Table 2.3** Characteristics of material and mental processes

|  | Participant roles | Grammatical characteristics of process type |
|---|---|---|
| Outer (i.e. material) processes | Actor (inherent) Goal Beneficiary | **unmarked present tense:** progressive **participants:** animate, inanimate but not facts **'projection'** of another clause as quote or report? No **'two-way' processes?** No |
| Inner (i.e. mental) processes | Senser (inherent) Phenomenon | **unmarked present tense:** simple **participants:** Senser must be animate, Phenomenon can be fact **'projection'** of another clause as a quote or report? Yes **'two-way' processes?** Yes (*like/please; fear/frighten*, etc.) |

This distinction is one relevant to recent developmental theory which addresses the question of when children develop 'a theory of mind', an ability to construe other persons as conscious beings whose behaviour is dependent on their perceptual and cognitive intentions and experience[3] (Astington 1994). But the distinction between outer and inner processes is not the only one made: our human experience as semiotic beings naturally leads the grammar to make languaging itself part of the theory of experience. This is done in two ways. Experience of language as communication is construed by 'verbal' processes of saying, telling, promising and the like, while the nature of symbolizing itself – including reference, denotation, realization and categorization – is construed through 'relational' processes which do not construe events but set up an identity relation (*Fido is my dog*) or a classificatory one (*Fido is a dog*). Four, rather than two, principal types of process must therefore be recognized.

The grammar of processes, participants and accompanying 'circum-stances' (time, place, manner, etc.), known collectively as TRANSITIVITY, constitutes the central core of the 'experiential' component of the ideational metafunction. The TRANSITIVITY system (like the interpersonal MOOD system) comprises choices available for a clause, and the functional parts of the clause (participant, process, circumstance) are realized by smaller units: nominal group, verbal group, prepositional phrase, as marked in Example 2.2.

*Example* 2.2

| CLAUSE RANK | My beautiful boxer dog | is racing | down the street |
|---|---|---|---|
| | participant | process | circumstance |
| GROUP/ PHRASE RANK | nominal group | verbal group | prepositional phrase |

It should be noted that these smaller units have their own meaning structure, realized in smaller units again – words.

In addition to TRANSITIVITY meanings and the experiential meanings available for lower rank units, there is another component to the ideational metafunction, one which is not concerned with part–whole constituency relationships. This is the 'logical' component

> with which the grammar shows that processes are not all independent of one another; it sets up a network of possible relations that may obtain between any pair of adjacent processes. (Halliday, forthcoming)

One set of these inter-process relationships – those of addition, contrast, time, cause, condition, etc. – is construed largely by the class of conjunctions, while the other relation, that of 'projection', involves the mental and verbal process types. These latter can construct the status of a second process as a representation of what someone says or thinks, as for example with *Daddy says the cat is hungry.*

Thus the ideational metafunction has two components: the experiential and the logical. The former creates finite constituent structures of the clause (and of smaller units such as the nominal group), while the latter creates extendable, iterative structures, linking clauses or other units together in a logical series.

## 2.3 *Textual metafunction*

The textual metafunction, the third strand of meaning, which enables the effective creation of ongoing discourse, also makes a contribution to the structure of the clause through its organization into two components – those of Theme and Rheme. The Theme constitutes the speaker's orientation or 'point of departure' for the Rheme that follows and so occurs at the beginning of the clause. There will always be an ideational component to the Theme, but a speaker may on occasion choose to make a textual and/or interpersonal element thematic as well, as in Example 2.3.

Much of the work of the textual metafunction is concerned with meaning relationships constructed within the whole text rather than the clause. For example the 'REFERENCE' system serves to identify and keep track of participants within a text, as illustrated in the following fragment

*Example 2.3*

| On the other hand | maybe | the cat | is hungry |
|---|---|---|---|
| Textual | Interpersonal | Ideational | |
| Theme | | | Rheme |

from a child's story, where the pronouns *she* and *it* and the determiner *the* signal that the relevant participant can be 'recoverable' by the hearer:

> Once upon a time there was <u>a princess</u>, who had <u>a beautiful white horse</u>. **She** loved **the** horse, and every day **she** groomed **it** . . .

In this case the identity of the participants in the second clause can be understood from nominal groups present in the previous clause. This retrieval of identity from the co-text is 'endophoric' reference. Alternatively, a participant's identity might be retrieved from a shared situational context, as with a conversational exclamation *Look at that!* Here, the reference is 'exophoric' in that the identity of the participant coded as *that* must be interpreted from some shared non-textual context. Thus, in its relevance-creating function, the textual metafunction organizes meanings both at the clause level and across the whole text, creating links both to co-text and context.

In summary, the grammar of English, through the three metafunctions, provides a resource for enacting social relationships, construing experience and creating relevant and cohesive text. It does this through parallel, simultaneous systems of the clause, through meaning choices relevant for smaller grammatical units, through the logical linkage of clauses to one another, and through meaning relationships across clauses and from text to context.

## 2.4 Language as a tri-stratal semiotic

The potential for growth of the semiotic system increases enormously with the development of lexico-grammar. One aspect of this is the metafunctional diversity which allows for expansion across the three strands of meaning. Another aspect, not yet discussed, is an elaboration of the meaning choices into two layers, or 'strata', so that a layer of 'lexico-grammatical' choices is itself the realization of a layer of 'semantic' (Halliday 1994) or 'discourse-semantic' choices (Martin 1992a). This can be illustrated from an example within the interpersonal metafunction.

The lexico-grammatical choice of [declarative], which is realized in the clause structure as Subject ordered before Finite, can itself be regarded as realizing the semantic choice of [give information], or 'statement', shown in Figure 2.8. However, if a declarative structure were the only realization of the meaning of giving information, it would hardly be necessary to see two choices (statement and declarative) as being involved. But of course in the mature language, a statement need not be realized as a declarative structure, but might instead be realized by the lexico-grammatical choice of [interrogative], as in *Have I ever forgotten your birthday?* used to assert 'I have never forgotten your birthday.' Alternatively the [declarative] option might on occasions realize a (semantic) question, as in the case of *You've accepted the job, I take it?* used to seek information. In the developed language there is no one-to-one biunique relation between the semantic choices of SPEECH FUNCTION and the grammatical choices of MOOD. The [declarative] option may be regarded as the 'natural' or 'congruent' realization of a statement, in that the declarative structure evolved to construe that very meaning of giving information. But through 'stratification' of the meaning potential, countless additional meanings become possible through the many-to-many realizational possibilities between semantic and grammatical choices.

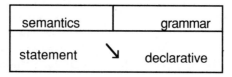

**Figure 2.8** Grammatical choice realizes semantic choice

The model of language as tri-stratal, with the meaning options (i.e. those of the non-phonological strata) organized metafunctionally is schematized in Figure 2.9.

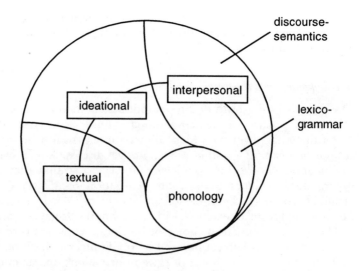

**Figure 2.9** Language as a tri-stratal, metafunctional system

The lexico-grammatical stratum of options that eventually emerges therefore evolves as a splitting into two levels of the meaning choices of the semiotic, which begins to occur at the time the meaning choices become metafunctionally organized (see Painter 1984: 214–19). An important corollary of this interpretation of grammar, as options for meaning which realize 'higher' options for meaning, is that the relation between the semantics and the grammar is seen as a 'natural' one, rather than being merely arbitrary and conventional, like the relation between semantics and phonology. This in turn means that structural realizations of grammatical options are viewed as configurations of meaning and are assigned meaning-oriented functional labels, such as Actor, Subject, Theme. It also means that an analysis of the lexico-grammatical structures of any text is necessarily an interpretation of the meaning of the text.

## 3 Language in use

### 3.1 System and process

SFL theory, as outlined so far, clearly avoids the dichotomizing of meaning and form so characteristic of Chomskyan linguistics and of psycholinguistic approaches to language learning. At the same time it avoids dichotomizing the system and the use of the system. It models language in terms of an elaborate network of paradigmatic relations (sets of meaning options), and these relations imply a rich realizational potential of 'words and structures'. On any particular occasion of use, particular meaning choices are made and particular lexico-grammatical forms are actualized. In other words, a particular spoken utterance or exchange is a specific instance of the systemic potential. This way of modelling the linguistic system as a paradigmatic resource and the text as an instantiation of choices from that system embodies the semiotic principle that meaning is relational, constructed by oppositions, and avoids the notion that form is symbolic and meaning is not. It also avoids Chomsky's dualism between knowing a form and knowing its use, a dualism which ultimately amounts again to seeing form as autonomous, something to be filled with or attached to meanings which have to be separately construed and then matched up with language-as-form.

Further than this, it is the recognition that language encompasses both system and use – both paradigmatic potential and actualizations of that potential – that helps explain the possibility of development and change in the meaning potential. When modelled as a system network, language is being viewed synoptically (Martin 1985), and appears static, a finite set of meaning options. But precisely because meaning is an intersubjective activity, there can be no meaning without the actualization of those possibilities for meaning, as text. And it is in the instantiation of meaning options in speech that the system is not only created but maintained and changed. A linguistic system can thus be viewed from the perspective of the totality of meaning possibilities at any hypothetical moment in time ('the system'), or it can be viewed in terms of particular instantiations of that system which have taken place ('the process', 'the text').

To clarify this relation between language as system and process, Halliday uses the analogy of the climate as a system, in comparison with the weather as instances of that system:

> A climate is a reasonably stable system; there are kinds of climate, such as tropical and polar, and these persist, and they differ in systematic ways. Yet we are all very concerned about changes in the climate, and the consequences of global warming. What does it mean to say the climate is changing? Climate is instantiated in the form of weather: today's temperature, humidity, direction and speed of wind, etc., in central Scotland are INSTANCES of climatic phenomena. As such they may be more, or less, TYPICAL: today's maximum is so many degrees higher, or lower, than AVERAGE – meaning the average at this place, at this time of year and this time of day. The average is a statement of the PROBABILITIES: there is a 70 per cent chance, let us say, that the temperature will fall within such a range. The probability is a feature of the SYSTEM (the climate); but it is no more, and no less, than the pattern set up by the instances (the weather), and each instance, no matter how minutely, perturbs these probabilities and so changes the system (or else keeps it as it is, which is just the limiting case of changing it).
>
> The climate and the weather are not two different phenomena. They are the same phenomenon seen by two different observers, standing at different distances – different time depths . . . So it is also with language: language as system, and language as instance. (Halliday 1992a: 26)

So in discussing the way the linguistic *system* develops and changes, it has to be remembered that this is possible because language is being continually instantiated in the form of speech. Children construe the system of language from the innumerable occasions of text which they observe and in which they participate, while at the same time it is the system which enables them to participate in text. This continuous dialectic between system and process can be related to the Vygotskyan notion of the zone of proximal development, in that a child may be enabled, in dialogue with the conversational partner, to create texts that are slightly beyond the current systemic potential. These collaboratively produced texts perturb the system, in that they are being processed as well as produced, so that in time the system extends to accommodate the new possibilities. Thus language is interactively constructed with respect both to text and to system.

### 3.2  Language and context

In addition to providing a way of relating system and use, the modelling of language as a paradigmatic resource provides a way of describing different kinds of linguistic variation. One kind of variation – functional or 'register' variation – is a matter of the way that language is used differently in different kinds of contexts. That is, the English used during a family mealtime conversation is very different from that of a business meeting, a church service, a television real estate advertisement, a child's fairy story, and so on, and yet one would want to recognize that all make use of the same English grammar. This kind of variation according to use can be explained in terms of different selections from the semantic resources being made in different situational contexts, resulting in different tendencies in the lexico-grammatical realizations.

If different meaning choices come into play in different situations, then clearly it is necessary to have a means of modelling the contexts for language in use. And here it needs to be recognized that language is a social phenomenon, not just in being interactional between individuals, but in the fact that any interpersonal interaction takes place within a broader sociocultural environment. Halliday (1978a: 189) takes account of this when he describes a situational context for speech as 'a temporary construct or instantiation of meanings from the social system'. This means the extralinguistic environment for a text is being interpreted as an instance of the social system, while the extralinguistic environment for language as system is understood to be the social system itself:

> The context for the meaning potential – for language as a system – is the context of culture . . . the context for the particular instances – for language as processes of text – is the context of situation. And just as a piece of text is an instance of language, so a situation is an instance of culture. So there is a proportion here. The context for an instance of language (text) is an instance of culture (situation). And the context for the system that lies behind each text (language) is the system which lies behind each situation – namely, the culture. (Halliday 1991a: 7)

This proportionality is illustrated in Figure 2.10.

|  | Environment | Language |
|---|---|---|
| Meaning potential | Social system (culture) | Linguistic system |
| Instantiation | Social context (situation) | Text |

**Figure 2.10** The social environment for language as system and text

In this interpretation, the social system, or culture, is regarded as a complex system of meanings, and its relation to language is one of realization, comparable to the relation between semantics and lexico-grammar. This is not of course to suggest that it is only through talk that the social system is manifested and made accessible. The point is rather that the social system is conceived of as semiotic in nature and the other ways it is manifested – through forms of art, codes of dress, through the legal and educational systems, through social institutions like the church and the law – are themselves seen as symbolic systems. But these more visible systems are no more important in realizing the meanings, values, structures of the society than is everyday casual conversational interaction.

In sum, the systemic model suggests that just as language can be viewed in terms of system or instance, so the social system can also be viewed from these two perspectives. As already discussed, the child only has experiences of language in use – texts – from which to construe the systemic potential of language, and in a similar way it is from social contextual instances that the child must construe the social system. Since those social contextual instances are being realized largely (even though not exclusively) through linguistic choices which create texts, it follows that it is through participation in individual texts that particular social contexts are largely constituted for the child, and thus ultimately it is principally from instances of text that the child construes the social system.

Clearly this approach can also be readily aligned to Bernstein's work on socialization, where his original argument that different social groups favour different lexico-grammatical patterns has been developed in terms of different groups having different 'semantic styles' (Halliday 1978a: 111). These semantic styles can be seen as different habitual meaning choices, different pathways through the semantic and grammatical meaning potential favoured by different social groups. While register variation concerns different linguistic choices for different social purposes, Bernstein's codes involve different linguistic realizations by different social groups of some common extralinguistic social context, such as regulation of the child by the parent.

The general point, then, is that in learning language, a child is never learning an autonomous formal system. The grammar construes meaning and the meanings ultimately derive from the culture. In this way 'the child's focus moves easily between microsemiotic and macrosemiotic environment' (Halliday 1978a:124). Halliday illustrates this point informally, with an example from his case study of Nigel:

> So when Nigel's mother said to him 'Leave that stick outside; stop teasing the cat; and go and wash your hands. It's time for tea', he could not only understand the instructions but could also derive from them information about the social system: about the boundaries dividing social space, and 'what goes where'; about the continuity between the human and the animal world; about the regularity of cultural events; and more besides. He does not, of course, learn all this from a single instance, but from the countless sociosemiotic events of this kind that make up the life of social man.

The argument is that, just as instances of language in use are the child's data for construing the underlying language system, so instances of language in context provide the child with data for construing the underlying social system and the values and ideologies with which it is imbued. This is a position which would appear to be compatible with the approach and findings of ethnographic studies of the role of language in socialization, such as those of Heath or of Ochs and Schieffelin, as well as with Bernstein's theory of codes as different subcultural orientations to meaning.

In discussing the relationship between culture and language, context and text, Halliday emphasizes that the relationship is one of realization and not cause and effect:

> The situation is 'realized' in the text. Similarly the culture is 'realized' in the linguistic system. This does not mean that the one somehow **causes** the other. The relationship is not one of cause. It is a semiotic relationship; one that arises between pairs of information systems, interlocking systems of meaning. (Halliday 1991a: 15)

It is not therefore a case of culture causing language or language determining culture – the two have coevolved. And in terms of the instance of language and the instance of culture, the same relationship applies – the context of situation does not determine the text, but is realized as text, which in that realization constructs the context. Thus the two are simultaneously construed by the child.

### 3.3  Metafunctional construal of context

There is a further step in the systemic analysis of context, relevant to the problem of making principled links between contextual choices and linguistic ones. Clearly, in addition to a theoretical recognition that instances of language occur in social contexts, it is necessary to have some way of further describing the social context so as to be able to track some realizational path from contextual options to linguistic ones. An important move in this direction is the analysis of the social context for a text – the 'context of situation' in Malinowski's (1923: 306) terminology – as a three-part semiotic construct which relates to the three metafunctions of language (interpersonal, ideational and textual).

The three components of the context of situation are its 'tenor', which refers to the roles and relationships of the interactants, its 'field', the term for what the interactants in the situation are doing, and its 'mode' – the role assigned to language in the enactment of the situation. Each of these three components will be both actualized and constituted by choices in one of the three linguistic metafunctions (as well as by choices made from other semiotic systems, such as gestural, kinesic ones).

### 3.3.1  Tenor

The social roles and relationships of the interactants are a crucial aspect of any context for language in use. The power relations holding between interlocutors (in terms of both authority and expertise), the degree to which they are known to each other, the social roles being taken on in the particular instance and the nature of the affectual relations holding between them are all aspects of the context for a text which have a bearing on the options for meaning taken up by each party to the discourse. (See Poynton 1989.) And conversely, the linguistic options taken up in the course of an interaction will serve to construct the interactant roles and relationships. These linguistic options will be those of the interpersonal metafunction – choices in SPEECH FUNCTION, MOOD, MODALITY, INTENSITY and so on.

### 3.3.2 Field

The field has been described by Halliday as the social action being undertaken on any occasion of language in use. It is

> that which is 'going on', and has recognizable meaning in the social system; typically a complex of acts in some ordered configuration, and in which the text is playing some part, and including 'subject-matter' as one special aspect . . . (Halliday 1978a: 142–3)

The field component of the context will be realized by ideational linguistic choices

> in transitivity, in the classes of things (objects, persons, events, etc.), in quality, quantity, time, place and so on . . . (Halliday 1978a: 143)

Martin (1992a: 292), developing the notion of field as a semiotic system, defines fields as 'sets of activity sequences oriented to some global institutional purpose'. He gives the following examples of fields: 'linguistics, tennis, cooking, winemaking, gardening, dog breeding, film, architecture, sewing, car racing, philosophy, sailing, building, chess, war, politics, religion and so on', and adds that 'obviously there are fields within fields and subfields within these'.

He suggests that

> as a first approximation, these activity sequences can be broken down as follows:
> i. Taxonomies of actions, people, places, things and qualities
> ii. Configurations of actions with people, places, things and qualities . . .
> iii. Activity sequences of these configurations. (Martin 1992a: 292)

The taxonomies are the semantically organized 'classes of things' that Halliday refers to, and elements from these configure into structures realized linguistically through the clause systems of TRANSITIVITY. These activities are sequenced with respect to one another to constitute the activity which is the field or subfield.

One aspect of 'the culture' viewed as a semiotic system is thus argued to be a network of fields and subfields describable (though this has not yet been done) in terms of taxonomies of participants and sequences of activities, which may gain expression in the ideational component of language. So, for example, an everyday activity such as 'catching the bus' will instantiate options from various semantic taxonomies, such as forms of passenger transport, the personnel involved (drivers, passengers, fare collectors, etc.), locations where passengers board and leave, ticket types, and so on. Configurations of such elements constitute the activities involved in taking a bus ride, which are carried out in sequence. These activities (in Sydney) include the passengers walking to a bus stop, waiting, hailing the bus, mounting in turn at the appropriate entrance, perhaps checking the destination and/or fare with the driver, then paying a fare or showing a pass or validating a previously purchased ticket (each involving its own micro sequence of actions), taking a seat or standing in the centre aisle, signalling with the bell when planning to alight, and so on.

This particular example of a social process is one in which linguistic acts of meaning will be only minimally involved. However, all the activities constituting the social process are meaningful, and the 'knowledge of the world' brought into play in carrying them out and interpreting their linguistic component is itself semiotic in nature. A recognition of this would seem to be implicit in the metaphor of 'scripts' used within the artificial intelligence and psychological literature to address knowledge of sequences of events together with the set of actors and players involved (Schank and Abelson 1977; Nelson and Gruendel 1979), an approach which has also been used to take a more text-oriented approach to children's language development (Nelson and Seidman 1984).[4]

Although catching a bus is a social process which requires very little use of language for its achievement, giving instructions to a child or foreign visitor for travelling by bus, or recounting a particular bus trip, calls for an explicit linguistic representation of at least some activities within the sequence and it will be the ideational grammar of lexical taxonomies and of participants and processes that will be deployed to do so.

### 3.3.3 Mode

The differing role of language in the actualization of social processes, mentioned above, is the contextual variable of 'mode'. Where language is simply a tool to facilitate a social process that can be carried out through non-linguistic behaviour, language can be said to have an 'ancillary' or accompanying role. On the other hand, where the social process consists entirely in linguistic behaviour, as in the drawing up of a contract or the narrating of a story or the teaching of history in school, language has a 'constitutive' role (Halliday and Hasan 1989: 58).

The effect of differences in mode can be seen most clearly when two social processes which share aspects of the field are considered. For example, a television commentary on a football match has a more ancillary mode than a written newspaper report on the same game. While

there is likely to be some similarity in the ideational meanings expressed –
the same things will be referred to, the same activities talked about – there
will be a great difference in the deployment of textual grammar. Clearly
the text more distanced in time from the activity being discussed, and for
which there is no ongoing shared visual setting, will rely more heavily on
the language to organize the information, will need to be much more
explicit about what things are being referred to and will need to construct
the sequence of events explicitly in language. To do this there will need to
be a different mobilization of the resources of the textual metafunction –
for example, a different use of thematic organization, a greater use of
anaphoric reference and conjunction, less ellipsis, and so on.

The situational context in which a text occurs can therefore be seen in
terms of three crucial components – tenor, field and mode – which are
related to the three components of the linguistic system – the
interpersonal, ideational and textual respectively, as shown in Figure 2.11.

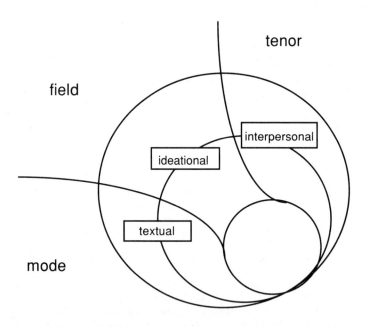

**Figure 2.11** The relation between context and text

Thus discourses in contexts with the same tenor and mode variables but
different fields would be predicted to differ with respect to the ideational
systems of the semantics and grammar. Discourses in contexts with the
same field and tenor, but different mode variables would be expected to
differ chiefly with respect to selections for the textual metafunction. And
similarly, discourses alike in field and mode but differing in tenor relations
would be expected to differ chiefly in the nature of choices from the

interpersonal metafunction. Neither the three aspects of the context nor the three components of the linguistic system are of course seen as entirely independent, but sufficiently so for this kind of patterning to be expected.

Recent work within systemic theory by Martin (1992a) attempts to begin characterizing the contextual components as a generalized potential in terms of networks of options. A particular situation providing the specific context for a particular text is then described in terms of the selection of options at the contextual level. In Hasan's work (Halliday and Hasan 1989), a similar distinction is made between the potential constituted by the contextual variables and the particular values taken up on a particular occasion which constitute the contextual configuration for that text. Thus while the uniqueness of any particular situation can be allowed for, similarities of patternings allow for the notion of situation 'type'. Situations and texts, therefore, can be understood as unique occasions, but more importantly, can also be recognized as systematically similar or in contrast with other occasions by virtue of belonging to the same or different generalized situation type.

In considering the relation between text and context as instances of language and culture, it is important to repeat that there is a mutual relationship between the two. Texts are one of the forms in which contexts gain expression, but those contexts themselves are in turn partly, or entirely, constituted by the language that takes place within them. The linguistic choices made on a particular occasion not only reveal contextual values but construct them. Thus the culture itself is seen as a set of semiotic systems which both gain expression and are continually created through other semiotic systems, of which language is perhaps the most important.

## 4  Systemic linguistics as a theory of learning

> When children learn language, they are not simply engaging in one kind of learning among many – rather, they are learning the foundation of learning itself. The distinctive characteristic of human learning is that it is a process of making meaning, a **semiotic** process; and the prototypical form of human semiotic is language. Hence the ontogenesis of language is at the same time the ontogenesis of learning. (Halliday 1993b: 93)

In this section an attempt will be made to summarize or elaborate on aspects of systemic theory in order to focus specifically on how the theory considers the question of learning. Learning is generally considered and discussed using the constructs and metalanguage of cognitive psychology, involving 'conceptual development', 'cognitive processes', 'thought', and the like. Indeed, as seen in the earlier discussion of the conduit metaphor, these are the terms in which commonsense, non-technical talk about understanding and communication take place. What SFL offers is an alternative way of formulating these issues, based on the principle that learning is essentially a semiotic enterprise.

The earlier discussion of the developmental literature on language and thought provided some evidence that when learning is conceived of in mentalist terms it can be difficult to bring language into the picture. Since learning is seen as involving conceptual development, the learner's concepts, existing in some non-symbolic mental medium, need at some point to be brought together with the symbolic forms of language. This issue tends to be resolved by according language the conveyancing role of making public inner conceptualizations (see Chapter 1, Section 1.2). Unfortunately, such a view readily leads to an educational approach which may elide language altogether, as argued by Hirst (1974), addressing the question as a philosopher rather than as a psychologist or linguist. He warns that if the medium in which thought occurs is seen as composed of 'ideas' or 'concepts' upon which operations of thinking such as abstracting, inferring or deducing occur, then all of these mental operations 'can in principle occur quite independently of any use of language in which thoughts can be expressed' (Hirst 1974: 70). The business of education is then likely to be directed at cognitive processes without reference to language.

As we have seen, however, Trevarthen has shown that newborns are social beings, designed to learn from other people, while work on prelinguistic vocalization and gesturing suggests that symbolic exchange with others begins much earlier than the first mother-tongue words and structures. Vygotsky in turn has argued that the 'natural', biological line of mental functioning, which proceeds initially, is transformed by linguistic interaction. All this work points to the role of symbolic exchange in the learning process. Similarly, Halliday argues against trying to relate language and thought as distinct lines of development, suggesting instead that cognitive processes are most usefully interpreted as being semiotic processes, with language as the most important of these. From this perspective, conceptual development is the development of semiotic potential, most particularly the development of a linguistic meaning potential:

> [Cognitive and linguistic processes] are not two different things; they are two different ways of looking at the same thing. We can interpret such processes cognitively, as thought, or semantically, as meaning – as one aspect of the total phenomenon we call 'language'. (Halliday 1988b:1)

The great advantage of adopting this approach is that the manifestation of cognitive processes can then be looked for in the lexico-grammatical and phonological realization of meaning:

> We can then relate [cognitive processes] to the other, more observable aspects of language: its wording ('lexico-grammar'), its writing and its sounds. Since language is not only the primary means by which a person learns but also the primary evidence we have for judging what that person has learnt, it is helpful to conceive of learning in linguistic terms. (Halliday 1988b: 1)

In this way, issues of 'cognitive development' become issues of semantic development and can be addressed through an exploration of the wordings of a learner's texts, since these are the actualizations of the learner's meaning system.

An account of learning language within this approach thus becomes a description of the development of resources for meaning (in psychological terms, resources for thinking) – and hence the development of the means of learning itself. The systemic account of language development argues that children construe a language in interaction with others to gain both control and understanding of their environment. The language which is developed shows evidence of this impetus in being organized on a metafunctional principle as resources for acting in the world and resources for understanding it. And it is the simultaneity of acting and reflecting when these resources are instantiated as text which is the key to learning through language.

Making meaning, even when exploring the objective world, is achieved interactively, and in suggesting that the linguistic system is a tool shaped partly by the need to make sense of the world, it is recognized that that world is not available to the child 'raw', awaiting private understanding. From the beginning, reality is being continuously interpreted to and by the child with the 'significant others' of his/her first meaning group – the world available for knowing, including the child's own subjectivity, is a semiotically, and hence intersubjectively, constructed one. And this semantic construction of the environment takes place with every instantiation of the meaning system in all the countless conversational and other semiotic exchanges of everyday life.

During these conversational exchanges, very young children are simultaneously developing the linguistic system of their meaning group and the social semiotic systems which gain their realization through language (as well as through other semiotic systems with their own planes of expression). The semiotic systems of field, mode and tenor have been mentioned and the model may be further elaborated to allow for further representing the social system in terms of semiotic systems of genre and/or ideology beyond these (Martin 1992a). Through the relationship of realization all these non-linguistic meaning systems find their actualization in lexico-grammatical and phonological/graphological form – an actualization which simultaneously serves to construe the higher-level systems.

This learning of and through language takes place through conversation whose overt goal is simply to get on with the business of everyday life. Children learn language and become socialized into the culture at home by others who may have minimal conscious knowledge about either language or the social system. The effectiveness of everyday talk as a means of initial apprenticeship into the culture indeed lies in the very implicitness of what is taught and learned – the 'commonsense' knowledge that can henceforward be taken for granted as the basis for living.

As a particular resource for coming to know the phenomenal world, the ideational component of the mother tongue is developed by the child. This component is a meaning potential which constitutes a theory of experience. That is, the ideational resources constitute an interpretation, since experience must be construed – as discussed earlier in this chapter, 'nothing real "just is"' (Shweder 1990: 4). In interaction with other persons, and in the processes of enacting social relationships, children come to achieve this construal according to the theory provided by the language:

> What makes learning possible is that the coding imposed by the mother tongue corresponds to a *possible* mode of perception and interpretation of the environment. A green car *can* be analyzed experientially as carness qualified by greenness, if that is the way the system works. (Halliday 1975: 140)

> Nigel's experience of how things are is such that it can be represented in terms of processes, of people and things functioning as participants in these processes, and of accompanying circumstances. Not that reality can *only* be represented in this way, but this is a *possible* semantic interpretation; the fact that Nigel adopts this form of representation rather than another one is because this is the way it is done in the language he hears around him. (Halliday 1975: 106)

One of the first ideational achievements of the move into the mother tongue is the generalization of experience achieved through naming. Different aspects of experience are named by different classes of word – process by verbs, participants by nouns, their qualities by adjectives, etc. Nouns, verbs, adjectives are all 'common' words, that is words for construing classes, for recognizing different individual, specific experiences as being in some sense the same. Although for some children the very first move into the mother tongue will involve proper names, construing unique individuals (e.g. Halliday 1975: 67), the model of the mother tongue very quickly enables the child to generalize experience through word classes.

An important aspect of the ideational grammar as a resource for learning is that it is not a rigid, inflexible grid imposed on the learner, but provides for multiple perspectives on experience. For example, Halliday (1994) argues that in English the grammar of TRANSITIVITY allows an event configuration to be interpreted 'transitively' on the model of an Actor doing, with or without a Goal (*he's building/he's building a castle*), but also 'ergatively' on the model of a Medium participating in a process, with or without an Agent (*the clothes are drying/the wind is drying the clothes*). The different process types themselves – material, mental, relational – are not discrete categories, but shade into one another through minor intervening categories which share features of types on either side, forming a 'flexible semantic space' (Halliday forthcoming). Different perspectives are again offered by the two components of the ideational grammar. The experiential component suggests a particulate, constituency model of experience, while the logical complements this by representing experience on a more dynamic, flowing, recursive model. Thus, 'the grammar of daily life is rich in multiple perspectives of this kind' (Halliday 1993b:108). Through such means, this multifaceted meaning resource allows us to 'transform experience into the coherent – though far from consistent – patchwork that we learn to project as "reality"' (Halliday 1993a: 10).

One aspect of learning language, then, is the construal of reality through the resources of the ideational metafunction. And since language itself is part of the totality of experience, it too can be an object of reflection as well as the means of reflection. This complex situation is possible because of the self-reflexivity of semiotic systems. Not only does language in use create discourse which must itself be organized and referred to by means of the textual metafunction, but language as system and text also becomes available for reflection using the resources of verbal and relational process within the ideational metafunction. Thus, using language to learn *through* language inevitably entails learning *about* language (Halliday 1980).

This takes place at the implicit, unconscious, everyday commonsense level (for example in the way speakers use the 'conduit metaphor') and also in the building of explicit theories about language:

> By the act of meaning, consciousness imposes order on the phenomena of experience. When protolanguage evolves into language . . . meaning becomes self-reflexive: and in two senses. On the one hand, it imposes order on itself: the TEXTUAL metafunction . . . construes a reality that is made of meaning. On the other hand, we can TALK ABOUT the way we mean, and examine the nature of the order our way of meaning has imposed. As well as a grammar, a theory of experience, we have a GRAMMATICS . . . a theory of theories of experience. (Halliday 1992: 31)

The point here is that while the grammar constitutes an unconscious and implicit theory of experience, it is also the resource for consciously building designed, explicit theories – about language (grammatics, linguistics) and about anything else at all.

Consciously designed theories such as linguistics, sociology, physics, and so on, constitute the realm of uncommonsense, educational knowledge discussed by Bernstein, involving what Vygotsky described as scientific concepts. This kind of knowledge, the disciplinary knowledge of school and academic study, can be seen as different field systems, different systems of interpreting/structuring reality, which can only find their expression through the linguistic system actualized as text.

Educational knowledge differs from commonsense knowledge both in its nature and in the way it is learned. Unlike the gradually accumulated and possibly contradictory nature of commonsense reality, discipline-based knowledge aims to be highly systematic and is thus 'represented by definitions, taxonomies, ordered progressions and logical relations' (Halliday 1988b: 1). As Vygotsky pointed out, rather than being learned in an unconscious, implicit way, through conversational discourse whose explicit goal is simply the conduct of everyday life, educational knowledge is oriented to explicit reflection on meanings and the conscious understanding of their interrelationships.

In comparison with commonsense knowledge, educational knowledge is realized much more exclusively as linguistic meaning and form, and those realizations are in particular the forms of written rather than spoken language. This is not simply a matter of a graphological, as opposed to phonological, substance in the form of expression – though of course mastering the written medium itself requires uncommonsense understandings about language – it is a matter of new ways of using the meaning resource to organize experience. These new ways involve what Halliday has called 'grammatical metaphor' (Halliday 1989, 1994; Halliday and Martin 1993).

Grammatical metaphor is possible because the content level of language is stratified into two planes, the semantic and the grammatical. On the semantic plane, a particular experience of physical action, such as clapping, may be construed as a constellation of participants and process. Typically this would involve a lexico-grammatical choice of [material process], involving a configuration in which the participants are realized by nominal forms and the process by a verbal group, as with *people applauded the singer.* There is also, however, the possibility of realizing such a meaning with alternative grammatical choices and these are especially prevalent in written forms of the language.

Grammatical metaphor involves the use of nominal forms (nouns and their modifiers) to construe experiences that are prototypically construed by verbs or other word classes. Halliday (1996: 348) gives the following example to illustrate the difference between the spoken language, organized grammatically around the process, and the 'nominalized' written form:

| spoken | written |
|---|---|
| when she accepted people applauded | her acceptance was followed by applause |

The 'metaphor' here lies not in the lexis, as with the more usual understanding of the term, but in the grammatical patterning, since the written version construes as participants phenomena that are more congruently interpreted as processes. This reconstrual has flow-on effects in the structure so that the logical semantic relation of temporal succession between the two events of accepting and applauding is represented in the written version as a process (*followed*) linking the two nominalized participants. The effect, as with any metaphor, is to achieve an additional layer of meaning, as the *activities* of accepting and applauding are recovered by the hearer at the same time as they are being interpreted as *participants*.

The justification for regarding the spoken style, organized around the process, as the more 'congruent' and the nominalized written style as the 'metaphorical' is that the written style is a later development in various respects, including the ontogenetic one:

> [T]here are three distinct histories in which 'accept' is construed as a verb **before** it is construed as a noun
> 1. diachronically, in the history of the language;
> 2. developmentally, in the history of the individual;
> 3. instantially, in the history of the text. (Halliday 1996: 349)

Nominalization facilitates the systematizing of knowledge and the creation of technical lexis. By naming events or changeable states with nouns, they can readily be placed into taxonomies (*erosion – water erosion, wind erosion*), can be measured precisely (amounts or rates of *growth, speed, reproduction, temperature, acceleration*, etc.) and can generally become subject to all the kinds of modification possible for nouns within the nominal group. However, this is not the only function of grammatical metaphor. The less technical educational knowledge of the humanities also favours highly nominalized forms, and this is a crucial means of creating the appropriate textual structures demanded by the more static and monologic written mode (see Eggins *et al.* 1987; Halliday 1987; Halliday and Martin 1993). So, although different 'bodies of knowledge' have their own particular favoured types of text and their own linguistic characteristics, the grammatically metaphorical forms of written language will be generally relevant. And this is usually the case even where the specialized knowledge is not in the written medium; the spoken texts will still tend to use the forms of written language.

While there are no published longitudinal studies detailing the development of grammatical metaphor, there is plenty of evidence in the child language literature that the speech of very young children is indeed 'congruent' in Halliday's terms. Macnamara (1982: 142) is one who explicitly examined his case study data on the language of two children up to the age of about two-and-a-half, to check on the relation between word class and meaning, and found the language to be perfectly congruent. Halliday himself (1989: 96) suggests that grammatical metaphor is 'unlikely to be mastered until the age of eight or nine'.

More certain than the age at which grammatical metaphor is controlled is the correlation between the ability to use grammatically metaphorical forms of language and success in understanding educational knowledge. It could not be otherwise if by 'knowledge' is meant systems of meaning, and if the systems in question are very largely realized in the metaphorical written style. On this view educational success cannot but be a primarily linguistic matter.

Given the nature of educational knowledge – as systematic, more compartmentalized than commonsense knowledge, dealing with technical meanings understood in terms of explicitly defined relationships to each other and realized through written language – it is unlikely that it can be learned in the same way as everyday, commonsense reality is built up. As a system of meanings, any area of educational knowledge will still need to be construed interactively, since meaning is an interpersonal endeavour. However, the fact that this kind of knowledge is taught and learned in an institutional setting is a recognition that the model of implicit, unconscious, unstructured apprenticeship through casual conversation is not an appropriate way of learning these new systems of meaning.

SFL-based educational research and practice in Australia has argued on the one hand for the meanings of uncommonsense knowledge to be construed interactively, and has developed a pedagogy which foregrounds teacher–student discourse, including the joint production of written texts, as well as student group work (Macken 1989, Macken-Horarik 1996, Christie et al. 1992, Cope and Kalantzis 1993). On the other hand it has argued the need for students to develop not just 'the language of the discipline', the particular registers and forms of discourse relevant to that system of meanings, but a language for talking about them. This follows from seeing the discipline as a system of meanings realized as language texts. On that basis conscious reflection on that system of meanings will be enabled by overt exploration and deconstruction of texts realizing them. To become a party to such an exploration, however, the learner needs ways of talking about the meanings of the text, meanings which are realized in the metaphorical lexico-grammatical forms. The metalanguage thus becomes a tool in the mastery of grammatical metaphor and the conscious control of the discourses of the field. It provides the means of accessing the knowledge, values and ideological positions realized in them and reflecting on them in a critical way (Rothery 1989, 1993, 1996).

While the more strongly compartmentalized discipline-based knowledge is the province of the secondary school in Australia, it is in the primary school that the initiation into the written mode of language begins. In fact the main expectation of the first years of formal schooling is that children should learn 'reading and writing' together with the new semiotic of 'arithmetic'. These are the 'basics' that there are regular calls for a return to, whenever politicians, parents or teachers become concerned with children's educational achievements. And they *are* foundational in that without a successful control of the written medium and the writing system there can be no control of grammatical metaphor and no accessing the specialized fields of the secondary school.

From the beginning, gaining control of the writing system is itself a move out of commonsense knowledge in that it involves the construal of abstract objects:

The patterns of writing create systemic properties which are then named as abstract objects, like the **beginning** and **end** of a page or a line, **spaces** between

**words** . . . Children learn that **writing** is different from **drawing**; and that whereas 'what I have drawn' is named with reference to my world of experience, such as a cat or a house, 'what I have written' is of a different order of reality: either it has its own name, as an object created in the act of writing ('you've written a "c" '), or it is named with reference to another symbol – to an element of the language, usually a phoneme or a word ('you've written /**k**/'; 'you've written **cat**'. This last is of course very complex, since it is a symbol standing for a symbol. (Halliday 1996: 341–2)

The ability to deal with abstract categories – those denoting or referring to symbolic rather than tangible entities – is, according to Halliday, something which is not usually developed in the early years before school. With reference to his case study of Nigel, he suggests that 'children have difficulty with abstract terms typically up to the age of about five' (1989: 95). Again, child language texts reported in the literature would seem to support this, or at least would support the claim that abstract terms are absent from very young children's speech, but there are no details available as to exactly when and in what circumstances such language is first used.

The idea that language development is complete by age 3 or 4 is clearly not a tenable one from the perspective of systemic theory. The system develops to fulfil the demands placed upon it; initially this means developing as a stratified, metafunctionally organized semiotic and this is certainly achieved by age 2 or 3. However, as long as the child is using language in new contexts of situation, enacting new social relationships, construing new fields, creating new kinds of discourses, the meaning system will grow as a response to the new demands. And as argued earlier, the linguistic meaning potential is in large part the same thing as the cognitive potential; a study of linguistic development is necessarily a study of cognitive development.

Access to a child's developing language – the developing meaning potential (cognitive potential in psychological terms) – is achieved through accessing the child's texts, which simultaneously instantiate and build that potential. The text is a semantic unit, a unit of language in use, language functioning in a context of situation, and its meanings are coded into the observable words and structures of lexico-grammatical form. Thus within a systemic theoretical context, a longitudinal study of a child's grammar in use leads to an understanding of that child's potential for thinking and learning.

## 5  The present study: a case study of learning through language

The next four chapters of this book will provide a longitudinal case study of one child's grammar in use, with the aim of describing the way language was mobilized and developed as a resource for learning during the pre-school years. Stephen, the child in question, was aged two-and-a-half when data collection began and was 5 years old when it was completed, beginning school three months later. By focusing on this age period, the study can provide a link between previous SFL case studies of the very early development of language and more recent research using the theory to explore the development of literacy in school.

Stephen is the researcher's son, the second child in the family, and four-and-a-half years younger than his brother, Hal. Samples of his language were recorded without his knowledge as he went about the business of everyday life. The research is therefore in the tradition of parental diary studies which have been used to explore language development over the past century (e.g. Leopold 1949; Bloom 1973; Halliday 1975, 1984b) and shares the particular advantages and limitations of this approach. The advantages relate to both the quality of the language recorded and the information which can be brought to bear on its interpretation, while the disadvantage is that the extent to which the findings can be generalized beyond the one subject cannot be determined without further research.

The most important reason for choosing to collect data in this way – from a family member who can be observed and recorded using language quite unselfconsciously in the contexts of everyday life – is clearly that the data run the minimum risk of being contaminated or limited by the fact of being collected. Alternative models of data collection for a developmental study would include the utilization of an experimental procedure, the collection of non-elicited data within a semi-structured setting and the collection of naturalistic data 'by proxy' from a number of subjects. Each of these methods has the advantage that a wider range of subjects can be studied, but all have disadvantages with respect to the quality of the data and the interpretation possible.

Experimental approaches to data collection have an appeal within theoretical approaches which seek 'clean', 'objective' data to test specific hypotheses in a context where it is believed all variables other than those under attention can be identified and carefully controlled. However, researchers conceiving of language as a social practice, and meaning as intersubjective in nature, have long argued against the very premises upon which experimental data collection takes place (see e.g. Newson 1978; Shotter 1978). Certainly, simply to recognize that an experiment to elicit linguistic data is itself a semiotic context that will have a strong bearing on the language produced is to appreciate the extreme difficulty of obtaining data which will provide insights into how language is used outside that experimental situation.

In the attempt to collect more naturalistic data, many language researchers have traditionally set up semi-structured situations where mother and child are left alone to play and interact with various toys and props (e.g. Howe 1981, Bloom 1993). These sessions can be repeated at intervals over time to track development, or longitudinal depth can be simulated by recording children of different ages. Such an approach obviously has an advantage over a diary study in that a number of different children or dyads can be studied. However, it still has the disadvantage that data are collected in only one type of situational context – a one-to-one interaction between parent and child, focused on visible material props with no goal other than to pass the time through talk. Even if this particular type of situation is one typical of that child's experience – which should not be taken for granted – it is unlikely to tap the child's full range of linguistic resources.

Another possibility for data collection, which may overcome this limitation, is to record subjects 'remotely' as done by Wells (1986) and Hasan (1988). In the former study, children wore radio microphones stitched into their vests which were repeatedly activated for 90-second bursts between 9 a.m. and 5 p.m., while Hasan, who was comparing the speech of children of a similar age, requested mothers to record several hours of talk between themselves and their children over a two-week period, as they carried out their usual routines in their own homes. The data collected in each case are thus rich and uncontrived, but still not entirely without problems. Wells' method has the advantage that the speaker is quite unaware when recording is taking place, but it faces the problem that such short random bursts of recording do not honour the text as a unit. Hasan's methodology does not have this problem but would be difficult to employ over a very extended period of time. Moreover a disadvantage with both methods is that non-participants will be interpreting the meanings being exchanged. This not only raises questions where participants and observer do not share the same social positioning, but is a limitation for a developmental study in that the observer will have no insight into the intertextual history of any particular utterance or text.

Against these limitations, a parental diary study has distinct advantages. As with Wells' research, the child's unselfconscious language can be recorded in any variety of situations in the course of carrying on everyday activities. Moreover the parent as participant–observer will not only have participated in construction of the meanings being interpreted, but will also be familiar with the unrecorded texts which provide an important aspect of the context for the recorded ones. Because of this, new developments are readily noticed, the typicality or unusuality of a particular aspect of the recorded language is appreciated and background events and texts relevant to the recorded instance can be understood.

Appreciating that using language is an intersubjective affair, it is of course undeniable that consciousness of being recorded on the part of one speaker may affect the speech of both interactants. It is hoped that this is mitigated in the present case by three circumstances. The first of these is that the control of the recording was in the hands of the recorder, so there was no need to worry about outsiders hearing anything that might prove embarrassing, and thus no reason to be 'on guard' when the tape recorder was active. Secondly, interactions with a very young child are in any case so demanding of a parent's attention that consciousness of being recorded would be hard to maintain. And thirdly, a decision was taken that no attempts would be made to keep to regular timetables for recordings, to keep the child near the recorder when it was activated or in any way to adapt the flow of everyday activities so as to facilitate the collection of data.

It could of course be argued that, however unselfconscious the speech recorded, taking an interest in the child's language and learning of itself affects the process. This was not seen as a problem for this research since such concerns are entirely consonant with the parent's role, as interpreted and enacted in a middle-class Anglo-Australian family like Stephen's, and there was thus no conflict between the attention given to the child's development by the parent as parent and as researcher. Overall, it can be asserted with reasonable confidence that the data represent speech samples which are as 'natural' and 'spontaneous' as it is possible to obtain.

While the data are rich in terms of the possibility for longitudinal depth, contextual breadth, spontaneity and 'insider' interpretation, they are limited in being collected from a single subject and it will obviously take further comparable studies to explore further the findings of this research. From the perspective of the informing theory of language as a social semiotic, however, it can be supposed that there is every probability that the patterns of meaning developed by Stephen in interaction with his inner circle will be highly comparable with those of other middle-class children learning English as a mother tongue. This group is, of course, an 'advantaged' one in educational terms and so the study will represent the experience of children who make the transition into formal education with the least difficulty. The research should thus illuminate the way in which such children are indeed prepared for school learning by the semiotic experience of the first few years of using the mother tongue.

### 5.1 Data collection for the case study of Stephen

As discussed above, data sought for this study were samples of Stephen's unselfconscious conversational interactions as they arose in everyday settings. These were recorded using audiotapes and also pencil and paper notes. Data were collected during two phases. Notebook observations were recorded for a few weeks at 2 years and 6 months (2;6) after which a four-month phase of intensive collection began, using audiotapes and field notes. Then for the next four months audiotaping ceased but handwritten notes continued to be taken. Then, when Stephen was aged 3 years 3 months (3;3), intensive data collection was resumed and continued up until his fifth birthday.

During the period of the study, Stephen attended a childcare centre each weekday during school term times. At home he spent time in the company of his brother and of neighbourhood children of his own age and younger, as well as with his parents and (on annual visits from overseas) his grandparents. No recordings were made at the childcare centre apart from conversations taking place when Stephen was dropped off or collected. It was not practicable to record in the centre, where in any case Stephen spent much of his morning outside, actively using the varied range of playground equipment, and most of the afternoon asleep.

It was found that recorded interactions between Stephen and his brother at home, when an adult was not present, provided relatively little useful data. Usually the language was used as a minimal adjunct to a noisy game and was often barely intelligible when it came to be transcribed. Partly then for practical reasons, a decision was made after a few months to concentrate on interactions where the observer was present, though not necessarily the only person interacting with Stephen.

Audiotaped recordings were made using a small portable cassette recorder and were transcribed within a day or two, so that contextual details could be recalled as fully as possible. In order to minimize the intrusiveness of the data collection process and to allow for variations in the amount of time available for transcription week by week, no attempt was made to record at specific times or locations or for predetermined lengths of time. The recorder was simply switched on when convenient, in a variety of situations: at meals, playing with parent or sibling, bath time, bedtime story, on car rides to and from childcare, on outings to the park or zoo, and so on. Between three and six separate recordings of 15 to 45 minutes in length were recorded each month during the 'intensive' periods of collection, the general aim being to tape about 30 minutes of conversation each week. A total of 39 hours of audiotaped conversation was collected. Throughout the study Stephen remained unaware of the recording function of the cassette player and when he noticed the machine was on without anything playing, he assumed tapes were being rewound.

In addition to audiotaped material, pencil and paper 'diaries' were kept continuously. These handwritten notes amounted to a substantial supplement to the taped material and noted new developments, 'favourite' forms, brief snippets of talk, such as question–answer sequences, and also longer exchanges when Stephen was interacting with other people. Stephen understood that, like the 'rewinding' of tapes, the notebook writing was to do with his mother's 'work', which he did not connect with himself.

## 5.2 Analysis and presentation of data

The focus of the study is on the child's building of knowledge – the mental construction of the general field of 'everyday experience' – and on the development of language to achieve this after the age of thirty months. SFL theory predicts that ideational systems of the language will be chiefly implicated here, as the child's task is one of building semantic taxonomies, configurations of participants and processes, and activity sequences. The work of building semantic taxonomies involves construing experience as a world of discrete phenomena categorized by lexical items. This is a matter of vocabulary development, which in turn requires the development and use of relational processes with which to identify, classify and describe nameable things. Things themselves are ultimately construed grammatically by nominal groups (noun phrases), whose modifying elements contribute to description and specification of the objects and persons of experience. On the other hand, the representation of events and activity sequences involves other TRANSITIVITY options, particularly the use of material process configurations, together with choices from the logical metafunction to make temporal or other linkages between events. Finally, there is the special place of language itself as an aspect of reality to be construed, not only in terms of abstract things like sounds and letters, but also in terms of the activity of exchanging meaning. This latter area involves the remaining area of TRANSITIVITY, that of mental and verbal process types. Table 2.4 summarizes the relation between each different aspect of experience and the ideational grammatical system most centrally involved in its construal.

**Table 2.4** Ideational systems predicted as relevant for development of field

| Aspect of experience | Linguistic system implicated |
| --- | --- |
| Things, qualities, etc. | • lexical taxonomies<br>• relational transitivity to identify and taxonomize (*X is Y, X is a Y, X has a Y*)<br>• nominal group modification to identify and describe (*the X with a b c properties, the a, b, c X*) |
| Material events | • material transitivity (*X happens, X did Y*) |
| Activity sequences | • logical relations (*X happens, then Y happens, X should have happened but Y happened, X happened because Y happened*) |
| Semiotic events | • mental and verbal transitivity |

In the context of this framework, Stephen's utterances, and those of his conversational partners, were initially coded according to PROCESS TYPE and the logico-semantic relations between clauses (i.e. conjunctive links and patterns of quoted and reported speech and thought). As well, nominal groups were coded according to the type and modification of the Head word. The texts in which these various meanings were instantiated were continually re-examined in terms of their contexts of occurrence and this suggested further meaning systems that should be taken into account, such as the textual one of REFERENCE and the interpersonal one of MODALIZATION. As the analyses progressed and patterns of language development and use became clearer, so too did certain developments in Stephen's 'thinking' begin to emerge.

In order to keep the focus on learning through language, and on the constellation of different linguistic resources that might be implicated in any particular intellectual development, the data will not be presented language system by language system in the chapters to follow, but rather in terms of the different aspects of field being engaged with. This means that the following three chapters present a description of Stephen's use of language to interpret 'reality' between thirty months and five years, by looking at his representation of different facets of experience. First, his identification and classification of the world of things and qualities is discussed and then his representation of the world of process configurations. The description of the latter is spread over two chapters, the first of which considers the linguistic representation of 'outer' events by means of material processes and conjunctive relations, while the next describes the representation of semiotic activity by means of mental and verbal processes and relations of projection.

In the sixth chapter, the data are revisited once more to describe in greater detail one particular linguistic resource which proved relevant in the interpretation of all three domains: the logico-semantic system of cause–effect relations. The goal here is to refocus on the systemic potential – on language as an expandable resource – as well as to extend the earlier description of activity sequences. It is hoped that by foregrounding different perspectives in turn, first the experiences being understood (leading to expansion of the language) in Chapters 3 to 5, and then the language being expanded (resulting in new understandings) in Chapter 6, it will be possible to see more clearly how learning language and learning through language are indeed facets of a single process.

The case study is thus presented not as a single continuous narrative of development, but as a series of longitudinal descriptions, each focusing on different areas of meaning. Initially each chapter is briefly contextualized in terms of the developmental background and the linguistic systems relevant to its particular domain, following which a description of Stephen's use of language is presented. The method chosen to describe the patterns of development is to take the data up to age 3 as one data set, that collected between 3 and 4 years as a second set for comparison with the first and that collected between 4 and 5 years as a third set. Thus, for each topic, the changing patterns of meaning are described broadly in terms of a comparison between Stephen's speech in the third, fourth and fifth year of life.

The account of Stephen's language in every chapter is illustrated throughout by very brief text examples. These are dated in years, months and days, with, for example, 2 years, 9 months and 4 days represented as 2;9;4. The conventions used in the transcriptions of speech are set out in Table 2.5.

After the four passes through the case study data have been made, a number of illustrations of the system–process relationship will have been provided, suggesting various ways in which using the language (creating text) enables development of the meaning systems. It will also be possible to consider overall trends in the patterns of development over the pre-school years, as a basis for considering the extent to which a child like Stephen has become prepared for the new demands of learning 'educational knowledge'. The case study as a whole should thus provide an extended exemplification of the theoretical position put forward in this chapter that learning is a linguistic process.

**Table 2.5** Transcription conventions

| Transcription convention | Interpretation |
| --- | --- |
| (?   ) | unintelligible |
| (?hat) | unclear but with probable utterance given (here, *hat*) |
| ... | omitted speech |
| ha- | interrupted speech (e.g. here of *hat, haven't, happen*, etc.) |
| [ <br> [ | overlapping utterances |
| <u>hat</u> | contrastive stress on word (here, *hat*) |
| it [= hat] | clarification of meaning (*it* refers to *hat*) |

Where relevant, rankshifted (i.e. embedded) elements are indicated by square brackets:

| [  ] | embedded phrase |
| --- | --- |
| [[  ]] | embedded clause |

Embedded phrases and clauses are indicated only when texts are cited specifically to illustrate the use of embedding.

### Notes

1 Names given to system options, or 'features', are conventionally enclosed in square brackets.
2 Names of systems are conventionally written in capitals.
3 See further Chapter 5.
4 See further Chapter 4.

# 3 The construal of things: classification and identification

The case study of Stephen's pre-school language will open with an account of how experience was interpreted in terms of categories and instances. This aspect of field concerns things, and qualities (and to a lesser extent, actions) as nameable, describeable phenomena construed into semantic taxonomies. The texts discussed will be concerned with what something 'is' (rather than with what it is doing), with what things are called and conversely with what a name denotes.

## 1 Developmental issues

The most significant move in the child's prior linguistic history, as far as the classification and naming of phenomena is concerned, is obviously the initial emergence of lexis at the end of the protolinguistic period, at about 16 months. This has been described in some detail from an SFL perspective in Halliday (1975) and Painter (1984, 1989) and will not be pursued here. More pertinent to the age of the child in this study is the question of the child's ability to group objects into classes at one or more levels of a taxonomic hierarchy, about which there has been some debate.

One strongly maintained position, supported by Piagetian theory, has been characterized by Katherine Nelson (1979: 66) as follows:

> It is frequently observed that young children do not grasp the principle of semantic or conceptual hierarchies. They use few superordinate terms and have difficulty with conceptual classification and with part-whole class relationships.

Despite this observation, it is striking that, where diaries are used as the data source, children can be observed to have taxonomic organization of vocabulary at a very young age. For example, Macnamara (1982) expresses certain reservations about the abilities of two-and-a-half-year-olds based on his experimental data, but his own parental diary demonstrates (p. 108) that, as early as sixteen-and-a-half months, his son used both *animal* and specific animal names appropriately. Similarly, a diary study of Stephen's brother, Hal, shows him, at twenty-two-and-a-half months, having lexical terms at two hierarchical levels (Painter 1984: 192–3), while Halliday (1980) has a particularly interesting example where his son at almost 20 months struggled to categorize a toy engine and a toy bus as members of a common class, saying: *two . . . two chuffa . . . two . . . two*, and then giving up. This incident illustrates how the discrimination of two categories at what Rosch *et al.* (1976) refer to as the 'basic object' level (the most imageable, functional level in a taxonomy) may bring to consciousness the need for a superordinate name even at a very early stage of language development. Given the paucity of naturalistic data addressing the question of everyday semantic hierarchies, the data here will be used to explore further the possible depth of lexical taxonomies that construe commonsense knowledge.

Perhaps the main concern in the literature has been with the criteria by which children construe category membership. Perceptual similarity has been reported as the basis for both 'underextension' in young children's prompted speech (Anglin 1977) and 'overextension', including metaphorical uses, in their spontaneous speech (Clark 1973, 1975). Perceptual similarity of specific exemplars is also seen as one basis for category learning in experiments carried out within the framework of prototype theory (Rosch 1977). Similarity of function is also widely reported to be an important criterion for establishing categories (Bloom 1973, Barrett 1978, Rescorla 1980, Anglin 1983, Nelson 1974, 1991a). In some disagreement with these views, however, is Macnamara's claim that 'true' categories cannot be established on perceptual or functional criteria, since, for example, a plucked one-legged canary would still be a canary despite failing to meet perceptual criteria, and 'an orange would still be an orange even if the whole human race lost its taste for oranges' (Macnamara 1982: 200). In effect Macnamara argues that only when the scientific basis for a category is determined (e.g. the biological criteria for a canary, the botanical criteria for an orange, the chemical composition of water) has a true category been established.

The SFL approach, as discussed in Chapter 2, emphasizes that any structure inherent in material reality is capable of multiple interpretations and that the environment is a social construct:

> It does not consist of things . . . it consists of human interaction, from which the things derive their meaning. The fact that a bus moves is by no means its only or even its most obvious perceptual quality, as compared, say, with its size, its shininess, or the noise it makes; but it is its most important semiotic property, the meaning with which it is endowed in the social system. (Halliday 1975: 141)

A social-semiotic approach to meaning does not need to privilege either an object's function or a feature of its appearance as being invariably its most criterial property. Nor does it need to privilege the construction of reality in terms of any single culture, language or field as the single unitary 'truth'. But it can predict that a name learned as part of a commonsense field is likely to categorize in terms of socially salient and observable characteristics (e.g. *measles* in terms of spots), whereas uncommonsense fields will use different kinds of categorization criteria which have greater explanatory power in terms of the social goals of the field (e.g. *measles* in terms of viral disease). In the discussion of Stephen's speech, the kinds of descriptors used by parent and child to characterize things during everyday conversation will be noted in order to provide a basis for exploring whether and in what terms categories and criteria for classification are actually discussed and whether and how definitions are construed by and for the child.

In addition, this chapter will concern itself with issues arising from the observation made in Chapter 2 that children develop different classes of word to construe different aspects of reality (nouns for things, verbs for processes, etc.). Two related aspects of development which have remained largely unexamined concern the point when 'abstract' meanings (denoting non-tangible experience) may be construed, and the point when the congruent relation between meaning and word class may be displaced in favour of a grammatically metaphorical construal. Given the postulated importance of these developments for the understanding of 'educational' knowledge, this chapter will explore Stephen's earliest moves into abstraction and metaphor.

The following issues will therefore be taken up in the case study description provided in this chapter:

- the relation of names to their contexts of use
- the depth of lexical taxonomies that construe the commonsense fields
- the articulation of criteria for forming classifications
- the construal of definitions
- the concreteness of the categories embodied in the child's vocabulary
- the degree of congruence between meaning and word class

## 2 Relevant linguistic systems

As discussed in Chapter 2, lexical semantic relations are a central linguistic realization of the child's taxonomic understandings, as is the use of relational processes to classify, describe and define (Halliday 1994: Section 5.4). In addition, an exploration of this area of meaning involves considering the form and use of the child's nominal group, the linguistic structure for representing experience as things. Finally, the semantic system of REFERENCE (Halliday and Hasan 1976), or PARTICIPANT IDENTIFICATION (Martin 1992a), will be relevant as a linguistic means of introducing things into the discourse and managing ongoing reference to them. Each of these areas of the language will be discussed briefly before considering Stephen's use of his developing system.

## 2.1 Lexical relations

In Martin's (1992a: 295) modelling of field, the taxonomies which realize any field are of two kinds: those construing superordination relations (the 'is a' relation – 'an oak is a tree'), and those construing compositional or part–whole relations (the 'has a' relation – 'a tree has leaves'). These are 'hyponymy' and 'meronymy' relations respectively in terms of Halliday and Hasan's (1989) account of cohesion, the former known also as 'class inclusion' relations (Piaget 1977). Illustrations are given in Table 3.1.

**Table 3.1** Hyponymy (superordination) and meronymy (part–whole) relations

| Hyponymy relations (class inclusion) | Meronymy relations (part/whole) |
| --- | --- |
| sport – team sport – hockey | team – player |
| flower – rose | flower – petal |
| vehicle – car – Mazda 626 | car – door – handle |
| literature – poetry – lyric poetry | universe – galaxy – solar system – star |

Terms at the same level of a taxonomy, such as rose, tulip and daffodil, or petal and stamen, may be referred to as co-hyponyms or co-meronyms, respectively. Synonymy and antonymy relations are also an important aspect of the 'is a' relationship and both are treated by Martin (1992a: 300*ff*) as a kind of co-hyponymy.

## 2.2 Relational process clauses

It is the experiential clause grammar of relational processes which chiefly functions to classify a participant, to assign it qualities or to identify one participant with another. For the purposes of this discussion, a simplified version of the relational process system, as shown in Figure 3.1, will be sufficient (see Halliday 1994: 119).

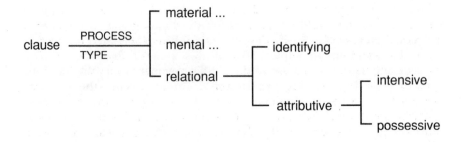

**Figure 3.1** Relational process options in English

The basic distinction represented in the network is between identifying and attributive structures. Examples of the two, with the participant roles labelled, are given below as Examples 3.1 and 3.2.

*Example 3.1*

| identifying | Simon | is | the best artist |
|---|---|---|---|
| | Token | | Value |

| The best artist | is | Simon |
|---|---|---|
| Value | | Token |

*Example 3.2*

| attributive | Simon Simon | is | talented an artist |
|---|---|---|---|
| | Carrier | | Attribute |

| talented an artist | is | Simon Simon |
|---|---|---|

As can be seen, there is a semantic difference between the two and a formal reflex of this is the fact that only the identifying clause is reversible. The semantic difference is characterized by the different pairs of participant roles recognized for the two types of clause. For an identifying clause, one participant role is a category, meaning or value (Value) and the other is an exemplar or instance (Token) of that meaning. These clauses serve to identify and define phenomena. In an attributive clause, one role is that of a participant (Carrier) which is assigned an attribute (Attribute), which may be a quality (e.g. *talented*) or membership of a class (e.g. *an artist*).

Attributive clauses which classify, such as *Simon is an artist*, or which assign a quality, such as *Simon is talented*, realize the feature [intensive] in the network shown in Figure 3.1. Another early relational clause structure is that of the possessive attributive clause. This construes both ownership, as in *Simon has a studio*, and also meronymy relations, as in *The studio has a wooden floor*, the latter being an important means of creating compositional taxonomies.

### 2.3 Nominal group structure

The things of experience are construed grammatically as nominal groups (pronouns, nouns, or nouns together with their modifying elements). The structural functions of the adult nominal group are identified by Halliday (1994: 180*ff*) as in Table 3.2.

This analysis provides for a description of the group in terms of its logical structure, which is one of successive modification of a Head, and also in terms of its experiential structure, since different Modifier slots have developed particular experiential meanings. The Head of a (non-elliptical) nominal group has the experiential function of Thing (i.e. that which is being construed), and may be a noun or a pronoun. If it is a noun, a modification structure is possible, with the Deictic and Post-Deictic functioning to identify the Thing, the Numerative to quantify, the Epithet to describe and the Classifier to subclassify. The Qualifier role adds further modification in any of these ways, usually where a unit larger than a word is needed to realize the meaning. The Qualifier role therefore typically has a prepositional phrase or clause embedded within it. (Single square brackets indicate an embedded phrase and double ones an embedded clause.)

**Table 3.2**  The structure of the nominal group

| Pre-Modifier | Pre-Modifier | Pre-Modifier | Pre-Modifier | Pre-Modifier | Head | Post-Modifier |
|---|---|---|---|---|---|---|
| | | | | | *he* | |
| *a* | | | *large* | *breakfast* | *tray* | |
| *all* | | *twenty* | | | *girls* | *outside* |
| *those* | *other* | *two* | *old* | *mahogany* | *wardrobes* | *[with mirrors]* |
| *the* | | | | | *boy* | *[[I spoke to]]* |
| **Deictic** | **Post-Deictic** | **Numerative** | **Epithet** | **Classifier** | **Thing** | **Qualifier** |

Nominal groups may be elliptical in their realization, in which case a Deictic (or Numerative) may function as the Head of the group, as in the example in Table 3.3, where the Head of the group is in bold type.

**Table 3.3**  Elliptical nominal groups

| *those* | **books** | *(are mine)* |
|---|---|---|
| **those** | | *(are mine)* |
| Deictic | Thing | |

*2.4  REFERENCE*

The textual system of REFERENCE is deployed to bring an entity within an intersubjective frame and to allow interlocutors to locate and keep track of it during the discourse. Once something has been introduced into the discourse, such as *a tall man* in *I saw a tall man*, it is tracked by means of 'presuming' reference items, such as *he* or *the* in *the man lit a cigarette before he got into a car*. Since entities are construed grammatically as nominal groups, it is within this structure that REFERENCE choices are realized, either in the Thing role or the Deictic role. In the Thing role, presuming reference will be realized by a personal pronoun (*I, he, she, him, them,* etc.) while in the Deictic role, personal and demonstrative pronouns and articles are possible realizations (*my, his, this, those, the,* etc.).

In discussing the identification of participants, Martin (1992a: 98) makes a distinction between nominal groups which are 'phoric' and those which are 'non phoric'. A phoric group is one which presupposes or presumes information. In such a case the identity of the Thing is coded as known to the addressee, because recoverable from the context. The context may be the cultural context (homophoric reference), the immediate context of situation (exophoric reference) or the wording of the text itself (endophoric reference). Examples of phoric groups are given in Table 3.4 with the phoric item in bold.

**Table 3.4** Contexts for recovering identity of a participant

| Context for recovery of participant identity | Type of reference element | Example |
|---|---|---|
| culture | homophoric | ***The** Prime Minister announced a tax cut.* |
| situation | exophoric | *I want **that** one.* |
| text | endophoric | *Two boys entered. **They** looked menacing.* |

While phoric groups 'presume' a participant's identity, non-phoric groups in Martin's description serve to 'present' or introduce participants to the addressee. A simplified version of part of Martin's (1992a) system network for participant identification is reproduced as Figure 3.2.

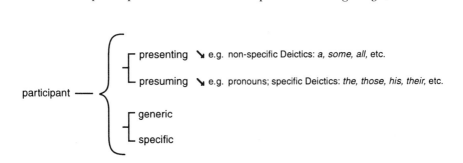

**Figure 3.2** Simplified IDENTIFICATION system (following Martin 1992a)

As can be seen, this description also indicates that an entire generic category may be constructed as Thing. Such a participant can be presented (introduced into the text) in various ways, but probably the most typical realization in texts construing commonsense fields is by a plural noun in the Thing role with no Deictic element in the structure, as with the nominal group *tigers* in *tigers are being hunted to extinction*.

## 3  Stephen's language 2;6 to 3;0 years

In the description to follow from the first data set, the characteristics of Stephen's explicitly 'naming' utterances will be discussed first, followed by a discussion of the taxonomic relations construed in his speech. Finally some consideration will be given to the concreteness of the vocabulary and the congruence between semantic choice and lexico-grammatical realization. The description as a whole will then be summarized as a basis for providing a comparison with the data from the fourth year.

### 3.1  Naming through relational processes

Children's early talk is greatly concerned with trying out and learning names as a means of interpreting things. One striking feature of Stephen's utterances with this function is that exophoric retrieval of presuming reference was invariably used on such occasions. What was being named was brought into the semiotic context by means of a reference item such as *that* or *it*, which functioned as a Carrier in an attributive clause structure, such as *That's an X* or *What's that?* The identity of exophoric *that* here had to be recovered from the context of situation. Examples are given below, with the exophoric presuming item in bold:

2;7;30    (S is playing with nesting cups and toy figures)
       S:    **That**'s two red ones (pointing to part of stack) . . .
           **They**'re all mens (indicating toy figures he is playing with).

2;8;4    S:    (drawing) **It**'s a hedgehog . . . **that**'s his tongue (drawing it).

2;9    (S watching M dress)
       S:    What are **those**?
      M:    Nipples.
       S:    Nipples.
       S:    What's **that**?
      M:    **That**'s my belly button.
       S:    Hal laughs at belly button.

These naming clauses therefore invariably involved a participant whose identity needed to be specified by reference to something outside the text. This characteristic is unlikely to be idiosyncratic to Stephen since, for example, Macnamara's (1982) diary data show exactly the same 'restriction' in his subject's early language.

Another restriction in Stephen's 'naming' speech was that all his early uses of the metalinguistic verb *call* involved proper names, as in the following case:

2;9;2    S:    What's this bear called? (picking up *Smokey the Bear* book)

Using *call* with a proper name makes explicit the fact that unique individuals are identified by means of linguistic names. This may provide a stepping-stone for children, allowing them to interpret the speech of others in which *call* is used more generally, as in the following example:

2;7;1    M:  And do you remember what that is? (= picture in book)
         S:  Mm.
         M:  What is it?
         S:  It's a house.
         M:  It's a house, special house and what's it made of?
         S:  Oh (pause) snow.
         M:  Yes, that's right, it's made of ice.
         S:  Made of ice.
         M:  And it's called igloo.
         S:  Igloo.

Stephen's *it's a house* classifies the entity referred to by *it*, while his mother's *it's called an igloo* does a similar job while making explicit the naming function of language and the distinction in abstraction between the thing referred to and the name. Once the child has attained an understanding that unique individuals are called by a (proper) name, such instances from the adult have the potential to help the child arrive at a more conscious understanding that common nouns also serve to name, albeit categories rather than individuals.

Stephen's first recorded query about categorization using *call* occurred towards the end of the third year:

2;10;7   (S fiddling with raincoat in back of car)
         S:  I need a coat- a coat- what's it called? (*it* referred to a
             missing toggle)
         M:  Raincoat (misunderstanding what S wanted the name of).
             You need a button on your raincoat.

Taking the perspective that language is a system for making meaning, it can be argued that in using this identifying process, *call*, Stephen was developing the understandings that assigning a name to something is giving it a meaning and that categorizing is achieved through language. This first metalinguistic term thus lays a foundation for reflecting on the potential of language in the process of using it to produce text. And this was to prove a key characteristic of Stephen's language development and language use after age three.

Although the introduction of *call* into the system is a significant first step in this respect, it is important to stress that, in all these early examples of the use of *call* by Stephen, he introduced the thing being named by means of exophoric reference (*it* in the above text). In other words, there were again no examples from Stephen where both Token and Value were

named categories. Such a possibility was, however, modelled at times in the
adult talk, as in the final utterance of the following text:

2;8;18    (S is singing 'Mary had a little lamb')
          S:   Fleece, not feece, no; not teece; not teece (laughing).
          M:   No, not teeth.
          F:   (sings) Teeth were as white as snow.
          S:   No, not teeth, fleece.
          M:   Yes, fleece; fleece is the wool on the lamb.
               **All the lamb's soft wool is called the fleece.**

### 3.2 *Defining*

From the texts cited above it can be seen that there was some explicit talk about
*naming* by both child and adult in this period up to 3 years of age. But there was
a noticeable absence of such talk about *meaning*. And it is probably not
coincidental that the only occasions when Stephen's parents were pushed in
this direction were those when a text became an 'object' available for
reflection. A nursery rhyme which is regularly recited and sung provides such
an example, giving rise in the above text to the parental explanation *Fleece is the
wool on the lamb*. Written texts provide another opportunity for language to
become the object of reflection, as in the next example:

2;7;1    M:   (reading aloud) '"Your shadow" chuckled Trumpet.' (turns
              from book to S) D'you know what a shadow is?

(However, in this case M went on to 'explain' by moving her hand against
the light, demonstrating physically, rather than verbally, the meaning of
*shadow*.)
  On Stephen's part there was only a single recorded example where he
made a direct enquiry as to meaning, and this was right at the end of the year:

2;11;5   S:   What's a pet? (having heard it in talk between M and H)
         M:   A pet is an animal who lives in your house; Katy's our pet.
              (later)
         S:   What's a pet called?

  In this example M first tried to explain the category by giving a fairly
classic definition, in the form of a Token-Value structure in which the
Value is a nominal group with a superordinate term as Thing and a
defining relative clause in the post-modifying Qualifier role. The clause is
analysed in Example 3.3.

*Example 3.3*        *A pet*    *is*    *an animal [[who lives in your house]]*

| Token |   | Value   ↘ nominal group |   |
|-------|---|---------|---|
|       |   | D | Thing | Qualifier ↘ relative clause |

This definition is the only example of its kind in the data from Stephen's third year and, perhaps intuiting that this was something outside his normal linguistic experience, his mother then attempted to explain *pet* by making it the Value in an exemplifying clause. Her second utterance is analysed as Example 3.4.

*Example 3.4*    *Katy   's  our pet*

| Token | Value |
|-------|-------|

That these attempts were insufficient to clarify the meaning of the category for Stephen is clear from his follow-up enquiry later in the day. His 'erroneous' use of *call* – his only metalinguistic verb – in *What's a pet called?* can be interpreted as an attempt by him to use his current linguistic resources to make a new move towards talking about meaning rather than about 'reality' directly.

Stephen himself attempted no classic definitions, but did occasionally reword a meaning in order to clarify it. This involved linking clauses or phrases in an 'elaborating' (or 'i.e.') relationship. Examples of defining through implicitly elaborating utterances are given below:

2;9        (S is building a tower of bricks)
           S:    I'm making a hard one; a high one.

2;7;13     (S goes to sit on the chair the cat is on)
           S:    (to cat) 's alright, you can stay there.
           M:    You can share it.
           S:    Yes I share it, with Katy. He go there (pointing to cat on her
                 half) and I go here (pointing to his half).
           (pause)
           S:    I share with Katy.
           M:    Yes.
           S:    I share with Katy.

Explicating the meaning in this way (*a high one; he go there and I go here*) clearly differs from a classic definition in that it elaborates the meaning of *hard* or *share* only as relevant to this one particular occasion and exemplification. And this was characteristic of all such occasions.

### 3.3 Taxonomic relations

To supplement the account of Stephen's naming and elaborating clauses which construe particular categories, the texts of this period will be considered with respect to value relations between lexical items, both as implicitly assumed and as actively constructed.

### 3.3.1 Hyponymy

Almost any excerpt of Stephen's conversation demonstrates the taxonomic understandings already reached by him, although any particular text is likely to provide evidence of no more than two lexical levels. These might be distinguishing subcategories of a 'basic object' class, as in the following example, where *fire engine* acts as a subclassification of the more general car:

2;7;1    M:  (rummaging in toy-box) Let's see what cars we've got.
          S:  (picks one out) Fire engine one.

Alternatively, such 'basic object' classes might be provided with superordinates, as in the following example, where *clothes* is used as a general category for shirt:

2;8      (S has new clothes, not yet seen by F)
          M:  Show Daddy your new shirt.
          S:  (runs into bedroom) Where's my new clothes?

However, since oppositions at *named* levels also construct the semantic space for a superordinate category – whether or not the child has a productive lexical item to realize it – the semantic hierarchy may be deeper than such examples suggest. The following text illustrates this:

2;7;24    (family at breakfast)
          S:    Crocodiles die.
          M:  Yes, crocodiles die.
          S:    And spiders die, and ants die, and giraffes die . . .
          (continues through zoo animals seen two weeks before).
          S:    And aeroplanes die (looks at M).
          M:  No, aeroplanes don't die, they just break.
          S:    Aeroplanes break . . . (continues catalogue of creatures + die).
          H:    And Stephens die.
          S:    (indignantly) No, Stephen's not dying.
          H:    Ye-
          M:  Oh, don't start an argument.
          S:    Caterpillars die . . . (continues with parallel examples). And cars <u>break</u>.
          M:  Yes.
          S:    And they drive all the way home.

Only basic object level categories of things are named in this text, but in naming different creatures and comparing these with different classes of vehicular transport, the text is also serving to build this higher level of categories, even though they are not named. Moreover simply to place classes of living creatures in opposition to classes of modes of transport is to deploy a semantic opposition between animate and non-animate 'movers'. Thus two non-named superordinate levels of entities are implied, as indicated in Figure 3.3.

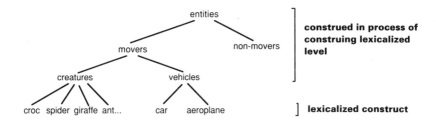

**Figure 3.3** Semantic taxonomy implied by 'Crocodiles die' text[1]

This text also exemplifies the fact that processes as well as participants are taxonomized: *break* and *die* are clearly being contrasted by the end of the text and thus implicitly there is a superordinate notion of 'ceasing to function' being explored.

A number of taxonomic understandings can therefore be inferred from a spontaneously occurring text such as this, but it seems open to question whether the child would, or indeed could, have demonstrated all of them in the context of an experimental sorting task. This must therefore highlight the value of diary data in providing input to the working hypotheses on which experimental work is premised.

The text above is also an illustrative one when it comes to raising the issue of how the child comes to construe the semantic relationships of the adult language at this early stage before linguistic meaning can be talked about. The two principal facilitating strategies appear to be the use by the child of the cognitive/semantic strategy of comparison and contrast and the use of the interactive process of dialogue. It can be seen that in this text the repetition of lexical items and the deployment of hyponymically linked vocabulary in the context of repeated clause structures (as well as the use of intonation) served to mobilize the comparison and contrasting meaning relations. At the same time, monitoring the adult's validating or contradicting responses was an equally crucial aspect of Stephen's achievement of new knowledge.

The role of the dialogue partner in making superordination relations visible was not, however, limited to a responding role. One of the most striking features of the data is the way the adult talk constantly laid out hyponymic relations, for example in the way unshared information was probed:

2;10;7    (M asking about the 'cooking' done at preschool)
          M:  Did all the children make the lunch, or just – just the big boys?
          S:  The big boys.
          M:  The big boys and girls, eh?
          S:  Not all the little boys.
          M:  Not all the little babies.

The 'or' question which initiated the text lays out the two levels of taxonomy under focus, and S's follow-up *not all the little boys* (amended by M to *babies*) shows that he understood this by specifying what *big boys (and girls)* was in opposition to.

   Similarly, in the following text, hyponymy relations were implicitly rehearsed by the strategy of an open invitation to discuss animals, followed immediately by the adult's specification of a hyponymic example of a class of animal:

2;8;20    M:  Tell me all the animals you saw today. You saw the lion?
          S:  Yes.
          M:  And you saw the monkey?

A parallel strategy can be seen in typical adult offers of this period when a preliminary offer using the general category (e.g. *Anyone want a drink?*) was followed by questions specifying the possible co-hyponymic options (such as *orange juice, lemonade*). Thus while the child was actively mobilizing his language in dialogue to explore lexical relations, the adult was simultaneously making those relations accessible, not by metalinguistic explanation but by making the potential visible in text.

### 3.3.2 Meronymy

In the literature, it is hyponymic (class-inclusion) taxonomies which have been focused on. However, Tversky (1990) and Martin (1992a) point out that meronymy relations ('partonomies' in Tversky's terminology) are an equally crucial aspect of classification. One of the respects in which 'like' things are alike is in sharing the same parts. This can be seen in the following snippet of conversation, where the possessive attributive process is deployed.

2;8;20    S:  I got a pocket today?
          M:  No, not today.
          S:  Pocket in my trousers?
          M:  No.
          S:  Why?
          M:  I don't know; they – those trousers haven't got a pocket, darling.
          S:  I think my jean has got pockets.

Stephen's initial question focused on the predictability of the meronymy relation between trousers and pocket, while his final utterance suggested that because *trousers* and *jean* are in a co-hyponymy relation they will share the meronymic attribute of having a pocket. At the same time, M's use of <u>those</u> *trousers* in the above text implies that some parts are non-essential as far as category membership is concerned, pockets not being criterial for trousers. While this is all information which can be inferred from the conversation recorded here, it can be seen that none of it was talked about explicitly: knowledge of what are and are not to be construed as characteristic or essential parts was built up very implicitly during this period.

The strategy of comparing instances was repeatedly used to explore empirically whether all instances of a class have the same parts:

2;7;1     (S checking wooden puzzle pieces)
          S:   That one's got a knob, that one's got a knob, that one's got
               a knob too.

However, when it came to exploring the attributes of family members, it is not clear whether it is each person's unique individuality which was being explored or their status as examples of broader categories:

2;9;6     (S notices M's earrings)
          S:   <u>I</u> haven't got earrings.
          M:   No, you haven't got earrings.
          S:   And <u>Hal</u> hasn't got earrings.
          M:   No, Hal hasn't got earrings.
          S:   And <u>Daddy</u> hasn't got earrings.
          (reaches to F's face) Daddy's got <u>bristles</u>.
          M:   Mm, he has, hasn't he?
          S:   <u>I</u> haven't got bristles.

In this text, Stephen did in fact establish a likeness between the three males which was not shared by the female, and also a difference between the adult and child males, but these differences were explicitly construed only in terms of the specific individuals involved.

Entities which are construed as co-hyponyms can be expected to share characteristic component parts. Thus building compositional taxonomies to cross-classify the superordination ones is an important aspect of constructing knowledge about the things of experience. However, this ambiguity as to whether observed component parts of an entity were simply characteristic of the observed individual or were criterial for establishing the class was endemic at this period. This was true not only in Stephen's talk but also when his parents offered or elicited meronymy statements following or preceding classifications – something they were very likely to do in 'naming' conversations. The meronymy relation might be realized by possessive relational clauses (with *have* or *have got*) or by nominal group Qualifiers realized by a prepositional phrase, *with X*. All the following examples occurred when parent and child were looking at picture books together early in the period:

2;7       S:   (looking at picture in book) Camel.
          M:   What's it got?
          S:   Got hump.

2;7;5     M:   What's that?
          S:   It's a tiger.
          M:   Mm. It's got beautiful stripes.

2;7       M:   (indicating picture) Man with a hat.

2;7;1     (naming characters in book series from pictures on back cover)
          M:   This one with a stripe, that's Growl the tiger.

Adopting this model Stephen would frequently produce this pattern unprompted:

2;8;16    S:   (reading) Baby . . . got a face, and 's got a big tummy.

2;8;23    M:   What did you see at the zoo today?
          S:   Elephants, and they got big trunks.

2;8;27    (M and S standing outside shop with two large dogs outside)
          S:   Big dogs . . .
          (one dog lies down, S looks at it closely)
               He's got big teeth and a big nose.

2;10;23   S:   (stroking cat) She's got a cold nose.

2;7;23    S:   (sorting out toy cars) There's a fire engine one with a ladder.

2;8;4     S:   (looking at picture-book) A pink man with scarves on.

What is striking here is that these descriptors were often of parts that might constitute criteria for discriminating the instance as a member of the class, e.g. *got hump, got big trunks* or *with a stripe*, but cannot be distinguished from other occasions where the description is relevant only to the very particular instance, e.g. *with a hat*. The same linguistic resources were being drawn on to construe both individuality and typicality through a description of parts. Thus, specific observations by Stephen, such as *they got big trunks* referring to specific observable (pictorial) elephants, were a valid means of characterizing the instance but also had the potential for being construed more generally as characterizing the class.

### 3.3.3 Qualities: antonymy and similarity relations

Although the parts into which any thing can be decomposed are specific to the kind of thing it is, anything at all can be considered in terms of qualitative dimensions such as size, shape, colour or texture. These kinds of descriptors are organized primarily in terms of synonymy and various kinds of antonymy relations, ranging from direct oppositions (*dead/alive*) to clines of various kinds (*blue/red/yellow/green* . . . ; *boiling/hot/warm/cool*) (see Lyons 1977).

These oppositional relations were made visible in adult speech just as were hyponymy and meronymy relations. In the two examples which follow, one reflective and one active in mode, the lexical sets realizing the antonymy relations are in bold.

2;8;20   M:  I don't think you saw a snake.
          S:  I did!
          M:  . . . **Big** one.
          S:  No.
          M:  **Little** one?
          S:  No.
          M:  **Middle-size** one?
          S:  No.
          M:  Not **big**, not **little**, not **middle size**?
          S:  No.
          M:  What was it like?
          S:  (saucily) Nothing.

2;7;8   (M and S playing with set of plastic baskets that stack)
          M:  Keep looking for the **big**gest; they're all **little** ones.

These examples illustrate the way quality terms are available for describing very different things on different occasions. By using *big* on different occasions for different classes of object an implicit likeness is construed between these otherwise unrelated things.

Stephen himself construed the same quality as relevant for very different things on different occasions. For example, *hot* was used at different times with reference to hands, to food, to the ground, to a light bulb, and so on. In addition to such an implicit construal of likeness between disparate things, he had also begun quite explicitly to draw a likeness between things interpreted as belonging to unrelated categories, as in the following examples:

2;9;12    (S brandishing a cone-shaped object)
          S:    That's my sword . . . 's like an ice-cream.

2;8    S:    (reflects on his 'drawing') Looks like a koala.

However, in such texts, the quality in terms of which the likeness was construed, such as size, colour, texture or (as here) shape, was invariably left unstated.

These utterances exemplify one function for this structure which was to interpret a semiotic representation, such as a toy or picture, in terms of the (non-present) thing that it signified. The other function of this clause pattern was to provide a way for Stephen to clarify for himself that visual appearance might be misleading when categorizing:

2;7;14    S:    That's fire; that's not fireworks; (pause) that looks like fireworks but it's not fireworks, it's fire.

This was very strongly modelled in the parent talk, partly due to a reluctance to reject the child's meaning:

2;9;12    (M and S looking at drawing of a fat sandwich triangle)
          M:    What do you think is in that sandwich?
          S:    Some cake.
          M:    Looks like cake; but I think it's a sandwich.

2;10;7    (M and S looking at the fine spray blown from a fountain)
          S:    It's steam.
          M:    Well, it looks like steam, yeah.

In all these examples, however, it was still the case that the qualitative features in terms of which these different things were visually similar were left unspecified.

There was in fact only a single recorded example when Stephen was able to draw an explicit analogy between disparate experiences in terms of a shared quality:

2;9;3    (S watching M dishing up spaghetti)
          S:    That's slippery. (pause) Sometimes the floor is slippy;
              when there's water on it goes splat and – and the swimming
              pool (?    ) (tails off unintelligibly)

In drawing this analogy, never modelled for him, between spaghetti sliding off the fork and people slipping on a wet floor, Stephen was taking what might be termed a 'creative' step in his thinking. That is to say he was using his meaning resources to construe a new connection between familiar interpretations of experience.

### 3.3.4 Commonsense categories

Just as descriptions in terms of parts were ambiguous as to whether the part ascribed to a specific instance was typical or even criterial with respect to class membership, so were descriptions in terms of qualities. And again the ambiguity was present in the parental talk. Moreover, on those occasions where the adult talk did hint that a particular quality was a defining criterion for some category of thing, this was not necessarily 'accurate' in terms of the adult language. For example:

2;7;1    (looking at picture-book)
      M:  What's that?
      S:  It's a bub- um (pause) a fish.
      F:  Yes, good boy, it's a whale.
      S:  I thought it's a whale; it's – it is a fish.
      M:  Yes, a big, big, big fish.

M's final statement in this excerpt appears to imply not just that this whale is big but that bigness is criterial when it comes to distinguishing whales from 'other' fish. This means that although she herself did not count whales as fish, she chose, in talking to the child, to do so, treating observable size as the implied criterion for whalehood rather than attempting to distinguish whales from fish by reference to unobservable facts about them. Thus in relation to Macnamara's (1982) claim that perceptible features are inadequate as a basis for establishing criteria for classification, it can be argued that the child's categories will be 'unscientific' initially precisely because they do need to be based on features open to observation and action in social contexts relevant to the child's experience. In this case, as well as similarity of habitat and appearance and visible parts (observable from books and television) which suggest shared category membership for whales and fish, differences between them that do arise from the child's experience, such as the latter being a source of food or being a possibility for a pet, are similarly interpretable in terms of the whale's great size. Thus commonsense semiotic experience will lead to the construal of categories that are likely to be revised in later life.

### 3.4 Rankshift and abstraction

In discussing naming and describing utterances so far, reference has been made several times to their context-dependence and to the fact that observable characteristics were of importance in discriminating things into categories. However, this should not be taken as implying that all occasions focusing on classifying and identifying involved visibly present things in the 'here-and-now'. Sometimes a broader context was relevant. For example, an enquiry *Where's the blue ball?*, which uses a presuming Deictic *the*, is obviously not construing a visible blue ball. The utterance involves homophoric reference, having an interpretation with reference to some shared context in which a single specific blue ball would be a part, in this case the set of balls that were used in the household in which the speakers lived.

Moreover there were a few occasions when Stephen attempted to identify an absent object for another person even when the name of the object was not known or was perhaps forgotten. In such a case Stephen used a 'general' lexical item like *thing* or *stuff* as Head of the nominal group, with a post-modifying clause or phrase as Qualifier. This post-modifying Qualifier would be the source of retrieval for a presuming item occurring as a Deictic, in a form of reference termed by Martin (1992a: 123) 'esphoric' reference. For example:

2;7;1     (S is examining a puzzle piece without a knob)
          S:    Where's the thing [[go on there]]?

2;8       S:    (examining ball) The blue stuff is off.
          M:    What stuff, darling?
          S:    The stuff [off the red ball] (i.e. blue Velcro stripe off the red ball).

In each case here, the nominal group identifying the object contains a Deictic whose reference is retrieved within the text (within the nominal group itself in fact), as illustrated in Figure 3.4.

**Figure 3.4** Esphoric reference

However, it is true that the nominal group Qualifier itself contains an exophoric reference item, so ultimately the identity of the thing in question can only be resolved by reference outside the text, as in Figure 3.5.

Nonetheless, this use of esphoric reference would seem an important first step in the distancing of identification from the non-textual context. Moreover, these examples display the phenomenon of rankshift (embedding) which may itself be an important first step in achieving a kind of abstraction through language. The term rankshift is used for the situation where a unit of one rank, or constituency level, operates as a

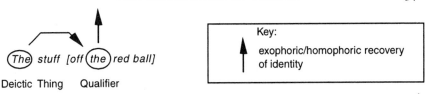

Figure 3.5 Exophoric reference within the Qualifier

functional constituent of another unit at the same or a lower level. Thus the example in Figures 3.4 and 3.5 has a prepositional phrase *(off the red ball)* acting as part of a nominal group even though groups and phrases are at the same rank. The other example above (2;7;1) has a clause *(go on there)* acting as a constituent of a group, even though a group is of a lower rank than a clause. See Figure 3.6.

Figure 3.6 Rankshift in nominal group structure

The importance of this in a discussion of language development is that Halliday treats rankshift as one kind of experiential grammatical metaphor, the phenomenon whereby the congruent relation between semantics and grammatical form is skewed to achieve a double layer of meaning. The double layer in this case arises from an event (process^circumstance: *go^on there*) being construed as a quality of a thing.

The control of experiential grammatical metaphor is a late development ontogenetically and its deployment is associated with control of written language. This kind of rankshifted structure in more formal written language will additionally involve the construal of something other than a concrete entity as the Thing/Head of the nominal group. None of the few examples of rankshift found in this data set are abstract in this sense. Moreover the embedded clause *go on there* is itself perfectly congruent in the way it construes an action as a verb and a location as a prepositional phrase. Similarly, in the other context in which rankshift occurs in the data (that of mental process clauses of perception) the rankshifted clauses themselves are again quite congruent in that the meanings expressed are perfectly 'concrete'. An example of rankshift in such a case was when Stephen called out *See [[what do my cheeks]]* when he wanted an audience for his cheek-puffing antics. As actions are as observable as things, a perception clause of this kind is a natural site for rankshift.

Although in themselves these examples of rankshift (also visible at a similar age in Limber's (1973) data) hardly qualify as the kind of abstraction characterized by adult grammatically-metaphorical language, it may be that this is an entry point to more abstract language as far as the child is concerned, in that the structure itself is in a sense 'non-congruent' because it violates the canonical constituency pattern whereby larger units are made up of smaller (lower-rank) units.

Apart from the formulaic exclamation *That's a good idea!* , established by 2;8, the only instances of anything other than a concrete entity being construed as a noun in the third year involved the use of the 'frozen' metaphor of Material Process^Range TRANSITIVITY structures (Halliday 1994: 146–8), where the participant role rather than the process role specifies the activity, as in *take a walk*. Examples from Stephen's language were: *do a big laugh; do a big kick;* and from language addressed to him: *do a big blow* (of nose); *make a big mess; have a last pee.* There is little variety in Process^Range structures used at this stage, and their highly coded status in the language means they do not have the force of true grammatical metaphor. Thus in general, the data from Stephen up to age three corresponds with that of Macnamara's subjects in that meaning and lexical class are congruent with one another.

### 3.5 Summary: 2;6 to 3;0 years

During the period up to age 3, identifying, classifying and 'defining by rewording' was achieved by Stephen by means of utterances characterized by their context-dependence. Overt classification involved placing an observed instance of a category into that category using an exophoric reference item to signify the observed instance (e.g. *that's a dog*). Similarly, things given an identity through explicit naming with *call* were signified with an exophoric reference word. In addition, when words (such as *share*) were self-clarified they were given a highly specific kind of contextualized definition through rewording.

Towards the end of the period, with the development of the first metalinguistic term, *call*, the relationship between meaning (categorization) and wording became explicit to the child, and there was an isolated instance of enquiring about the meaning of a common noun (*pet*), in which *call* was pressed into service, as the child groped for a way to talk about meaning. However, apart from this one occasion, there were no definitions of terms recorded, even from the parent.

Illustrative examples from Stephen's language also show that he was deploying a lexical semantic system in which hierarchical organization was evident. Although any individual text would be likely to reveal only two named levels of a taxonomy, an accumulation of different texts and an appreciation of the unnamed levels constructed by the named ones suggests that in some areas at least four levels can be inferred.

Both parts and qualitative properties of specific things were readily named and, in addition, instances of different categories were recognized as sharing perceptible characteristics such as bigness, hotness or blueness. However – with a single exception – when comparisons were drawn, the specific qualities shared by members of different classes were left unstated. Moreover there was a lack of explicitness by both child and adult concerning the definitional status of descriptions of parts and qualities of an entity. Parental talk implied that certain features of an object, always of an observable nature, might be criterial to the object's classification but was not explicit about this.

The adult talk did, however, make the various semantic relations between words relatively transparent in the talk, while Stephen, for his part, monitored the adult's responses to his categorizations and deployed the strategy of comparison and contrast to construe taxonomic relations of all kinds and to make imaginative links between things construed into different categories (e.g. a sword and an ice-cream; slippery spaghetti and slippery floor).

Stephen's vocabulary was all of a 'concrete' nature in that the qualities, things, and processes named were tangible and observable. There were no abstract nouns and there was as yet little evidence of experiential grammatical metaphor, although some routine Process^Range structures provided a model for construing an action as a noun. The first more productive lack of congruence in the system was the occasional use of embedding. This occurred not only in mental process clauses where an event might be construed as a perceived participant, but also in nominal group structures like *the thing (that) go in there*. In the latter case, in order to identify a non-present object linguistically, Stephen was able to use esphoric reference and construct a clause into the Qualifier role in a nominal group.

## 4 Stephen's language 3;0 to 4;0 years

In this section, the second data set covering the period from 3 to 4 years will be described and a contrast will be drawn between this data set as a whole and that of the earlier period. In general, the most striking difference which emerges from an examination of identifying, classifying and describing utterances is that, in the fourth year, Stephen was not only more explicit in identifying particular things but began much more consciously to explore the relations between categories and the criteria for class membership. Indeed reflection on these matters appeared to take up much of his attention during this year. This, of course, is an interpretative judgement, but it is one based on several differences in the use of language in this period which, taken together, make sense on the basis of such an interpretation.

The developments in question, which will be discussed and exemplified in turn, are the following:

1. The favouring of non-phoric nominal groups in relational clause structures.
2. The explicit specification of criteria for classification.
3. The first definitions of categories, leading to grammatical metaphor.
4. The identification of specific things through rankshifted structures.
5. The development of text reference and grammatical metaphor.
6. The construal of abstract meanings.

### 4.1  Use of non-phoric groups when identifying, classifying or describing

One respect in which the talk from Stephen as a 3-year-old was different from his talk as a 2-year-old was in his construction of relational clauses. Whereas before one participant role in such a clause had always included an exophoric reference item, so that the participant's identity was signalled as recoverable from the context of situation, such participants were now constructed by nominal groups in which there were no presupposing reference items. This change will be interpreted here as the functional reflex in grammar of a more conscious concern on Stephen's part with relations between the elements in his meaning system. That is, Stephen displayed an overt interest in the taxonomic organization of categories, rather than simply attempting to construe classes referentially through the naming of instances.

To clarify this point, it can be noted again that texts in the third year had used relational processes such as *it's a —, those are —* to classify observable instances of phenomena into categories. Descriptive clauses like *it's got a hump* had similarly tended to focus on the characteristics of the instance under attention, which might or might not be typical or criterial of the class. While these kinds of utterances were also plentiful in the fourth year, it was equally likely by then that observing and commenting on an instance would immediately lead to explicit reflection on the category itself and on the status of the instance as typical of the category.

For example, when Stephen noticed a plane in the sky, he said:

3;7    S:    (looking up at plane) Do aeroplanes have wheels?
       M:    Yes.

What is different from earlier queries about objects is that Stephen did not here ask whether the particular plane he was looking at had wheels. Although his perceptual attention was focused on one individual plane, he was inquiring about meronymy relations for the class of aeroplanes generally. Because of this he used generic reference, realized by absence of a Deictic element within the nominal group (*aeroplanes*).

In the following example, the movement from observing the particular to deriving an explicit generalization is worked through in the text.

3;7;5    (S talking about the 'big shoes' laid out by the door)
        S:   Hal has [big shoes] and you have and Daddy has; grown-ups
            have.

Comparing similar instances with a text such as *Hal has and you have and Daddy has* was a very long-standing strategy. The new development was the explicit construal of the taxonomic generalization to be drawn from such a comparison of instances. Here a superordinate term, *grown-ups,* was used to make explicit the fact that the named individuals were being construed as representatives of the class – a class characterized by having a particular attribute.

The next examples are even more overtly focused on the class rather than the instance, because of the use of the non-specific Deictic *all.*

3;5;11    S:   (sees horse) Ooh horsey . . . All horses have tummies don't
            they?

3;9;6    (S notices gum tree with smooth peeled trunk)
        S:   Not all trees grow bark trees, you know . . . Not all trees
            grow bark trees- not all trees have bark t-
        M:   Well, they all have bark, but some kinds of trees the bark
            peels.

The use of *all* as a Deictic in the group emphasizes Stephen's concern with the generalizability of the meronymy relation, even though a specific observed horse or tree provided the stimulus for the enquiry.

In the 2-year-old talk *(not) all, (not) every,* and stressed *some* had only been used in conjunction with a specific Deictic to signal totality or partiality of instances of a particular known group (all the children in the preschool, every Smartie in the packet, some of the blocks in the box, etc.). After age three, however, these non-specific Deictics were used outside the context of any specified group. They constituted an experiential means of exploring the notion of a class and the typical characteristics shared by all or some members of a category.

As well as the generalizability of a meronymy relation, the generalizability of qualities of a class might be explored in this way:

3;8;19    S:   Look a van car. Are all van cars coloured?
        M:   They're different colours, yeah.
        S:   Are only vans all the time coloured?
        M:   Vans and cars can be different colours.
        S:   Yeah, some are scruffy and some are beautiful.

Thus all these examples show how an observation of an individual entity typically led to a comment on the qualities or meronymic relations obtaining with respect to the class to which the individual was construed as belonging.

In addition, observations of specific things now led to investigation of the taxonomic status of the category, rather than of the specific thing. The following examples illustrate this:

3;7;13    S:  Are all cars are motor cars, Mummy?
          M:  Yes.
          S:  Oh no, sport cars aren't ordinary.

3;8;7    (S looking at animal jigsaw puzzle pieces)
          S:  There isn't a fox [i.e. on this jigsaw]; and there isn't – Is a platypus an animal?

3;8;14    (M and H have been talking about dolphins being mammals and sharks fish)
          S:  Are seals dolphins?
          M:  No, but seals are mammals too, they aren't fish.

In these examples of the fourth year, there are for the first time comments and enquiries about classification that embody two named levels of taxonomy in the one clause. The importance of this is that whereas an attributive clause such as *That's an animal* categorizes a specific instance of a class into that class, an attributive clause of the form *A platypus is an animal* sorts out hyponymic relations between two classes. So from creating text in order to make sense of non-linguistic phenomena, Stephen had moved towards using language to make sense of the semantic potential itself. Thus the self-reflexive character of language was coming to the fore in a new way.

It is partly because of this that the character of conversation with a child at this stage of development is so different from that with a child who has only recently moved into the mother tongue. The following longer excerpt of a conversation illustrates the nature of this difference:

3;8;5    (M reading Easter Bunny book to S – shows him the word *dog* and asks him if he knows the word)
          S:  No.
          M:  It's an animal.
          S:  Rabbit?
          M:  No, it's 'dog'.
          S:  (?Dog's) not an animal!
          M:  Yes it is. (pause) What is it then?
          S:  It's – it's just a dog.
          M:  Yes, but dogs are animals.
          S:  No, they aren't.
          M:  Well, what's an animal then?
          S:  Um, (?a) giraffe's an animal.
          M:  Oh, I see, you think animal is only for zoo animals.

S:  Yeah.
M:  Dogs are animals too, they're tame animals. And cats, cats are animals too. Did you know that?
H:  (chipping in) And people, we're animals.
S:  We're NOT!

On the surface, the language used here is simple. In terms of the syntactic structures in which child language is frequently discussed, Stephen's utterances appear unremarkable: simple Subject^Verb^ Complement structures in positive or negative form. But a year earlier such a conversation would have been out of the question. Until two named levels of a taxonomy can be constructed into a relational clause (*dog's not an animal*; *cats are animals*), this possibility of using language to discuss semantic categories and clarify mismatches between the adult's and child's taxonomies in a 'context-free' way could not be realized.

Gaining this new knowledge and mobilizing his metalanguage to do so was sometimes a struggle, as can be seen in the following example:

3;6;25   S:  A bus isn't a truck is it, Mum?
         M:  No.
         S:  What is it?
         M:  A bus is for carrying people.
         S:  No, what is a bus called? I said, a bus, what is it called?
         M:  It's called a bus; that thing (points) is just a bus and it's –
         S:  (plaintively) Oh, why is it just a bus?

With hindsight, it would seem that what Stephen wanted to know was what superordinate category *bus* belonged to. But since *vehicle* (much less *mode of passenger transport* ) was not a sufficiently everyday term for M to use, he received a definition which did not provide a superordinate. A classical definition would have done this and then qualified it by suggesting the function of the thing. In this case M provided the qualifying function part of a classical definition (*for carrying people*), but not the taxonomizing part. Stephen's apparently inappropriate use of *call* here was probably his attempt to signal that he wanted the superordinate name, since *call* specifies the process of naming and he had no metalanguage to refer to taxonomic levels. However, because M could not understand why he should ask for the name of something he already had the name for, she was reduced to naming the instance (*that thing*) as a member of the class *bus*, much to Stephen's frustration.

One respect in which languages vary is, of course, in what semantic categories are lexicalized, and this text illustrates that one of the things children have to learn in using language to construe things is the limits of the lexical system for doing this. Perhaps Stephen's initial question was prompted by some awareness that there is a gap in the lexical taxonomy here in everyday English, a gap which he needed to probe.

### 4.2 *Specification of criteria for class membership*

The nature of most qualities as categories in terms of which any thing can be described is underlined when specific instances of different categories are compared in terms of a shared named quality. In the previous data set, there had been only a single explicit example comparing slippery spaghetti and slippery floor (see text 2;9;3, p. 94), but by the fourth year, such utterances were common:

3;10;4    (S talking about a car)
        S:    It's burgundy, like Hal's toothbrush.

Comparisons of this kind allow the qualitative feature (such as colour) to be focused on as a dimension sharable by different particular things. Thus by specifying the terms in which examples of two different kinds of thing are alike, both the generalizability of the quality and the individuality of the observed instance was construed.

Alternatively, however, the recognition of an unusual property may be the child's only means of interpreting something unfamiliar. This can be seen in the following example:

3;9;5    (S is looking at picture of Lord Mayor in regalia)
        S:    This looks like a swimming person and he's got a gold medal.

Construing a likeness between different things using *looks like* was not new, but what Stephen was now able to do was to specify the respect in which two things were observably similar: in this case the mayoral chain of office called to mind the Olympic champions who had been seen repeatedly on television. This resemblance between things which arose in different contexts was in turn a way for the child to begin to interpret an unfamiliar instance (*this*) in terms of a more familiar category (*a swimming person*).

Thus the first text (*It's burgundy like Hal's toothbrush*) suggests an understanding that the same attributes might be freely shared by things otherwise unlike (a particular car and a particular toothbrush), while the second text could be read as suggesting that different instances might be given a similar category interpretation because of some particular shared attribute.

Certainly one of Stephen's concerns during this year was to explore such matters and, while descriptive clauses detailing the parts or appearance of specific things were still common in the parent–child conversation, the most striking feature of such talk now was the much more overt reflection on what observable features might be criterial for the class concerned. This can be achieved simply by using a descriptive attributive clause with generic participants, for example when Stephen challenged his parent's categorization of a harbour ferry as a *boat* in the following text:

3;5;7    M:  (correcting S) <u>This</u> is a boat; <u>those</u> (pointing) are ships.

          S:  No, boats aren't big.

Or when Stephen remarked on observing a lizard:

3;8;19   S:  Snakes and worms, they don't have legs.

          M:  They don't have what, darling?

          S:  Legs. Snakes and worms don't have legs,

          M:  Ah no.

          S:  But lizards do.

Obviously when parts and qualities are assigned to things construed as generic nominal groups, then those parts and qualities are constructed as generalizations about the category as a whole.

### 4.2.1 Use of internal cause

An additional key way the language can be deployed to construe criteria for classification is by inferentially linking a specific thing and its characteristics by means of an 'internal' causal relation (Halliday and Hasan 1976: 257*ff*). An example would be the *cause* link presented in bold in the following text:

3;7;24   (M says something about her 'best boys')

          H:  We have to be your best boys 'cause we're your only boys.

          S:  And Daddy.

          H:  He's not a boy, he's a man.

          S:  **He is a boy, 'cause he's got a penis.**

          H:  He's a male, we're all males.

          S:  He's a man and a boy too.

In this text, Stephen's meaning can be paraphrased as 'I know he is a member of the class "boy" because . . . ' or 'the reason I say he is a member of the class "boy" is because . . . '. The causal link is 'internal' to the text, serving to explain the speaker's reason for asserting or inferring something, rather than construing an obligatory relation between two external events (see Chapter 6 for further discussion). Using an internal causal relation in the way Stephen does here cannot be achieved until the child is able to bring to consciousness and articulate the positive criteria involved in naming. Thus although the development of an internal causal logical relation is a development in a quite different area of the grammar from both relational TRANSITIVITY and REFERENCE, it can be argued that the developments described in all three areas have a similar functional impetus, that of using language to reflect on categorization.

Other examples of the use of this internal relation to elucidate criteria for classification are given below:

3;5;7     (M teases that the zoo bears fancy some 'juicy boys' to eat)
          S:   We're not juicy boys, 'cause we haven't got juice in.

3;7;8     (S relaying confused account of a mouse at preschool)
          M:   Really! There was a mouse there?
          S:   Yeah, but it wasn't a strange mouse, 'cause a strange ones go
               – 'cause strange mouses bite you.

3;9       (M refers to airship as 'spaceship balloon')
          S:   Not a spaceship – an <u>air</u>ship – 'cause a spaceship has bits
               like this (gestures) to stand it up.

3;11;11   S:   That's fifteen because it's got a 5; that's fourteen because it's
               got a 4.

3;11;15   S:   Our cat is an animal because it's got fur.

The last two examples at the end of the fourth year were probably repetitions of things that he had heard said to him by his brother, who was often anxious to impart his more specialized knowledge to Stephen. But in all cases the explicit criteria for class membership were observable characteristics of the things talked about, just as the implied criteria had been in the previous year.

### 4.2.2 Context for category name

A new development, however, was that Stephen now began to specify linguistically a context in which a particular name (and therefore categorization) would be appropriate, as in the following case:

3;4;5     (S has been served spaghetti bolognese – a favourite)
          S:   So this is bolognese. (pause) So that's bolognese (poking
               it). When you eat it, it's bolognese, isn't it?
               It's still bolognese when you eat it, isn't it?
          M:   (puzzled) Yes.
          S:   Yeah, but we call it meat, don't we? We call it meat, don't we?
          M:   You make bolognese with meat.

In this example Stephen was clearly puzzling over the taxonomic relations between *meat* and *bolognese*, and whether consuming the food provided a context in which the culinary term *bolognese* might be replaced by *meat*. He attempted to make his problem explicit to the interlocutor by specifying linguistically the context in which a particular category might or might not be appropriate. He did this with a hypotactic *when* clause in which *you* was used in its sense as a generalized participant.

In the following example, *we* was used as a generalized participant in a similar way to *you* in the previous text:

3;6;29     (S in bed, holds up hands to M)
           S:    Know what we call nails when they're nice? When we cut
                 them, they're called fingernails!

This use of a *when* clause to build a general specification of context into
the naming utterance as a means of exploring field restrictions on the use
of names was a new development in the fourth year, although (as will be
discussed in Chapter 4) *when* clauses to sequence activities were not new.
Thus the attempt to explore the basis of categorization with the addressee
provided one pressure for Stephen to expand his system of temporal
logical relations, as well as providing the impetus for the new internal
causal choice.

### 4.3 Definitions leading to grammatical metaphor

Overt discussions of the relations between aspects of the language system
were not restricted to consideration of categories of things. The meaning
of an action could also be explicitly discussed now through identifying
clauses providing definitions. In such clauses, the process term is
constructed into the Token role and an alternative linguistic formulation
is constructed into the Value role, by means of a rankshifted clause. For
example:

3;7;5      (M is going to shampoo S and wants him to put his head right
           into the bathwater to wet the hair)
           M:    C'mon. Drown.
           S:    Not drown! Drown is [[go down to the bottom and be dead]].
                      Token     Value

The creation of definitions as a means of reflecting upon the meaning
system thus necessitated the deployment of a degree of grammatical
metaphor. This arose in the fact that neither of the grammatical participants
in the clause was construed by a noun or a nominal group: a process word
(*drown*) was construed as the Token, while a coordinated pair of clauses was
construed as the Value.

Moreover, unlike the earlier attempt to elaborate on the meaning of
*share* through exemplification in text 2;7;13 (see p. 87), this rewording of
the meaning of *drown* came closer to having relevance across different
contexts, and to being textually 'self-contained'. This was true also of
defining clauses in which a class of things, rather than actions, was
defined, such as:

3;8;7      H:    I'm going to do a pee.
           S:    It's wee, not pea.
                 Pea is things [[that you cook and you eat them]].
                 Token     Value

Here the Value role is realized by a nominal group with a rankshifted clause-complex as Qualifier and, apart from the fact that the Head of the group is a general word (*things*) rather than the appropriate superordinate, this utterance approaches a classic definition. It was rare in this respect, but it is the use of non-phoric groups on each side of the defining process that allows for the possibility.

During this period Stephen also began to use the metalinguistic term *mean* for the first time to signal relations between terms within his linguistic potential. (It had been used earlier only to signal a self-correction as in *That's Hal's – I mean Daddy's – money.*) In the following example Stephen used *mean* to try out a definition of the process *balance*:

3;9;30    (S shows M complicated Duplo structure)
      S:    Balance means [[you hold it on your fingers and it doesn't go on the floor]].

This example resembles earlier attempts to elaborate meaning in that the 'definition' given is actually specific to the current context of situation. And this, of course, was often the case both in definitions offered by Stephen and those supplied to him, such as the following:

3;7;8    (M and S enter house dripping with rain)
      M:    (to F) Oh, we're drowned!
      S:    What does drown mean?
      M:    Means [[we're all wet]].

3;7;17    (discussing route while waiting at traffic lights)
      M:    We're going straight on.
      S:    What does straight on mean?
      M:    Means [[we're not going to turn at all]]. See? We're just going straight across.

Stephen also used *mean* to define quality terms as well as process and thing words:

3;7;17    S:    . . . speeding. Speeding means fast.

3;9;30    S:    When you look out the window it looks like flood.
      M:    Oh, does it?
      S:    Flood means windy.
      M:    Oh, no, flood means wet.

Attitudinal expressions could also be explicated:

3;7;24    S:    Sucked in means (chants) na-nani-na-na.

This could be done, as in this case, by presenting an attitudinal synonym, or alternatively an attitudinal expression could be reworked into experiential language:

3;7;3      M:  You're naughty boys to throw them up there.
           S:  Hal did it, by accident.
           M:  Well, Hal's naughty then.
           S:  No, by accident; that's not naughty, that's mean (pause) [[you say sorry]].

What is clear from all these examples is that Stephen no longer had to infer meaning only from contextualized observations of language in use and from observing responses to his own attempts at meanings. He continued to do this, of course, and will do so for the rest of his life, no doubt, but the striking characteristic of the talk between three and four years was the use of the linguistic system both to explore and to expand that system itself.

The advantages of using language to develop itself in this way can be illustrated by Stephen's attempts to understand the (non-congruent) expression *traffic jam*. For a month after he first heard the term he attempted to understand it by checking every time the car queued at traffic lights whether this was an example of a traffic jam. As the route to the childcare centre was a very busy one, there were repeated opportunities to do this. A few examples are given below:

3;5;8      (car waiting to turn right at lights)
           S:  Is this a traffic jam?
           M:  No, it's (pause) just waiting at the lights.
           S:  No, is this called a traffic jam?

3;5;13     (car stationary at lights)
           S:  Is this a traffic jam, Mum?
           M:  Well –
           S:  Is this a traffic jam?
           M:  No, not really.

3;5;14     (car stationary at lights)
           S:  Is this a traffic jam?
           M:  (fed up with this question) Oh, it's a little jam.
           S:  No, it's a big jam, a big traffic jam; there's all cars. (pause) Is it a traffic jam?

3;5;26     (car stationary at lights)
           S:  Is this a traffic jam?
           M:  Not really; a traffic jam is when there's lots of cars.
           S:  But there is lots of cars, Mum; there is lots of cars and trucks; there is. That's a traffic jam.

Attempting to understand the expression by checking whether every possible instance was an example of the meaning was not proving efficient for a category not readily 'point-at-able'. In the last text M had, for the first time, tried to resolve the matter by supplying a definition (*A traffic jam is when there's lots of cars*), rather than giving a qualified yes or no to the classification. And Stephen finally began to be satisfied when this definition was refined some weeks later:

3;6;23    (M explains that now they are in a real traffic jam, because when the light goes green they still can't go because there are too many cars.)
M:   A traffic jam is when you can't go even when the light is green.
(The car then stops again as the light ahead goes red.)
S:    (?. . .) It means when it's green it's called a traffic jam, but this is not a traffic jam cause it's red; a green one is a traffic jam.

The use of metalinguistic explanation provides a valuable short-cut for establishing intersubjective agreement on the extension of any category (cf. 'what's an animal?', text 3;8;5 on pp. 102–3). However, for a category which construes a phenomenon which cannot readily be ostensively identified, it becomes not simply useful but a quite essential tool for understanding.

### 4.4 Identifying specific things: rankshifted structures

While identifying clauses defining categories provided a very important context for embeddings, those clauses identifying specific things also used rankshift in a comparable way, as can be seen in the following example:

3;6    S:   Oh look, Mum, a white petrol truck over there . . .  look there, that's [[what I was talking about]].

By the end of the year embeddings within embeddings were routine:

3;11;10    (S points from car)
S:   That's [[where we went yesterday and saw the thing [[that lifts up]]]].

These are similar to very early identifying utterances in that they depend on an exophoric reference item as Token, but what is new is the prevalence of rankshifted clauses as Value. Common to most of these examples was the fact that the use of embedding enabled the object (or location) picked out to be identified in terms of Stephen's previous experience with it. It is interesting to see that the phenomenon of rankshift, so often marshalled in adult written discourse to summarize previous *text* (Halliday and Martin 1993), was used prominently by

Stephen in these early years to summarize previous experience as a means
of establishing intersubjectivity.

A related new development was that Stephen was now able to identify
for someone else a non-present non-visible entity by using rankshift in a
nominal group structure with a lexical Head rather than a general word
like *thing* or *stuff*: for example, *biscuits* in the following text.

3;4;6     (S explaining what he ate to M)
          S:  Little crunchy round biscuits [with 'tanas in].
          M:  Cor!
          S:  You don't – we don't have one of them do we? We don't
              have one of them do we?
          M:  No.
          S:  We have only little round biscuits [[that not crunchy]], we
              have only little round ones [with worms in] [= butter
              through holes].

The use of these nominal groups is part of the picture of using purely
linguistic means for establishing the identity of the item under attention,
though it should be noted that the contexts in which Stephen did this
were not at all similar to 'referential communication' experiments
exploring egocentrism, which also call for nominal groups of this kind. In
the latter, these structures are called upon to construct a description which
will discriminate for an addressee one and only one of a series of pictures
or designs of which the speaker has no previous experience (Dickson
1981). In these data, on the other hand, the child speaker is representing
the object linguistically in terms of some feature (sultanas, crunchiness)
which is particularly salient in terms of his own experience.

Alternatively the identification provided in the nominal group Qualifier
may rest on previous experience with the object, just as in the identifying
clauses discussed earlier:

3;7;5     S:  I saw a orange truck [[that we haven't seen for a long time]].

3;7;21    M:  What did you do in the park with Jason?
          S:  I played with the dog [[that we stroked yesterday]].

In this way the grammatically metaphorical post-modifying structure
allows the speaker to encapsulate an experience into a descriptor. This
enabled Stephen to create an appropriate textual structure to organize his
information. Instead of establishing intersubjectivity by bringing to shared
attention the previous experience and then giving his new information, he
could use the capability of embedding to 'downrank' the status of the
experience in terms of the information exchange. The importance of
embedding as a means of organizing monologic written text has been
emphasized in systemic writing (e.g. Halliday 1989). In these examples of

3-year-old talk, it is possible to see comparable text-organizing pressures responsible for some of the earliest examples.

### 4.5 Text reference and grammatical metaphor

In the discussion of defining clauses, the use of *mean* as an identifying process was illustrated, together with the use of experiential metaphor in the construal of the participant roles of Token and Value. Three further examples of the use of *mean* will be discussed here because they exemplify a further metaphorical move, which is where the process itself functions metaphorically. That is to say, rather than being used to construe a simple synonymy relation, *mean* is used to express a logical relation, the internal causal relation.

There were three recorded examples of this in Stephen's speech:

3;5;6     (regarding his toast)
          S:   It's got a plate and that's mean [[it's tea]].

3;6;12    S:   (checking book) There's words; that means [[it's a story]].

3;9;21    (S is describing an imaginary flying machine)
          S:   A propeller it's got on, and it's got two wings there and two
               wings there and that means [[it's a biplane]].

Here, the internal causal relation has been built into the clause structure itself rather than being expressed conjunctively. A more congruent construction of the meaning would have been in the form of clause complexes linked by a conjunction:

> *It's a story because there's words*
> *There's words so (I conclude) it's a story*
>
> *It's a biplane because it's got two wings*
> *It's got two wings so (I conclude) it's a biplane*

In these congruent versions, the characteristics of a particular thing are construed as explaining the inference to be made concerning its class membership, as in many examples already given in this chapter. And it is possible that initially *that means* was simply a formulaic expression substituting for *so* and functioning as an internal conjunction in Stephen's speech. In favour of this interpretation is the fact that there were no variations of tense or modality in the realization of *mean* to make it clear that it functioned as a Process element. However, in the previously cited example *That's mean you say sorry* (3;7;3 on p. 109), *that's mean* cannot be interpreted as an internal conjunction, which suggests that there is a genuine grammatical metaphor being deployed here.

Even if this is not accepted, clearly such a 'formula' used as a conjunction could provide a stepping stone towards the metaphorical use. *That*, in other contexts, was unambiguously an anaphoric reference item; *mean* was already used as an identifying process and embedded clauses had already developed, so the potential for creatively constructing an inferential causal link in the form of an experiential clause structure was certainly present.

If *that* in these texts is taken as a reference item proper, rather than simply part of a conjunction, then it can be suggested that these examples also show Stephen using the system of REFERENCE in a new way. In the examples above he was not simply referring exophorically or homophorically to an entity in the context nor referring endophorically to a linguistic construction of an entity. In these cases, the demonstrative *that* links anaphorically with the whole of the preceding proposition and construes it as a fact using 'text' reference. In other words *that* is equivalent to *the fact of having two wings*.

As Martin (1992a: 416) points out, text reference of this kind involves a degree of grammatical metaphor. This is because a meaning which is not semantically a participant is being construed by the grammar into a participant role in the second clause. The use of reference by Stephen in these examples can therefore be seen as another part of the move in abstraction and towards talking about meaning rather than about experience directly.

## 4.6 The construal of abstract meanings

Another aspect to the question of abstraction concerns whether referents for lexical items are concrete entities or not. During this period it was still the case that lexical items were overwhelmingly used to construe only concrete and observable things, but there were a few tentative moves beyond this. Apart from adopting the term *traffic jam*, discussed earlier, the moves into abstract nominals occurred in three areas: in Stephen's use of *problem* to make a complaint, in his attempts to construe time, and through his growing acquaintance with language in a written form.

In the speech going on around him, Stephen heard many expressions where behaviour was treated as a thing (in being construed by a noun), particularly when his elder brother received admonitions such as *That's disgusting behaviour; That's bad manners.* However, apart from the Process^Range constructions of the previous year and the use of verbs to realize a participant in defining clauses, the only recorded instances by Stephen himself were at the very end of the year, when he adopted the term *problem* to construe a situation, as in:

3;11;7    (S examining nails)
          S:    Mummy this thumb is still sharp; it's still sharp and this finger
                – it's the problem that you have to cut my fingers all the time.

Taking up the word *problem* may have been related to the frequency of *What's the matter?* in the adult talk, a case of 'frozen' metaphor like the Process^Range structures. It was certainly the case that abstract nouns were not yet part of Stephen's everyday language. The route into non-congruent representations was through embedding of clauses, the representation of actions as participants (in defining clauses) and the beginning of text reference rather than use of abstract nouns.

However, one domain of everyday language which inevitably encourages some move towards abstraction is in the expression of temporal meaning, since the language allows for the location and quantification of time as well as for sequencing of events. During the fourth year, the noun *time* itself began to be used:

3;5;24    S:    He [=F] has to do it later cause (?not time) – 'cause it hasn't – we haven't got time.

This phrase was, of course, a frequently heard excuse for deferring action, although in this case Stephen was not offering it to negotiate his own (lack of) action, but simply reflecting on why he was eating muesli rather than the porridge which his father usually cooked.

Towards the end of the year *time* occurred within a phrase, such as *for a long long time*, to construe an Extent, a kind of circumstance not found in the previous year. Moreover, nouns began to be used to identify 'points' in a temporal sequence, as in *next month, next week, tomorrow*, etc. While they were not used accurately, such expressions did orient Stephen towards construing the experience of time as something segmentable and locatable, and doubtless provided a model for treating non-tangible experience as a thing.

Easily the most important experience in this regard, however, was Stephen's growing familiarity with written language. One manifestation of this was his recognition of both *story* and *joke* as nameable types of text. The latter developed because his brother frequently read jokes to the family from paperback joke collections and, over a period of several months, Stephen imitated this behaviour, announcing that he was making a joke:

3;3;21    S:    (holding book open) Mum, I'm going to tell you a joke.
          M:    All right, what is it?
          S:    Why does a cat moo? (looks expectantly)
          M:    I don't know; why does a cat moo?
          (S grins, but does not know how to proceed)

3;6;11    S:    ('searching' in Hal's joke book) I'm going to do a joke; how does a cat (pause) go (pause) word bomb!?

It was probably because it had come to Stephen's attention via the material object of the book, that Stephen was able to focus on the joke as well as the story, as a unit of discourse, classifiable as a 'thing', although not of the same tangible order of reality as most other things construed by nouns.

His other concern with written language was with the medium of writing itself. Attending to this had led him to see words as entities with parts consisting of letters:

3;9;6     S:   Handbag has got 'b' and tummy has got 'm' and belly button is 'b'!

And when he began 'writing', then letters too were decomposed:

3;10;2    M:   That one isn't an F; it's got a stroke down there: it's E.
          S:   And a F has two ones.

But although he was talking about symbols, he was considering them as material entities, so there is nothing essentially new here. However, when he discussed spelling, he adopted the prevalent metaphor which treats the word as a process with a beginning, middle and end, even though he himself could not write:

3;8;16    S:   Ireland start with a I 'cause it's I-land.

By the latter part of the year he was also becoming familiar with numerical symbols as material entities:

3;10;2    S:   It's a upside down 9, and a upside down 9 makes 6!
               (later)
               Upside down 6 means 9, upside down 9 means a 6.

and also as symbolic ones:

3;11;7    (S overhears F mention '50')
          S:   Is 50 a number?
          F:   Yeah.
          S:   How does it go?
          F:   It comes after 49.
          S:   A hundred comes after 49.
          F:   A hundred comes after 99.

A number can only be perceptually experienced as a material graphic. The graph of the numeral can be observed and talked about like other things, but as a number it is only an 'object' of the symbolic world and – especially if it is a high number – can only be understood relationally, not referentially. In other words, a number is a meaning not a thing. Without the development of the relational clause structure already discussed,

Stephen could not have begun to understand it in this way because he could not have framed an enquiry in which a numerical symbol is placed in its 'meta' category (*number*). Now he was able to do this and, in further attempting to understand the symbol, he reconstrued the material processes *go* and *come* metaphorically as relations and discussed the sequence of enumeration by construing it (following F's model) in terms of relative locations.

In all of this Stephen was moving away from a completely congruent kind of representation of tangible things. It was experience of the written medium of both linguistic and numerical representations which pushed him into stretching his language use in this way. While the potential for construing abstract 'things' is manifested to a degree in our everyday language to talk about time, the first grapplings with the business of schooling extended Stephen's language use further in the direction of abstraction and metaphor.

### 4.7 *Summary: age 3;0 to 4;0 years*

This section has described and illustrated a number of changes in Stephen's language and language use related to the construal of things as individual cases and as classes. Many of the changes concern a shift away from classifying observable instances only to classifying categories as well. They involve the use of language as its own metalanguage and a few steps towards the use of grammatical metaphor.

In order to categorize categories rather than things, Stephen for the first time deployed generic nominal groups (e.g. *cars, seals*) in attributive clauses (e.g. *are seals dolphins*). He also developed new non-specific Deictics to specify explicitly that an entire or partial class was under focus (*all, every*, stressed *some*, etc.). While comparison and contrast continued to be used to explore value relations (e.g. differences between snakes and lizards, similarity between celebrity swimmers and Lord Mayors), a new move was for Stephen to verbalize the criteria he had construed for classifying something. He did this by explaining his classification in terms of the attributes shared by members of a category. This required the use of *because* as an 'internal' linker, and on at least three occasions even resulted in the use of text reference and grammatical metaphor to do the same thing (using *That means [[      ]]*).

Stephen could now probe the relevant contexts for using particular names (such as *bolognese*) by construing in language a context for their use, using a newly developed *when* (=whenever) clause to do so. He also related linguistic meanings through synonymy, forming definitions using *be* or *mean*. And in achieving this, he constructed non-thing meanings into participant roles within the relational clause in an early form of grammatical metaphor.

Grammatical metaphor was also deployed in the form of rankshifted Qualifiers within nominal groups (with a lexical category as Thing). This occurred when Stephen used language to identify an individual thing for the addressee (e.g. *biscuits with 'tanas in*). Through this structure the linguistic identification of particular objects was further freed from dependence on shared experience. Instead, on many occasions Stephen's own experience with an object could be crystallized into a Qualifier (e.g. *the dog that we stroked yesterday*) as a way of creating a shared understanding through language alone.

While the relation between meaning and word class was overwhelmingly congruent, Stephen could now use the resources of relational grammar to begin to understand non-tangible 'things' like a *traffic jam* or a *number*, and the attempt to construe observable symbols as symbols rather than as material objects generally required a beginning move into abstraction and grammatical metaphor.

## 5  Stephen's language 4;0 to 5;0 years

The major breakthrough in the construal of taxonomies occurred in the previous period with the development of linguistic tools for construing meaning without reference beyond the linguistic system. This section will deal only very selectively with data from Stephen's fifth year to illustrate briefly how those developments were built on over the next year. It will involve a consideration of Stephen's ability to learn from definitions and from further moves towards abstraction and grammatical metaphor.

### 5.1  Learning from definitions

In his fifth year Stephen enjoyed looking at illustrated information books on natural history. In mediating the less commonsense knowledge they contained, his parents were continually modelling definitions in the context of taxonomizing. Each consideration of a picture in the book might lead to a defining statement being offered to Stephen in the following way:

4;7;21  M:  An arctic fox; that's a kind of fox that lives in the snow . . .
That's called a frilled lizard; it's a kind of lizard that can puff out.
These reindeer are called caribou; they're the reindeer that live in Canada.

Stephen was therefore becoming very experienced in attending to definitions in the context of subcategorizations.

His own early attempts at context-free definitions were enabled by the development of rankshift as described for the previous period (cf. 3;7;5, p. 107) *Drown is [[go down to the bottom and be dead]]*), though with very general nouns as Thing/Head of the nominal group (cf. 3;8;7, p. 107) *Pea is things [[that you cook and you eat them]]*). During the fifth year, he began to exploit these structures more confidently, and in the next example he can be seen attempting a definition as a means of generalizing from the immediate context, thus bringing together two of the characteristics of the previous year's talk:

4;5;8    (driving past the Royal Agricultural Society Showground at Easter)
         S:   I saw a cowboy on a horse. (pause) Any person who's riding a horse who's got a round hat on is a cowboy. (no one responds) Any person who's riding a horse who's got a round hat on is a cowboy.
         M:   Yeah, if they're going to the show, they probably are cowboys.

Having observed and commented on a particular individual here, Stephen tried out a context-free definition of *cowboy*. This appeared quite a self-conscious move and he was certainly looking for a response to check on his efforts. (As it was not entirely satisfactory in adult terms, however, it was only validated by M within the actual context of observation.)

The same pattern of movement within the discourse from the immediate context to a generalizing definition can be seen in the following example:

4;2;7    (S waves his tennis racket around instead of hitting ball to M)
         M:   C'mon! Don't do exercises while I'm standing here.
         S:   Is that exercises?
         M:   Yes.
         S:   Anything you do is exercises.
         M:   Yes, 'cause it all makes you strong.
         S:   Is food exercises?
         M:   Oh no, has to be actions, running about and stuff.

Once again Stephen took the discussion further than clarifying whether the specific here-and-now behaviour (which could be signified by exophoric *that*) was categorized as *exercise*, and attempted to formulate a definition that would hold without reference to the immediate context. But a new development is also illustrated here. This is Stephen's ability to draw an immediate inference from the definitions given and use it to take the dialogue further in the exploration of meaning. In the above example, M's supplementary information, that things count as exercises because they make you strong, immediately led Stephen to check whether (eating) food, which he had often been told 'makes you strong', therefore counts as a kind of exercise. This immediate bringing to bear of newly received information on older knowledge was a development apparent in the fifth year.

In the next example, Stephen's understanding of the meaning of *meat* was extended by his ability to draw the appropriate inference from his mother's playful remark:

4;7;23    S:   I wonder where you get tiger food.
          H:   Tigers eat meat.
          M:   Give it a little boy!
          S:   (seriously, after a pause) Is a boy meat?

At an earlier age Stephen might well have concluded that tigers eat meat *and* little boys, since he was not aware of any connection between the two, but by this time he was continually inferring new connections in the course of participating in a single conversation, and then checking out the new taxonomic relation construed.

This ability to draw an immediate inference from a definition that he was offered is even more clearly illustrated in the following conversation:

4;4;10    (M and S are discussing whether whales kill people)
         M:   There may be one kind of whale that can kill people, but most whales are nice creatures.
         S:   They're not creatures, Mum, they're whales.
         M:   Yes, creature is anything that's alive.
         S:   Are <u>we</u> creatures?
         M:   Yeah.
         S:   (laughs) No we're not!

Stephen's experience in using the language to develop itself further was now sufficient that, without intervening experience or exemplification from which to construct value relations, he could see the implications for his current taxonomic system of new categories for which he had received only 'positive' definitions.

### 5.2 Uncommonsense categories

Although Stephen now had the resources to learn from definitions, some of the things he began to ask for the meaning of could not be answered in taxonomic terms. This is because Stephen lacked relevant knowledge of social institutions or scientific principles. An example is the following text where he asks *What's the Council?*

4;6;3    (M warns Hal not to wreck the stool he is on)
         S:   Can you throw a stool away?
         M:   Yes.
         S:   How can you?
         H:   Easy (miming) shoo-oom!
         M:   You have to put it out for the Council Clean-up.
         S:   What's the Council?
         M:   The Council are (pause) the garbage men (pause) they – they – they pay the garbage men. Sometimes there's a special garbage day and you can put out big things like old mattresses or furniture.

In the end M answered the question *What's the Council?* by describing one thing that it does, since to answer what it *is* would require locating it in terms of a taxonomy of government levels, which in turn would require explanation of the relation between the citizen and authorities providing services, and so on.

Similarly in the following example, Stephen's question was answered in terms of what something does rather than what it is:

4;2;13    (M warns S not to play with wall socket)
      M:  It's a switch for electricity.
      S:  (?But what is it?)
      M:  It's for electricity.
      S:  But I don't know what it looks like.
      M:  No, well, you can't see it. The electricity makes things go . . .

It would seem that a commonsense understanding of uncommonsense things like local councils or electrical current amounts to some understanding of an activity or sequence in which it participates rather than a location in a taxonomic hierarchy.

### 5.3 Abstract categories

In Stephen's fourth year abstract categories had arisen in two main areas: the domain of temporal meaning and the exploration of symbols encountered as written graphics. There were further developments in both these areas after age 4, as will be exemplified below. First, though, a new domain of abstraction will be described – the construal of qualities in nominal form.

### 5.3.1 Objectifying qualities

During the fifth year there were developments in the way qualities were construed, especially when things were being compared. Finding a point of similarity between two things of different categories was a familiar strategy (cf. 2;9;12 *My sword . . . 's like an ice-cream*), and in the previous year Stephen had also begun to specify the respect in which different things were alike (cf. 3;10;4 *It's burgundy like Hal's toothbrush*). Such comparisons were now developed further by relating things of such different orders that the polysemy of the adjective was emphasized.

For example in the following conversation, early in the fifth year, Stephen related a number to a person in terms of a shared quality:

4;0;8    (M and S are discussing when people first learn to swim)
      M:  I should think quite a lot when they're six.
      S:  (Laughing) Or a hundred!
      M:  (laughs)
      S:  That's big, like Daddy.

In fact a number is big in a very different way from a person, but presumably using the familiar and material as a benchmark to make sense of the less familiar and semiotic allowed Stephen to come to grips with the meaning of *big* (high numerical value) in a mathematical sense.

A related new development in the fifth year was the attempt to specify the respect in which two things/actions were alike, using *same* as a Post-Deictic in the nominal group and construing a qualitative feature of an object or action as the Thing:

4;6;8    (M and S discussing S and his friend)
         S:    You said we're both the same size.
         M:    Same age.
         S:    Mm.

4;8;30   (F says the current (hired) car can't go as fast as the usual one)
         S:    I thought – I thought all cars could – all cars could go the
               same – all cars could go the same (pause) fast.
         M:    The same speed.
         S:    Yes, same speed.

In examples like this, the Thing role embodied the feature or dimension in terms of which individuals or classes were seen as alike. This form of realization has the advantage that the sameness of the qualitative dimension – considered as a dimension (size, speed) – can be focused on, rather than the sameness of the specific attribute (big, small, fast, slow) shared by the individual or class. Although one example of this kind of abstraction (where a quality term is the grammatical Thing) was familiar to Stephen at a much younger age, in the interrogative *What colour is X?*, it was not until he was 4 years and 6 months of age, after long experience of comparing things in terms of specific colour, shape and size properties, that he began to try to construe other qualities as nouns.

One impetus for developing nominalized quality terms was therefore an attempt to 'measure' qualities and there are hints of a change in orientation towards such a task. Assessment of a quality can be achieved interpersonally through various systems of 'grading', such as lexical clines (*hot, warm, cold*) or comparative forms (*hot, very hot, hotter*), as well as through prosodic means (Martin 1992b). However, coming into contact with uncommonsense ways of measuring – through scales of temperature, speed or length, with 'objective' units – seemed to create for Stephen the beginnings of a tension between the familiar commonsense interpersonal ways of measuring a quality and the more 'experientialized' forms.

Stephen not only developed the term *measure* at 4;7, but attempted to use some more precise, experiential indications of degrees of a quality. For example:

5;0      S:    There was a giant one – (indicates) from that wall to over there.

Here, the attitudinal description *giant* is immediately 'unpacked' into a more objective form of measurement, by comparing the size with an observable space. The following text makes a similar attempt with a different kind of quality:

4;7;2    (discussing their blue clothes)
      M:  I'm blue and grey and so is Daddy.
      S:  Daddy's isn't the same [i.e. colour grey].
      M:  No, mine's a bit darker.
      S:  About this much (indicating space between hands); about this much darker (adjusting the space).

Again Stephen appears to be groping for a way to quantify more precisely a qualitative difference. And in a final example, he can be seen trying out an objective scale:

4;6;25    (S watches a motorbike overtake them)
      S:  He's beating us by – (pause) he's beating us by twenty-three metres.

Here the experiential, uncommonsense measurement *he's beating us by twenty-three metres* is preferred to the longstanding interpersonal, common-sense, graded form *he's going faster than us*.

In the fifth year, then, Stephen began to construe qualities in an 'objectified' way under the pressure to create intersubjectivity about personal judgements. This led him to construe qualitative dimensions nominally, so that different manifestations could be identified as the same or different. And it led him to seek ways of expressing comparisons other than through interpersonal grading. This is exactly the task of uncommon-sense, scientific construals of knowledge – to express such meanings positively and through standardized units, rather than relationally and interpersonally through grading. Thus Stephen's language was moving in the direction that would be required for later school learning. Verbal contact with older children and adults led him in this direction, of course, but in addition it was his contact with the various visible symbols of uncommonsense knowledge that was an influence, since it was at this time that he was trying to interpret the symbols on rulers, measuring-tapes, speedometers, size labels on clothes, and so on.

## 5.3.2 Time as an object

In considering further the construal of abstract categories in the fifth year, certain developments in the interpretation of temporal meanings can be noted. Among the non-tangibles named in the previous year were duration/locations of time, using nominal groups such as *a long time, next week, month, year*. Having gained experience in the contextualized use of such expressions, Stephen now began to elucidate these terms explicitly, just as he had previously done for more concrete expressions. Some examples follow:

4;2;16   H:   And next year you'll be five and you'll go to school.
         S:   When's that going to be?
         H:   Next year.
         S:   When is that? Is that when I wake up again?
         H:   No, it's after next Christmas, a long, long, long time.
         S:   Oh (wails plaintively) I don't want it to be a long, long time;
              I want to be like you.

This attempt to locate *next year* depended on the possibility of a rankshifted clause of time being pressed into service within an identifying clause structure:

Example 3.5        *Is that [[when I wake up again]]?*
                   Value            Token

In the next example, the time expression is identified by distilling 'when you wake up again' into the noun *sleep*. Having been objectified as a nominal group Thing it can be enumerated and construed as a meronym of the thing that is *a week*:

4;5;7    S:   Mummy, is a week a long time?
         M:   Seven sleeps.
         S:   Oh, is a week seven sleeps?

Stephen's question can be analysed as follows:

Example 3.6

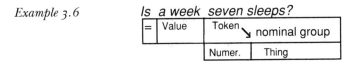

Thus the possibility of representing a duration of time metaphorically in nominal form allowed Stephen to explicate a duration through a Numerative^Thing structure. It also enabled him to characterize it as having size through the use of a modifying Epithet. This was seen in his formulation of the following enquiry:

4;10;12  S:   How come it's a bigger day when it's summer?
                     D Epithet Thing
         M:   I don't know, the sun just stays there longer.
         S:   Does it go down slower?

So although temporal expressions like *day, sleep, time* had been used circumstantially in the previous period (*today, after sleep, for a long time*), the additional metaphorical step of construing them in participant roles made it possible for Stephen to attempt definitions and to enumerate, grade and qualify the terms in the course of conversations which explored their meaning.

### 5.3.3 Language as an object

Beginning to treat language as an object had been a feature of Stephen's language in a small way during the fourth year, when he had identified two categories of discourse as identifiable things (*story* and *joke*) and had begun to talk about words and letters as things, and words and numbers as symbols. In the fifth year there were developments in both these areas.

The text-types identified in the previous year had been made visible to Stephen through their association with texts in a visible, material sense (i.e. books). Having become more conscious of text as object through the written medium, Stephen by 4;6 was also recognizing spoken language interacts as identifiable things:

4;6;9     S:   Mummy, it's a question that you don't eat porridge with
               your fingers. (pause) It's a question that you don't eat
               porridge with your fingers.
          M:   That's not a question it's an order.
          S:   What's an order?
          M:   It's something that you tell somebody and they have to do.
          S:   I meant an order.

Developing a name for a speech act can be considered as a kind of abstraction, since it involves seeing as segmentable and classifiable something which is experienced as a process.

Much more prominent, however, at this time, was an interest in decomposing and naming the smallest spoken and written units of language in an attempt to relate them to one another. This was undoubtedly because of increasing exposure to the written medium, although he could not yet read himself. In the following three texts, the naming of a letter is indicated by placing the letter in quotation marks. The first example illustrates Stephen's ability to name a sound by naming the letter which represents it:

4;3;15    (S tries to teach his young friend, C, to articulate the initial /s/
          in *skateboard*)
          S:   /s/ 's' 's' skateboard.
          C:   Gateboard.
          S:   's' (to H) He doesn't know what 's' is; it's a word but–
          H:   It's not a word.

By the end of the year, he had settled on *sound* as a nominalization to construe phonemes.

4;10;12   (M and S are discussing the letter 'g')
          S:   Like Ge-raham.
          M:   Yeah, Graham, and gorilla.
          S:   And (pause) Georgie (from label on peg at preschool?).
          M:   Georgie, yeah, that's spelt with a 'g' too, but it's like a /dʒ/.
          S:   They have two sounds: /dʒ/ and /g/.
          M:   Yeah. Boy, don't you know a lot!

However, this commonsense nominalization is ambiguous since the writing system cannot be discussed without distinguishing the two ranks of phoneme and syllable. A final example shows how Stephen had sorted out *letter* from *word*, but discovered that written letters do not construe the most salient spoken unit, the syllable:

4;4;10    (S talking about how he can write his name)
          M:   Oh, you'll have to learn how to do – (pause) Mum. Think
               you can do Mum as well?
          S:   How? (pause) Mum-my.
          M:   Or Mummy, yes. You could do that because you know how
               to do an 'm' . . .
          S:   Yeah, I know how to do a /i/.
          M:   The 'y' at the end.
          S:   Yeah, yeah, yeah, I know – I know – I know, Mum-my.
          M:   Mm, that's right.
          S:   Um, just two letters, just two. Do you just have two?
          M:   No, there's two <u>bits</u>: Mum-my, but there's more than two <u>letters</u>.
          S:   Oh, how does it go?
          M:   You have 'm' and then you have the letter 'u' . . .

Obviously the very first steps in becoming literate push a child into conceiving of language as an object and then into more sophisticated considerations of that object as actualized in different media. Using language to reflect on language introduces some technicality – *word, letter, sound* – but strains the child's resources because these acceptable everyday terms do not make enough discriminations among the elements involved.

Even though Stephen was only grappling with one aspect of written language – the alphabetic writing system of English – the task was pushing him into abstract construals. As a graph, a letter is a material object to be discriminated and decomposed as Stephen had been doing in the previous year. But as a representation of a phoneme, a letter construes something much less tangible – not just a sound qua sound, like a bark or a crash, but a sound as a form of semiotic realization.

### 5.4 Summary: 4;0 to 5;0 years

In Stephen's fifth year there was no dramatic change in the nature of identification and classification, such as was apparent between 3 and 4 years of age. Rather, what can be seen is how the changes described earlier continued to be built on as Stephen came into closer contact with uncommonsense knowledge.

The use of definitions as a means of learning became more entrenched, involving rankshifted clauses both within the nominal group and acting as Value in an identifying clause. Furthermore, experience with this form of learning, and with explicit discussion of categorization generally, provided Stephen with a new ability to make inferences from definitions and to reflect overtly on the implications for his current meaning system of information received in a current conversation.

Finally, the tentative moves towards abstraction noted in the previous year continued. The long-standing strategy of finding likeness between different things led to the development of a metalanguage for qualities, with nominal forms such as *age, size, speed*. Also, tentative steps were taken to measure rather than grade qualities. At the same time temporal meanings were construed more metaphorically as countable, measurable things, and a nominal metalanguage was developing for referring to written and spoken units of language.

## 6  Overview: classification and identification 2;6 to 5;0 years

In this opening section of the case study the focus has been on Stephen's construal of the phenomena of experience and their conceptual or semantic organization into taxonomies. To that end, Stephen's naming and categorizing behaviour has been tracked over the period from 2;6 to 5 years. This focus means that as well as the lexical sets themselves, particular experiential systems and their deployment in text have been under attention. These are the relational processes (which serve to identify, classify, describe and decompose phenomena) and options within the nominal group, the structure which serves to provide a linguistic representation of a thing. In addition, it was found that in the creation of discourse to achieve classification and identification, options within the textual system of REFERENCE were deployed in new ways and there were also developments in the logical linking of clause-complexes.

### 6.1  Developments in the grammar

Perhaps the first point to be made then is that a continuing intellectual exploration of the phenomena of experience led to new linguistic forms. In other words, learning through language entails learning language itself. Although at the beginning of the study Stephen had a taxonomically organized vocabulary, used a variety of relational process options, created clause complexes and had a full nominal group structure, there were new developments with respect to all these areas over the period studied. Table 3.5 lists some of the main linguistic developments discussed in this chapter as realized at clause, clause-complex and group rank. All the developments listed resulted from the cognitive pressure to understand the world and to organize it as meaning.

**Table 3.5** Selected developments in linguistic realizations, 2;6 to 5 years

**Relational processes**
**2;6 to 3 years**
classifying, identifying

| | | | | |
|---|---|---|---|---|
| attributive | *be* | | Carrier:exophoric reference item | *it's a house* |
| identifying:symbolize:name | *call* | earlier | Token: exophoric reference item | *he's called Smokey* |
| | | | Value: nom. gp with proper noun | *the bear* |
| | | later | Token: exophoric reference item | *it's called an igloo* |
| | | | Value: nom. gp with common noun | |

comparing

| | | | |
|---|---|---|---|
| attributive:circumstantial | *be, look* | Carrier: exophoric reference item | *it's like an ice-cream; that looks like a sword* |

**Relational processes**
**3 to 4 years**
classifying

| | | | |
|---|---|---|---|
| attributive | *be* | Carrier: non-phoric nom. group | *are seals dolphins?* |
| identifying: exemplify | | Token, Value: non-phoric nom. gps | *a dog's an animal* |
| identifying: symbolize: | *mean* | Token: noun, verb or adjective | *drown means [[go* |
| decode | | Value: word or rankshifted clause | *down to the bottom and be dead]]* |

comparing quality

| | | | |
|---|---|---|---|
| attributive | *be* | Attribute linked to Comparison circumstance | *that's burgundy like Hal's toothbrush* |

**Clause complex (linkage to relational process)**
**3 to 4 years**

| | |
|---|---|
| universal 'when' clause linked to identifying clause | *when we cut them they're called fingernails* |
| internal 'because' clause linked to attributive clause | *he's a boy 'cause he's got a penis* |
| | *It's got two wings there; that means it's a biplane* |

**Nominal group structure**
**2;6 to 3 years**
classifying, describing

| | | |
|---|---|---|
| all of D, PD, E, N, C, T, Q functions | Thing: 'concrete' noun | *two dirty shirts* |
| | | *the other car transporter* |
| when name unknown | Thing: gen. word^Qualifier:[[embedded clause]]; Deictic: specific, realizing exophoric reference | *the thing [[go on there]]* |

**3 to 4 years**
classifying, describing

| | | |
|---|---|---|
| | Thing construing symbol | *joke, a number, 'm'* |
| | Thing (unrestricted) ^ Qualifier | *biscuits [[that not crunchy]]* |
| | Deictic: variety of non-specifics | *all, not all, some* |
| | Deictic realizing text reference | *. . . that means.* |

**4 to 5 years**
classifying,
comparing quality

| | | |
|---|---|---|
| | Thing construing unit of time | *a week, seven sleeps* |
| | PD: *the same*^Thing construing quality | *the same size* |

## 6.2 *Developments with respect to mode*

All the developments listed above have already been illustrated with text fragments from occasions when Stephen was constructing the everyday knowledge that is built into non-specialist lexical taxonomies. In this section it will be suggested that all these changes in the linguistic potential and in the way it was used during the period studied can be characterized generally in terms of the register variable of mode. Three interrelated aspects of mode development will be discussed: context-dependency, metalinguistic development, and abstraction and grammatical metaphor.

### 6.2.1 Decreasing 'context-dependency'

Mode is discussed in the following terms by Halliday (1978a: 189) in his discussion of the three components of the context of situation:

> If we are focusing on language, [the] last category of 'mode' refers to what part the language is playing in the situation under consideration.

Martin (1992a: 513) refers to mode in a similar way as 'the role language is playing in realising social action'. And when mode concerns the status of language with respect to the *experiential* dimension, he argues that 'mode mediates the semiotic space between action and reflection'. This, in general terms, is a matter of context-dependency – 'the extent to which a text constructs or accompanies its field'. Thus an interpretation of Stephen's linguistic development in terms of mode implies a change over time in the role assigned to language in the contexts which gave rise to the texts being examined.

Part of Martin's network outlining basic options within the action–reflection 'semiotic space' is reproduced as Figure 3.7.

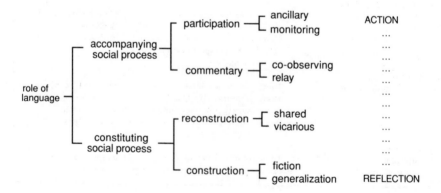

**Figure 3.7** Mode: degrees of abstraction (from Martin 1992a: 522)

This network is clearly designed to classify a much broader range of texts than the set being considered here, but the basic opposition between [accompanying] and [constituting] is highly relevant in the interpretation of Stephen's attempts to classify and identify phenomena. The argument being put forward here is that in the process of construing material experience through linguistic identification and categorization, Stephen initially created texts which were highly context-dependent, as phenomena were categorized in the process of using language to monitor and co-observe specific things. In the fourth year, however, the texts created were more context-constitutive, as language was distanced from the specificity of experience. In terms of the network above, the major change in the use of language for classification after Stephen turned three was a move towards [construction] and taking up the [generalization] option.

Before elaborating on this, it needs to be acknowledged that the ability to generalize is in some sense exhibited long before this – even by the protolinguistic child. In order to create a protolinguistic sign, a child has to construe a particular situation as being a functional context of the same kind as some earlier occasion when a protolinguistic sign was successfully used. So even a protolanguage system involves some generalization of the specificity of experience. And even more clearly, with the move into the mother tongue, the development of common noun names involves generalizing. A name is a category and naming involves the interpretation of individual, specific, particular phenomena as belonging to classes of things, events, qualities, and so on.

Thus even before the development of any clause structure for naming, this achievement in generalization is taking place by means of single-word utterances, when a particular thing may be pointed at and given a category name. Hasan (1985: 26) makes the point that working out the categories initially is problematic for the learner because the meaning of any category depends on its relation to other categories, but those value relations can only be established as understanding is reached concerning the domain of signification constructed by related categories. She concludes:

> If the sign system is as pervasively arbitrary as the system of language is, then the only way the signification of signs can begin to be learnt . . . is through the regularity of the correspondence between the sign and what the sign stands as the sign of. From this point of view, those contexts are more important in which such correspondence is immediately observable.

In other words, the initial language learning experience must take place in contexts where, in terms of mode, the language used is least distant from the phenomena being engaged with or observed. This does not mean that very young children cannot talk about the past or the future, but it does mean that initial learning of lexical categories would be unlikely to take place if the child only experienced 'displaced' talk where the job of constructing the context in which the names had relevance also depended entirely on language.

A consideration of the typical classifying utterances of the first period of the case study, such as *that's two red ones*, or *it's a house*, shows that Stephen was using such language in non-displaced contexts in which he was attending to specific concrete things (or pictures of these). Rather than being pointed at physically, as in single-word speech; the thing was constructed linguistically by means of pronominal or elliptical nominal groups with a presuming reference item as Head, such as *that* or *it*. In this way the specific entity under consideration could be recovered from the shared context via exophoric reference if the object was visually perceptible, or via homophoric reference where shared familiarity with the relevant context allowed for this.[2]

During his third year, then, Stephen had considerable occasion to enquire about and practise classification with respect to specific things in this way. These specific phenomena could be readily brought into intersubjective focus either through being jointly observed or because the shared life of the speakers enabled them to be recalled or invoked with a minimum of linguistic work. On such occasions a classifying utterance certainly served to generalize experience because it treated a particular material phenomenon as being an exemplum of a category, but nonetheless (in its deployment of reference) the language was context-dependent and the talk was concerned with specific experiences.

During his fourth year, however, many categorizing utterances had moved to a new dimension of generalization in that they served not to classify specific instances of phenomena, but to classify other lexically realized categories. This occurred with queries like *are seals dolphins?* or observations like *a bus isn't a truck*. In such utterances there is no concrete, specific, observable phenomenon that is being categorized; rather one category is being interpreted in terms of another. In other words, value relations are being explored directly rather than through signification.

Value and signification as two aspects of meaning are compared by Hasan (1985: 23) as follows:

> Value is system-internal, being defined by the relation of one sign to another in the system . . . Signification, on the other hand, is not a system-internal relation; it is concerned with the relation between the sign and what the sign is a sign for.

Thus when the child moves from building value by engaging in signification to engaging directly with value relations, there is a shift in mode. The categorizing utterance itself becomes interpretable without reference to any particular context of situation. In terms of mode, then, the language generalizes across contexts in a way in which the earlier naming talk did not.

This distancing of classification from specific 'here-and-now' or 'there-and-then' contexts also prompted an expansion in the potential for linking clauses through hypotaxis. Whereas previously *when* had realized only a temporal meaning of succession (*when Daddy comes, we can buy some chips*) (see Chapter 4), it now began to be used in classifying utterances with a sense of 'universal' time, as in *when we cut them they're called fingernails*. This too is a development in mode terms, since the context for the particular name choice is being constructed linguistically rather than left implicit, and the context is being constructed in terms of a generalization, *when* as 'whenever' rather than as some particular moment.

Experience in creating intersubjectivity through linguistic explicitness also carried over into the linguistic construction of very specific things, as in utterances like *biscuits [[that not crunchy]]* or *the dog [[that we stroked yesterday]]* where a clause was rankshifted into the nominal group structure as a Qualifier. When this happened it was often to allow previous experience with an object to become an identifying characteristic. In later years embedding will be used in monologic text to summarize previous text as a point of departure for providing new information (Halliday and Martin 1993). In early childhood it may develop partly to summarize previous experience so that it can provide an identifying descriptor as the child uses language to build relevant experience into the current context as a means of achieving an intersubjective focus.

## 6.2.2 Metalinguistic development: learning about language by learning through language

A key aspect to the new distancing in mode is that it involves a move by the child towards overt exploration of the systemic meaning potential. The meaning potential is the language system, the system of value relations, which the child is continuously constructing and reconstructing from experience with text – text being the manifestation of the (shared) system on a particular occasion of use. The shift that Stephen made from categorizing specific instances to categorizing the categories themselves can be characterized as a shift in attention from the instantiation of the language system to the relations holding between the terms in the system itself. In other words, when creating text in the fourth year, Stephen was not simply building the system but was exploring it. In this sense he was not simply learning language but was simultaneously learning *about* language.

It is important to emphasize here that there is no suggestion being made that a child *first* 'labels' things (by signifying) and *then* works out taxonomic relations (value). On the contrary, any child construes value relations in the process of trying out signification, and attempts to name on the basis of the value relations currently holding in his system. That is, learning names by assigning instances of thing-experience to a category simultaneously requires the learner to relate categories to one another and indeed to construe unnamed categories in the process.

Thus, right from the beginning of this study Stephen was undoubtedly building and using a lexical system in which the options were systematically linked through semantic relations of hyponymy, co-hyponymy, meronymy, synonymy and antonymy. It could not be otherwise if he on one occasion named 'the same' thing as a *drink* and on another as an *orange juice*; if he could respond to a question like *what colour is it?* with lexical items only from the set of colour terms; if he expected to find pockets on items of outer clothing but not on underwear and not on pieces of furniture. Such linguistic behaviour demonstrates the semantically organized nature of his lexical system. Stephen at age two-and-a–half was therefore carrying out the very task of making sense of specific phenomena by naming them and in the process constructing a systemic potential.

However, once a systemic potential was in place, new possibilities arose. To quote Hasan (1985:45):

> the very inter-relatedness of the terms within the linguistic system acts as an advantage, once an effective entry into the system has been made . . . It is this systematicity of language which also permits its use as a meta-language, permitting paraphrase, explication etc. And these too are ways of learning meaning, even though these means of learning how to mean cannot be used with the infant.

What Stephen was able to do, then, in his fourth year, was to use language as its own metalanguage and to set up those interrelations in order to reflect on them. Thus a key characteristic of language development and language use described in this chapter relates to the self-reflexive character of the linguistic system, its ability to make itself an object of exploration using the tools which evolved to make sense of the non-linguistic world. On such occasions the child is still learning from text, learning by using the linguistic potential, but the goal of the text thus created is to explore the potential directly rather than with reference to any particular, identifiable instances of the phenomena being explored. The texts created, therefore, realize non-specific deixis and generic reference within the nominal groups acting as participants of the relational clause.[3] And by the fifth year, a single dialogue could produce a renovation of the taxonomy through inferences drawn from a definition provided by the addressee.

Of course specific 'here-and-now' instances of phenomena were still classified, but a strategy for reflecting on the system in such a case was also developed. This was the use of an internal causal relation to articulate the defining characteristics for the category in question, as in *Our cat is an animal because it's got fur.* And while the defining characteristics were always observable parts, qualities or behaviours at this stage, the possibility clearly existed now for a category to be explained in terms of something not readily observable, as will be the case with many concepts of educational knowledge.

Direct enquiries about language as system were facilitated by the use, in the same period, of an identifying process which specifically signals that the meaning potential of language is being explored, namely *mean*. In the earlier period, Stephen had been limited to setting up an identifying relation between a material object and a lexical category (or, more accurately, a material object or a non-linguistic symbolization of it in the form of a picture) using *call*, as in *That's called an igloo*. Once language can be explicated in language using *mean*, then what receives this linguistic identification need not be a linguistic construal of a tangible entity, action or quality. The way is open for abstractions like 'a number' or 'a week' to be given linguistic translation.

### 6.2.3 Abstraction and grammatical metaphor

So far, developments in mode have been discussed in terms of a freeing of the texts from anchorage in a localized context and in terms of the use of language as its own metalanguage. An additional aspect to these developments was the beginning use of abstract and grammatically metaphorical language. Developments in this area are summarized in Figure 3.8. Sections of this figure labelled (a) to (l) will be referred to in the following discussion.

Although the texts cited in the language development literature provide ample evidence that the language of very young children lacks abstract concepts and is congruent in terms of the relationship between meaning and grammatical word class, there has been no systematic study of the development of these more adult features of language. This case study would suggest that most of the early moves away from a completely congruent linguistic representation develop as an aspect of the moves in mode which occur as the child uses language to identify and classify.

Figure 3.8 shows that up till age 3, there was little evidence of any non-congruence, and two of the three minor areas in which it occurred were not concerned with identification and classification of things. These were the nominal realization of a participant role to construe an action, found in routine Process^Range structures (a), and the rankshifted clausal realization of a (Phenomenon) participant within a perception clause to construe an entire event observed (b). Apart from these, the only lack of congruence in the language was in the violation of the rank-based constituency organization which occurred when a clause was rankshifted into the Qualifier slot within the nominal group (c). When this happened, it was in an attempt to describe something for which no lexical item was known. In such a case, the attempt to achieve a shared meaning with the addressee, when no shared word was available, pressured the language into construing event configurations as descriptors.

In the fourth year, however, the moves towards linguistically constitutive texts and towards exploring value relations directly led to a number of small developments away from completely congruent speech. One effect of language playing a greater role in the achievement of identification of specific things was the extension of rankshifted Qualifiers to nominal groups with lexical Heads (d). Sometimes this was again to compensate for lack of vocabulary, for example the lack of a single-word Epithet for *that not crunchy*

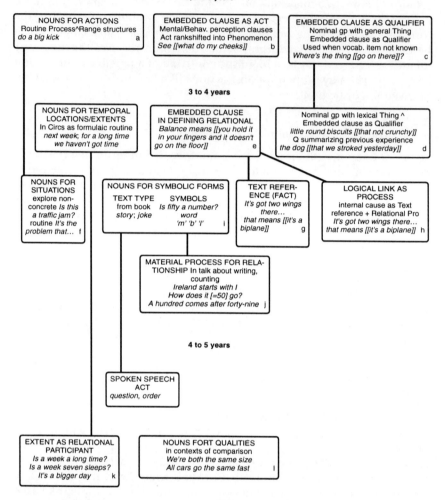

**Figure 3.8** Developments in abstraction and ideational grammatical metaphor, 2;6 to 5 years

in describing biscuits. At other times it was to bring previous experience to bear as a means of identifying the thing, as with *the dog that we stroked yesterday.*

The move into using language as its own metalanguage created several points where abstraction and metaphor resulted. For example, the pressure to relate language item to language item in an identifying relation required the rankshifting of a clause (or even clause-complex) so that it could act as one role within a defining clause (e). This might be necessary where a synonymy relation could not be constructed with a single lexical item in each of the Token and Value roles, as for *drown is [[go down to the bottom and be dead]].* The development of everyday metalanguage also allowed the exploration of everyday metaphors like *traffic jam*, used by other people (f).

Another example where the exploration of the meaning system resulted in grammatical metaphor was in the construal of the internal causal relation (to make explicit the criteria for a classification) as discussed earlier. In an alternative form of representing this conjunctive relation, anaphoric text reference evolved, where a 'fact' rather than a 'thing' was construed into a participant role realized by *that*, as in *it's got two wings there; that means it's a biplane* (g). This form also entailed the use of a verb, *mean*, to construe the logical relation of causality (h).

Finally it can be noted that the explicit construal in language of both hyponymy and synonymy relations also enabled the first explorations of categories represented by nouns but with no tangible referent, such as numbers (as symbols rather than graphs) and types of text (as symbolic rather than material phenomena) (i). Moreover, once written symbols were construed as things, they were decomposed into parts or 'located' with respect to other symbols by using 'material' verbs to construe relationships rather than actions (j). This again can be counted as a form of grammatical metaphor which has developed as part of the mode shift already described. Further developments in the fifth year included the construal of extents in time as 'things' that could be defined, enumerated and described and qualities as 'things' that could be compared (k, l). Thus, Stephen had taken a number of very small but significant steps into ideational grammatical metaphor between two-and-a-half and five years.

To sum up, the various changes in Stephen's linguistic system and its use in relation to classification and identification have here been interpreted in terms of a movement between two poles, as shown in Table 3.6.

**Table 3.6** Developments in mode in the identification and classification of phenomena

| Language up to age 3 | New aspects of language after age 3 |
| --- | --- |
| attend to material instance | + attend to semiotic category |
| create text relevant to specific context | + create text relevant across contexts |
| build system from text | + explore system with text |
| represent concrete phenomena | + begin representing abstract/ symbolic phenomena |

It is not, of course, that the child ceases to be concerned with the foci displayed in the left-hand column, but rather that those of the right-hand column are new possibilities which arise, possibilities which will be crucial to later school learning.

## Notes

1 Within the formalism of systemic theory it would be unproblematic to offer an alternative representation of such taxonomic relations in terms of semantic features which cross-classify various categories (such as animacy, gender, age).

2 It is not the case that anaphoric reference had not yet developed, but that overtly categorizing utterances at first only involved anaphoric reference where the dialogue partner had already introduced the entity linguistically, as in: M: *Want some rice?* S: *It's hot?*

3 The use of non-specific Deictics within the nominal group was not itself new – requests such as *I want a biscuit*, for example, were common early on, but the deployment of non-phoric groups in both roles of an attributive clause was new.

# 4    The construal of events

To consider knowledge only in terms of the identification and classification of things, qualities or processes would be to suggest a somewhat static picture of construed reality. To balance this, it is important also to focus on experience as a world of happenings in the interpretation of which taxonomies of things and processes are drawn upon in the formation of structures which interpret reality more dynamically. This chapter will therefore concern itself with Stephen's linguistic interpretation of events. In terms of Martin's (1992a) model of field as a semiotic system, this means considering clause-level TRANSITIVITY realizations of events and also the relations which hold between activities to constitute an 'activity sequence'.

## 1  Linguistic and developmental background

The system of TRANSITIVITY is built up and deployed to represent reality in terms of processes in which entities participate in different roles and different settings. Such a representation produces a structure where a process element is configured with one or more participant roles and, in some cases, one or more circumstance roles, as in the following example:

| *My daughter* | *may have thrown* | *the toys* | *over the fence* |
|---|---|---|---|
| participant role | process | participant role | circumstance role |
| Actor | Material | Goal | Location |

In this example, the activity is represented as a Material process in a configuration with an Actor ('doer') participant and a Goal ('done to' ) participant, together with a circumstance which construes the spatial Location of the process. The participant roles are realized by nominal groups, the process by a verbal group and the circumstance by a prepositional phrase.

However, although it is the deployment of the experiential structure which is under focus in this chapter, it needs to be remembered that any clause uttered as text will also construe an interpersonal structure. Thus the example given above also embodies interpersonal choices of [finite] from the system of FINITENESS, [declarative] from the system of MOOD and [low / probability] from the system of MODALITY, [positive] from the system of POLARITY and [tone 1] from the phonologically realized system of KEY.

While a single event can be configured linguistically as a structure of process and participant (with optional circumstances), successive events may be linked to form a larger structure – that of the 'activity sequence', realized by clause complexes and larger text structures. Martin (1992a: 537) cites Barthes' work on narrative theory as providing a relevant notion of activity sequence:

> A sequence is a logical succession of nuclei bound together by a relation of solidarity (in the Hjelmslevian sense of double implication: two terms presuppose one another): the sequence opens when one of its terms has no solidary antecedent and closes when another of its terms has no consequent. To take a deliberately trivial example, the different functions order a drink, obtain it, drink it, pay for it, constitute an obviously closed sequence, it being impossible to put anything before the order or after the payment without moving out of the homogeneous group 'Having a drink'. (Barthes 1977: 101)

As this passage points out, any particular nameable activity sequence like 'having a drink' has various component parts. In addition, these components may in turn be broken down into their own parts (e.g. 'pay for it' comprising 'take out wallet, hand over money, receive change'). Alternatively the whole ('Having a drink') may function as a single unit in a larger sequence (e.g. 'Going home from work').

Where developmental studies are concerned, investigation of children's understanding of activity sequences has been taken up most prominently by Katherine Nelson and her colleagues (e.g. Nelson 1978; Nelson and Gruendel 1979; Nelson and Seidman 1984; French and Nelson 1985) using the notion of 'scripts' from artificial intelligence (Schank and Abelson 1977). Nelson's research shows that middle-class pre-school children can verbalize and/or act out familiar activity sequences when asked a question like *What happens when you have lunch at McDonald's?* and prompted with further questions to add details. The children are seen as calling upon knowledge in the form of scripts which are 'models of familiar experiences that are called into play in the appropriate verbal or situational contexts' (Nelson 1978: 256). These familiar experiences are described in terms of 'event sequences', the component parts of which 'theoretically . . . can be of any size; that is, a child might refer to an element as small as taking a bite of a hamburger or as large as eating lunch' (Nelson 1978: 261).

Their compositional nature is thus one aspect of activity sequences, whether these are theorized in semiotic or cognitive terms. The other factor of agreed importance is the relation of activities to one another in a sequence. A sequence is recognized where an expectation has been construed that the component events will follow one another. If the predictable sequence is disrupted, then the countering of expectation is likely to be realized linguistically, perhaps in the form of a 'concessive' conjunction. Thus in the following text,

> Becker served for the match in the third set
> **but** double-faulted three times
> to level the set

the conjunction *but* 'marks the fact that Becker's double-faulting was unexpected in the field' (Martin 1992a: 323).

Although temporal conjunctions are obviously the fundamental means of explicitly sequencing verbal representations of actions, a temporal sequence is also inherent in the use of causal links. Where two TRANSITIVITY structures are linked by means of a causal rather than a temporal conjunction, Martin (1992a: 193) suggests that 'the connections between events are "modulated" in such a way that one event is seen as ... *determining* the other rather than simply preceding it'.

> [T]he connection between events is modulated through 'obligation': *we won* **because** *we trained hard* means that the Cause determined the Effect. (Martin 1992a: 193)

This interpretation links causal relations *between* clauses with the interpersonal systems of MODALITY, which intrudes a speaker assessment into an individual clause, as summarized in Table 4.1 for cause-consequence and cause-condition.

**Table 4.1** Modality and causal conjunction (after Martin 1992a)

|  | MODULATION | MODALIZATION |
|---|---|---|
| cause:consequence (*so, because*) | obligation | — |
| cause:condition (*then, if*) | obligation | probability |

In this view, causal linkers, as well as construing ideational logico-semantic relations, also constitute an interpersonal intrusion into the field in a parallel way to the clause-level systems.

It should be noted here that conjunctive relations may be realized linguistically in a number of ways: through paratactic and hypotactic linking of clauses into clause complexes, through cohesive linking of different clause complexes, and (at least in the case of temporals and causals) within the clause as a circumstantial role. The different possibilities are set out in Table 4.2 for temporal and causal relations.

**Table 4.2** Examples of realizations of temporal and causal relations

| Linkage | Time | Cause |
|---|---|---|
| Parataxis | He studied **and then** rested. | He worked hard **and so** he passed. |
| Hypotaxis | He rested **after** he studied. | He passed **because** he worked hard. |
| Cohesion | He studied. **Then** he rested. | He worked hard. **Therefore** he passed. |
| Circumstance | He rested **after his study.** | He passed **because of his hard work** |

In addition, conjunctive relations may be cross-classified as 'external' or 'internal' in type (Halliday and Hasan 1976; cf. Dijk's (1977) semantic/pragmatic connectives). The examples given so far have all been external in type since it is these that construe links between activities within a sequence. An internal link, on the other hand, construes a relation between moves in the text rather than between the events represented in the text. It is a text-internal way of organizing the discourse as can be readily seen in a sequence like *First he takes no exercise, secondly he eats far too much and thirdly he chain-smokes,* where the three activities listed do not constitute a temporal sequence in terms of the field, but only in terms of their organization in the text.

The move from single words to experiential structures has been described in some detail from a systemic perspective in Painter 1984 and 1989, where it was argued that ergative and transitive interpretations of experience initially developed in different contexts of use. In the description of Stephen's language this will not be an issue and it will be assumed that Stephen had had up to a year's experience of interpreting events through the system of TRANSITIVITY before the period with which this case study is concerned.

This chapter will consider some of the developments which took place in Stephen's use of language to construe activities and activity sequences between 2;6 and 4 years. That is, an account will first be given of characteristics of Stephen's deployment of language up to age 3 and this will be compared with characteristics of his speech in the fourth year taken as a whole. The language of the fifth year will not be described here as the most relevant issues will be taken up in the following two chapters concerned with the construal of semiosis and the construal of cause–effect relations.

Issues to be explored in this chapter include the following:

- the situations in which activities were regularly construed, decomposed and sequenced linguistically;
- the evidence for Stephen's holding of expectations concerning the relation between process and participant, activity and activity;
- the circumstances in which causal as well as temporal links between activities were construed;
- the evidence for a shift in mode in the construal of events;
- verbalization of explicit generalizations about 'what happens' and 'who does what to whom'.

## 2 Stephen's language 2;6 to 3;0 years

In terms of his ability to represent an event experientially by the second half of the third year, Stephen had developed a full range of material process structures, as shown in Table 4.3.

**Table 4.3** Stephen's range of material process structures by 2;10

| Transitivity roles | Examples |
| --- | --- |
| Actor^Process | *Katy's sleeping* |
| Actor^Process^Range | *I didn't do a big kick* |
| Actor^Process^Goal | *She going to bite it* |
| Actor^Process^Recipient^Goal | *She gave us some stuff* |

His speech at 2;10 also provided examples of varied circumstantial roles (see Halliday 1994: 149*ff*) with the exception of Role, Matter, Extent and Contingency types. However, circumstances of Cause:reason were limited to the question word *Why?*, while Location in time was restricted to a few routine phrases (e.g. *today, yesterday, in a minute*).

The description of Stephen's use of language up till the age of 3 will consider the kinds of situations in which activities gained linguistic realization and will explore the extent to which event configurations and activity sequences were construed as predictable by Stephen – that is, the extent to which he can be seen to expect that certain kinds of participants participate in certain kinds of processes or that one event will follow another in a predictable sequence. Evidence for this will be sought in his use of language to predict, to construe causal links between activities and to express counter-expectation. Finally, a small set of texts will be discussed which illustrate a new move towards a more overt exploration of the generalizability of TRANSITIVITY relations and which flag the direction of developments in the fourth year. The use of language in the fourth year will then be described and a comparison made between the two data sets.

### 2.1 Construing individual sequences of events

Young children can learn about many activities relevant to their daily existence simply from observing those around them and participating in routines of social life. However, in families like Stephen's, language is used throughout the early years of childhood to comment on what the interlocutors are doing, or have done, to facilitate the accomplishment by the child of everyday tasks and to negotiate what will and will not be done by family members. In this way TRANSITIVITY structures are constantly used in 'here-and-now' contexts where the meaning is most readily accessed and temporal links emerge in the verbalization of ongoing activities.

### 2.1.1 Ongoing commentary

One of the first ways to construe experience as language is through commentary on what is enacted, observed and recalled. For example, ongoing commentary on the child's own actions and those of others takes place from the beginning of the move out of protolanguage and was still a facet of Stephen's speech in the third year:

2;7;7      (drawing a picture)
           S:   Did draw a balloon. (pause) I'm colouring in the balloon.

2;7;8      (observing seagull landing among pigeons eating scraps)
           S:   He's – he's chasing them; oh, he's taken their chips.

To do this requires no prior holistic understanding of the activity as a sequence of component parts, since each individual action can be represented as it occurs, but presumably the verbalization helps the child to build up expectations of sequences.

### 2.1.2 Accomplishing an activity

Another situation type in which activities may be construed linguistically very early in a child's life is when adult and child accomplish a task together. In these data, shared tasks were always likely to be accompanied by a shared verbalization of the component parts of the activity and their sequencing. For example:

2;7;29     (M and S playing with nesting barrels)
           M:   Oh, what about the green one? That comes first.
           S:   Mm.
           M:   Get that one first.
           S:   That goes like that, then it goes like – there? then you put it
                on here; then you put it on here; you put it on here now.
           M:   Yes, that's right. And then put the red one on top.
           S:   Then you put it in here; we put it in here, then (fall–rise
                tone) . . .

As can be seen, the temporal sequencing here was linguistically foregrounded to aid the structuring of the task, resulting in the use of cohesive and paratactic links by both parties (*then, first, now*). However, where language was in an ancillary mode like this with both speakers engaged in the non-linguistic action, the representation of the activities themselves was likely to be inexplicit.

It was when adults gave instructions to Stephen to enable him to complete an activity by himself that the component parts of an activity sequence were made more explicit, even though the mode was still language accompanying action:

2;7;1    (S struggling to open door to get out of room)
        M:  Turn the handle first.
        (S turns handle)
        M:  That's it; mind your toes . . .

2;8;21   (H is telling M about his sports results, when S enters)
        S:  I did a wee.
        M:  Press the button.
        S:  What?
        M:  Press the button.
        H:  Our lowest score is one.
        S:  What press the button?
        M:  Press the toilet button.
        H:  Our lowest score was nil.
        S:  (?Where . . . ?    )
        M:  In the toilet; where do you think the toilet button is!
        S:  (softly) In the toilet.

2;10     M:  Do you want to wash your handies here? . . . Then put your
             sleeves up, plug in (?    ) That's a boy.
        S:  I did.
        M:  Good boy.
        (S washes hands, then lifts them out of water)
        S:  (?    ) dry on the towel.

In all these texts the adult was deploying language as an instrument for mediating the child's solo accomplishment of physical actions, teaching the child both the linguistic realization of an activity sequence and, incidentally, the value of language as a tool for learning physical tasks.

The latter can be seen in the following example which illustrates that, at this point, language could not simply substitute for observational experience when the task was unfamiliar:

2;7;13   (S cannot reach door handle of fridge. For the first time he
            fetches something to stand on)
        M:  Put it [=stool] at the side; don't put it in front of the fridge.
        (S places stool in front of fridge)
        M:  How can the door open, if it's there? The stool's in the way.
        (S looks at M, gets on stool, reaches handle and finds stool is
        blocking the door)
        S:  Oh, stool's in the way.
        (moves it to one side and opens door)

Although Stephen did not make use of the verbal instructions to modify his original plan, he did adopt his mother's formulation of the problem at the end and on later occasions he was observed following instructions to place the stool to one side.

Where a particular activity sequence was more familiar, Stephen was evidently able to make use of his language-mediated experiences to verbalize it for himself. In the following text, he seems to be verbalizing the details of the activity as a means of thinking through in advance what is involved in a small domestic task:

2;9;23    (S asks M for drink. She tells him to look in kitchen, thinking there might still be one out from lunch)
  S:  I will ask Hal. (goes over to H) Can you come in kitchen with me?
  H:  What for?
  S:  To bring the orange juice, put it in a cup and drink it. All right?
  H:  Okay.

Thus, although language could not entirely replace 'hands-on' experience, Stephen was in a continuous process of learning the value of representing activity in language as a tool for learning.

All the above examples were also very typical of Stephen's conversations at this time in that the components of the activity specified in the talk were relatively small-scale. Nelson (1978: 257) suggests that it is while in the process of learning such 'scripts' that a young child would be most readily able to verbalize all its parts explicitly. Later on, when it can be taken for granted that 'opening the door' requires turning the handle and moving aside as the door is pulled towards you, and that pulling sleeves up, putting the plug in, running water, drying afterwards are all part of 'washing hands', that 'getting a drink' involves putting it into a cup, and so on, it may be less easy for these details to be made linguistically explicit. Whether or not this proves to be so, it is certainly the case that in households where language is favoured as a means of aiding the learning of activities, these 'micro'-level activities are likely to be laid out for and by the child.

### 2.1.3 Negotiating a 'place' for an activity

As well as helping Stephen to accomplish an activity, parental directives also served to verbalize what could or could not count as a culturally appropriate component of an activity:

2;7;7    M:  You can't do that when you've got food in your mouth.

2;7;7    M:  You're not writing while you're having tea.

2;8;21    S:  Mummy can I have that?
  M:  Not till you've finished your muffin.
  S:  Not till finished y- my muffin.

As can be seen from these examples taken from different occasions of Stephen 'having tea', this involved modelling temporal links of various kinds as various of Stephen's actions were construed as prohibited or to be postponed for the duration of the eating activity. In this way, as well as through observation and commentary, Stephen learned what kind of action was expected to be part of eating a meal.

Where two actions have no expectancy or solidary relation construed between them, it may be necessary to construe them into a sequence linguistically in order to negotiate a place in the course of events for a desired activity. From Halliday's (1984b) data, it would appear that this was the function for which temporal conjunctives first emerged for his son, examples of whose early hypotactic and paratactic clause-complexes are given below:

1;8;28    N:   When New-World finish, song about bús.
          [high rising tone signals a clause making a demand of the addressee]

1;10;1    N:   First Daddy finish talking, then go in park.

Although it is not known whether taxis relations first emerged in this way for Stephen, the use of temporal links to relate TRANSITIVITY structures construing distinct activities was frequent in the speech of both child and adult:

2;10;7    S:   Later, when Daddy comes, we can buy some chips.

2;7;6     (M is working in the kitchen; S wants her to play with his wooden blocks)
          M:   Just let me put these things away and then I'll come and do blocks.

Thus, the brief text illustrations given so far of the verbal representation of individual events and sequences show that they were represented in the form of commentaries and also in the negotiation of speaker/hearer action. Both provided means of learning predictable sequences. In the negotiation of action, particularly, the linguistic representation of temporal sequencing was prominent. The achievement of physical tasks resulted in the linguistic specification of relatively small components of an activity sequence with hypotactic (*when*), paratactic (*then*) and cohesive (*first, now, then, later*) conjunctive links used to represent the relation of succession. Parental prohibition of certain activities as being legitimate parts of a sequence led to the modelling of a variety of temporal linkers, while both parties used language to sequence desired activities with respect to distinct prior activities.

## 2.2 *Implicit representation of the typical*

By his third year, Stephen was less concerned to construe everything done and observed into language than to understand the predictable relations between one activity and another, or between participant, process and circumstance. Evidence for this can be found in the various ways in which Stephen achieved an implicit representation of 'what happens'. These include the first construal of causal links between events, the use of language to predict on the basis of past experience and the linguistic signalling of an implied contrast between what was expected and what was observed.

### 2.2.1 Obligatory links between events

It has already been shown that the mutually satisfactory management of activities involving child and/or parent provided an impetus for the use of temporal conjunction. In addition it was in the negotiation of speaker and hearer action, rather than the construal of observed experience, that causal links between activities were first developed. For example, the first *why?* utterances recorded from Stephen were concerned with challenging adult prohibitions and refusals, as in:

2;7;8     (S is cramming dry cereal into his mouth)
          M:  Oh, oh, Stevie! Don't eat it like that!
          S:  Why?
          M:  Now do you want this?

Although in this case Stephen's *why?* was ignored, such challenges did often result in the explication of an activity sequence:

2;7;7     M:  Would you like some salmon?
          S:  And peas too.
          M:  Peas? Peas have all gone, darling.
          S:  (disgruntled) Why?
          M:  Because you ate them.

As discussed earlier, the relation between the two actions (or the action and resulting state) within an activity sequence is one of temporal succession, but further than this any activity introduced as a cause is construed as making the effect follow obligatorily. Thus, *they have gone because you ate them* means not only 'you ate them and then they disappeared' but that there is an invariant relation between eating food and its disappearance. In this way, causal relations, even when created in the context of here-and-now negotiation, encourage generalizing from the particular case.

At this time, causal explanations were not only provided by the parent in response to the child's demands. Very often, too, the adult would, without prompting, provide an explanation for a command – an explanation which was often an account of the undesirable next action following the child's own current or likely activity:

2;7;10     M:   Oh, don't play with that umbrella, darling; you'll make it all open up.

2;10;7     M:   Don't put your fingers in [fish tank] though, 'cause you might frighten the fish.

Stephen can be seen beginning to adopt this model of supplying a linguistic representation of a possible consequence to a contemplated action in examples like the following:

2;7;24     S:   Won't touch it [=caterpillar], 'cause it might sting you.

2;8;17     M:   Just put it [=pin] down, I think.
           S:   It might (pause) cut you.

Adopted from texts where adult and child negotiated action, it is not surprising that sequences coded in this way tend to foreground the child as participant in one or both clauses. The fact that Stephen was remembering texts addressed to him in managing these clause complexes may also explain the regular use of *you* in the earliest examples, since he did not normally confuse the deictic reference of pronouns.

Another important result of the negotiating origins of these clause complexes is that an element of probability as well as obligation was introduced into the relation between the events. This occurred because the reason given was for not doing some action. Thus the second action in the sequence of material events being considered was modalized since it would only follow if the first action were actually carried out or continued with. There is an implicit conditional relation, as follows:

Won't touch it because, *if I touch it*, it might sting me.
Put it down, because, *if I don't*, it might cut me.

These characteristics of early causal clause-complex relations in Stephen's .speech are not idiosyncratic to this one child. As will be discussed more fully in Chapter 6, other non-experimental studies reported in the literature have also found that causal utterances from 2-year-olds and 3-year-olds refer in the main to commands and statements of intention and 'often with some negative aspect to the situation' (Hood and Bloom 1991: 342).

Although Stephen produced no conditional clause-complexes himself, it was certainly the case that conditional clauses addressed to him at this time were very strongly oriented to negotiating action, for example to specify the location for an activity:

2;7;6    M:  Look, sorry, go in your room if you want to play; we're eating up here.

or to lay out the only acceptable sequence of activities:

2;8;14    M:  If you want to go outside, you get your clothes on.

Thus the logico-semantic relation of causality, which Martin argues is a means of intruding the modal assessments of obligation and probability into the construal of events, has been found to emerge in the negotiation of speaker/hearer action. Its importance in the construal of field as activity is that setting up a causal relationship between two actions is to imply that the action in question – whether desired (going outside) or feared (being stung) – will be contingent upon the other action construed, not only in this situation but by implication in every comparable situation.

### 2.2.2  Predicting sequent events

So far, the examples given of using language to predict an activity sequence have been in contexts where language served to negotiate action and a causal relation was construed. At least as important for understanding activity sequences, however, were those occasions where actions were predicted simply to reflect on and interpret what was going on. In these cases it was temporal rather than causal links which were explicitly construed. By age two-and-a-half, Stephen was confidently using enhancing temporal clauses, not only to negotiate a desired event as discussed earlier, but to predict a next event – in a sequence which did not necessarily involve himself as a participant.

Such sequences were predicted on the basis of repeated (language-mediated) observation or repeated verbalizing of particular written texts. For example:

2;8;22    S:  (looking at picture of deer in story book) When the fox comes, he's gonna chase it away.

2;9       (in the car, waiting at traffic lights)
          S:  When that one goes green then that one will go red and then that one will go re- (light changes) go green!!

2;10;7    S:  (looking at empty park in rain) When it stops raining, then there might be lots of horses.

In such examples, it is a specific individual activity sequence that is being construed – the actions of the deer in the picture or the traffic light in front of the car or the rain currently falling. Nonetheless, the ability to predict depends on the speaker having construed an expectation from previous experience that the way one event has followed another in the past is the way it is certain or likely to occur again. Whether the source of his understanding was repeated talk or repeated observation, Stephen was using language here to construe his sense of the way the world works in terms of one event predictably leading to another.

The importance of verbalizing as a means of learning and understanding the predictable routines of life was apparent when Stephen commented on sequences that were taken for granted by others. The last example above, concerning traffic lights, is a case in point, as is the following:

2;10;7     (S and M in car)
           S:   I've got a dirty shirt.
           M:   Have you?
           S:   Mm.
           M:   (Turning round to see) Ooh, yes. Never mind. Put it in the
                wash [= basket for dirty clothes].
           S:   Later make it nice and wet.
           M:   (chuckling) Mm.
           S:   Don't say that.
           M:   Don't say what?
           S:   Laugh.

Stephen was offended here because he felt that what for him was a perfectly serious comment – that after going in the laundry basket the shirt would be made thoroughly wet – had caused amusement.

The importance of talk in sorting out everyday activity sequences was apparent when Stephen had to enquire about sequences of events that were too taken for granted to be the subject of incidental talk by others. Personal observation and experience may not be sufficient to allow a child to make sense of the world even when adults provide considerable commentary on their own ongoing, anticipated and obligatory actions. On those occasions the child may request that the activity sequence be verbalized. For example, there was a period of several weeks when Stephen repeatedly sought verification of where household stores came from, particularly bottles or packets placed on the table at mealtimes.

2;8;6      (M takes bottle of milk from fridge to table)
           S:   We did buy that in the shop?

Stephen rarely went supermarket shopping, but through language he could validate his inference that a shopping activity had preceded the appearance and use of the goods in the house. Such an occasion is comparable to the prediction *Later make it nice and wet* in the previously cited text, in that it shows the child using language to reflect on an activity sequence that will thereafter be simply taken-for-granted 'background knowledge of the world'. And although he was not here representing explicitly the generalization that everything consumed at home is first bought in a shop, some such implied generalization must have lain behind his questions.

Moving beyond the everyday, a slender new strand in Stephen's talk which began in this third year involved the beginnings of predicting events in his own 'life story' from the talk of others:

2;9;15    S:    When I'm two to go in a birthday.
         M:    No, when you're three.
         S:    Oh, when I'm three (pause).
         M:    You'll have a big birthday-
         H:    With a big cake.

2;9;23    S:    One day my tooth will come out and I will have $60!

Predictions of this kind arose from implicit comparisons of himself with his brother and from the talk which accompanied events in the older child's life. They are interesting in that this attempt to represent events which were more distant from those currently being engaged in required the construal in Theme position of a location in time. The temporal circumstance, *one day* – known to him as a ritual marker for written narrative – was pressed into service in one case above, while in the other, the temporal hypotaxis found in other predicting utterances was deployed (*when I'm two . . .* ). In this one text, however, the link between the clauses was not to sequence two events with respect to one another (cf. *when the fox comes, he's gonna chase the deer*), but rather to provide a temporal location for the event being predicted. Thus the attempt to predict more distanced events extended the language by calling for a clausal specification of temporal location.

Whether the actions predicted were immediate or non-immediate, all these occasions when Stephen represented a temporal expectancy between events (and/or states) indicate that he had construed activity structures with more than one component, or was in the process of deploying language to do so. Through language in use he was coming to understand the way things are done or the way things happen in the world of commonsense experience.

### 2.2.3 Signalling counter-expectation

Another way that Stephen expressed his understanding of the predictable course of events was by signalling when some violation of his expectations had occurred. For example, a representation of an ongoing event in Stephen's third year was often imbued with exclamative intonation to signal the violation of expectation:

2;10;7    (observing a game of tennis proceeding at a familiar court)
          S:   Play tennis in the <u>rain</u>!! (rise–fall tone)
          M:   It's not raining much now. Anyway people don't mind getting wet when they're playing a good game.

2;10;13   (F and S in kitchen. F drops transparent biscuit barrel from high shelf)
          S:   Daddy smash the biscuits! Daddy smash the biscuits! (rushes into brother's room) Daddy smashing the biscuits!
          H:   (entering) Where's Daddy smashing the biscuits?
          F:   I didn't smash them, I dropped them, 'cause my hands are cold.

In these cases the anomaly lay in the circumstance providing the setting for the event or in the realizations of participants and process.

On other occasions, the normal and the atypical were explicitly contrasted, as in the following brief recount:

2;8;24    (S returning from park with F and H and soccer ball)
          S:   I didn't do a big kick up in the air [i.e. as usual].
          M:   Didn't you, darling? Did you do a little kick?
          S:   No; I did a big kick right over!!

In fact, as time went on, the fact that an event was spontaneously recounted was enough to signify its salience as disrupting a predictable, if unstated, sequence, as in:

2;8;17    (S and M walking together. S recalls incident from a few days before)
          S:   I spilt it at the restaurant; I spilt it at the restaurant.
          M:   Yes.
          S:   Dropped it at the restaurant.
          M:   Mm, made you cry, didn't it?

Stephen's sense of the unusual, and by implication the normal, in what happens can also be observed in a very new development. This was the very occasional use – on only four occasions – of a *why?* question which was neither a challenge to the adult's authority nor an expression of discontent at what was happening, but a means of exploring an unexpected event. For example:

2;9;15    S:   There's no smoke coming out of the car.
          M:   No, it doesn't always come out, darling.
          S:   Why? Why? Why doesn't it come out?
          M:   Well, it's not supposed to come out much, love.

2;10;7    (in car, a very light sprinkling of rain on the windscreen)
         S:    What – what – why not the drips are coming down?

Where processes and participants configure in ways predictable from previous experience, that can be accepted as the way the world is and there is no need to question them. In other words, in terms of commonsense experience, there is no need to ask why drips roll downwards or (given the age of the typical Australian car) why smoke comes out of an exhaust pipe. Only violations to the expected need to be explored by asking *why?*

In sum, there were overall a number of different ways in which Stephen used language to represent indirectly his understanding that the specific event or sequence being verbalized either conformed to or violated construed norms about 'what happens' in the world. Predicting sequential events, whether using causal or temporal relations to do so, implies that the succession construed is either obligatory or typical and not unique to the particular occasion. Conversely a construal of the typical was implied when the child signalled that an observed event or sequence was not expected. This could be done through the use of intonation, through overt comparison of the normal and the remarkable or, less explicitly, through the selection from memory of what to verbalize. It was also implied on the rare occasions when the child sought an explanation for something observed.

### 2.3 Explicit generalization of process–participant relations

The uses of language discussed so far have been concerned either with the representation of activity (sequence) or with various linguistic ways in which – without overtly representing a generalization – Stephen demonstrated that he had construed one. Finally, some account will be given of occasional texts where Stephen construed a generalization quite overtly.

While all the text illustrations provided so far demonstrate that Stephen confidently used TRANSITIVITY structures to represent events, there were a few occasions when he also created texts which functioned to explore the configurations themselves and to generalize about what kind of participant engaged in what kind of process. Before discussing Stephen's texts, however, it can be suggested that the strategy he used, that of deploying comparison and contrast relations to substitute different participants into a TRANSITIVITY structure, was not a new one, nor one idiosyncratic to this child.

Examples from other case studies show that from early on different specific participants may be construed into a TRANSITIVITY structure in successive utterances as a way of understanding the configurational possibilities of processes and participants. For example, in the following text from Scollon (1976: 120) the creation of parallel participant^ process structures (*duck swim*; *Brenda swims*; *Mommy swims*; *Charlotte swims*) was achieved cooperatively, since the child, Brenda, was producing only single-word utterances at this stage:

1;8     B:   duck
         M:   Hm?
         B:   duck; swim; swim; swim; swim; duck
         M:   Can duck swim?
         B:   Brenda
         M:   Brenda swims?
         B:   Mommy; swim; swim
         M:   Mommy swims too
         B:   Charlotte
         M:   Uh hm. Charlotte swims too

Seen in purely formal terms, such a text can be described as a joint construction of a TRANSITIVITY structure. However, acknowledging that the formal patterns actualize meaning allows the text to be seen as primarily an exploration of experiential meaning – an exploration that, to be explicit, might be glossed in the form of enquiries such as *What does swim mean?*, *Do only living things swim?*, *Is what the duck does in the water the same event as what Mummy does?*, etc.

Children who have already configured structures continue to use the adult partner to verify their explorations, as in the following example from Halliday's (1984b) data:

1;9;10   N:   Eat chuffa?
          F:   You can't eat trains!
          N:   Can't eat blue chuffa.
          F:   No you can't eat the blue train.
          N:   Can't eat red chuffa.
          F:   No you can't eat the red train.
          N:   Can't eat man (looking at wooden toy).
          F:   No you can't eat the man.
          N:   Can't eat that book.
          F:   No you can't eat that book. You can't eat any book.

Again this is not mere 'pattern practice', but a playful way of validating understandings about what constitutes eating and what counts as (in)edible.

Stephen, in his third year, similarly explored participant^process relations in an example like the following:

2;9;3    S:   Can you talk?
        M:   Yes, I can talk, darling; can <u>you</u> talk?
        S:   Yes, I can talk, and Hal can talk, and Daddy can talk.

> M:  And Katy [=cat], can she talk?
> S:  No; she goes 'au au'.

Although the generalization that only people talk is not constructed explicitly, this text marked a new development for Stephen in that it was one of only three recorded examples in the third year where *can* was used with a third-person participant in its meaning of potentiality or ability. Overwhelmingly, *can* was used with speech role participants in the negotiation of action, as in *Mummy can you do blocks with me?* or *Can I go and get a heater?* Otherwise, *can* was virtually restricted to comments on Stephen's own ability (e.g. *I can say 'accident'; I can't do that*, etc.). This extension of *can* to use in third-person clauses was to prove important in the following year, when there was a new focus on generalizing.

This new focus was first heralded in the third year in a very few exceptional texts where the familiar text pattern of repeated parallel TRANSITIVITY structures was deployed, but with new kinds of realizations for the participant and process roles. The new choice realizing the participant role was a plural nominal group with no Deictic element, while the new choice for the Material process role was a verbal group making the marked choice of present tense.

As discussed in the previous chapter, a nominal group of this kind construes a generic category, rather than any actually or potentially identifiable member of the class, and a material process clause which has selected (simple) present tense similarly generalizes the action represented. The unmarked present tense choice for a material process clause is [present-in-present], as in *the car is breaking*, while the marked option, often called 'universal' present tense, removes the proposition from any specific location with respect to the ongoing context of situation and construes a generalization.

An example of a comparison and contrasting text where Stephen has removed the deixis from the proposition was cited on p. 88 and is repeated below.

2;7;24    (Sunday breakfast)
> S:  Crocodiles die.
> M:  Yes, crocodiles die.
> S:  And spiders die, and ants die, and giraffes die . . .
>      (continues through zoo animals seen two weeks before).
> S:  And aeroplanes die (looks at M).
> M:  No, aeroplanes don't die, they just break.
> S:  Aeroplanes break . . . (continues catalogue of creatures + die).
> H:  And Stephens die.
> S:  (indignantly) No, Stephen's not dying.
> H:  Ye-
> M:  Oh, don't start an argument.

S:    Caterpillars die . . . (continues with other parallel examples).
       And cars <u>break</u>.
M:   Yes.
S:    And they drive all the way home.

This text has been discussed as one which enabled Stephen to construe
implicitly new levels of hierarchy in his taxonomy of moving things. A
crucial aspect of this, however, is that the relation of different classes of
participant with different classes of process was being explored.

The text was very striking at the time because it was so unusual in its use
of a generic nominal group (*crocodiles* rather than *the crocodile*) configured
with a non-deictic verbal group. Up to the age of 3, there were only four
other recorded examples. Three were in comparison and contrast texts of
this kind, and all these were concerned with the potential for behaviour of
different age groups of children. In the next example it is the
circumstance being substituted in each successive utterance:

2;7;5    (S watching a baby being strapped into its stroller by adult)
          S:    Babies go in the prams sometimes.
          M:   What?
          S:    Babies go in the prams sometimes.
          M:   Yes, they do.
          S:    And babies go in the shops.
          M:   Oh yes, babies go in the shops.
          S:    And babies go to the Easter show sometimes.
          M:   Yes . . .

In this case, Stephen's suggestions that babies (like older children) also go
on everyday outings (such as to the shops) and holiday outings (such as to
the Easter show) were verified by the adult, perhaps validating a view of
babies as family members (but unlike, say, the family pet).

In the following text, Stephen places himself, by implication, outside the
category of 'little boys':

2;7;20   (sitting at kitchen counter. S puts drink down carefully)
          S:    Only <u>little</u> boys put on edge.
          M:   Mm.
          S:    'cause little boys are naughty.
          M:   Well, little boys spill it by accident.
          S:    Only little boys do accident. I can say 'accident'!!
          M:   Yes you can, can't you?
          S:    (leaning over on stool) Little boys do that sometimes and
                 they fall off the stool and they cry.
          H:   Sometimes big boys cry.
          S:    No, little boys cry.
          H:   No, big boys cry too. Remember Stephen fell off the stool,

and Stephen's a big boy and Stephen cried.
S:   I didn't fall off.
H:   You did.
S:   I didn't.

These last two texts also contain the USUALITY Adjunct, *sometimes*, used on only four other occasions overall. Its presence underlines the focus on the typical and possible rather than the actual. The two other third-person examples involving USUALITY are given below.

2;9       (S watches M dry herself after shower)
          S:   (pointing) Bottom.
          M:   Mm.
          S:   Sometimes poo does come out.

2;10      (M driving S. They wait at traffic lights)
          S:   Sometimes it goes green and orange and red.
          M:   The traffic lights.
          S:   Mm.

In these cases, rather than predicting a next event based on past experience, Stephen used that past experience to form an explicit generalization by means of the non-deictic TENSE choice and the USUALITY adverb.

French and Nelson (1985: 13) found evidence that in response to a question about habitual activity, children as young as three could use 'timeless speech' of this kind. Moreover several of their 3-year-old subjects reporting familiar 'scripts' used USUALITY adverbs such as *sometimes*. However, they note that previous studies had reported that children did not or could not form such generalizations until much later. Certainly in these data, collected from Stephen up till his third birthday, the spontaneous use of these forms was rare and marked a new departure in the interpretation of experience.

In the construal of material events, then, a few texts stand out in the third year because they were explicitly concerned with construing an event as a generalization which was not tied to any specific context of situation. At the same time, it will be seen that such conversations were much more typical of the kind of talk that took place during the following year, well after Stephen had turned three. Yet, despite their 'advanced' nature, three of the four comparing and contrasting examples (those concerned with babies and little boys) actually occurred at 2;7, very early in the first data set. They appear to be examples of what Halliday (1992b) has recently called the 'trailer' (i.e. 'preview') phenomenon, when a very restricted use of a new development foreshadows its crucial deployment in a later period when it spreads to new contexts.

Examples of this can be found in other systemic case studies. In

Halliday's (1975) account of Nigel's early language, he observes how the combination of different meaningful tones with a lexical item was used by his child at first only with proper names. Then a little later this distinction emerged as the foundation for a major reorganization of the system, with every utterance having the potential for two different functional meanings signalled by the choice of tone. In the case study of Hal, the use of language in the new function of giving unshared information was seen to have its origins in the recounting of incidents where his person or his feelings were hurt (Painter 1984: 133–4).

Stephen's occasional explorations of generalizing are perhaps also typical of new developments in that they were strongly connected to a particular meaning area which was invested with strong feeling on his part. He had been upset on various occasions when witnessing insects die in the garden or animals being killed on TV documentaries, and so the issue of mortality explored in the *crocodiles die* text was certainly a salient one to him. In the other comparison and contrast texts, it was the issue of being a baby or a little/big boy that was being explored. Just as the names of his inner meaning circle were of particular affectual significance to Nigel, and painful moments to Hal, so was this issue of growing up very salient to Stephen. The importance of size/age as a way of categorizing children comes through in comments from parent and child alike. Moreover, Stephen was one of the 'big' children at his childcare centre (which took babies and toddlers up to age 3 only) but at the same time he was ever conscious of being the 'little' boy in the home context.

The focus on 'little boys' was particularly prominent in adult talk focusing on rules. And while the adult talk in the third year did provide many more examples of generic reference than Stephen's talk overall, the formulation of rules relating to 'little boys' in contexts of control was one of the most predictable uses. The following texts are examples.

2;7;13  S:  (complainingly to M) Daddy didn't give some nuts to me.
        M:  Well, nuts are not for little boys.
        S:  Why?
        M:  Well, because sometimes they get stuck (points to throat) and make you cough.

2;8;17  (S wants some of M's wine)
        M:  No, little boys can't drink wine.
        S:  (pause) 'Cause it makes sick.

Thus the social contexts of Stephen's life made the categorization of individuals as babies, little boys, big boys or grown-ups of particular concern to him, and a site for reflection which extended his use of language. Of course, it is not being suggested that the semantic domains of greatest concern to Stephen will prove to be generalizable to other children. But what may be suggested as typical in language development is that particularly salient areas, especially those invested with interpersonal, affectual prominence, may be the site of new developments which are at first entirely restricted to this one domain.

### 2.4 Summary 2;6 to 3;0 years

Whether negotiating speaker–hearer action or construing observed experience, much of the everyday conversation between parent and child served to build up activity sequences relevant to everyday domestic experience. On the whole, the activity sequences were small-scale, and when language accompanied physical action the representation of events might be inexplicit or fragmented. However, the parent's use of language to facilitate the carrying out of physical activities did model the linguistic representation of sequences and may also have oriented Stephen to the value of language as a substitute for material trial and error in the accomplishment of tasks.

In 'active' contexts of use, the systems of TRANSITIVITY and of temporal CONJUNCTION were mobilized by Stephen to initiate desired activities and to help accomplish a manual task. And in the negotiation of speaker/hearer action Stephen began also to construe causal links between events, as he reflected on the possible consequences of his actions. This constituted a development towards implicit generalization, since a consequence cannot be predicted except on the basis of a regular succession of events within an activity sequence.

Sequential actions were also anticipated in a more reflective mode when predicting a next event, something achieved through the temporal linking of clauses. On the very rare occasions when more distant activities were predicted, a temporal circumstance was deployed to locate the future event. Again the ability to predict suggests an expectation, not present in a simple running commentary, that one event follows another to comprise the sequence being considered.

Stephen's expectations were also manifested when disrupted. Any such disruption to the norms being construed created surprise which gained linguistic manifestation. This might involve the construal of an anomalous observed event, overlaying the experiential structure with an exclamative intonation contour, or it might involve the selection from memory of a particularly salient event for shared recall. Alternatively, the typical and actual might be overtly compared (*I didn't do X, I did Y*) or an explanation might be sought from the addressee as to why the predictable was not taking place. Thus through the causal or temporal linking of current and future event, together with various manifestations of counter-expectation, Stephen used language to represent events in a way which demonstrated that he had inferred that particular participants and processes or particular activities 'go together' to form an activity structure or sequence.

In the light of developments to be discussed in the next section, one of the most significant developments in the third year was the way a specific observation might give rise to a linguistic construal that was not tied to any specific context of situation. Such clauses were removed from their anchorage in the deictic present by a choice of non-deictic TENSE or MODALITY in the Finite, and occasionally an additional choice of USUALITY, to make it explicit that general rather than specific relations were being construed. The events generalized chiefly related to the behaviour of the class of 'big boys' or 'babies', and in texts of this kind, language was being used not simply to construct or reconstruct lived or observed experience as a way of interpreting it, but was being used to generalize that experience as a way of further reflecting on it.

## 3  Stephen's language: 3;0 to 4;0 years

In considering the construal of the world of events in the fourth year, attention will be given to developments that relate to Stephen's understanding of what is typical and what is anomalous in experience. First, new aspects to the implicit construal of the typical and of expectancy relations will be considered. Then a number of developments will be described involving the explicit generalization of activities and activity sequences. Finally, a new strand in the talk will be described where the world of events was problematized, where generalizations were tested and possibilities explored.

### 3.1  Implicit construal of the typical

It was apparent from the data of the third year that Stephen was already inferring from his specific experiences what was normal and what was exceptional. In the fourth year, the implicit construal of generalizations about the world of events continued to be apparent, and was manifested in four additional ways. With respect to the representation of single events, one development involved the use of comparison and contrast to focus on norms of behaviour of the interactants as participants, while another involved the use of the interpersonal system of MODULATION to construe the normal or expected. Where activity sequences were concerned, Stephen had begun to recount brief sequences involving some disruption to what was expected and had also developed a new capacity to construe observed events as causally related.

#### 3.1.1  Exploring norms of child/adult behaviour

In the previous year, a single use of a hypotactic *when* clause was recorded, where the function was to locate rather than sequence an event. Its use was motivated by a new attempt to construe a relatively distant event. In the fourth year, predicting or recounting events distanced in time from the here-and-now was much more frequent, as was the use of a locating *when* clause.

These two abilities in managing a larger time frame were brought together with the comparison and contrast strategy of the previous year, used to focus on participant^process relations. A new aspect here, though, was a particular concentration on child-speaker or adult-addressee in the participant roles. Although focusing on the two individuals, these texts can perhaps be interpreted as attempts to understand better the different behaviour appropriate for different people depending on their age classification. For example:

3;10;7    S:    When I'm four I <u>still</u> have to go to kindy [i.e pre-school].
          M:    Yes, and when you're five you will go to school.
          S:    And when I'm seven I will go to school;
                and when I'm eight I will go to school;
                and when I'm a hundred I will go to school.

Both the use of the Modal Adjunct *still* and the repetition of the TRANSITIVITY configuration *I will go to school* highlight the sameness of the predicted event, which will occur regardless of the variation in the temporal context. Stephen's text was clearly reflecting upon his own future life, but in doing so was implicitly construing the reality that children attend school for the entire term of their childhood.

Similarly, in the following examples, Stephen considered himself as an adult or as an older child and reflected on the difference this would make to participant roles:

3;6;12    (M has lifted S up for a cuddle)
          S:    When I'm grown up, will I pick you up and cuddle you?
          M:    I hope so.

3;7       (F carrying S to bathroom upside down)
          S:    (laughing) Could you carry me when I'm four?
          F:    Yes.
          S:    Could you carry me when I'm five?
          F:    Yes.
          S:    Could you carry me (pause) when I'm four?
          F:    Yes.
          S:    Could you carry me when I'm six?
          F:    No.
          S:    Why?
          F:    Because you'll be too big then.
          S:    (laughs delightedly)

In these conversations, Stephen was exploring the understanding that what was a normal role for him at age three would not continue to be so. Sometimes changes in norms of behaviour were regretted, and the following text was striking in that he construed himself as a third party to strengthen the contrast between his current and baby self:

3;7;4     (M invokes rule of dress before breakfast)
        S:   When I was two (holding up two fingers carefully) before, I used to be a baby and <u>he</u> didn't get dressed, <u>he</u> just had pyjamas.

Another strand in this exploration was to shift perspective in another way and consider the parent in the role of child. The following text, like that above, was constructed in the course of negotiating action:

3;6;29    (M teasingly asks for share of boys' ice-cream in restaurant)
        H:   (refusing) You don't let me have your wine.
        M:   I'm not allowed to give you wine.
        S:   You're not supposed to have ice-cream. (pause) When you were a little boy, you had ice-cream.[1]

Other examples were more simply reflective:

3;6;16    S:   (poised to run) One, two, three, four, five, blast off!!! (rushes off)
           (on returning) Would you do that when you were three?
        M:   Oh yes, I ran down slopes when I was three.

3;7;13    (S shows off, running and doing head-over-heels)
        S:   Could you do that when you were a little boy?
        M:   When I was a little girl, yes.

In these last texts Stephen was considering his mother as he had never known her, by using language to construe her as a member of the class to which he himself belonged (*three (years old); a little boy*). He could then explore whether, as members of the same age group, they were alike in their abilities. By doing this he clearly enriched his understanding of the other individual, as someone who had had experiences he could envisage without ever having witnessed them. Equally importantly, though, he could consider his own behaviour as representative of typical 'childlike' behaviour, rather than simply a particular action he was enjoying at the moment. Thus these examples, like the others, provided a way of reflecting upon himself as an exemplary rather than unique participant.

## 3.1.2 Construing the unexpected

In the fourth year, Stephen's construal of the unexpected was achieved not only through the expression of surprise, but by intruding his personal attitude into the representation through a modal OBLIGATION choice. For example, when experience failed to meet predicted expectations, Stephen began to construe the expected configuration of participant and process as a normative rule using *should* or *supposed to*:

3;7;8     (S attempts to rock his recently mended stool)
            S:    This – this stool's stopped wibbling (wobbles it violently).
            M:    Oh darling, what are you doing?
            S:    (disgruntled) It's supposed to wibble.

3;9;6     (looking out of car window on familiar route)
            S:    Where's the smashed car? There's supposed to be a smashed car on the grass.

Obligation modalities had been used by Stephen in the previous year in the negotiation of action, when he tried to change a situation by influencing others. Here, however, he used modulated propositions, not to act on the world but simply to express his sense of the way it ought to be in comparison with the way he observed it to be.

In addition, the expression of surprise continued to be prominent in Stephen's representation of material experience. By the fourth year, Stephen produced many brief recounting texts where two or more sequential actions were reported. These might still involve everyday experiences of washing, dressing and playing and so on, but were notable in that they were related to convey Stephen's sense of a disruption to an 'unmarked' sequence of events having occurred.

Very often negative polarity signalled the frustration of a predicted element in a sequence, according to Stephen's expectations:

3;5;7     (S watching chimps at zoo)
            S:    You know that baby monkey he likes to cuddle up in the mother and he doesn't scratch her.
            M:    No, he doesn't because she's got thick fur and skin and it doesn't hurt her when he grabs her fur; that's how he's supposed to hold on.

3;5;15    (in the car)
            S:    I saw a cement-mixer [=truck] and the thing's not going round.
            M:    Oh, perhaps it was empty; perhaps they used all the concrete up and they're going home.

3;8;20    (M and S tidying bathroom after S's bath)
            S:    I was standing there [= in bath] when the water was getting hot and (indignantly) it didn't get hot!
            (M explains that the hot water in the tank has all been used up)

The following example offers a variation on this theme in that a negative situation produced an unexpectedly positive result:

3;10;2   S:    Look Mum (showing hands). There wasn't any soap (?      )
                 I put lots of water and then it made it clean!

(M explains that superficial dirt soaks off in plain water but advises that soap is needed for 'really' dirty hands)

These examples are typical in that explicit 'concessive' conjunctions were not made use of to signal the move from normal to exceptional, and this was perhaps because the counter-expectation could be adequately signalled through POLARITY and KEY (intonation) choices, as well as by an implicit appeal to the adult's shared expectancies.

That there was an implied counter-expectancy link can, however, be suggested when the adult's responses are taken into account. Whenever Stephen's current experience led him to a certain expectation of a sequent event which was then not realized, and he shared his sense of surprise, there was an opportunity for the parent to offer an explanation. This might involve the articulation of marked and unmarked sequences and the modelling of causal relations between different events.

### 3.1.3 Linking the unusual to a preceding cause

In examples like those above, when Stephen expected a certain sequent event which was then not realized, there was an opportunity for the parent to offer an explanation. In addition, Stephen at this time regularly construed explanations for himself of unusual events.

In the previous year, when the first cause–effect sequences of activities were construed by Stephen, they arose particularly in the shared production of warning utterances, where Stephen was advised not to do something in view of the likely consequential action. In the fourth year, there was an increasing tendency for Stephen to construe observed events as causally linked to one another. These arose from noting an unusual event and seeking to construe a prior event as a cause, just as the adult partner supplied explanations for him in the examples given above (and in those of the previous year; cf. F: *I dropped them 'cause my hands are cold*).

Stephen began for the first time therefore to suggest a prior cause for an observed state or action that was noteworthy:

3;5;1     (S is playing with a bag with a hole in)
          S:  It's got a hole in it 'cause Hal banged it [S had witnessed this event the previous day].

3;5;11    S:  A red tow truck pulling a car, because its engine's broken [S would have heard such explanations before, cf. 3;5;12 p. 164].

In both these cases his causal interpretation, whether or not he had witnessed the sequence, had been guided by the talk of others. On another occasion he construed a causal interpretation for himself:

3;8;17    (S and M discuss indicator in car which has been mended after
          breaking)
          S:   You went the wrong way, that's why it broke.[2]

Here Stephen brought to bear one observation, that M often got lost while
driving (or perhaps he was recalling also a specific occasion), with another,
that the direction indicator had broken, and he construed a causal
connection between the two. This particular connection had not been
modelled for him and the fact that he made it suggests a new inclination
to see events as obligatorily linked to one another. It was no longer enough
for Stephen simply to observe the unusual – such as the fact that it broke –
he now looked for some preceding action that could be construed as the
cause.

     And if he could not construe the preceding cause for himself, he got
help from his conversational partner:

3;5;12    (S observes a man pushing a car backwards across junction)
          S:   Why's he pushing the car, Mum?
          M:   I don't know, darling; engine must have broken.

Direct enquiries as to the cause of unexpected actions by others, which
had just begun in the previous year, constituted an important means of
learning during the fourth year.

     Thus, through the use of third-person OBLIGATION choices, through the
continued use of POLARITY and INTONATION and through the representation
of causal relations between specific actions, Stephen expressed in an
implicit way his understandings of what constituted an 'unmarked'
combination of process and participant or of action and action.

### 3.2 Explicit generalizing

In addition to the implicit representations so far described, Stephen's use
of language in the fourth year was very much oriented to the explicit
construal of generalizations. This occurred in the representation of an
event as a single clause structure and also through the representation of a
sequence of two or more actions.

### 3.2.1 Generalizing process-participant configurations

As discussed previously, in the earlier data set it was only in one or two
conversations involving highly salient areas of interest that the exploration
of an event in terms of different classes of things and actions was
prominent. After age 3, however, the focus on non-specific TRANSITIVITY
structures had spread to all field domains, as Stephen overtly explored the
potential as well as the actualization of field.

     One of the chief grammatical reflexes of this change has been discussed already: the use of generic reference in the nominal group, together with non-deictic present tense in the verbal group, in the construal of the experiential clause configuration. The following occasions were typical of the fourth year in that an observation of a particular participant led immediately to reflection on the behaviour of (or towards) the class, thus focusing on the potential rather than the actual event:

3;4;25    S:    (observing cat bristle) Why don't cats like dogs?

3;5;6    S:    (sipping his drink) Drinks don't go bad, do they?

3;5;11    (S observes horse in park)
          S:    Ooh horsey! You don't pat them on the bottom, you pat them on the top.
          M:    On the neck.

3;6;23    S:    My eye's got better. How does it make it to get better?

3;8;17    (S observes horse in park)
          S:    A galloping horse; a big galloping horse. There's – there's a – there's a little one. I saw a little – I saw one big galloping horse and one little galloping horse. They gallop around. Some horses don't gallop around; some horses don't gallop around on the grass.

3;9;14    (S watches motorbike overtake them)
          S:    Could motorbikes go faster than cars?
          M:    Well, some can and some can't.

3;9;6    (S has been observing a caterpillar)
          S:    There was a caterpillar on the path, and it started to bleed! And there was another one – a stingy one . . .
          (takes M out to look at the caterpillars)
          S:    Did you know caterpillars could do poos?
          M:    Yes.
          S:    But they can't see their bottoms.

This movement from engagement with or observation of a particular instance to a general comment or enquiry is also found in Halliday's (1984b) data. Although it appeared in Nigel's speech at an earlier age, the children were at a comparable stage of development, and Nigel moved into this kind of text only after a long period of construing observations, recounts and predictions of particular experience. In the following text a recalling of specific experience with a cat led to an enquiry about cats in general:

2;10;22　N:　And you [=I] saw a cat in Chania Falls.
　　　　　M:　Yes, you saw a cat in Chania Falls.
　　　　　N:　And you picked the cat up. Mummy, do cats like meat?
　　　　　M:　Yes, they do.
　　　　　N:　Do cats like bones? Do cats like marrow?

　　In most of the examples given above, the questions or statements were generalized by removing their anchorage in a time frame which relates to speaker now. This was achieved through the use of the 'universal' present tense choice. Another way to avoid locating the process in any specific time is to modalize the Finite, an option Stephen repeatedly took up. When he did so, he used *can/could* (or *can't*) in its meaning of 'potentiality' (cf. Halliday 1994: 281), making explicit the fact that he was exploring the potential a particular class of entity has to configure with a particular class of process.

　　For example, in the following text Stephen appears to be exploring the classes of birds that can configure as participants with the process *talk*:

3;8　　　　(S has been talking about a white cockatoo feather)
　　　　　S:　Cockatoos can talk.
　　　　　F:　Yes, cockatoos can talk.
　　　　　S:　And parrots can talk.
　　　　　F:　Yes.

This text, like the following one, also shows how comparison and contrast continued to be deployed to explore the possible relation between the elements construing an event:

3;7;5　　S:　Cars could go speeding and (?　　) could go speeding and a truck could go speeding and a sport car could go speeding; everything could go speeding; (pause) 'cept houses; they're stuck.

Sometimes the comparison was left implicit, as in the next example:

3;5;11　　S:　Can shoes break? Can shoes break? Can shoes break, Mummy?
　　　　　M:　Yes.
　　　　　S:　What's inside them?
　　　　　M:　Nothing's inside them.
　　　　　S:　Can they break?
　　　　　M:　Yes.
　　　　　S:　What's inside them?
　　　　　M:　Nothing's inside them. When a shoe breaks, (demonstrates) this bit comes away from this bit.

This text was probably building on an unstated contrast between the processes of 'mending' and 'breaking', since the conversation followed an earlier one in which Hal talked about mending his shoes. Presumably because 'mending' was opposed to 'breaking' in Stephen's taxonomy of events, he needed to check up on the possibility of *break* configuring with *shoes*.

It should be noted again that up till the age of three, *can/can't* had been used almost exclusively with speech role Subjects in the negotiation of action, within the meaning area of OBLIGATION and INCLINATION, in making requests, seeking permission, and so on. By age three there were four recorded cases of *can* used more reflectively to enquire or comment on ability, such as *can you talk?* Now, in the fourth year, however, the principal use was with generic third-person Subjects to construe the meaning 'Is it possible for Xs to —? / Are Xs able to —?', a clearly reflective orientation aimed at exploring the event configuration itself.

### 3.2.2 Generalizing an activity sequence

It was not only the representation of single events that were generalized at this time. In a similar way, Stephen also began to concern himself with the activity sequence as a potential rather than as a specific actualization. To do so, temporal or conditional hypotaxis was used to represent the usual or necessary relations between events. On those occasions the conjunction *when* realized the meaning of *whenever*, as in the following:

3;5;17   (road near preschool)
       S:   When they go to work, they leave their cars here.
       M:   Who do?
       S:   The peoples.
       M:   The people at kindy?
       S:   No, the people who goes to work, (?people's) mummies.

3;6   (in car)
       S:   We're always stop when the cars coming.

In this last text, the modal Adjunct *always* additionally contributes to the construal of the typical, the original USUALITY realization *sometimes* now being part of a system which included other values (namely *always* and *never*).

Examples of the use of the newly developed relation of hypotactic condition to represent a general relation between two events are given below.

3;5;29   (discussing how to carry his Lego structure)
       S:   If you hold it two hands close together, it will crash.

3;10;2    (S observes cat sniffing at something M has left on counter)
      S:    If you put it there Katy will eat it.

As can be seen, these examples were reflecting on the undesirable consequences of speaker or hearer action. But expressed as a conditional relation between processes, they were removed from the immediate speaker-now context, to construe a more general relationship between the processes.

This manner of generalizing can be seen again in the following example where a parental command is elaborated by Stephen into a conditional sequence:

3;10;14    (in car, S has packet of balloons)
      M:    Oh, don't open them now. Wait till you get home. Here-
      (turns and puts balloon packet into her bag).
      S:    If you open the balloons when (pause) you're not at home, you will <u>lose</u> them.

A text such as this contrasts with the jointly constructed cause–effect sequences of the previous year, where a specific intended action was linked to a possible consequence. Here, instead of agreeing *I won't open them because I might lose them*, in which a possible consequence of a particular action is predicted, Stephen created a more general rule by relating the processes through condition and generalizing the Actor as *you*.

### 3.2.3 Construing a single occurrence as a generalization

In the examples given so far, Stephen was drawing on a history of repeated specific experiences and observations when he construed an explicit generalization. However, there were also a dozen recorded occasions during the fourth year when he inferred a generalization from a single experience or observation. This can be seen in the following two texts, again deploying a hypotactic link of general time or condition:

3;10;16    (S in back of car picks something off his trouser leg)
      S:    When something's on my leg,
      M:    Mm-
      S:    and it's a black thing,
      M:    Mm-
      S:    I could just drop it, and it will fall down.

3;9;27    (in back of car, S sneezes)
      S:    Sometimes if you look at the sun, you go tishoo.

On both these occasions Stephen was reporting on his own ongoing or immediately completed action. But rather than simply being monitoring through language, the actions were construed explicitly as a sequence that would always hold once the first action had initiated it. The use of modality in these texts (and the generalized participant *you* in the second one) are further evidence that Stephen's interest was in characterizing the specific occasion as a generalizable one and in characterizing his own action as typical of persons in this situation.

Equally striking were occasions when a specific incident from the non-immediate past was recalled and presented as a timeless generalization rather than being recounted as a particular event. Thus in the next example, Stephen chose not to comment directly on the specifics of the previous night's story which had involved a toy duck which 'laid' toy eggs, but simply to check on the generalizability of this. (The answer he got, however – presumably because of the doubtfulness of the generalization in this case – simply acknowledged their shared experience of the specific example.)

3;5;10    S:   Mum, some toys lay eggs, don't they?
          M:   Yes, in our book last night the toy duck laid eggs.

In such cases, *can/could* modality was again frequently used by Stephen to underline his focus on exploring a participant-process relation, rather than simply recalling an event:

3;7;8     (S flapping plastic bag which H had blown up and burst the previous day)
          S:   You know you could pop shopping bags.
          M:   Can you?
          S:   <u>Hal</u> can, <u>I</u> can't.
          [S had previously understood that only paper bags could be burst]

3;8;22    (recalling an incident from previous day when F accidentally smashed a melamine plate)
          S:   (eating) You know, plastic plates can break, can't they?
          M:   Mm, we know now they can. I didn't know they could, but they can, can't they?

3;8;25    (on previous day at zoo, M and S had seen a lion pounce onto some meat lying on a shelf in its cage)
          S:   Lions could jump up their things to eat.
          M:   Lions could jump up their things to eat?
          S:   You know, at the zoo.
          M:   Oh yeah, jump up <u>on</u> their food.
          S:   Yeah.

All these examples illustrate how Stephen chose not to relate the particular incident that had been part of his observational experience, but to represent the event linguistically as a potential that would be relevant across contexts.

### 3.2.4 Problematizing the potential/actual relation

It is clear from the texts cited above that Stephen had begun to short-cut the process of building knowledge by construing a single observed instance as a generalization. This, however, did not always lead to a representation that would be validated by the dialogue partner, and thus a further characteristic of reflective talk in the fourth year was the problematizing of the potential/actual relation.

Sometimes the impetus for this came from the parent, as in the following:

3;6      (S looking at a park from the car)
        S:   That can't be shut 'cause it hasn't got a gate. (pause)
            All parks can't be shut 'cause they haven't got a gate.
        M:  Well, <u>some</u> parks have gates. Centennial Park has gates.

Here M challenged Stephen's generalization by citing an instance of experience familiar to him which contradicted his statement.

The continuance of a text already cited provides another example of a challenged generalization:

3;8;1    S:   Cockatoos can talk.
        F:   Yes, cockatoos can talk.
        S:   And parrots can talk.
        F:   Yes.
        M:  <u>Some</u> parrots can talk.

Here M added the Modifier *some* to the nominal group *parrots* to indicate that the process only applied to a subgrouping of the participant class. The text then continued with Stephen himself offering specific experience in support of the negotiated generalization:

3;8;1    M:  <u>Some</u> parrots can talk.
        S:   We went to school and – and I saw a parrot and he was blue
            and red and (?all) lovely and – and – and he said hello to
            him – and he said hello to me.

At other times, specific experience was introduced by Stephen to challenge a generalization the parent had given or validated:

3;6      S:   We're always stop when the cars coming.
        M:  You certainly do.
        S:   <u>You</u> didn't stop.

3;6;13   S:   Why can't we have two [houses]?
         M:   Everybody only has one house, darling.
         S:   But on the TV some people they went to another house.

3;6;30   (F and S are discussing sports cars)
         F:   . . . and they [=sports cars] go fast 'cause they've got a big engine.
         S:   But that [=one we're looking at] doesn't go faster than us. See? (as they move off from lights) We will go faster.

In such texts, as in the last two cited here, Stephen would often introduce his counter-example with a cohesive conjunction *but*, one which construes the 'internal' meaning of 'despite what you say'. (An implicit relation of this type is also evident in the first text of the group (3;6 above).) This link is different from the 'external' meaning of 'despite what happened' which was implicit in the examples cited earlier where Stephen recounted an activity sequence where the predicted course of actions was disrupted. In effect the discourse here was structured not in terms of something unexpected in the activity sequence, but rhetorically, in terms of an argument structure where counter-evidence is brought to bear on an earlier proposition.

### 3.3 Exploring alternative activity sequences

Another important development in the fourth year was the exploration by Stephen of different possible activity sequences. The conditional relation was one resource which could be brought to bear to consider alternative possibilities. In the following example, Stephen did not appear to be challenging his parent, but genuinely exploring:

3;6;26   (M encourages S to clean his teeth)
         S:   What happens if you leave them all white?
         M:   Well, they don't stay white. If you don't clean them, then they go all brown and smelly.
         H:   And people won't want to look at you.
         S:   If you don't clean them, will you die?
         M:   No, you won't die, but your teeth will go bad.

Prominent in this fourth year also was another way of exploring an activity sequence. This was by putting forward in dialogue alternative possible steps in the sequence. For example, on finding that a car which was regularly to be seen standing on a steep driveway, leading to a garage, was not there, the following conversation took place:

3;10;2   S:   Hey, look, look, the falling-down car is gone.
         M:   Oh, it's not there, no.

> S:  It's g- maybe it's gone under the garage.
> M:  Yeah, maybe it's gone right inside.
> S:  Yeah, cause maybe it's gonna rain; maybe it doesn't come these days.

Stephen appeared to be enjoying bringing to bear his understandings of how events are connected, to suggest alternative explanations for the car's absence, introducing each possibility with the modal Adjunct *maybe*.

Often, Stephen liked to suggest an alternative explanation to one offered by the dialogue partner. For example:

3;9;2  M:  Oh, what's happened to make that terrible stink?
       H:  Probably a bushfire somewhere.
       S:  Or could be a very, very smelly bus has gone past.

3;9;6  S:  Where's the smashed car? There's supposed to be a smashed car on the grass.
       M:  Is there?
       S:  Mm.
       M:  They must have taken it away.
       S:  Maybe the wind flyed it away.

His suggestion in the last case was clearly a playful one, made as a contribution to building the text as a series of alternatives rather than to argue a point of disagreement.

When it was a case of negotiating his own action, though, Stephen was more concerned to disagree with the adult and would suggest an alternative action to that proposed by his parent. MODALITY was deployed again, this time to signal an as yet unrealized future action rather than a possible preceding one.

3;6;5  (M asks H to tidy Lego into sorting trays)
       H:  I'm waiting for Stephen.
       M:  He doesn't really know where the pieces go, so it's better if you do it anyway.
       S:  (looking up at M) He could teach me.

3;7  (M says they can't go on the train now)
       S:  Why?
       M:  'Cause we're in the car.
       S:  But we could park it somewhere.
       (M mentions her heavy bags that she wouldn't want to carry)
       S:  We could leave them (?at home).

3;9;1  (S complaining about his raised car seat)
       M:  If you were down there [i.e. where Hal sits] you wouldn't be

able to see anything.
F: You'd be stretching up all the time.
S: But I could lie down.
M  Ah no. You're not supposed to lie down in the car. That's silly.
S: Hal does.

An implicit or explicit countering internal *but* was once again deployed here. It linked the adult's and the child's proposal, since the alternative step in the sequence was intended to replace rather than add to the parent's suggestion. And in the final move of the last text cited there is a further example of the argumentative strategy described earlier of challenging a generalization with a specific case.

All these final texts demonstrate that the capacity to control one's own and others' actions through argument depends on a shared understanding of activity sequences (knowing follows teaching, cars can be parked when no longer wanted, etc.), but also crucially on the ability to build on the addressee's statement, rather than tracking changes in the observable environment. Thus in both these kinds of texts, where alternative inferences are made or counter-suggestions are put forward, the monitoring and negotiation of everyday events has moved well beyond the post-protolanguage goal of interpreting individual observed events into linguistic structures.

## 3.4 Summary: 3;0 to 4;0 years

In Stephen's use of language to represent events in the fourth year, the most important developments involved the construal of norms of experience and the construction of argumentative moves based on understandings of those norms.

One continuity with the earlier language use was in the implicit and explicit use of comparison and contrast to help construe what is 'normal'. This was particularly evident in texts where the past and future actions of the interlocutors were compared with the present ones. Through this means, the different behaviours appropriate to different age groups could be inferred by Stephen, although he did not construe any such inferences into linguistic form. In achieving the relevant comparison, the use of a thematic *when* clause to provide a context for the 'distant' event being represented had become routine, building on the single occurrence of the previous year.

Stephen's expectations about the predictable actions of a participant or of particular sequences of events were made linguistically visible when he implicitly or explicitly compared the expected and the observed. The expression of counter-expectation, using interpersonal grammar, was another continuity with the previous year, one which led to a new use of OBLIGATION to construe normality (e.g. *it's supposed to wibble*) and also to the production of brief texts embodying an implicit external conjunctive link of counter-expectation (e.g. *the water was getting hot and (yet) it didn't get hot!*).

The expression of counter-expectation in these latter recountings of disrupted sequences was important in providing occasions when the adult would respond by supplying an explanation for the unexpected event. Stephen himself had indeed learned to expect that anomalous events would be explained in terms of a prior causing event and began to construe such causes himself for the first time, sometimes linking causally two sequent events that the adult saw as unrelated.

One of the most striking new developments in the fourth year involved the regular and explicit representation in language of many generalizations that were based on repeated observations of events. The majority of these generalizations (e.g. *horses gallop around; caterpillars could do poos*) were formulated as an additional reflection when his attention was caught by a particular participant and its current activity. To achieve this additional layer of reflection, the TENSE choice of simple present was regularly taken up in conjunction with generic participants and MODALITY systems were further developed. This latter development took the form of a new deployment of third-person Subjects in clauses modalized with *can* or *could* and a newly frequent use of USUALITY, together with the development of additional options within this system. In addition, to achieve the explicit generalization of activity sequences, new logico-semantic options were developed. These were an additional temporal meaning – that of general time ('whenever') realized by *when*, and that of condition, realized by *if*. The impetus to draw a general understanding from the particular case was in fact so strong at this time that Stephen also construed isolated single occurrences of an action or sequence as generalizations.

Whether Stephen's generalizations were construed on the basis of repeated experience or by inference from a single observation, he did on occasions 'over-generalize', and when this happened the more knowledgeable dialogue partner might cite a specific instance of experience to draw his attention to this fact. Stephen himself also did this, construing as problematic generalizations that he had himself formulated or which he had learned from adult talk, but which were then apparently contradicted by some witnessed instance. In these explorations new patterns of discourse were created in which challenging counter-evidence was introduced by means of an internal cohesive conjunctive relation realized by *but*. This expression of counter-expectation organized the text rhetorically in terms of the argument rather than experientially in terms of a sequence of construed activities.

Argument structures were also created when Stephen challenged an adult proposal by suggesting an alternative possible activity to that put forward by the addressee. Modal Finites were used in the verbal group to construe the hypotheticality of the proposition and the internal conjunctive *but* was again deployed by Stephen to bring his utterance into a challenging relation with the addressee's. Stephen's basis for offering an alternative was his now extensive 'background knowledge of the world' that enabled him to suggest alternative moves in a sequence rather than accepting the adult's construal. On other occasions, he also rehearsed such alternative possibilities cooperatively, using MODALITY and conditional relations to build a series of alternative construals.

## 4  Overview: the construal of material events from 2;6 to 4;0 years

This chapter has considered Stephen's linguistic construal of everyday knowledge in so far as that concerns relations between participants and processes and between one event and another. The focus has therefore been on the construal of field as it concerns the representation of event configurations and activity sequences rather than classificational and compositional taxonomies of things. Just as with the construal of taxonomies of things, however, the most striking developments between the third and fourth year can be interpreted as changes with respect to mode.

In very general terms, developments in the representation of field as activities took the route shown in Figure 4.1.

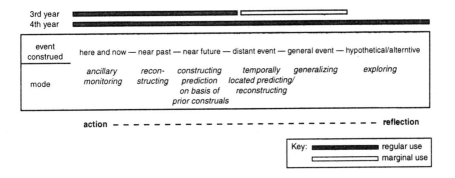

**Figure 4.1** Outline of developments with respect to mode in the representation of events

Figure 4.1 represents mode options in a simplified form as a continuum between action and reflection. It shows that the construal of an event in the third year took place principally in contexts where the linguistic representation either accompanied the action taking place or was temporally not far removed from it. In the fourth year, there was additionally a representation of events more distant in time or removed from time altogether in being generalized or hypothetical events. This developmental shift along the mode continuum was accompanied by developments in the linguistic system being called upon to create more constitutive texts.

The attempt to construct more distant events led to the experiential rather than logical realization of time. That is, time was realized as a circumstance within the clause structure, as part of the process rather than a relation between two processes. This occurred not only with adverbial realizations such as *yesterday* but in the hypotactic linking of two clauses, where the dependent clause introduced by *when* served to provide a location for the main clause construing an event (*when I'm grown up, will I pick you up and cuddle you?*). This shift from a sequencing to a locational use of *when* can be explained by the additional pressure placed on the language to represent not only the event but the context of its occurrence. This is because, in the representation of a distant event, a shared speaker/hearer temporal orientation needs to be constituted by the language in a way not called for when construing next or previous events.

The further moves towards the reflective end of the continuum occasioned a series of other developments all related to each other. The relevant reflective texts are described by Martin (1992a: 521) in the following terms:

> Generalising texts neutralise TENSE, DEIXIS and PERSON in order to construct social processes as potentials underlying and cutting across particular manifestations.

This characterization touches on the nature of these texts, which lies in their orientation towards field as system rather than as actualization, and suggests an explanation for repeated linguistic choices manifested in Stephen's speech of his fourth year. These were choices of [present] from the TENSE system or alternatively a preference for a Modal Finite rather than one selecting for TENSE. USUALITY options were another new development serving to remove the construal from any deictic location. These choices were taken together with that of [generic] from the REFERENCE system (thus removing any expression of DEIXIS from the nominal group) and/or the generalized pronoun *you* from the PERSON system.

In terms of Stephen's linguistic development, all these options were clearly associated with the move towards generalizing texts. Although the use of Modal Finites was certainly not new, it was only in his fourth year that third-person choices of ABILITY and OBLIGATION became prominent (e.g. *plastic plates could break; the stool is supposed to wibble*). Where third-person forms occurred in his third year, it was on occasions which were similarly oriented away from the immediate context of situation (*I can talk and Hal can talk and Daddy can talk*). Changes in the forms and uses of MODALITY are summarized in Table 4.4.[3]

**Table 4.4** Developments in Finite and Adjunct realizations of MODALITY 2;6 to 4 years

| MODALITY | 2;6 to 3 years | | 3 to 4 years | |
|---|---|---|---|---|
| | Finite, Adjunct forms | Uses | Additional Finite, Adjunct forms | Uses |
| PROBABILITY | *might* | negotiating, planning, predicting | *could, would, must('ve); maybe* | generalizing, explaining |
| OBLIGATION | *have (got) to; can/can't* (speech role Subjects) | negotiating | *should(n't); supposed to; allowed to* (3rd p. Subjects) | generalizing |
| | *not allowed to* (1 example 3rd p.) | recounting | | |
| | *should* (1 example 3rd p.) | counter-expectation | | |
| ABILITY | *can/can't* (speech role Subjects; 4 3rd p. examples) | reflecting on ability generalizing | *can, could* (mainly 3rd p. Subjects) | generalizing |
| USUALITY | *sometimes* (7 examples, mainly preview texts) | generalizing | *always, usually, never* | generalizing |

In addition to the developments in clause and group systems, there were parallel developments with respect to choices for linking clauses together. For example, the meaning of usuality within a sequence was achieved through a new use of *when* in its meaning of *whenever*, a development from its earlier use to construe a specific temporal sequence.[4] The meaning of obligation within a sequence was achieved through the development of *because* to join representations of temporally related events, construing them as necessarily linked in that sequence. And in the exploration of hypothetical events, the development of *if* enabled the linking of two events in a necessary sequence, with the additional meaning that the first event had status only as a possibility. The parallels between developments in clause and clause complex systems during the fourth year are summarized in Table 4.5.

**Table 4.5** Parallel developments in clause and clause complex systems in the construal of events

| | USUALITY | OBLIGATION | PROBABILITY |
|---|---|---|---|
| Clause | *always, some times . . .* | *should, supposed to* (3rd p.) | *could* (3rd p.), *maybe* |
| Clause complex | *whenever* | *because* | *if* |

When considering how children come to form the generalizations that may eventually be realized explicitly in these ways, this case study suggests that the deployment of comparison and contrast plays a crucial part. As illustrated from other case studies, this is a cognitive/semantic strategy used in the earliest stages of the mother tongue. It is from comparing instances that the child builds up a sense of what is normal, and it is a sense of what is normal that lies behind the ability to predict the way one event will follow another. It also underlies the expression of counter-expectation when an unlikely event configuration occurs (such as biscuits being smashed or Stephen kicking a ball right across the soccer pitch or hands becoming clean without first being soaped). In the expression of counter-expectation there is always an implied understanding of the way the world goes and this is built up by implicitly or explicitly comparing and contrasting different instances of experience. Thus comparison and contrast enables the development of temporal and concessive relations between clauses as well as the more explicitly generalizing relations shown in Table 4.5.

Figure 4.2 outlines the development of the external conjunctive links discussed in this chapter, showing how all those which generalize have drawn upon comparison and contrast relations.

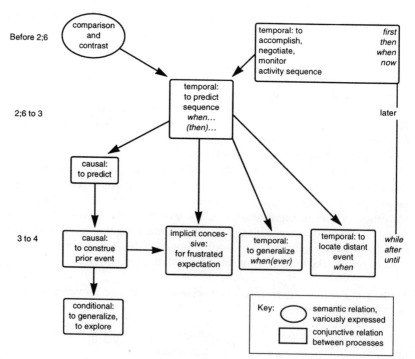

**Figure 4.2** Outline development of conjunctive relations between processes

Finally, in discussing other developments in Stephen's use of language which have been described in this chapter, it will be useful to elaborate the notion of 'constitutive' texts in a reflective mode, to make a distinction between texts which Martin (1992a: 517ff) calls 'field structured' or 'iconic' texts and those he terms 'genre structured' or 'non-iconic':

> One way to scale texts along this action/reflection dimension of mode is to take the activity sequences aspect of field as a base line and see to what extent texts are structured with respect to these sequences. Texts can then be divided into those organised primarily with respect to activity sequences (iconic texts) and those organised along different lines (non-iconic texts.)

The distinction being made is one between texts whose generic structure is provided by the activity sequences being construed (e.g. narrative, biography, instructions) and texts which are not organized around a sequence of events (e.g. expository texts such as book reviews and editorials).

The mode continuum of Figure 4.1 essentially outlines some principal options for iconic or field structured texts. However, one interesting characteristic of Stephen's language use over the period studied was his participation in texts structured along other lines. The 'preview' comparison and contrast texts in the third year provide one example of texts construing actions but structured in an alternative way to that of an activity sequence. When a single activity is repeatedly construed with alternative participants or circumstances substituted in succeeding utterances, there is no temporal link implied in the use of *and* (e.g. *babies go in the prams sometimes; and babies go in the shops; and babies go to the Easter Show sometimes*). The link is instead an (implicit) comparative one ('similarly'), whereby the utterances are organized according to a principle internal to the text, which does not reflect the construal of activities in terms of a script or sequence.

In Stephen's fourth year, a new non-iconic text-type was created in the exploration of the sometimes problematic relation between an event as an aspect of field potential and as an observed instantiation of that potential. Such texts manifested a rhetorical structuring in terms of counter-expectation, not in relation to a sequence of activities, but in relation to the previous speaker's assertion (e.g. *They go fast . . . – But that one doesn't go fast; Everybody only has one house – But on the TV they went to another house*). In the process of dialogue, Stephen used an explicit internal cohesive conjunction to organize the utterances textually rather than in terms of any activity sequence.

Thus at the same time as an internal causal link (*because*) was developing to enable Stephen to construe a relationship between a classifying utterance and a representation of the criteria which were relevant to it (see Chapter 3, Section 3.2.1), he was also developing an internal link to construe a rhetorical relation between a generalization and a counter-instance. In both cases, the development took place as a means of reflecting on the system or the potential which cuts across different manifestations. In the construal of events just as much as in the construal of things, then, Stephen was beginning to construe the meaning system itself as something to be reflected upon.

Table 3.6 (see page 135) can therefore be extended to include the further aspects of mode changes indicated in Table 4.6.

**Table 4.6** Developments in mode in the construal of events

| Language up to age 3 | New aspects of language after age 3 |
|---|---|
| Construe observed, recalled, predicted events; negotiate current actions | + explain events |
| Construe actual events | + construe generalizations |
| Focus on the actual | + focus on the potential |
| Organize sequences of events | + organize sequence of rhetorical moves |

The next chapter will explore this theme further by examining how Stephen represented semiosis directly as a process of his experience.

## Notes

1 Similar justifications were often given to Hal to explain 'favoured' treatment of the younger child.
2 The development and use of different realizations of causal and conditional linkers (including *that's why*) will be detailed in Chapter 6.
3 Mental process realizations of MODALITY will be discussed in Chapter 5.
4 See Chapter 3, Section 3.2.2, for its comparable use with classifying clauses at this time.

# 5 The construal of semiosis as process

This chapter describes Stephen's use of language to interpret the activity of symbolizing. In doing so, it takes further the description of the language in ways that relate to each of the previous chapters. On the one hand it will develop the theme of 'learning about language' that was shown to be an important aspect of the use of language to construe relationships of identification and classification. On the other hand it will extend the description of the previous chapter by continuing to describe Stephen's interpretation of experience as a world of activity. The events under attention now, however, are those of communicative rather than physical activity, and are represented by mental and verbal processes, rather than material ones. This means too that the most important logico-semantic relationships between one process and another to be considered here will be of quoting and reporting rather than of conjunctive relations.

## 1 Developmental background

Ontogenetically, the representation of communicative activity builds on the development of the informative function of language, which takes place in the 'transition' phase after the abandonment of protolanguage. As soon as a child moves into the mother tongue, he or she has a means of representing 'content', and so sharing a construal of experience with another person. Children do this from the beginning of the transition, talking about things both speaker and addressee are attending to and very soon also talking about things (or activities, etc.) from shared past experience. Initially, however, the possibility of offering the addressee a linguistic representation as a *substitute* for shared experience is not taken up immediately. In other words the child does not at first tell the addressee things they do not already know. As Halliday (1978b: 87) has pointed out, information is unlike other things negotiated by means of language, in being itself created by language and having no existence except by means of language. Because of this complex situation, it may be some time before infant talkers come to recognize that in addition to being a resource for semiotically monitoring or recreating shared experience, language can be used to create and make known hitherto unshared experience. That is, it may only be after some experience of exchanging linguistic meaning that children appreciate that, through the telling of unshared experience, new information or knowledge can be constructed for the addressee.

The emergence of the informative function is a critical development of the transition phase, and two children studied within a systemic framework both made apparent their consciousness of it by developing or adapting MOOD structures in an idiosyncratic way, specifically to signal that an utterance had the status of information being given (see Painter 1984: 252). At this early stage of development, then (at about 1;6 to 2;0), it was from their use of interpersonal resources that inferences could be made about the children's growing understandings of the nature of information and of speaker roles taken up during its exchange. The question to be explored here will be when and how the child *represents* such understandings linguistically.

Within the developmental literature as a whole, the issue of children's ability to think and talk about language arises under the topic of 'language awareness' (Sinclair *et al.* 1978) or 'metalinguistic abilities' (Hakes 1980). On these topics, investigations range from a consideration of children's spontaneous self-corrections (Clark 1978) to experimental studies of children's acceptability and grammaticality judgements (Gleitman *et al.* 1972; Pratt *et al.* 1984). The latter take their inspiration from the concerns of formalist linguistics, and are preoccupied with distinguishing 'syntactic competence' from comprehension of meaning, rather than with how children construe information exchange in speech.

Another relevant area of developmental research is that of children's 'theory of the mind', exploring when children come to construe other persons as intentional beings with their own thoughts, feelings and beliefs (Astington and Gopnik 1991; Astington 1994; Bartsch and Wellman 1995). Much of this research is not in fact linguistic in nature but comprises experimental work investigating children's ability to deceive others and to understand 'false belief' – for example by predicting where someone will look for an object which has been moved in their absence. The findings – that in comparison with 4-year-olds, '3-year-olds truly have a conceptual deficit' (Astington and Gopnik 1991: 11) – are often drawn from what children say in response to experimenters' questions, but the focus of attention is not on language as such.

However, within this field there are also researchers whose particular interest is in young children's early linguistic communications about the mental world. For example, Bretherton and her colleagues collated data from a number of studies to determine whether and what labelling of internal states takes place in infancy. They conclude (Bretherton *et al.* 1981: 356):

> From a theory of interfacible minds which is implicit in infants' first attempts at intentional communication at the end of the first year, young children progress

to an explicit, verbally expressible theory of mind that begins to emerge at the end of the second year. At this stage in their development, children become capable of exchanging verbal information about internal states as experienced by themselves and by others.

This work is not framed to distinguish between language which indirectly signals mental states (e.g. *Ooh!* might signal surprise) and instances more relevant to the concerns of this chapter, where language is used to directly represent mental processes (e.g. *Emma understood*). Nor could it present all the utterances reported in the context of the particular speaker's developing grammar, so it is not possible to assess such matters as which utterances come from rapid or slow developers or whether *I want* reported from any particular child is a genuine declarative mental process, or simply a baby imperative form. Nonetheless, one relatively firm conclusion which can be drawn from this study is that children talk about cognition later than they talk about perception or feelings. Bretherton *et al.* (1981: 350) observed that the only utterances in the mental domain recorded with any frequency were 'about seeing, wanting, hunger, fatigue and feeling pain'.

This pattern is corroborated by the longitudinal case study presented in Painter (1984). The data reported there show that by two years of age, Hal's vocabulary concerning semiotic activity included only *see, want* and *say*. Similarly, the research of Bartsch and Wellman (1995), using conversational data from ten children, found that 'the young child's construal of people may be bereft of a conception of thoughts and beliefs' (p. 111) since 'genuine reference to the subjective mental state of desire occurred around two years of age, much earlier than reference to beliefs' (Astington 1994: 82). It would seem, then, that in the very early stages of language development, there is little or no construction of knowing, understanding, believing, etc., as goings-on that can be represented linguistically. Despite the amount of learning taking place, the inner processes involved are not actively construed by the child's grammar during the transition phase.

The work of Wellman and Bartsch (1988, Bartsch and Wellman 1995) is also important in distinguishing between 'conversational' and 'psychological' uses of vocabulary for mental states in the conversations of ten children. This distinction was first made in an earlier study based on naturalistically collected data, which was carried out by Shatz, Wellman and Silber (1983) on the early uses of 'cognition verbs'. In this research, one longitudinal case study from 2;4 to 4 years was examined and supplemented with recordings from thirty two-year-olds. The authors distinguished between mental verbs used with 'conversational functions', as in *I think the car's outside*, and such verbs used experientially in 'reference to mental states', as in *they thought about the car*. (See further below, Section 2.1.) They found that in every case conversational uses preceded referential ('psychological') ones.

## 2 The grammar of semiosis

From a linguistic perspective, the representation of symbolizing activity involves the use of both mental and verbal process types, jointly referred to by Christian Matthiessen (1991) as 'symbolic processes'. Verbal processes represent the activity of saying (giving information) and mental processes the activity of construing (as when receiving information).

Adopting Halliday's perspective that the ideational resources of the language constitute a theory of experience, Matthiessen discusses the grammar of process types in the following way:

> The kind of 'world view' that emerges . . . is, not surprisingly, centred around human consciousness. The ideational metafunction draws a boundary between the domain of human conscious processing and what is outside this domain. (Matthiessen 1991: 83)

Matthiessen represents this diagrammatically as in Figure 5.1.

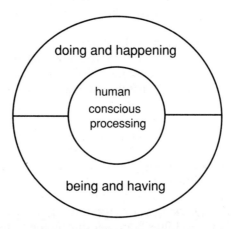

**Figure 5.1** 'The ideational centre of the universe of processes' (Matthiessen 1991: 84)

In Matthiessen's interpretation, following Halliday (1994), mental process clauses stand apart from other types with respect to their key characteristic of having a conscious nuclear participant. That is to say, one participant role – which Halliday terms 'Senser' – must be interpreted as being endowed with consciousness. This can be illustrated by Examples 5.1 and 5.2 below, where the second participant role of 'Phenomenon' (that which is 'sensed') is also labelled:

*Example 5.1*

| The woman | enjoyed | the movie |
|---|---|---|
| Senser | Mental | Phenomenon |

*Example 5.2*       *The movie*        *delighted*        *the woman*

| Phenomenon | Mental | Senser |
|---|---|---|

*Example 5.3*       *The train*        *regretted*        *the delay*

Clearly, an example such as 5.3 could only be made sense of by attributing consciousness to the train.

The clause as mental process construes 'inner' experience, the experience of consciousness. Matthiessen (1991: 83) describes it as follows:

> Human conscious processing is interpreted as a combination of a cognizant participant and conscious processing . . . it spans perception (seeing, hearing, feeling, etc.), cognition (thinking, knowing, believing, remembering, wondering, etc.), and affection (loving, hating, wanting . . . ).

There are thus three broad subclasses of mental process, as shown in Figure 5.2.

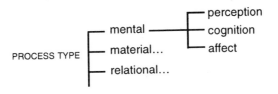

**Figure 5.2** Mental process choices in English

These subtypes of mental process share the grammatical characteristic of selecting 'simple' present as the unmarked choice of present tense as well as that of requiring a human (or conscious) participant.

Given the meanings they construe, the fact that mental processes require a conscious participant is in no way surprising, and one might expect that verbal processes, such as *say* or *tell*, would be like mental ones in respect of precisely this semantically natural grammatical characteristic. However, this is not the case; verbal processes do not require a conscious participant in the nuclear 'Sayer' role, as the following examples show (see Halliday 1994: 140):

*Example 5.4*       *The hall clock*        *says*        *it's three-thirty*

| Sayer | Verbal |
|---|---|

*Example 5.5*       *The barometer*     *warned*     *everyone*        *that a storm was likely*

| Sayer | Verbal | Receiver |
|---|---|---|

It follows, then, that mental and verbal processes are not grammatically aligned as 'human' processes. Instead, the grammar aligns humans with other symbol sources, such as clocks, barometers and books. This implies that the interpretation of experience inherent in English is not one where persons are construed primarily as animate beings along with other sentient creatures, but one where persons are interpreted primarily as semiotic sources:

> The human centre is in fact expanded, but the expansion is not along biological or cognitive lines to include our animate neighbours but rather along semiotic lines, to group us with documents, signs, instruments and so on as symbol sources. (Matthiessen 1991: 84)

The grammar does, however, treat mental and verbal processes as together forming a central domain, in that they both share the potential for 'projecting a situation as a semiotic construct' (Halliday 1994: Chapter 7.5). In other words, either a mental or a verbal process clause may be linked to a secondary clause through a relationship of quoting or reporting. Table 5.1 exemplifies this.

**Table 5.1** Examples of projection

| Type of process in projecting clause | Relationship to secondary clause | Example clause complex |
| --- | --- | --- |
| Verbal process | paratactic (quote) | *He said 'she is enjoying the movie'* |
| | hypotactic (report) | *He said that she was enjoying the movie* |
| Mental process | paratactic (quote) | *He thought 'she is enjoying the movie'* |
| | hypotactic (report) | *He thought she was enjoying the movie* |

Because of their shared capacity for projecting a secondary clause, Matthiessen (1991: 84) argues that mental and verbal processes together constitute the central domain of experiential meaning, which must be viewed as concerned with 'symbolic processing'. He extends the earlier figure to show this, and to include the grammatical characteristics of the two process types (see Figure 5.3).

As mentioned above, this interpretation, aligning mental and verbal processes, rests on their shared potential for 'projecting' a situation as a secondary clause. This is a potential not shared by material processes nor by the 'borderline' group of 'behavioural process' which construe semiosis as material activity (cf. Halliday 1994: 139). Behavioural processes, realized by verbs such as *watch, listen, meditate, laugh, talk* do require a conscious participant ('Behaver'), but in other respects are like material processes. That is, they adopt present-in-present (present continuous) as the unmarked present tense and they cannot project a secondary clause. These are the grammatical reflexes of their semantic status as processes which interpret semiosis as physical activity.

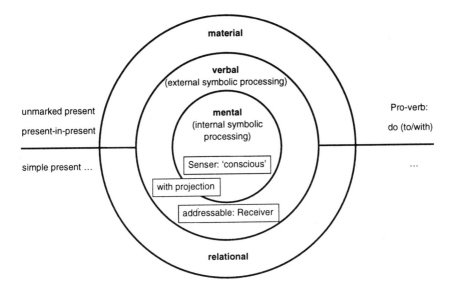

**Figure 5.3** Semiotic extension of human centre and corresponding grammatical categories (Matthiessen 1991: 87)

The relation of projection which distinguishes the mental and verbal processes from the behavioural type is described by Halliday (1994: 250) as being

> The logical-semantic relationship whereby a clause comes to function not as a direct representation of (non-linguistic) experience but as a representation of a (linguistic) representation.

This representation of a representation he terms a 'metaphenomenon':

> The projected clause . . . represents a second order phenomenon, something that is itself a representation. We will refer to this as a 'metaphenomenon'. (Halliday 1994: 252)

Thus through the relationship of projection, a secondary clause is instated as second-order representation, either a 'locution' (a construction of wording projected by a verbal process), or less directly as an 'idea' (a construction of meaning projected by a mental process). Table 5.2 illustrates the terminology.

**Table 5.2** Types of metaphenomena

| Projecting clause | Projected (secondary) clause | (Metaphenomenon type) |
|---|---|---|
| *He said* | *'That suit is a disgrace, Bill'* | locution (construction of wording) |
| *He thought* | *Bill's suit was a mess* | idea (construction of meaning) |

In summary, systemic theory argues that mental and verbal processes constitute a central domain of the grammar of English concerned with construing semiosis or 'symbolic processing'. The interpretation of reality inherent in this grammar is one in which knowing and telling are mutual processes, and in which knowledge is seen as emanating from human and non-human symbol sources alike.

### 2.1 Interpersonal grammatical metaphor

In addition, there are particular circumstances in which the symbolic processes function as a grammatical metaphor for interpersonal meanings – something which proves to be quite significant when the ontogenesis of this area of the grammar is explored. To explain this, reference can be made to Matthiessen's presentation of Halliday's argument that while semiosis is *represented* by means of symbolic and relational processes, it is *enacted* interpersonally as dialogue, in which the interactants can also intrude their affective and cognitive/modal attitudes.

> Semiosis is enacted inside dialogue by you & me, here & now; the rest of the world does not take part in this dialogic interaction – the outsiders, non-interactants, are 'they', 's/he' and 'it', the third person of traditional grammar . . . We can call the inside the **deictic centre** of the interpersonal universe since it serves as the frame of reference for various kind of deixis. (Matthiessen 1991: 92)

While enactments and representations are always coordinated by the clause grammar through the mapping of MOOD and TRANSITIVITY choices onto one another, it is also possible for them to 'coincide'. This occurs in a present tense construction of a mental or verbal process when one of the interactants ('I' or 'you') is construed as the participant (Senser/Sayer) in the transitivity structure, as in *I think (they are coming)*, or *I tell you (they are coming)*. In such a case, the structure constructs a double meaning. The mental or verbal process can be taken as an overt representation of the mental or verbal action that is necessarily going on, but it can also stand as a (grammatical) metaphor for an interpersonal meaning such as 'probably' or 'statement'.

Table 5.3, slightly abbreviated from Matthiessen's paper, exemplifies the kinds of utterances which constitute metaphorical representations of MODALITY and MOOD (cf. Halliday 1994: Chapter 10.4).

**Table 5.3** Metaphorical realizations of MOOD and MODALITY using symbolic processes

| Process | Speaker-oriented | Listener-oriented |
|---------|------------------|-------------------|
| Verbal | *I tell you* | *Tell me; could you tell me?* |
| Mental | | |
|    cognitive | *I wonder; I'd like to know;* | *Do you know?* |
| | *I think/believe/reckon* | *Do you think/ believe/ reckon?* |
|    affective | *I want you to* | *Do you want me to?* |

Halliday (1994: 354) argues that it is their status as interpersonal metaphors that explains the characteristics of these symbolic process clauses with respect to 'tagging'. In a clause complex, it is the primary (main) clause which construes the proposition being negotiated and so it is the primary clause whose Subject and Finite are repeated in the tag, as with *The fight didn't start before the police arrived, did it?* Since a projecting clause is the primary clause (with the projection a dependent one), it is normally the case that this projecting clause is the one whose Subject and Finite will be echoed in the tag, as with *The jurors might decide she is guilty, mightn't they?*

However, it has often been noted that first-person, present tense mental process clauses are not normally echoed by a question tag which repeats the Subject and Finite of the projecting process. For example, *I think he's coming, don't I?* is a marked structure only possible in certain constrained contexts of argument. Example (a) in Table 5.4 illustrates the way a question tag for such constructions will instead more normally relate to the secondary, projected clause.

**Table 5.4** Question tags with mental process clauses

| a | 1st person present tense: tag on projected clause | *I think he's coming, isn't he?* |
|---|---|---|
| b | 1st person past tense: tag on cognition clause | *I believed he was coming, didn't I?* |
| c | 3rd person pres. or past: tag on cognition clause | *His mother thinks he's coming, doesn't she?* |

Example (a), with the mental process in first person and present tense, differs from the others in that the apparently dependent clause carries the tag. This fact suggests that in such cases, the ideational meaning of a mental process gives way to, or coexists with, an interpretation where the projected clause is the proposition being negotiated (and therefore taggable). The mental process structure clause itself construes an interpersonal modal meaning, as shown in Example 5.6.

| *Example 5.6* | *I think* | *he* | *'s* | *coming* | *isn't* | *he?* |
|---|---|---|---|---|---|---|
| Interpersonal | Modal | Subject | Finite | Predicator | TagFinite | TagSubject |
| Experiential | | Senser | Mental Process | | | |

Thus, projecting processes may – when the deictic centre and the experiential représentation coincide – function as interpersonal grammatical metaphors of MOOD and MODALITY. The 'conversational uses' of mental verbs described by Shatz, Wellman and Silber (1983) will fall into this category of grammatical metaphors.

In sum, then, the theory of experience embodied in the ideational grammar argues for mental and verbal processes as a core realization of the construal of the inner and outer processes of symbolizing. At the same time, the interpersonal system of dialogue is based upon a fundamental role choice of giving and demanding with respect to two kinds of 'commodities' being negotiated: goods and services, or information (Halliday 1994: 68). To represent these roles experientially is to use mental and verbal processes to talk about persons as wanting or requesting something or as knowing, telling or asking. When the interactants in the current dialogue are represented in this way, the experiential grammar becomes a resource for metaphorically coding interpersonal meanings.

The rest of this chapter will describe Stephen's development of this area of the grammar, as a basis for considering his model of learning and the role of language within it. In the first place this will involve an exploration of how the roles taken up in the enactment of dialogue are represented using symbolic processes. Particular attention will be given to the representation of roles involved in information exchange, where a speaker who is telling adopts the role of 'primary knower' and assigns the addressee the role of 'secondary knower' (Berry 1981). As well as this, this account will show how the relation between external semiosis (saying) and internal semiosis (seeing, knowing) was enacted, discussed and problematized by Stephen during the period 2;6 to 5 years. Finally, the description will track the development of an understanding of non-human semiotic sources of knowledge.

## 3  Stephen's language 2;6 to 3;0 years

By the first period with which this study is concerned (2;6 to 3 years), semiotic activity was already being construed by Stephen both as physical behaviour (using behavioural processes) and also as symbolic processing (using mental and verbal types). In fact, all three mental process types (perception, cognition, affect) are attested in Stephen's language from this period, together with various verbal process realizations, such as *say*, *ask*, *shout* and *tell*. Despite this, there was only a limited construal of the domain of symbolic processing by Stephen up to the age of three years. This is because mental processes were restricted with respect to realizations of the Senser role while verbal processes projected locutions only in certain kinds of contexts. These limitations will be described and discussed in more detail below, beginning with an account of the use of mental processes and moving to a consideration of verbal processes and the projection of locutions.

### 3.1  Representing the interactants: affect and cognition processes

All three kinds of Mental process clause (cognition, perception, affect) can serve to construe the dialogic process of exchanging knowledge or exchanging goods and services. Information can be represented as known or perceived (or not) in the process of its exchange, and goods and services can be desired (or not). And during the period up to three years, most occurrences of mental processes were in fact concerned with construing the dialogic interactants – that is, they were largely constructed with speech-role (I/you) pronouns as Senser. Only one instance of a third-person cognition clause was recorded and there were no third-person mental processes of perception. At this stage, it was only mental processes of affect that were involved in the construal of third parties outside the deictic centre of dialogic exchange. Stephen's speech was by no means unusual in this, and Bretherton *et al.*'s (1981) collation of data from different sources shows a similar pattern, with third-person Sensers being especially infrequent for perception and cognition clauses.

In Stephen's language, moreover, the overwhelmingly frequent choice for the Senser was in fact the first-person pronoun used in present tense constructions, which allows the clauses to be interpreted as metaphorical realizations of interpersonal choices (as 'conversational' uses in Shatz, Wellman and Silber's terms). For example, an *I want* clause, easily the most frequent realization of [affect], can be read as an 'indirect command' of '(you) let me' or '(you) do' rather than simply as an experiential representation of the speaker's desire. The following text illustrates this.

2;10;7   (M chuckles at something S has said)
      S:  Don't say that.
      M:  Don't say what?
      S:  Laugh . . .
          I don't want you to laugh.

This conversation was concerned with negotiating action (albeit semiotic action) rather than exchanging information. And the move from a direct imperative *Don't say that* to the formulation *I don't want you to laugh* confirms both the meaning of the latter and its metaphorical status (since Stephen clearly had an alternative congruent (imperative) realization for a command).

Similarly, the most frequent cognition process in Stephen's conversation, a projecting *I think* clause, as in *I think the left [seat belt] is best,* can be viewed as a metaphorical choice of PROBABILITY. (Congruent representations of PROBABILITY were already available with the modal verb *might* and the modal adverb *maybe.*) This metaphorical manner of construing MODALITY appears to underlie most of the early use of cognition processes. Thus, while it is true that in these clauses the child does construe himself as a thinker and the information he is giving as a representation of his thought, the interpersonal meaning of modal assessment appears to be more important than any explicit reflection on the processes of consciousness.

Unfortunately, there were no recorded occasions where Stephen tagged the projected clause in the utterance (e.g. *I think **the left is best, isn't it?**). In such a case there would be clear evidence that the proposition being negotiated was that of the projected dependent clause and the metaphorical status of the *I think* would be unequivocal. Nevertheless, the elliptical responses by the addressee in the following examples come close to having the same effect:

2;8;3     M:  Where's the blue cup?
          S:  I expect Daddy's got it.
          M:  Has he?

2;8;23    S:  I think my jean has got pocket.
          M:  Your jeans have, yes.

On other occasions the mental process experientialized an intention which Stephen recognized might need to be negotiated with the addressee:

2;8;15    (M and S reading. M offers to write S's name in book)
          M:  Oh, I haven't got a pen; we'll write it on later, darling.
          S:  (getting up) I think I will get one.
          M:  Right, you get a pen.

2;8;20    (S interrupts game with M)
          S:  I think I do the piano [= toy keyboard].
          M:  Oh, right, good idea.

Supporting an interpretation of these latter utterances as interpersonal metaphors is the fact that on other comparable occasions a modal Adjunct, *just* (see Halliday 1994: 82), appeared to function in a very similar way to *I think*. That is, it functioned to head off an interpretation of the speaker's intention as non-compliant:

2;7;1     (M and S are in S's messy room)
          M:  Shall we fix up these puzzles?
          S:  I'm just going to show these to Hal.
          M:  All right, but he's watching television now, you know.
          S:  (going to door) I'm just going to show them to Hal.

2;8;20    M:  You ready for bath, my darling boy?
          S:  No.
          M:  No?
          S:  I just want to – read – read books just a minute; I just want to read books.

During the early period, then, Stephen's mental processes were more concerned with negotiating information or action than with construing himself as a learner. As was the case with Shatz *et al.*'s (1983) subjects and those of Bartsch and Wellman (1995), interpersonal uses preceded experiential ones. In fact it would seem that the representation of mental processes arises in order to extend the interpersonal resources of MOOD and MODALITY, rather than for representational purposes. Nonetheless, in being 'metaphorical', the representation of the self as participating in a mental process was still one aspect of the meaning created. These interpersonally oriented utterances can therefore provide an entry point for the more reflective, ideationally focused construals of cognition which began to emerge in the third year and which will be discussed shortly.

There may well be a stronger experiential point to representing the self as a cognition Senser when that involves construing oneself explicitly as a non-knower in the course of dialogue, when unable to respond as requested:

2;8;20   M:   Where's Catherine's one?
         S:   I don't know [where Catherine's one is].

Once the nature of dialogue has been understood, it is no longer appropriate for children simply to choose to remain silent when they have been assigned the role of primary knower. So, when unable to answer, Stephen needed to respond by construing himself as lacking knowledge, with *I don't know*. Again, however, it could be argued that the most important thing achieved here is the management of the immediate interpersonal negotiation, which requires the giving or disclaiming of information to count as a compliant response. Thus the experiential meaning – the explicit representation of himself in the role of cognition Senser – functions primarily to achieve the enactment of dialogue rather than any reflection upon it. (Shatz, Wellman and Silber (1983) found this was one of the earliest uses of mental processes and classed it as a conversational rather than referential function.)

However, in the parent talk, especially that centred on story-reading, there was considerable use of cognition processes to represent Stephen as a knower or potential knower, and here the experiential strand to the meaning was much more foregrounded. For example:

2;7;1    M:   (reading) '"Your shadow!" chuckled Trumpet.' (turns to S)
              Do you know what a shadow is?
         S:   (quietly) Mm.
         M:   You see my shadow, here on the book? See that? . . .
              . . .
         M:   And do you know what Growl was frightened of? He was
              frightened of his own face in the mirror.

*Do you know?* often functions as a grammatical metaphor for an offer of information, when the addressee is assumed not to know, as in *Do you know what Growl was frightened of?* (standing for 'I'm going to tell you what Growl was frightened of'). Alternatively, *do you know?* can function as an 'indirect question' as in *Do you know what a shadow is?*, in which case the proposition being negotiated is the projection – in this example *what's a shadow?* On these latter occasions the adult reader was genuinely concerned with Stephen's knowledge, so the experiential meaning was an important strand. But at the same time, Stephen's murmured assent was not taken as evidence of his being a knower unless he also responded to the projection (i.e. explained what a shadow was in this case). The metaphorical structure thus had the flexibility of allowing Stephen to take it at 'face value' as a request for confirmation (requiring no display of knowledge), while allowing his mother to mean it as an indirect question, and if necessary to treat it retrospectively as an offer of information.

### 3.1.1 Reflection on changing knowledge

As far as Stephen's own construal of himself into the Senser role is concerned, the most important development during this initial period was the use of *I thought* to acknowledge new information which called for a reconsideration of his previous understanding. In such a case construing himself as a Senser does seem to have a clear ideational motivation. (Again, Stephen's use of language here is similar to that of two-and-a-half-year-old to 3-year-old subjects reported in Bretherton *et al.* (1981).)

Occasionally *I thought* was used simply when observational experience did not match expectations, as when a bowl previously only used for jelly turned out to have fruit in:

2;10;4   S:   It should be jelly! I thought it jelly!

However, usually the context was learning from text, as in the next example:

2;10;14   S:   I'm two and a half and-
          M:   Oh, you're two and a half, yeah, and Hal's seven.
          S:   No, Hal's four.
          M:   No, he's seven.
          S:   Oh, seven. I thought he's four.

Where the acknowledgement of information is concerned, a speaker need do no more than offer a minor clause (*oh*) or respond with non-verbal signals, so when Stephen began to acknowledge information received by projecting his 'understanding-till-now' using *I thought*, it was not simply to achieve a dialogic exchange, but served an experiential function. He was articulating his own previous understanding, constructing it in the process as a mental representation – as a meaning that contrasted with the meaning-in-wording that had just been offered him.

So although Stephen rarely reflected on other people's cognitions, he occasionally represented himself as without relevant knowledge, and had begun quite frequently to reflect consciously on his own changing state of knowledge. It is as though in doing this he was for the first time explicitly construing himself as a learner. Thus at the same time as he was, through the use of *call* (e.g. *what's that called?*), developing a way of talking about naming rather than simply engaging in naming, he was – through the use of this 'distanced' (past tense) mental process – stepping back and addressing his changing interpretations rather than simply engaging in the talk which adapted his knowledge. And, although he did not explicitly talk about this fact, his interpretation was changing because of the verbal interaction just engaged in: when he was explicit about reconstructing his knowledge it was on the basis of what he had been told much more frequently than on the basis of what he had observed.

### 3.2 Seeing/being told as ways of knowing

In addition to representing oneself as a learner by means of a cognition process as described above, perception processes can be used to construe information-receiving (*I see*) and verbal processes to construe information-giving (*I tell you*), when these are used with speech role pronouns.

Perception processes can construct either an entity or an action into the Phenomenon role, as in Examples 5.7a–b, taken from Stephen's speech.

*Example 5.7a*

| I | saw | a big lizard |
|---|---|---|
| Senser | | Phenomenon:Thing (nominal gp) |

*Example 5.7b*

| See | | [[my lips move]] |
|---|---|---|
| | | Phenomenon:Act (rankshifted clause) |

But in addition, perception processes can link to a secondary clause through the relation of projection. With himself identified as the Senser, Stephen on two recorded occasions projected a metaphenomenon using *see*:

2;8;22　(M and S are playing near window to street. S looks out)
　　　　S:　Where's Sarah [=child neighbour]?
　　　　M:　I don't know, Sweetie.
　　　　S:　I think I'll go and see if there's Sarah there.

2;10;23　(S talking about putting toy boat in bath)
　　　　S:　I want to see (gropes for words) it floats. I want to see does it float.

These can be analysed as shown in Example 5.8.

*Example 5.8*   *I'll go and see*          *if there's Sarah there*
                *I want to see*           *does it float*

| Projecting clause | Projection:Idea |
|---|---|

When a perception process is used this way, it gains a cognition meaning and could be glossed with *find out, ascertain*, or some other verb belonging clearly to a cognition set. What is interesting about these early examples, however, is that the literal perception meaning was also there for Stephen, since he was talking about ascertaining by seeing with his eyes. This means that the representation of himself as Senser, in these instances, was as one who learns from observation.

At this stage, while he did of course engage continually in verbal enquiry as a means of finding things out, he did not actually talk about this as a means of knowing. The nearest Stephen came to commenting on verbal exchange as a means of knowing was over a period of a week or two during which he became particular about who was being informed by his own telling. He represented his intended addressee explicitly in the role of Receiver in the TRANSITIVITY structure in these cases:

2;9;8   (in car. S makes a remark. F is not listening and M begins to respond)
        S:  No [= you don't answer], I'm just telling to Daddy.

Stephen's utterance can be analysed experientially as follows:

*Example 5.9*          *I'm just telling to Daddy*

| Sayer | ... | Verbal | Receiver |
|---|---|---|---|

Sometimes, indeed, Stephen appeared to assume that a hearer could not be construed as a knower unless specifically addressed:

2;9;13  (in park. H offers to kick ball with S, who is delighted)
        S:  (looks round at M, then to Hal) I'm just going to tell Mummy. (to M, standing alongside) Hal's going to kick the ball with me.
        M:  Oh, is he? Lovely.

As discussed earlier, when the informative function of language is first understood, information-giving utterances may be marked in some way and/or the dialogue roles of giver and receiver of information may be rehearsed and reflected on in role-play. After this, understanding of the mutuality between telling and knowing appears to become taken for granted, naturalized, unproblematic and unexplored. These few texts,

where the Receiver role gains prominence as an experiential representation of the secondary knower (information-receiver) in the dialogue,
not only provide evidence for Stephen's thorough understanding of the
informative function of language, but perhaps provide a hint that he
would soon begin reflecting more explicitly on the telling–knowing nexus.

There was one further occasion that also suggested that he was
beginning to reflect on the importance of talking as a means of coming to
know. Over breakfast one day, he was addressed as follows:

2;7;17     (at breakfast, M and F talk about height of tree in garden. S
           thinks something is happening outside and cranes his neck and
           rises to see)
           M:  There's nothing to see; sit down, darling, there's nothing to
               see, we're just talking.

Later in the day Stephen talked over with his mother a proposition of
concern to him (see pp. 200–1 for this text) and successfully clarified his
understandings. As the conversation concluded and they entered the
room where Stephen's father was, Stephen remarked *We're just talking,
Daddy*. This (surprising) remark echoes the occasion from earlier in the
day when Stephen was excluded by not understanding the conversation,
and could be interpreted as an attempt by him to represent the fact that
he was this time an insider to the talk, gaining information to which F, the
third party, was not privy. However, if this was the case, the text was unique
at the time in construing a relation between learning and talking.

### 3.3 Representing the interactants as Sayers

While Stephen's awareness of the informative function of language is
attested by his use of *tell* in the previous examples, it was not *telling* but
*saying* which was the process foregrounded in his speech during the first
period. When the dialogue interactants were represented as engaging in
outer semiotic processing, Stephen was concerned with the 'correctness'
of their manner of saying rather than with any relationship between telling
and knowing.

When representing himself in the role of Sayer, Stephen was most often
concerned with pronunciation, as in the following examples:

2;7;20     M:  Little boys spill it by accident.
           S:  Only little boys have accident. I can say 'accident'!

2;8;20     S:  I can't say that properly . . . can you say it properly?

2;9;6      M:  Are you ready for brekkie?
           S:  No. Br-r-r-eak-fast; say it properly.

Another concern of Stephen's when representing the interactants as Sayers was with their expression of the ritual wording associated with written texts. After a period of declaiming *one day* each time he turned the page of a story book, he began to switch to *once upon(s) a time*. Sometimes he reminded himself of the appropriate phrase:

2;9;2     (S opens book)
          S:   (to self) Say 'Once upon a time'; not going to say 'One day'.

At other times he corrected others:

2;9;5     M:   (reading) 'One day'-
          S:   No; say 'Once upons a time'.

Stephen's focus on such occasions was not on how saying impinges on knowing but rather on written text as being invariant, on the story as being a text object and perhaps on the wording itself as being authoritative. Coming to view written texts in these ways is likely to have an important bearing later on his orientation to knowledge, but at this stage there appears no close connection between this attention to saying and any reflection on meaning or knowing.

### 3.4 Representing others as symbolizers

### 3.4.1 Third parties as Sensers

While all mental process types are found in the data from Stephen's third year, only with the affect type was there any variety in the realizations of the Senser role. For this group (realized by *want* or *like*), there were third-person, as well as speech role, realizations of the Senser role (e.g. *Katy likes me*). However, apart from a single exceptional case, there were only speech role realizations of the Senser for perception and cognition processes.

Given that the Senser role in such clauses construes a person as a perceiver or thinker, the lack of third-person examples suggests that the perceptions and consciousness of others are not initially salient to the child learner. This is not of course to deny that the child's behaviour from a much earlier age implies that other people are accepted as endowed with sensory and cognitive qualities, such as memory, or the ability to perceive. (For example, as suggested by Bretherton *et al.* (1981), a child who talks at all is treating the addressee as endowed with hearing.) However, since Stephen, like the subjects of other case studies, only rarely at this stage used language to construe other people in the role of a perceiving or cognizing Senser, it seems that even in the second half of the third year, language was not used to explore the consciousness of others by representing other persons in this role.

Of course, as discussed in the introduction to this chapter, the inner world of other people can become visible by being manifested as activity, which can be construed by behavioural processes, 'corresponding' to verbal and mental ones, but even here the mental behaviourals were not deployed entirely freely. Cognition examples were entirely absent, while perception behaviourals were quite frequent, but mainly in the negotiation of action, with speech role participants (e.g. *Watch my legs*). As with the true mental processes, only affect behaviourals were used more reflectively with third-person participants. This is seen in the following text, where Stephen commented on his brother's reaction by interpreting him as a Behaver:

2;9      (S watching M dry herself after shower)
         S:   What's that (pointing)?
         M:   That's my belly button.
         S:   Hal <u>laughs at</u> belly button.
         M:   Does he? He thinks they're funny does he?

In sum, of the categories of inner semiotic behaviour construed by English grammar, only affect processes had come to Stephen's attention as observable activity carried out by third parties. In general it can be said that third parties were not construed as beings with thoughts and perceptions but were represented as having emotions. When this occurred, however, it was more often their outward activity (behaviour) rather than their inner (mental) processing that evoked comment.

There was, however, one instance of a third-person mental process of cognition which constituted an exception to the generalization which has just been made concerning Stephen's construal of other persons as symbolizers. The occasion was when M arrived home one evening and Stephen began to share with her what had happened in her absence:

2;8;4    (S sitting in pyjamas at his desk drawing, starts talking excitedly)
         S:   (? inaudible . . .) Daddy thought it was bedtime!
         M:   Did he?
         S:   Mm, and I thought it's bathtime!!

While it was not unusual for Stephen to quote (or less often to report) what someone had said as part of a recount of personal experience, this occasion was exceptional in that he chose to reconstruct the verbal events, not by replaying the wordings of the time, but reporting them further 'semioticized' as an Idea. Thus the focus was not on saying as an activity to be reported (see further below) but on the meanings that were exchanged. And this arose surely because of the disparity in the interpretations of the two parties in this case. So just as the *I thought* projections were occasioned by a reflection on the disparity between current information and previous understanding, the conflict of

interpretations underlying this text was the source of its being reconstructed in this way. In its representation of the consciousness of a third
party (*Daddy thought*) and in the reporting of meaning in the context of
recounting, this text previews much later developments and it remained
an exception in this first period.

### 3.4.2 Third parties as Sayers

Verbal processes, which construe the outer form of symbolizing, had no
restriction on the realization of the Sayer role, and third parties were
frequently construed as engaging in external forms of symbolizing. The
principal context for this was when Stephen quoted the speech of others,
either when including dialogue in his attempt to construct a story from a
picture book or when recounting some incident of personal past
experience in which a saying was one of the events recalled. Brief
examples follow:

2;7;16    (S 'reading' *Mr Bump* by himself from the pictures)
    S:    . . . and there's the stick and the dog comes and says 'You
    all right?'

2;7;16    (S 'reading' a familiar story, *Baby's Birthday*, by himself)
    S:    Um. 'He's saying "Wake up, baby" . . . and dressed up and
    he makes the cake and he wears birthday hat . . . and he says
    (sings) "Happy birthday to baby, happy birthday to you".'

2;10;7    (S talking of day at childcare centre)
    S:    We went in there and Sally said 'There's babies asleep'.

All these excerpts are typical in that they favoured incorporating the
dialogue into the story by means of a paratactic projection of a wording.
The construal of saying in these cases was in the context of narrating a
variety of events and it would seem that the projecting sequences counted
as just one of the activities in the sequence being constructed in language.
Earlier systemic studies (Halliday 1975, Painter 1986) show that
quoting of speech in the context of reconstructing past experience occurs
very early in children's language use, and initially without any projecting
clause. What was noticeable in this data set was that even after the
development of projection, illustrated above, salient sayings that Stephen
wished to reflect on were not presented as metaphenomena. This is
illustrated in the following example:

2;7;17    (evening. S is being dried after bath)
    S:    Big boys don't cry.
    M:    No, big boys like Stephen don't cry.
    S:    Hal cry.

M:  Yes, Hal cries sometimes. Well, everybody cries sometimes.
S:  (remembering hurting M's bare foot the previous day??)
    Somebody might step on somebody's toes.
M:  Oh yes, and then they might cry. Even Mummy cries then.
S:  Yes, even Mummy cries.
(they go through kitchen where F is busy)
S:  (to F) We're just talking, Daddy.[1]

*Big boys don't cry* was an expression used sometimes by staff at the childcare centre Stephen attended, and when uttered by Stephen here it had no application to the ongoing context. From the way he developed the dialogue it is clear that he was reconsidering this expression and its validity in relation to his own experience (since big brother Hal cried quite often). However, although Stephen projected locutions when narrating events he introduced this text into the current context as though it were his own construal. That is, he did not project it as someone else's locution. It appears that at this period, talking about people saying things occurred in the context of recounting what they did rather than reflecting on the validity of what they said.

*3.5 Non-human semiotic sources as Sayers*

A key characteristic of symbolic processing which was discussed in the introduction concerns the expansion of the Sayer role to include non-human semiotic sources. In exploring the extent to which non-human Sayers were represented in this early period, it emerges that it was through the alignment of relational processes with verbal ones that this expansion of conscious processing took place. This was possible because, alongside the use of *say* with a personal Sayer, this period after age two-and-a-half saw the first use of *say* as a relational clause.

In principle, there are clear grammatical differences between verbal processes and identifying processes, reflecting their different domains. The former construe the activity of communicating, while the latter are concerned with relations of identity. But as Martin and Matthiessen (1991) point out, there can be an overlap between the two domains when the identification relation concerns forms of symbolization. They represent the overlap in terms of the top right to bottom left axis on Figure 5.4.

In Stephen's life, the overlap between verbal and identifying processes occurred first when he began to interpret graphic symbols. On the first recorded occasion the identity relation was foregrounded as he appeared to be linking an exophorically indicated symbol with a spoken equivalent, by using *same as*:[2]

2;7;1    S:    That's (?same as) Daddy.

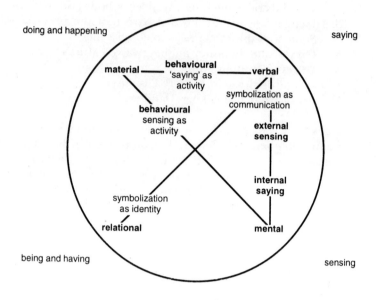

**Figure 5.4** Semantic terrain of process types (from Martin and Matthiessen 1991: 372)

Many other relational examples occurred at that time:

2;7;2    S:    (pointing at letters and symbols fairly randomly on title page) That's Daddy and that's Hal.

Then after a few weeks Stephen began to use *say* to indicate the identity relation:

2;7;13    (S and M looking at *Peter Rabbit* story book together)
          S:    (pointing to a random word) That says Peter Rabbit.

2;7;19    S:    (pointing to shopping bag with an S on) That says Stephen?
          M:    No, that says Food Plus; that's the name of the shop.

The next example was recorded with pen and paper, but the record notes that he adapted his intonation so as to quote the final word:

2;6;24    (M asks S to pass her a particular jar from shelf)
          M:    The blue jar with the yellow label.
          S:    Oh there; it's got words on; (?      ) says 'shop'.

In this case, the sign source (although possibly omitted from the clause structure) appears to have been construed as a Sayer in a verbal process. This interpretation of a sign source as a Sayer was clearly modelled for Stephen in the following conversation, which occurred when the car stopped at a junction and Stephen attended to the signs facing them (depicted in Figure 5.5).

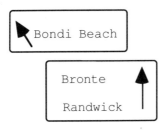

**Figure 5.5** Road signs discussed by Stephen (2;10;7)

This gave rise to the following conversation:

2;10;7    (driving, they reach a fork with a number of direction signs)
        S:    Oh, what's that there on the picture?
        M:    Where?
        S:    There.
        M:    Up on the sign?
        S:    Mmm.
        M:    That says 'Bronte over there' (points Bronte-wards).
        S:    Oh, and that says Bronte and that says Bronte (pointing at each sign).
        M:    No, that one says Bondi.
        S:    Oh. <u>That</u> one says Bronte.
        M:    Mm, the big one says Bronte and the top one says Bondi.

In one sense these utterances by Stephen using *say* simply expand the relational process options, as shown in Figure 5.6.

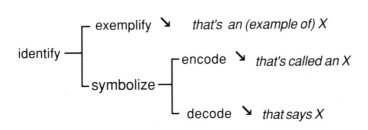

**Figure 5.6** Options for identifying

In support of this view is the fact that a structure like *That one says Bronte* spoken by Stephen here is of a comparable form to Stephen's other relational:identifying processes (see Chapter 3, Section 2.1). That is, it has in the Token role an exophoric Deictic which is interpreted by reference to some visible material entity, as shown in Example 5.10.

*Example 5.10*

| That | 's | an X |
| That | 's called | an X |
| That | says | X |
| Token | Identifying | Value |

However, it is noticeable that in the parent talk of the previous conversation there was a smearing of the verbal and relational meanings. While the road sign did not, of course, have 'Bronte over there' written on it, M chose to construct it into the role of Sayer projecting a locution as a way of clarifying the function of the traffic sign.

*Example 5.11*

| That | says | *'Bronte over there'* |
| Sayer | Verbal | projected locution |

One natural response to such data is to consider whether the original categorization of process types is faulty. However, Martin and Matthiessen (1991) demonstrate with numerous examples that almost any typological distinction which can be found in the linguistic system (such as process type categories) will prove to have areas of tension due to what they call 'topological' considerations. That is, subcategories which belong to distinct typological groups according to differentiating criteria may nonetheless be close to each other across a typological boundary because of their degrees of proximity within a shared semantic space. In this case, the shared semantic space is that of symbolizing, which can be construed by the language as communication (using verbal processes) or as identity of one thing with another (using identifying relational processes) (see Figure 5.4 above).

This accounts for there being, in Matthiessen's words,

> a similarity in the relationship between the projecting . . . and the projected . . . in the environment of saying . . . and the Token and the Value . . . in the environment of being. (Matthiessen 1991: 89)

Thus, there is a clear typological difference between Examples 5.12 a and b:

*Example 5.12a*

| The teacher | said | *the children must bring their lunches* |
| Sayer | Verbal | projected locution |

*Example 5.12b*

| The teacher | is | the best guide |
|---|---|---|
| Token | Relational | Value |

However, there is a blending of the two meanings in Example 5.13:

*Example 5.13*

| The sign | says | Bronte |
|---|---|---|
| Sayer | Verbal | Locution |
| Token | Relational | Value |

This is not grammatical metaphor – one meaning on the surface and another meaning lying behind it – but rather an overdetermination of the meaning. This particular overdetermination is discussed by Matthiessen in his consideration of the resources of English for construing semiosis. He states:

> Projecting onto another order of reality, semiotic reality, is like assigning a Value to a Token in a symbolic relationship. (Matthiessen 1991: 89)

This argument appears to be borne out by these developmental examples, which perhaps also suggest some of the contextual pressures which encourage the grammar 'to elaborate its options in ways such that divergent choices come to resemble each other' (Martin and Matthiessen 1991: 379). In this case the mother's goal was not simply to 'read' the sign, construing an identity relation between the graphic symbol and a wording or meaning. She aimed additionally to make visible to the child two further things: one was the fact that the sign is a semiotic source and the other was that the information it conveys is not simply the wording or meaning of the place name written on it but an indication of where the corresponding place is to be found. The simplest way to alert the child to all this without engaging in overt 'explanation' of how a road sign works was to construct the sign as a Sayer which quoted its two meanings of place and direction in the form of a locution. In this way the parent could be said to have exploited the topological parameters of the language to operate in the child's zone of proximal development.

In brief, then, experience with language in its written form led Stephen to construe a relation of identity – of 'stands for' or 'same as' – between written symbols and wordings. In the interactions which helped to reveal this symbolizing relation, the parent implicitly equated communicating and symbolizing. It appears that by this means Stephen was being guided towards an apprehension of the sources of written language as communicating meaning in a comparable way to the human speakers of his experience so far – an understanding that will be of crucial importance for the successful achievement of literacy in school.

*3.6 Summary: 2;6 to 3;0 years*

The picture of the child as learner in his third year is of one who was experienced in exchanging information, but was only just beginning to use his experiential resources to reflect upon himself as a learner whose state of knowledge was changing. When he did so, he might use *I thought* to instate his 'knowledge up till now' as a meaning (a metaphenomenon) to be reflected on. Apart from this, projection of meaning was engaged in primarily for interpersonal goals, either to negotiate action (using *I want*) or to negotiate modality/intention (using *I think*).

Even when the reorganization of his own knowledge was explicitly reflected on, using *I thought . . .,* the role of the talk in precipitating that change was not. Moreover, he did not *talk about* asking people things in order to find out, even though he was so much engaged in doing this. Nonetheless he did specify his own lack of knowledge when a dialogic response made this necessary (using *I don't know*) and he did occasionally hint that information was only available to those specifically addressed (*I'm just going to tell Mummy*).

Although the inner consciousness of others was not explored through language, an impetus in this direction arose when stated interpretations directly conflicted. It was often a conflict between the current construal of information by the addressee and his own understanding which led to the latter being construed as a metaphenomenon for public reflection (projected by *I thought*), as mentioned above. Moreover, the recounting of a particular occasion of conflicting interpretations led to the only recorded construal of a third party as cognizant Senser, with the construction of the two conflicting interpretations as projected metaphenomena (*Daddy thought, I thought*). Thus the ongoing attempt to interpret experience 'rightly' – in a way that made sense to him and was consonant with the interpretations of authoritative others – led to occasional reflection on the interpretations themselves rather than simply on the material phenomena being construed.

In general, however, this period can be characterized as one in which talking about knowing and telling was not dominant and in which exploration of problematic texts remained implicit. That is, when Stephen wished to use the addressee to help him reflect on a problematic text, this was not done by 'discussing' what someone had said. Instead the problematic text (such as *big boys don't cry*) would be instated not as a projection but as a 'first order' representation – as Stephen's own construal.

When the texts of others were reinstated as locutions, by being quoted or reported, it was during the narration of stories or the reconstruction of personal experience. And on these occasions, there appeared to be little differentiation between a verbal and a material activity as an event to be recounted. Nonetheless, in being projected, those texts were made available to be reflected upon and shared, just as were the reconstructions of material experiences.

Stephen also used verbal projection to instate a ritual wording (*once upon a time*) as a characteristic of written stories, an initial strategy for reflecting on the nature of written texts. This suggests that he had begun to conceptualize the written text as a source of invariant wording, an understanding that is fundamental in discriminating between the 'reading' of written and other visual symbols, such as pictures. Moreover, the adult, in negotiating written texts with Stephen, used mental projection to foreground the reader's role as a knower/thinker (or non-knower) in relation to the propositions in the text, thereby also contributing to the child's model of what a written text is. And a final effect of experience with non-human symbol sources – including notices, signs and advertisements as well as books – was the blending of identifying and verbal processes, allowing for the eventual extension of grammatical 'saying' to non-animate semiotic sources. In this process, only just beginning, an understanding of written texts as sources of meaning was necessarily being created.

The third year of life was therefore characterized by little representation of the processes of semiosis as a means of reflecting upon them, apart from reporting verbalizations as part of an activity sequence. Nonetheless the use of *I thought* provided the basis for exploring information as metaphenomenal in character, the use of the Receiver role suggested more conscious attention being given to the nature of information exchange and a number of small moves were made which contributed to an understanding of the semiotic character of written text.

## 4 Stephen's language 3;0 to 4;0 years

The fourth year of life initiated changes in Stephen's deployment of language to represent semiosis, which can be viewed in part as reflecting a more conscious articulation of a model of language as being a tool for learning. This will be discussed in terms of the following topics:

1. Representing the dialogic interactants: (i) knowers/wanters; (ii) informers;
2. Exploration of seeing/being told as ways of knowing;
3. Representing third parties as conscious symbolizers;
4. Representing non-conscious semiotic sources as Sayers.

### 4.1 Representing the interactants

#### 4.1.1 Representing knowers and wanters

In the discussion of Stephen's language up to age three it was noted that almost all mental process clauses were first-person ones and that the majority could be interpreted as interpersonal metaphors of MOOD and MODALITY. During the fourth year, the creation of interpersonal metaphors remained the principal use of mental processes and these increased both in variety and in frequency. At the same time, the experiential meaning coded on the surface of the metaphor appeared to be more important now. That 'literal' meaning involved the representation of dialogic roles such as giver or demander/receiver of information (primary and secondary knower respectively).

One new MOOD metaphor from Stephen was the use of a first-person cognition clause to construct an 'indirect question'. An example is the first line of the next text.

3;10;3    S:    (in car) I wonder where our Superman book and Batman book is.
        M:    Oh, it's at home I suppose.
        S:    What?
        M:    It's at home somewhere.
        S:    Mm.
        M:    It's in – it's probably in Hal's room.
        S:    It's probably lost. (trying out *probably* for the first time)
        M:    Do you think so?
        S:    (? No) (begins humming)

Here, rather than simply asking *Where is our Superman and Batman book?*, Stephen chose to make the enquiry by constructing it as what he was thinking. While the addressee 'read' the metaphor and treated the utterance as a demand for information, the experiential strand of meaning was also present. Through the metaphor Stephen could simultaneously engage in dialogue, seeking information, and present for self-reflection his own thoughts, by construing himself as a thinker and construing the information sought as a representation of his thought. (Unsurprisingly perhaps, when he used such a metaphor it was on occasions when there was no great urgency about obtaining the information at stake.)

The use of first-person cognition processes as metaphorical modalities continued as before, with *I betcha* joining *I think* and *I expect* as a high-value modal option. However, one big difference from the previous year in the use of interpersonal metaphor was the more frequent coding of the addressee (rather than the self) as the Senser.

One way this occurred was when Stephen began to introduce information with a thematic *you know* (where the *you* was rhythmically non-salient and the *know* took a level tone). This was not simply a meaningless routine, since on these occasions, where the addressee is literally coded as the knower, Stephen appeared to be introducing a topic for joint exploration. The *you know* thus appears to signal Stephen's orientation to the addressee as a knower who could contribute to his greater understanding of the knowledge being presented.

3;5;6  S: You know Ian's got two bikes and Hal hasn't got two bikes, he's only got one bike.
M: Yes, but it's a very good bike.
S: He's not lucky, is he? The ones who are lucky are supposed to have two bikes.

3;7;5  S: You know Batman punches holes through people like – like Superman; he punches people too.
M: Yes, they're rather the same, aren't they?
S: And – and they (?    ) and they punch walls and I can't 'cause I'm not strong enough.

3;9;1  (S asks M to draw him a picture)
M: All right, my darling.
S: You know Hal doesn't like to be a darling.

Just as *I think* can be read as a 'low'-value modality, so *you know* can be interpreted as a listener-oriented 'high'-value modality, assessing certainty. However, the surface construal of a cognition process also provides an aspect of the meaning. Taken at face value these utterances manage to construct a 'topic' for talk in terms of a representation of hearer knowledge. They construe as an idea something that did not arise from the immediate verbal or non-verbal context, providing a useful way of introducing it into the current context for shared exploration. So just as Stephen was able to deploy language to classify and identify phenomena outside the current context of situation at this period (see Chapter 3), he was also deploying second-person projection of ideas as a strategy for importing propositions into the current context.

In terms of the experiential representation of inner consciousness, however, the more significant occasions were when the addressee was construed as a Senser in interrogative clauses. One context for this was the use of *Do you remember?* to check on the establishment of intersubjectivity with respect to some situation being recalled, showing Stephen's understanding that shared recall cannot be simply assumed. But the more striking development was the way Stephen repeatedly coded the addressee as a secondary knower (the one not in control of the information) when he was introducing information by means of an indirect MOOD choice. Examples follow:

3;9;3  S: Do you know that 100 is more than 10?

3;9;7  S: Did you know caterpillars could do poos?

3;6;22  (S told the day before by his aunt how the pattern on his wooden snake had been burned on with hot wire)
S: (to M) Do you know how they make this? They (pause) put it on and it makes a pattern.

It should be noted that in none of these cases did Stephen specify the source of his knowledge, even when, as in the last example, it was a recent interaction with a specific individual.

Examples like these are MOOD metaphors. They are coded on the surface as questions about the addressee's knowledge, but they function to make it explicit that the projected clause is 'information', a linguistic construal of experience being offered to the addressee. The fact that the adult was not to display knowledge when 'asked' in this way was made clear on those occasions where the interrogative was taken at face value as an information seeker:

3;6     S:   Oh look, a scruffy car over there; that's a bit scruffy.
        M:   (laughing) Is it, darling?
        S:   Do you know what scruffy means?
        M:   Means all scruffy and dirty and-
        S:   No, don't tell. I tell, 'cause – 'cause it's a word that you don't say; <u>me</u> say.

Thus *Do/did you know?* at this period functioned to construct the information as not known to the addressee. Of course simply giving information in a declarative would also construct the addressee as a secondary knower, one to be informed. But this metaphorical MOOD choice allowed the nature of dialogue as information exchange to be made more explicit. This is because the information has been represented overtly in terms of what the hearer doesn't know rather than simply being exchanged.

It is important to note that the kind of information conveyed through these projected clauses was almost never personal information about what Stephen had seen or done in the parent's absence. Instead it had the status of being factual information that he was conscious (and proud) of having learned. This again suggests that the metaphor was deployed to enable some reflection on the information as knowledge. More everyday knowledge was often tagged with *you know*, offered in a rather superior tone, again highlighting Stephen's sense of power in being a giver of information, as in the following:

3;5;26   (M is looking round for jug of milk she poured earlier)
        S:   Daddy bought some milk you know (indicating new bottle).

Finally, in addition to all these occasions in which mental processes of cognition were partly coopted to interpersonal uses in the negotiation of information, there were new, experiential uses of first-person affect clauses. Up till the fourth year, first-person clauses (such as *I want*) had functioned in the negotiation of goods and services as indirect commands, and the representation of speaker desire was a somewhat marginal effect. (The only acceptable response was provision or negotiation of the goods and services rather than shared reflection on Stephen's desires.) However, during the fourth year, such clauses were very occasionally used outside the context of immediate negotiation. For example *I wish* was used by Stephen on several occasions to project a situation which was clearly not within the agency of the addressee to bring about. For example:

3;7;17    S:    I wish we had two Hals and two Stephens.
          M:    (laughs)
          S:    Two Hals, two Hals and two Stephens, I wish I had two
                Stephens and two Hals.

And there were also occasional past tense clauses when desire was reported on rather than negotiated (using *I wanted*):

3;8;5    S:    We didn't have the bikes at kindy and I wanted the hoops
               but they didn't give me any.

On such occasions, there appeared to be a new tendency for Stephen to reflect on himself in the role of Senser. A desired situation was projected, not to negotiate action, but simply to represent that construction to the addressee for comment and consideration. In doing this, Stephen was not simply revealing in language his feelings, but constructing a representation of those feelings which could then be talked about. As a result of all these moves, building on the early use of *I thought* (which continued in the fourth year), the reality to be represented for exploration through language was beginning to be explicitly coded in terms of metaphenomena – representations of Stephen's representations.

To summarize the discussion so far on the representation of the speaker and addressee through mental processes, the main point that emerges is that interpersonal metaphors continued to constitute the main use of this process type. However, while the *I want* and *I think* clauses of the previous year had appeared to provide little in the way of experiential reflection on cognition and desire, the choices made in the fourth year, using *I wonder* and (*do*) *you remember/know?*, offered a greater opportunity for the experiential component of the metaphor to gain prominence. Indeed, it would seem that the metaphor provided a way for the child to access that meaning.

In addition, Stephen continued to use *I thought* to reflect on his changing representations and had now also developed comparably experiential uses of first-person affect clauses. These latter allowed him to make available for reflection his own feelings outside the context of immediate reaction and negotiation.

### 4.1.2 Representing the addressee as information-giver

The speech roles of dialogic exchange can be construed not only through mental processes of cognition and affect but through a verbal process which represents the exchange of information in terms of 'I tell you that...' (give information) or 'you tell me' (demand information). Some intention to represent information-giving had been apparent in the previous year with statements like *I'm just going to tell to Mummy*, but in his fourth year (age 3 to 4), Stephen was much more explicit about his understanding that coming to know was a result of being told.

For example, there were occasions when he required the addressee to 'tell' about a topic. In commanding the addressee to tell him something, Stephen was coding his demand for information metaphorically, foregrounding in the process the fact that he would find out by being told. Typical texts are given below:

3;5;2    (S and M discussing spotted animals)
M:  You just saw a (spotted) horse; and giraffes have spots; and leopards have spots.
S:  Yes. (pause) Tell me some more animals.

3;7;5    (M and S discussing Superheroes)
S:  I haven't got strong muscles.
M:  Haven't you?
S:  Yeah – No (?      ) Only Batman and Superman.
M:  Well, they've got magic as well.
S:  Yeah, they've got magic as well. Could you tell about magic?
M:  Me?
S:  Yeah, could you tell about magic?
(M attempts to do so)

In these examples Stephen was able to name his topics as *some more animals* and *magic*. But if the experience he wished to explore was not nameable, he was pushed to construct a Matter circumstance using a rankshifted clause. For example, on one occasion F and S had missed M and H because one pair were looking for the other at the school while the other pair were looking for them at home. When they eventually came together there were lengthy explanations. Later, during the meal, Stephen initiated another conversation on this topic. Then the talk turned to other more immediate matters for several minutes, until Stephen, who had clearly not resolved the issue, interrupted loudly:

3;10;1  S:  <u>We should be talking about</u> – about when (? mutter) you – um – Hal was at school and we couldn't see him and – and – and – and – and – and – and Hal was – and Hal <u>was</u> at school – and Hal was at school but we couldn't see him so – so – s- we went back and I – and Daddy went over there and – and – and – then – um we couldn't find anyone to go there only Daddy and Stephen . . .

In this example, the addressees were not constructed as the primary knowers – presumably because they too had clearly been somewhat confused. But in his demand that they resume talking about the topic, Stephen demonstrated that the role of recapitulating talk in clarifying and understanding problematic experience had become very explicit to him.

When the information at stake was not simply personal experience, Stephen was in no doubt that adults were capable of adopting the primary knower role on any topic. Indeed he was likely to become indignant if the parent-addressee was unwilling to take on the role of teacher-teller:

3;6;2   S:   Why (?     ) clouds and it does rain.
          M:  Why does it rain?
          S:   Why – why – there are clouds and it does start to rain and we don't like it.
          M:  (confused) Why does it rain when we don't want it to?
          S:   Mm.
          M:  I don't know.
          S:   You have to tell something to me!

In all the above, the child's consciousness of the relation between telling and knowing is apparent. While this relationship itself was still not an explicit topic of talk, it is revealed in the choice of metaphors by which information was negotiated.

### 4.2 The exploration of seeing/being told as knowing

As well as a heightened consciousness of the role of talk in learning, Stephen became very concerned with the limits of construing information through visual perception. This concern manifested itself towards the end of the year in a series of playful attempts at misleading the perceptions of others and then revealing the 'truth' verbally. These explorations in turn build on the possible conflict which can arise when adults simultaneously guide children to learn from observed experience and challenge particular observations with verbally presented knowledge.

In the 'false belief' literature it seems that 3-year-olds have great difficulty in attributing to a third party a construal of experience different from their own. While it is true that Stephen, as a 3-year-old, very rarely represented the inner cognitions of third parties, he did begin to explore the possibility of misleading semiotic behaviour leading to 'false beliefs'. This was done not by talking about third parties but by checking on the information construed by the current addressee of his own messages.

During the last three months of the year, Stephen delighted in 'tricking' the addressee. On one occasion he simply imagined how one might do this by making a verbal play:

3;10;3    S:    When you forget <u>nothing</u>, you say 'Oh I forgot something'
                 and the person says 'What did you forget?' and you say
                 'Nothing!'

Here the deception lies in the possibility of construing a negativity as a
grammatical participant.

This was an exceptional example, however, and in other cases it was
tricking the addressee through a misleading visual representation that was
tried out, for example by displaying a 'wound' that was really a red texta
mark on his skin. The following text provides one example of many where
mental clauses of cognition and perception were deployed to explore the
possibility of false interpretations:

3;10;2    (S holds opaque plastic beaker to his lips)
          S:    Hey, you don't know (?wh-) I'm drinking or not when I do
                this!
          M:    Are you drinking?
          S:    (gruntings)
          M:    Are you? Oh you are!
          S:    (laughs) Yeah.
          M:    What a big glug.
          S:    You could see it, couldn't you?
          M:    Mm.
          S:    <u>Did</u> you see it?
          M:    I didn't see it, but I heard it.

On such occasions Stephen was insistent that the addressee explain how
they ascertained what was going on. If they were fooled, he relished
revealing (visually and verbally) the 'true' situation and discussed how they
could not tell because of his successful simulation. This fascination with
tricking other people through misleading their perceptions persisted into
the following year and can be seen as part of an exploration of both
observation and talk as sources of knowledge which began at this time.
    Stephen's awareness of this as an issue presumably arose from the
conflicts which inevitably arise in the construal of commonsense knowledge since understandings are gained in a fragmentary way from
perceptual and verbal input and from a variety of sources. One possible
conflict in constructing a consistent view of the world arises from
encountering fantasy representations in story books or on television and
relating these to personal experience. Stephen himself frequently initiated
conversations about his favourite television cartoon heroes as though he
were concerned to establish how to 'take' the experience presented there:

3;6;30    (S looking out of window of car which has drawn to a halt at the
          kerb)
          S:    What's in houses, Mum?

M:  You know what's in houses; rooms 'n' stuff and things in them.
S:  No. What's in houses when you go b-
M:  Oh, you mean, what're they made of?
S:  Yes, when we go bash and can someone crawl in them?
M:  No.
S:  Astro boy can.
M:  Oh well.
S:  Astro boy can fly.
M:  Yeah, but he's not real.
S:  He <u>is</u> real.

Despite his final assertion, Stephen's enquiries in this case probably stemmed initially from a wish to assess the realism of events depicted in cartoons, a visual semiotic source.

But it was not only observing events in an alternative semiotic world which created conflicts. For example, it had long been implicit in the parent talk that a learner's own perceptions might sometimes be misleading, since visual similarity had been used by the parent to 'excuse' Stephen's wrong identification of something (*It looks like a cake, but it's a sandwich*). Now, during the fourth year, other people both enjoined Stephen to construe knowledge from his observations and offered information which did not square with those observations. For example, one persistent theme in the adult talk was that you know something because you have seen it. This can be seen in the following conversation when Stephen talked about the need to buy more porridge.

3;5;24   M:  You buy the oats, you don't buy the porridge.
         S:  Do you <u>make</u> porridge?
         M:  Yes, <u>you</u> know that, you've seen Daddy make porridge.

Here the parent gives Stephen a piece of information verbally and then suggests that he could construe it himself on the basis of his perceptions.

In a similar vein, when Stephen expressed a faulty generalization, it was likely to be challenged explicitly on the basis of observational experience, as in the next example:

3;9;6    (discussing grey things)
         S:  Like – um like something that's grey, like – could be anything 'cept it can't be a dog.
         M:  Dogs can't be grey?
         S:  No.
         M:  You've never seen a grey dog? <u>I</u> have.

In the negotiation of information between the dialogue partners, then, a view of the process of perception as leading to knowledge was regularly presented to Stephen.

On the other hand, as discussed in Chapter 4, it was also made clear to him that personal observation was not a sure basis for construing a generalization. In the following text Stephen enjoins his father to 'see' that the latter's information is wrong, but it turns out that what they see is not taken as relevant:

3;6;30    (F and S are discussing sports cars)
        F:   ...and they go fast 'cause they've got a big engine.
        S:   But that [= one we're looking at] doesn't go faster than us.
            See? (as they move off from lights) We will go faster.
        F:   He's not trying; if he was really trying he could go much
            faster than us.
        S:   If he goes very fast he can – if he goes very fast he can beat us.

In this case F constructed a context linguistically in which his own original statement held good, through the thematic conditional clause *if he was really trying*. On occasions like this, then, Stephen was guided towards a privileging of verbal semiotic experience over his immediate perceptual construal.

The fact that by the end of the year Stephen was exploring the possibility of a person (a symbolic processor) construing 'false' information from a visual (or verbal) representation surely arises from his experience during this year, when on different occasions visual and verbal construals were validated and challenged by the adults he was learning from. And if, as reported in the false belief literature, 4-year-olds show a cognitive gain in this area, it should not be interpreted as a simple maturation. It is the result of considerable energy having been spent on developing understandings about how people come to know and how they may 'know' wrongly.

Through all the kinds of conversations discussed in this section, Stephen was building up some complex understandings. He himself was actively engaged in exploring the possibility of 'false' construals which may arise from perception. At the same time, the way his own interpretations were responded to in talk alerted him both to the importance of perceptual experience as a source of knowledge and of its possible unreliability. In some situations, adults encouraged him to learn from observations, while in others verbal semiotic experience was given greater authority than immediate perceptions. And alongside all this, the fictional representations available through different media were now being explicitly discussed as having a different status from experience directly observed or gained from conversation within the family.

### 4.3 Representing third parties as symbolizers

It is naturally enough from their own experience as learners that children build a model of what learning involves, and thus it is in conversations

where the interactants construe themselves as knowers, see-ers and tellers
that this will first become evident. However, construing semiosis more
generally involves also representing semiotic processing outside the
context of the current dialogue and interpreting third parties as symbolizers.

With respect to the coding of third parties as *inner* symbolizers, the main
point to be made is that this was still only rarely done. When it occurred, it
was still chiefly by means of affect (especially reaction) mental processes.
However, there was for the first time a behavioural representation of
cognition:

3;9;6      (Hal is finishing homework when M calls out that it's bath time)
           S:    (to Hal) You do one more write, okay?
           (H remains, pencil poised)
           S:    (to M) He has to think.

Clearly inner conscious processing had become sufficiently salient to
Stephen for him to interpret external behaviour as a manifestation of it.

Moreover, there were occasional examples where Stephen used the
generalized pronoun *you* as a Senser in a cognition clause as in Stephen's
joke *when you forget nothing,* or the following example:

3;11;7     (in car. S plans to look out for garbage trucks and cement
           mixers)
           S:    Sometimes you can't remember cement mixers, and then
                 (?    ) you can.

Perhaps Stephen was doing little more than reflecting on his own
conscious processing on such occasions, but there was also one recorded
occasion of a third-person mental cognition clause (*they don't know*). This
occurred in a conversation which began as a negotiation of action:

3;9;21     F:    Now stop it; don't annoy each other.
           M:    Just don't touch each other.
           S:    Or don't bite each other. Only animals bite – bite people;
                 only animals bite people because they don't know.
           M:    What don't they know?
           S:    Because – because the teacher says 'you don't bite'.

The rule about biting would have arisen at the childcare centre and it may
well be that animals not knowing any better was part of an original text
being recalled and reproduced here – a case of text running ahead of
system in Stephen's language. But what is also interesting in this example
is that the intention appears to be to articulate the understanding that
knowing something depends on being told about it.

Overall, while the inner consciousness of others outside the deictic centre of the current dialogue was represented in Stephen's speech occasionally when affect or perception was the domain, the construal of third parties as cognizing beings was still marginal. Nonetheless the possibility of interpreting behaviour as cognition had now arisen and at least one attempt to construe a third party as a knower had been made.

There was also a minor development in verbal projection which may be linked to this fledgling capacity for construing others as internal symbolizers. This is the use of projection to construe an imagined locution. As discussed earlier, by the time Stephen was two-and-a-half, he was well able to deploy verbal projection to represent third parties as communicators. However, it was only after age three that there were a few recorded examples where third-person verbal projection was used, not simply to report on verbal action or to construe it from a familiar narrative, but to represent another's consciousness.

For example, a quite lengthy conversation about parrots concluded as follows:

3;7;17    S:   But they don't bite you.
          M:   Well, they can do. If you poke your finger in the cage, they
               might bite you . . .
          S:   No, only little ones do.
          M:   Do they?
          S:   Yeah, because they – they say (loudly) 'Stop putting it out
               there cause I'm in there and I could bite you!'

Although he did not succeed in adjusting all the deixis to the bird's perspective (*out there* to *in here,* etc.), the strategy of projecting the bird's imagined locution as a way of considering and representing the bird's point of view was successful. This text shows how, in addition to using mental projection (e.g. *I wish*) to make shareable his own inner self, Stephen could now use verbal projection (rather than simply role-play) to construct a persona and represent the meanings in wordings of another.

Despite the expansion in the use of verbal projection, Stephen would still frequently adopt other people's meanings as his own construal:

3;10;2    (M is boiling some eggs, timing with her watch)
          S:   You don't put the thing that it whistles because you can't
               turn it off [referring to the very stiff timer switch on stove].
          M:   That's right.
          S:   Only Daddy can.

Here Stephen was not reproducing a text verbatim as with *big boys don't cry,* but was presenting as his own construal an explanation which he had overheard in a previous conversation between F and Hal, his understanding of which he wished to validate.

In a further example, Stephen presents as his own a claim from his friend Frank:

3;11;7     S:  What are vans made out of?
           M:  Metal and glass, same as cars.
           S:  Well, Frank's got a strong one; when it crashes into another
               car, it doesn't break.
           (M suggests this won't necessarily be the case)

In this excerpt, Stephen was presumably pondering Frank's boast about
his family's unbreakable vehicle, by checking on what vans are made of.
However, he did not actually instate the doubtful proposition about
Frank's vehicle as a metaphenomenon, but simply constructed it anew as
his own proposition.

What happens at this time is not that there is explicit discussion of
salient representations, explicitly attributed to different speakers, but non-
attributed judgements made by others were introduced into the discourse
as Stephen's own constructions to be negotiated in a new dialogue with a
new addressee. The interactions that ensued then alerted him to the fact
that what he had adopted as his own construction of reality, on the basis of
the verbal constructions of others, might be challenged when shared with
new addressees.

### 4.4  Non-human semiotic sources as Sayers

Representing a bird or animal as making meaning through their
vocalizations can readily be done by analogy with humans. Representing
non-human objects as meaning-makers takes a little more guidance. But as
a result of continuing experience with graphic symbols Stephen continued
to extend the grammatical category of Sayer to include non-human, non-
conscious semiotic sources in the way begun in the previous year.

The overlap between the symbolizing relation expressed in identifying
clauses and symbolizing through verbal projection was again apparent in
this data set. In the previous period, say was used as a relational process,
with the Token being expressed by an exophoric Deictic (That says Daddy),
and on one occasion Stephen appeared to use say as a projecting clause
with an implied non-human Sayer. Certainly there was evidence that in the
parent talk, the need to make visible the semiotic potential of written signs
and labels had led to a blending of the relational clause structure and a
projecting^projected relation. In this period, after age three, Stephen
several times adopted this strategy himself, construing written symbols as
Sayers projecting a wording.

It would normally be the case that an English speaker would construct
an individual symbol as a Token when reading it, although the text object
constituting the sign source might be a Sayer which projected a locution
or idea. The two possibilities are illustrated in Example 5.14a and b.

*Example 5.14a*     *That word*     *says*     X

| Token (symbol) | Identifying | Value |
|---|---|---|

*Example 5.14b*     *The notice*     *says*     'Do not litter'
*The notice*     *says*     *that you must not litter*

| Sayer (text object) | Verbal | Projection |
|---|---|---|

However, in the following case, Stephen blended the sign source with the symbol itself, allowing the latter to be construed as a Sayer as in Example 5.15.

2;5;7     (S jumps off the side of the pram slope at zoo)
        S:   It's not for Mummies. (points at a notice) And the word says 'For big boys; these things are for jumping for big boys'.

*Example 5.15*     *The word*     *says*     X

| Sayer (symbol) | Verbal | Projection |
|---|---|---|

On a later occasion, Stephen construed his 'writing' scribble as a Sayer:

2;9;5     S:   Look at my writing. It says 'This is for the birthday girl'.

It is clearly but a short step from this to a representation of the object that is the sign source as Sayer, as in *Hal's book says*, a step finally taken in the following year. As suggested earlier, it would seem that through the topological overlap with Token^Value structures, the grammatical alignment of conscious and other semiotic objects was becoming established. And in this way Stephen was learning to construe this aspect of experience in the terms of the theory inherent in the experiential grammar he was developing in partnership with more accomplished speakers.

### 4.5 *Summary: the construal of semiosis 3;0 to 4;0 years*

By age four, Stephen was becoming a little more conscious of inner processes as activities that could be recognized and represented through language. He was increasingly conscious of himself in the role of learner, and simultaneously interested in reflecting on his own desires (using *I wish* and *I wanted*) as well as reactions. Although it was still very rare for him to construe the inner processes of others except as reactions, there were isolated examples recorded where a third party was construed as a cognizant participant. Moreover, by imagining the locutions of another, he was indirectly representing them as able to make meaning. He also constructed possible locutions for various written sources of information such as noticeboards, consolidating his awareness of the meaning-making potential of inanimate semiotic objects.

It was in construing the roles of dialogic interactants rather than third parties that Stephen was best able to reflect on symbolic processing. He did this by exploiting the possibility of grammatical metaphor to represent semiotic exchange as it was enacted. The metaphors created included representing the addressee as a secondary knower when being informed (*do you know?*) and representing the addressee as a teller when Stephen wished to be informed (*tell me*).

In addition, the projecting structure created by the experiential representation of modality (*you know . . .* ) provided a strategy allowing Stephen to introduce his own still-to-be-explored construals into the discourse 'at one remove', as representations of the interactants' current knowledge. (His about-to-be-revised construals continued to be explicitly represented through the past tense projection *I thought.*)

However, although a meaning Stephen had construed from his own experience might be projected with *you know*, a meaning deriving only from a text heard in another context was not distanced by projection. That is, when a problematic construal was one originally constructed by a third party in another context, and Stephen wished to explore it, he did not at this stage introduce it explicitly as the locution or idea of a third party. Instead, he simply instated it in the current dialogue as his own representation – as in the previous year. Such a construal often needed some further negotiation to reach a form of 'valid' knowledge, providing Stephen with further grounds for differentiating different sources of knowledge.

During this year Stephen also began to explore different modes of receiving information by checking, through 'tricks', the extent to which seeing is knowing. At the same time, there is evidence that Stephen was beginning to ponder the relationship between fantasy events observed on the television and knowledge from personal observational or verbal experience. And conversations with adults were guiding Stephen to understand that seeing is a basis for knowing but simultaneously to accept that their verbal construals were a surer form of knowing.

Overall, the language of the fourth year provides a sharp contrast with that of the previous one in that the processes of semiotic exchange and the different sources of knowledge were for the first time a topic of talk. What remained similar, however, was that many of Stephen's explorations were still carried out relatively implicitly through the exploitation of grammatical metaphors and the 'trying out' of problematic sayings.

## 5  Stephen's language 4;0 to 5;0 years

Data from Stephen's fifth year of life show a consolidation of the trends of the previous year, leading to some significant new developments. In particular, Stephen's self-consciousness about himself as a learner and the addressee as a source of knowledge blossomed and extended further into an assessment of how other symbolizing entities should be regarded as sources of knowledge. In addition Stephen began for the first time to verbalize explicitly his understanding of the relationship between knowing and seeing or being told. A final aspect of this exploration of the processes of knowledge construction was that, for the first time, problematic information ceased to be simply naturalized as his own knowledge but was explicitly attributed to the source and renegotiated on that basis.

### 5.1  Representing the dialogic interactants

#### 5.1.1  Representing knowers

Continuity with the previous year is seen in some uses of projection where the speech roles were coded as knowers. As discussed earlier, when reference is made to the speaker's ongoing process of cognizing (inner speech) during the process of enacting dialogue (engaging in outer thought), this comes to be a way of intruding modal assessments into the interaction (i.e. using cognition verbs for conversational rather than referential purposes). From age two-and-a-half Stephen had been doing this, first with *I think* and *I expect*, then with *I bet* and now additionally with *I reckon*. In this fifth year, the dominant first-person projecting clause had become *I know*, which can clearly be taken as an additional modality coding the highest degree of probability.

In the following utterance by Stephen, *I know* is used as a modal acknowledgement to respond to information received:

4;5      (car halts at traffic lights opposite a derelict house with no doors)
         M:  You can see right through that house.
         S:   I know; I know; 'cause it's falling to pieces.

When used to initiate an exchange, I *know* can also be read as a metaphorical move in the dialogue, signalling that information is about to be given – a speaker-oriented version of the *do you know?* option described for the previous period. For example:

4;11;14  (the previous week, Hal had scoffed at S's overliteral construal of *run over*)
         S:   I know how your toe could be run over – you just put your foot down and the car goes p——g.

As interpersonal metaphors, these examples serve as explicit offers of information. At the same time, taken at face value, to project information with *I know* is to claim it as personal knowledge, a meaning which can also be taken from these examples. The possibility that the prevalence of thematic *I know* indicates Stephen's growing consciousness of himself as a source of information is supported by the following text where he seemed determined to formulate an explanation that he could insist on as his own opinion:

4;6;8    (in car, siren heard)
       M:  Ah, something – look, here's an ambulance.
       S:   Someone must have had an accident, or smashed into something.
       M:  Let's see what's going on. (pause) Something – there has been an accident.
       S:   I think – I don't think that; I think – I think the lights are broken, that's what I think.

In all these examples interpersonal meanings coexist with the experiential ones as before. This means that the experiential 'face-value' meaning is always available to the listener to be taken up as the negotiable proposition. This can be seen happening in the following example:

4;0;13    S:  I know what that one is – that's five.
        M:  Yes, you've got to know what all the numbers are.

While this example is no different in form from the others given so far, the addressee chose to respond in terms of the projecting mental process and not the projected relational one. This was probably because the information given by Stephen was in the area of uncommonsense knowledge and his pride in himself as a knower was therefore very clear to the listener. An example like this demonstrates that an interpersonal metaphor has the potential to be taken up experientially.

In fact a key development in the fifth year was that the majority of first-person mental process clauses not only *could* be negotiated in terms of their experiential content, but were exclusively concerned with experiential meaning. In the previous period, first-person affect clauses were described which were distanced from the ongoing negotiation and therefore did not serve as indirect commands. During the fifth year there were further examples of these but also many first-person cognition clauses which appeared to be simply negotiating propositions about Stephen's cognitions.

Uncommonsense knowledge was again to the forefront in the following fragment of conversation which foregrounded Stephen as a knower:

4;4;10    (S is busy with pencil and paper. M is not attending)
       S:  That's how you do an 's'; I can see; I know how to do an 's' now; I can do it lots of times now 'cause I know. I knew all the time how you do an 's'.

M:   Mm (beginning to tune in to the conversation).
S:   Except when I was three.
M:   How you write an 's'?
S:   Yes, I knew all the time except I was (?three).

Here Stephen states explicitly that his ability to do an 's' is explained by his knowledge – *I can do it lots of times now 'cause I know* – and then switches to the past tense to reflect on the longstanding nature of this knowledge.

In the next example too, having rejected the role of information receiver – stating explicitly that he does not need to be told because he knows – Stephen moves to a purely reflective proposition about his forgetfulness:

4;5     S:   Know how (?that one goes)? 'Three Blind Mice.'
        M:   'Three Blind Mice' (she sings it) ' . . . carving knife'-
        S:   (interrupts) Yeah, I know all of it now; you didn't have to do it all-
        M:   Oh.   [Sorry.
        S:        ['cause I know it.
        M:   (? Shall we sing it?)
        S:   I keep forgetting it.
        M:   Oh everybody forgets their songs, darling.

At 2;6, Stephen's earliest reflections on his own state of knowledge had been in examples where he commented on a representation that was challenged by the current conversation, using *I thought* to project his previous understanding. This continued to be an important strategy throughout the fifth year. For example, in the following text, Stephen not only made his feelings an explicit topic of reflective talk but was able to explain them by describing his misconception:

4;4;24   (on their way to childcare centre where a magic show is planned)
         S:   I'm a bit frightened of the magic trick.
         (M and F explain what kinds of things to expect)
         S:   (relieved) I thought he was going to turn a person into something, or something like that.

A new development, in the reflection on his own changing state of knowledge, was his frequent use of *I didn't know* to project a proposition as new information, foregrounding even more strongly his consciousness of himself as a learner as he clarified meaning.

4;5;8    (a car brakes suddenly)
         S:   I didn't know the cars could do skids. (pause) Oh yeah, I knew. (a few weeks before S had discussed tyre skid-marks on road with Hal)

4;5;13    (S and Hal discussing contents of the showbag S will get)
          H:   And bubbles [= bubble-blowing apparatus].
          S:   I didn't know there was bubbles; I thought there was only
               four things . . . I didn't know some things; I thought there
               was only three – two stamps, I thought.

In the following case Stephen was trying to follow a conversation
between Hal and his mother, when the former reported on building
renovations at his friend's house:

4;10;10   H:   . . . and they found a person's bones under the house!
          (M is sceptical about them being human bones)
          S:   I – I – didn't know there were people's bones.
          M:   Yes, inside you – you have a skeleton of bones.
          S:   I thought you meant like dogs' bones.
          M:   Like dogs eat bones?

Here in the negotiation of meaning Stephen was able to state what was
new information for him (*I didn't know . . .*), and – by using recursive
projection – to be explicit about the fact that his original construal was an
interpretation of M's speech (*I thought you meant . . .*).
     This ability to project a projecting clause to explain misconstruals was a
regular strategy from the beginning of the year:

4;1;6     M:   Shall I get you some chopped-up banana?
          S:   Yes please.
          (M brings it)
          S:   I thought you said chocolate banana!

In addition to experiential examples like these, where Stephen was
clarifying his understandings over the course of the current dialogue, he
could also report on what he knew simply as an aspect of a recalled
situation, in which case there is again no possible interpersonal reading.
In the following text he was describing how he once climbed up a tree to
reach the roof guttering:

4;7;17    M:   Up the tree, ah. What was in the gutter?
          S:   Um – just water. I put my hand in there and I didn't know
               that there was water in it.

Finally, it can be noted that Stephen's range of mental process
realizations was also growing, so that he could reflect in a variety of tenses
on a number of different mental processes:

4;3;7     (S enters room talking about his attempts at a manual puzzle)
          S:   I been thinking about that [=puzzle] but nothing imagines.

4;5;7    S:  In the night, when I was awake; in the night when I was
              awake and you were asleep
         M:  Mm
         S:  (after long pause) I dreamed (?      ) a big cough (? and
              there . . . ) Did you hear it?

In conclusion, then, the fifth year saw a continuation in the use of
interpersonal metaphors (using *I reckon, I know,* etc.) which have the
potential to be taken up interpersonally or experientially, and there were
clear examples when the experiential meaning of *I know* emerged as the
proposition being negotiated. During this period, a variety of first-person
realizations were also construed in other tense forms (*I knew/didn't know*; *I
keep forgetting*; *I've been thinking*; *I dreamed*) with no metaphorical meaning.
Thus, while continuing to serve interpersonal functions related to the
negotiation of modality and the achievement of successful dialogue, first-
person cognition processes were becoming an ever more important strategy
for reflecting on himself as an inner symbolizer, a learner and a thinker.

Comparable patterns can be found in the use of mental processes where
the listener was construed as the Senser. Just as in the previous year, the
addressee was repeatedly constructed as one to be informed. Around his
fourth birthday Stephen began to do this by representing the listener very
explicitly as a non-knower:

4;0;2    (earlier S had a minor accident, hurting his leg. Walks up to M
         and hits leg)
         S:  Mummy you didn't know that leg was strong.

4;3;10   S:  You didn't know I can count up to a hundred!

Here, *you didn't know* can be interpreted as a metaphorical way of
representing the listener as information-receiver and, by implication, the
speaker as informer. They are thus highly comparable to the *do you know?*
projections of the third year. However, these past tense declarative
utterances more readily allowed the mental process itself to be treated as
the proposition being negotiated:

4;0;8    S:  Mummy, look at that bus! Mummy, that bus!
         M:  Mm?
         S:  It's got – oh why didn't you see it? Has a (?      ) and some
              numbers at the side, they do.
         M:  Oh.
         S:  You didn't know they have those numbers at the side, did you?
         M:  Oh, I didn't really think about it, darling.

The fact that *you didn't know* was both echoed in the question tag and
negotiated by the addressee demonstrates that the proposition at stake

here was M's lack of knowledge rather than the bus having numbers at the side.

There were also many occasions when the addressee's knowledge or lack of it could only be construed non-metaphorically:

4;8;21    S:   A very long time ago, when you didn't know, we swapped beds.

4;0;8    S:   Mummy, do you know we've got a new person [=at pre-school] that you don't know?

In the last example, the opening phrase *do you know* is a metaphor of the kind discussed for the previous year (representing the current listener as about to be informed). However, the Qualifier *that you don't know* simply functions as an experiential descriptor of *person*. Embedded inside the nominal group the clause cannot operate as a MOOD metaphor.

Similarly, when what is known is simply a participant rather than a projected clause, only a cognition meaning seems possible:

4;1;12    (M gives S a special small 'bouncy ball' present from a friend)
         M:   For you, for Stevie; it's a bouncy ball.
         (S bounces it)
         M:   It's a very bouncy ball, so be careful.
         S:   (?It's hard.)
         (F enters)
         S:   Look what I got! A present! You don't know [[what it is]].

4;10    (discussing children at party)
        S:   There was Nicholas-
        H:   Who's Nicholas?
        S:   Um, you don't know him.
(cf. *I keep forgetting it*; *I didn't know some things* cited earlier)

Just as with first-person projection, then, second-person cognition clauses had followed a path from metaphorical uses which foregrounded the interpersonal meaning, to metaphors constructed in such a way that either meaning could be taken up by the addressee, to purely experiential reflections on the addressee as possessing or lacking the knowledge of which the speaker has control.

5.1.2 Representing the addressee as information-giver

A change from the previous year was that in addition to using the grammatical metaphor *(could you) tell me* to represent the addressee as the information-giver in the current dialogue, Stephen made continual reference to previous texts from the addressee by quoting or reporting their locutions. This was a move towards the purely experiential representation of the addressee as informer that parallels the non-metaphorical representation of the interlocutors as knowers.

Sometimes the addressee's speech was represented in order to engage in clarification of something which from the perspective of the present appeared puzzling:

4;2;4    S:  Sometimes – sometimes – sometimes – sometimes you say you went somewhere – you went somewhere – you went somewhere and you weren't alive yet.
         M:  No, sometimes I went somewhere and <u>you</u> weren't born yet.

4;6;6    S:  How much am I?
         M:  You're four-and-a-half, darling.
         S:  Am I? Am I four-and-a-half?
         M:  Yes, you're really four-and-a-half now.
         S:  But yesterday I thought you said I wasn't four-and-a-half.
         M:  No, you're four-and-a-half and a bit.

On these occasions Stephen can be seen to be negotiating information by explicating how he originally construed what the addressee had said. And equally often it was as a point of departure for a continued exploration of a topic that had clearly not been satisfactorily resolved in the earlier talk:

4;3;13   S:  How can something move your bones? You know you said last night . . .

4;3;14   (S picks up wire cake rack)
         S:  Yesterday [=two days earlier] you said 'silver is metal' or something.
         M:  Oh yes, silver is metal; and this is metal.
         S:  You said it could break.
         M:  I said you could bend the aerial and snap it off; this isn't an aerial.

These texts illustrate how a child will return to something that has been said but not satisfactorily understood, a characteristic which was not new at all. They also illustrate Stephen's control of the grammar for projecting locutions, paratactically and hypotactically, which was not new either. What was different now was the repeated bringing of the two together, mobilizing the latter in the service of the former. It was this ability to explicitly introduce the earlier text itself into the talk for further exploration, not just in the form of a proposition, but as a metaphenomenon, which was an additional important learning strategy now available. And it is a strategy which makes it explicit that it is representations of representations of experience that are being negotiated, that knowledge itself is semiotically constructed.

### 5.2 *The exploration of sources of knowledge*

Stephen's exploration of giving and receiving false information in visual and verbal modes continued during this year and the different status of fictional representations was further explored in conversation. There was, in addition, a significant new development in Stephen's reflection on the process of gaining knowledge, one which involved an explicit representation by Stephen of the link between seeing/being told and becoming informed.

The following texts can be cited as examples of Stephen's continuing attempts at visual and verbal misconstruals:

4;3;21   (S squashes two pieces of polystyrene foam closely together)
        S:   Do you think there's one on top?
        M:   (to oblige) There's only one, isn't there?
        S:   No, two! See! (separating them)
        (S hides one while M not attending)
        S:   Do you think I dropped one? Do you think one went in my gumboot?

4;5;14   (a few days before S and H had brought in some drawings to show M. They were labelled 'Hal' and presented to her as his work although all but one were done by S)
        S:   Hey, you know last night, last night I was tricking you; I was tricking you; Hal was helping me; I was tricking you.
        M:   Tricking me about what?
        S:   I was tricking you about my drawing.

4;1;9   M:   I'm not stopping.
        S:   Oh. Well, I am; I was just joking when I said I am.

4;2;11   M:   Would you like some marmalade on that toast?
        S:   Vegemite.
        M:   Oh all right (goes to cupboard).
        S:   I'm tricking you; I really want marmalade.

An example similar to the last two was also reported by Shatz, Wellman and Silber (1983: 307) from a child older than 3;8:

        F:   Did you have any dreams last night?
        C:   No, I didn't have any dreams at all.
        F:   Oh.
        C:   I didn't, 'cept I tricked you. I did have dreams.

The issue of a valid representation was also taken up when Stephen checked up as before on information presented in movies, cartoons and story books:

4;2        (S and M discuss film seen previous day)
           S:   Was it a real whale?
           M:   No, none of it's real . . .
           (later)
           S:   Hal, Hal; in that thing – in the movies, was the whale a real whale?

4;3;17     S:   (in car) Is there such thing as a wolf and a fox?
           M:   Oh yes.
           S:   Is there such thing as ghosts?
           M:   No.
           S:   But a person can dress up as a ghost.
           M:   Yes . . .
           S:   How can you be dressed up as a ghost if there's no such thing as a ghost?

4;4;10     S:   Hey, Mum, can dolphins eat boats?
           M:   No.
           S:   Why?
           M:   They don't want to eat boats; they eat fish. Are you thinking of *Pinocchio* (recently seen movie)?
           S:   Yes.
           M:   Oh, that was a whale. But they don't really swallow boats.

These examples show how the responses Stephen received continued to emphasize that not everything represented in fiction is 'real'.

By the end of the year, Stephen was puzzling over how these non-real things were made to appear real. The following conversation concerns a *Goodies* television episode which showed a giant kitten looming huge over skyscrapers:

4;10;10    S:   Was it really a person inside the cat?
           M:   (explains that the kitten was photographed to appear big) It's all pretend, they're not real, the Goodies.
           S:   On football, they're real – the people, like Hugh McGahan.
           M:   Who?
           S:   Hugh McGahan; he's the – what's he called? – we've got a football card of Hugh McGahan.

It is clear that Stephen was interested in finding out how the misleading semiotic effects were achieved, and by 4;10 understood perfectly well that the different things he saw on television had different statuses as semiotic representations (contrary to a popularly held view that children cannot distinguish 'truth' (a representation of actual material experience) from 'fantasy' (a representation of imagined experience).

But while exploring the possibility of false or fictional semiotic representation was a concern carried over from the previous year, a new concern was with the sources of adult knowledge. For the first time Stephen began to enquire about these, no longer necessarily accepting the knowledge of others as unproblematically 'given'. This can be seen in the following examples:

4;9       (S asking if hired car could go as fast as the new car)
         F:   No.
         S:   How do you know?
         F:   It's only got four cylinders.

4;10;12  M:  He likes it [=school] really.
         S:   How do you know? Did he tell you?

4;11;22  S:   How big do you think a tidal wave is?
         M:  Oh, I don't know, darling.
         S:   The sky?
         M:  Yeah, it would look like that (?    )
         S:   Have you seen one?
         M:  No.
         S:   Well, how do you know what a tidal wave is?
         M:  Oh I've read about it in books.

In these texts, Stephen questions the addressee explicitly as to the origins of their knowledge and suggests himself that observation and talk are valid sources of information.[3] These very explicit probes are an aspect of an important new development during this period which was Stephen's explicit construal of the process of his own coming to know things. The following texts illustrate this:

4;1;22   (they are driving behind a horse box)
         S:   I know there isn't a horse in there, 'cause you can't see its face.

4;5;17   H:  (discussing fruit) Some things don't have any pips.
         S:   I know, because I've seen mandarins have no pips.

4;10;10  (concluding the *people's bones* conversation cited on p. 225)
         S:   Anyway I know that a few birds eat the um – skeleton – the juice thing inside, 'cause I saw that on television.

So while between the ages of three and four years internal causal links were prominent as Stephen provided explicitly the criterion by which something was placed in a category, in this later period the semiotic status of what was being linked was itself made explicit. The difference being discussed here is that between the two possible representations shown in Example 5.16a and b.

*Example 5.16a*    *Some things don't have pips*    *because*    *mandarins have no pips*

| proposition (claim) | internal cause | proposition (evidence) |
|---|---|---|

*Example 5.16b*

*I know*    *that some things don't have pips*    *because*    *I've seen*  *mandarins have no pips*

| | projection of knowledge | external cause | | projection of perception |
|---|---|---|---|---|

In Example 5.16a, a typical utterance at age three, a 'claim' is supported by an explicit piece of evidence. But in Example 5.16b, the nature of the claim is construed explicitly by the ideational grammar as speaker knowledge and the nature of the evidence is specified as speaker perceptual experience. In grammatical terms, the claim is itself projected as a metaphenomenon, as a second order representation rather than a direct construal of experience, and in addition the basis for making that construal is similarly projected as a metaphenomenon, as a representation of a perception. The internal conjunctive link joining the two clauses in 5.16a is therefore 'experientialized' to an external one along with the experientialization of the status of the two clauses as inner construals.

This move is one from using language and observation to construe a phenomenon towards using language additionally to construe the process of construal itself. Stephen could now not only articulate the basis for asserting a proposition, but was conscious that this was what he was doing, relating perceptual construals and semantic (cognitive) ones.

On other occasions, the basis for knowing was specified not in terms of a representation of a perception, but of a representation of a verbal construction.

4;6;4    (S pulling bits of bark off tree in park)
M:  Don't do that.
S:   (scornfully) Mummy, it doesn't hurt the tree; the tree can't feel it 'cause it hasn't got a brain.
M:  How did you know that!?
S:   Hal told me.

4;7;28    S:   That's not very long; it's only eight sleeps.
M:  That's right!!
S:   I know 'cause Hal told me.

Stephen had therefore come to represent both perceptual and verbal experience explicitly as valid sources of knowledge.

However, just as he came to understand that not everything seen counts as valid knowledge, so his awareness was growing that not everything said should be taken as valid information. His verbal feints, characterized as 'joking' or 'tricking', were evidence for this, as was a new reflectiveness in the fifth year concerning verbal sources of knowledge. For the first time, Stephen began habitually attributing possibly problematic information to specific Sayers rather than simply naturalizing it all to himself. For example:

4;0;20   S:   Andrew said if he had a sore like that (indicating a scab), he would pick it off!
         M:   Well, Andrew's silly then.

4;6;16   (S sneezes)
         S:   At kindy they always say 'Put your hand over your mouth.'
         M:   Well, the main thing is that you turn your head away and don't sneeze onto anything.
         S:   They say it's so you don't get germs.
         M:   It's so you don't give germs to other people.

5;0;6    S:   Graham says if you look at the sun you go blind!!
         F:   Yes, that's right.

By projecting the information explicitly, Stephen avoided taking responsibility for a fact, or avoided 'internalizing' it as part of his own knowledge, until he had seen how it was responded to. This constitutes a new ability to distance himself from a proposition that he was nonetheless introducing into the dialogue for continued negotiation. Thus once again the familiar strategies of reworking problematic texts and reporting on the locutions of others were brought together as a crucial learning strategy.

*5.3 Representing the consciousness of third parties*

It was during the fifth year that it became perfectly routine for cognition Sensers to be other than the participants in the current dialogue:

4;1;9    (S is in the car on his way home from a party)
         S:   I'm going to put it [=whistle toy] in my pocket and I'm not going to tell Hal what it is.
         M:   Oh.
         S:   It's a secret.
         M:   That's right.
         S:   But you know what it is, don't you?
         M:   Yup, it's not a secret from me, but it's a secret from Hal.

> S:   It's secret for you and Daddy but not for Hal – it is for Hal
>       but he's got to guess what it is.
> M:   Mm.
> S:   He doesn't know what it is.

As in other conversations from the fifth year, the telling/knowing nexus is explicitly represented here.

Stephen had also become conscious of the different statuses of other persons as knowers. He had clearly made a link between knowledge and authority in the following exclamation concerning two staff members at his preschool:

4;0;3    S:   Jane's the boss and she doesn't even know that, and Kylie
              does.

He also frequently commented on the failings of his younger playmate, Simon:

4;3      S:   I didn't ask him because he – he – he – he doesn't understand.

4;2;15   S:   Simon knows some things – not as much as a big boy.

4;10;8   S:   When Simon gets bigger will he know more things? 'Cause
              he's three and he doesn't know anything!

And he was surprised that some younger children were more knowledgeable than himself:

4;10;2   M:   Boy, don't you know a lot!
         S:   Some things that I don't know that Fred knows and he's not
              as big as me.
         M:   What does he know? What sort of things?
         S:   I don't know; he knows things that I don't know but I forgot.

Third-person projection of ideas was an important way for him to consider the inner world of other people. There had, from 2;9, been very rare examples when a conversation had been recounted in terms of projected ideas, and this now became perfectly routine. As in earlier cases, a meaning might be projected to foreground conflicting opinion:

4;5;2    (S and M have been discussing 'He-Man' stamp marks on S's
         hand)
         S:   Grant thinks-
         M:   Mm-
         S:   those blue stamps-
         M:   Mm-

S: he thinks they're petal ones.
M: Petal?
S: Yeah, petal ones, I said he thinks; but they're not.

Or a projected idea might now simply serve to provide information which he had learned from talk:

4;5;7   M: You still haven't gone (to the museum) . . .
They [=pre-school] did tell you Monday, didn't they? Perhaps the driver's still sick.
S: He is. They thought the driver would be sick – would be sick – might get better; but he was sick then so he couldn't go.

A further new development was Stephen's ability to interpret non-verbal behaviour in this way:

4;0;24   (S is reporting on cat's reaction to his game with a friend which used a brush as a prop)
S: We used a bath brush and she [=cat] thinks – she thinks – she thinks it was her own one [i.e. for grooming]. It was a toilet brush!!

4;9;3   S: What thing does it [=a cat] come in?
M: Like a box?
S: Yeah.
M: Well, most people don't buy their cats . . . (she explains how their cat's mother just walked in and stayed with them and how they gave away most of her kittens)
S: Do cats decide they don't want to live in their home any more and they go and live in someone else's home?

4;10;5   (S anticipates his Grandpa's annual visit, and how he, S, will appear changed)
S: When Grandpa comes he'll think I'm a different person so he might go to another house.

These examples show Stephen not just interpreting observed, reported or even imagined behaviour into language, but inferring from these the mental/semantic constructions of the participants concerned.

Moreover, he continued to project imagined locutions with a similar function:

4;7;5   (M and S discussing Grandma who has not seen S for six months)
M: She won't believe any little boy can swim when he's only four.
S: But I'm not only four.
M: No, you're four-and-a-half, aren't you?
S: She'll say 'Oh god you're big and you're only three!'

He thus showed evidence of increasing empathy with others and was able to use projection as one strategy to consider experience very explicitly from a perspective other than his own, contrary to the supposed barriers of egocentrism. From having begun at age 2 with a view of other persons primarily as Actors or Behavers endowed with affect, he now construed them equally and equally explicitly as semiotic beings.

### 5.4  Representing non-human Sayers

During the fifth year, Stephen consolidated his understanding that written language projects locutions, as shown in the following example:

4;5;28    (S looking out of car window, M driving)
        S:    Look Mum 'o' 'no' ( /ounou/ ).
        M:    (turns briefly) I can't see.
        S:    O no, it's got an 'n' in the middle; 'o' then 'n' and 'o'.
        M:    Yes that is ono; I don't know why it should say ono.
        S:    Perhaps it's supposed to say 'I own the shop'.

Stephen was beginning to interpret the relationship between letters and sounds, but clearly had little understanding as yet as to the kind of text which might be constructed by a shop sign.

He probably had a better sense of what to expect from certain types of books since much more sustained interaction was centred on book reading. As before, these interactions were important occasions when adults constructed Stephen as a learner, indeed constructed both 'readers' as learners. They also highlighted both the value of factual information and the value of books as sources of information. The following utterances are a few taken from a single brief episode, looking at an illustrated nature book:

4;7;21    (S points at picture of starling in eagle's nest)
        S:    Is – is he supposed to live with them?
        M:    No, I don't think so. I don't know – oh, let's have a look.
            (reads silently) Yes! What he's done – look, he's a starling
            and it says he has built his nest inside the eagle's nest. Isn't
            that strange? I didn't know they did that . . .

        M:    This book's full of interesting things that I didn't know about.

        S:    What's that?
        M:    Oh, I don't know (pause) that (pause) is a frog (pause) a
            kind of frog.
        S:    No, the grey one.
        M:    Well, I'm just trying to read and see.

M:   Now, what do we want to learn about elephants? What do
      they tell us about elephants? They tell us that . . .

S:    (on reaching last page) Again!!
M:   You want it again. (turns to front) Look, which one's that?
S:    Um, a porcupine fish.
M:   Oh good boy!! You learn fast, don't you?

M:   He flies about most of the year; this one's flying over the sea.
S:    Even when it's raining?
M:   I suppose so, yes, but it doesn't tell you about that . . .

S:    What – what is it trying to do?
M:   Oh it's just – it's had a bit of an accident I think, I suppose;
      well let me see if it tells you-
S:    Does it tell what he's doing?

Under the influence of this kind of modelling Stephen could hardly fail
to become aware of the relevance of books as sources of information,
information that was specialized enough to be new even to the parent.
Thus Stephen not only questioned the adult who was mediating the
written information but was able to build on the developments described
earlier, to confidently construe the text as a Sayer in such utterances as
*Does it tell what he's doing?* When he did this, he was making visible his
understanding that the text itself was the original source of the
information and, given this, that knowledge was a semiotic construct.

### 5.5 *Summary: 4;0 to 5;0 years*

In the fifth year, semiosis finally became established as a topic of talk as
accessible as material activities. There were clear examples of the
representation of the speakers as engaged in inner semiotic processing,
not simply in the creation of interpersonal metaphors, but in the
negotiation of information about who knows what (*I knew, I keep forgetting,
you didn't know*) or in the clarification of unsatisfactory construals (*I thought
you said; I thought you meant*). Moreover, third parties were equally
represented as semiotic beings – their observed and imagined behaviour
was reported in terms of underlying meanings by being construed in terms
of semiotic processes (*she thinks; do cats decide; she'll say*).

During this year, Stephen showed a generally heightened consciousness
of the nature of learning and the role of talk in that process. He explored
further the different statuses of different knowers and of different semiotic
sources of information, which were recognized as being both human and
non-human, both perceptual and verbal. Observed experience and both
spoken and written texts were explicitly cited as sources of knowledge. As
such, written factual texts were treated authoritatively, while fictional

semiotic representations were recognized as not 'real' and the authority of spoken texts was understood as varying depending on the status of the Sayer. As part of these explorations, the grounds for knowing something became an explicit topic of discussion for the first time and problematic texts of third parties were explicitly attributed when cited for further exploration. This allowed Stephen to remain distanced from a received construal of experience until he had further negotiated and reflected on it. The groundwork had thus been laid for construing reality in terms of competing interpretations, something which gave Stephen's conversation a very different character from that of the previous year.

## 6  Overview: the construal of semiosis 2;6 to 5;0 years

This chapter has argued that an important domain of experience to be interpreted through language is that of semiosis itself. Following Matthiessen's (1991) interpretation of English TRANSITIVITY, based on Halliday (1985, 1994), symbolic processing has been seen as having an inner and an outer aspect construed by mental and verbal processes respectively (and also by associated behavioural processes). From the description of Stephen's development and use of this area of the grammar, three major areas of investigation can be identified: Stephen's interpretation of the participants who engage in semiosis, his interpretation of the process of learning (coming to know) and his representation of the products of semiosis (texts). In what follows the main points made in this chapter will first be outlined and summarized in a series of figures to represent Stephen's developmental path with respect to these matters. Following this, some of the implications of these developments will be briefly discussed.

### 6.1  The interpretation of the participants who engage in semiosis

#### 6.1.1  From enactment to representation of dialogue roles

One key aspect of Stephen's interpretation of the participants engaged in semiosis was his experientialization of the dialogue roles of primary and secondary knower and actor. In its most general terms, dialogue can be seen as the exchange of either information (knowledge) or goods and services (action).

When dialogue is enacted, the speakers adopt and assign complementary speech roles. For example, within any single information exchange, the speaker who provides information adopts the role of the primary knower, assigning the addressee a complementary role as the one to be informed, who is to know as a result of being told. Such speech roles are taken up continuously in the enactment of dialogue as speakers give or demand information and goods and services. While Stephen was experienced in adopting all these roles at the beginning of the study, the period between 2;6 and 5 years is one in which speech roles were represented ideationally by construing speakers as wanters, wishers, tellers and knowers (or non-knowers). This simultaneously involved construing the dialogue as a second order representation, so that what speakers say is represented as what they want or what they know.

For Stephen, as for other children studied, this experiential construal of speakers arose initially as a way of engaging in the interpersonal negotiation of information or action. But once established, it can become a way of reflecting on the nature of information exchange and in particular on the child speaker's role as a learner. This move was begun by Stephen in his third year, became prominent in the fourth and was still important in the fifth. These main developments are summarized in Figure 5.7.

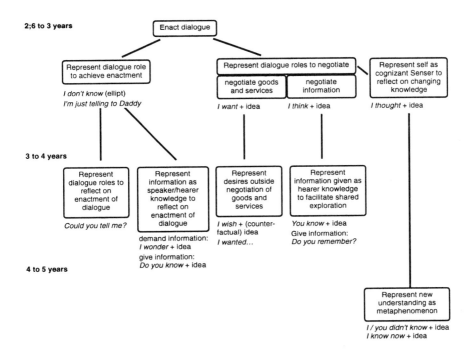

**Figure 5.7** Stephen's path from enactment to representation of dialogue roles

### 6.1.2 Construing the actions of symbolizers

Another aspect to the representation of symbolizers as participants concerns the way the actions of persons are interpreted as revealing their consciousness. From early on, other people were represented as speakers, and from age two-and-a-half, the actions of third parties were on occasions interpreted by Stephen as external representations of inner affect, using behavioural and mental processes. By the fourth year, material action could be explained by construing the participant's imagined speech, and action (or inaction) could also be construed as a manifestation of inner cognition (*animals bite 'cause they don't know*).

Finally, by age five, Stephen represented the imagined reactions of another by projecting their likely speech, and he interpreted the observed actions of another by reporting their thoughts. It can therefore be concluded that over the course of the pre-school years, Stephen had come to construe conscious beings as inner symbolizers and their speech as an outward manifestation of inner symbolic processes. These developments are outlined in Figure 5.8.

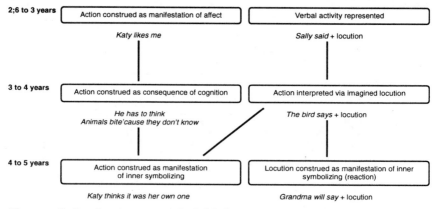

**Figure 5.8** Stephen's construal of third parties as symbolizers

6.1.3 The construal of non-human Sayers

A third and final strand to the construal of the participants in semiosis concerns the way written sources are gradually included in the construal of Sayers through exploitation of the verbal and relational senses of *say*. This development is summarized in Figure 5.9.

*6.2 The interpretation of the process of knowing*

At the beginning of this case study, Stephen had two coexisting 'implicit' models of learning. One was that one learned from enacting dialogue and the other was that one learned from observation of the material world. In the fourth year these models were explored. Through the use of interpersonal metaphor (*tell me*), the understanding of a relation between telling and knowing became more explicit, while the reliability of observation was tested out in play and the reliability of text was in turn tested out against observations. Then in the fifth year the two models were ideationally construed as Stephen specified explicitly that an observation

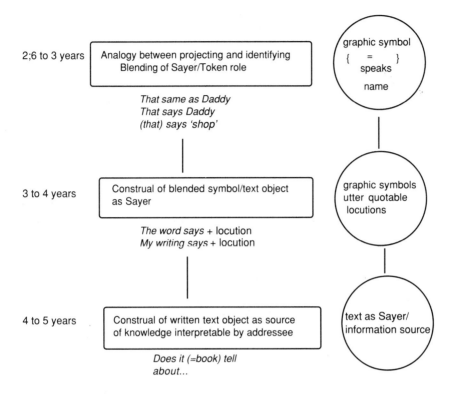

**Figure 5.9** Stephen's developing construal of written texts as information sources

or an experience of talk was the source of a specific metaphenomenon that represented part of his knowledge. These developments are summarized in Figure 5.10.

*6.3 Representing the products of semiosis*

The specific aspect of Stephen's representation of texts to be considered here concerns the way texts which had been part of the child's experience were introduced into a current dialogue. Reconstituting the texts of others in a new context and usually with a new addressee makes them available for renegotiation and reflection and can thus be an important strategy for learning.

By age two-and-a-half, recalled dialogue was often reconstructed but almost always in a narrating context where speaking was one of the activities in a sequence being reported. The child was presumably reflecting on the speech just as much as on the other events, but the quoted or reported locution was not a focus of negotiation in the new dialogue. Where the dialogue was reconstructed as a mental process

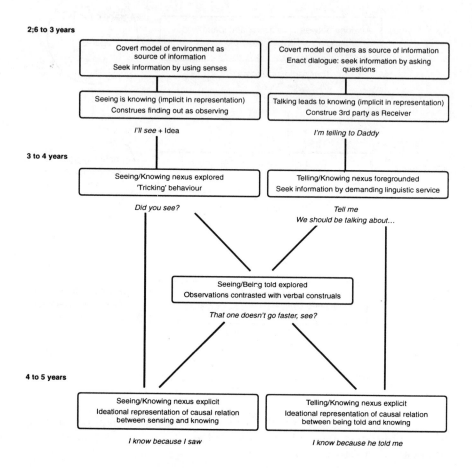

**Figure 5.10** Stephen's exploration of observation and talk as sources of knowledge

projection, which occurred only once in the third year, Stephen's reflectiveness about the text appeared to be more foregrounded. This was because some misapprehension on the part of one of the speakers was evident (a meaning of *he thought X but he was wrong*).

Most interesting were recalled texts whose wording was understood but which made generalizations or judgements which needed further exploration. These appeared to be reconstructed precisely for the purpose of having them renegotiated in the new context, but between 2;6 and 4 years these texts were introduced unprojected. Then in the fifth year, verbal projection was used to distinguish such utterances from Stephen's own construals. This enabled him to reintroduce an addressee's own text explicitly and demand further clarification of its content. It also allowed him to reserve judgement on whether to know something he was told by a third party until he had established its acceptability to other addressees. These developments are outlined in Figure 5.11.

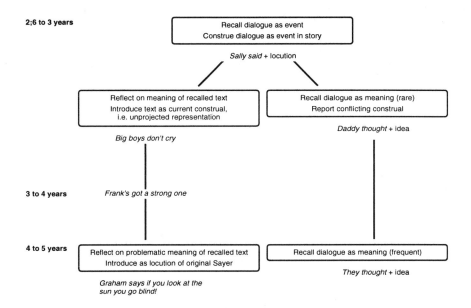

**Figure 5.11** Stephen's developing representation of the products of semiosis

This chapter has focused on Stephen's growing knowledge of language by examining the way he used the experiential grammar to represent the processes of semiosis. There was overall a dramatic development in his understandings between two-and-a-half and five years, with the most striking changes taking place in the fifth year.

From the perspective of psychological theory, researchers have found it most relevant to note the representation of the self as opposed to any other persons. And on this question Shatz, Wellman and Silber (1983: 318) suggest that 'once mental state expressions do start to appear, their domain of reference is not limited to the self for very long, if at all', a finding echoed by Bartsch and Wellman (1995: 62-3). However, taking a semiotic rather than psychological perspective, it is the self and addressee – the parties to the dialogue within the deictic centre – which are opposed to third parties. And it is apparent from these data that representing the knowing of third parties is a later development than representing the interactants of the interpersonal deictic centre.

The interpersonal character of the earliest representation of semiosis in fact has two facets. One is that the resources to represent meaning-making are developed in the first place, not to explore this domain of experience but to expand the interpersonal options for MOOD and MODALITY. The other aspect is that when the child's attention does turn to semiotic exchange as an activity to be represented, it is most readily explored by construing the ongoing dialogic process and representing the interactants of the speech event as participants. Thus where a Piagetian perspective distinguishes between the 'I' and 'others' and sees development in terms of decentring from an egocentric starting point, a semiotic perspective can suggest instead a moving out from the deictic centre of dialogue involving 'you and me' to the construal of the semiotic processes and products of third parties.

All the developments summarized in Figures 5.7 to 5.11 suggest that by age 5 years, children like Stephen have developed a number of key understandings that will prepare them for their future learning. Foremost among these are the ability to reflect on one's own processes of learning, and the ability to represent knowledge as metaphenomenal. Thus, building on a long experience of learning through language, Stephen had developed the ability to make public his own construals and misconstruals as such, so that they could become an object of reflection. Further than this, he could treat any text as an object of exploration, citing and discussing problematic conversations as well as discussing information from written sources. These are clearly central abilities for learning in school, where language both as system and text will need to become an object of reflection in any child's early and continuing development in literacy.

## Notes

1  This utterance is discussed on p. 197.
2  Unfortunately the audiotape is not clear enough to be quite certain that *same as* was used.
3  Astington (1994: 109) reports an anecdotal example of another child who similarly challenged the addressee's source of knowledge with *How do you know?* after age 4 years, while Bartsch and Wellman (1995: 61) also cite examples from 3-year-old children.

# 6   Cause–effect relations

The preceding three chapters have presented a case study of learning through language, attending to the construal of taxonomic relations and of material and semiotic activities respectively. The focus has therefore been on the texts which have mobilized language to address the problems of 'making sense' of each of these realms of experience. In this chapter, the analytical lens will be readjusted a little so as to focus directly on the development of one of the meaning systems through which learning is achieved across the different domains – that of causal relations. The purpose of this is twofold. On the one hand it will enable a closer consideration of the development of language as system. On the other hand, it will provide a context for revisiting some of the data already presented, together with further material, to illustrate the child's growing ability to learn by engaging in the semantic process of reasoning.

Causal relations have been chosen for particular attention, both because they have entered the description of all the previous chapters and because of their theoretical prominence within cognitive approaches to learning. The ability to infer cause–effect relations is fundamental to notions of 'logical' or 'scientific' thinking, and the fostering of the abilities to reason and hypothesize are prominent educational goals throughout the Western world. In particular, these matters have received considerable attention within the Piagetian developmental framework, where the ability to formulate alternative hypotheses, test them and draw relevant conclusions is seen as the hallmark of the highest stage of cognitive development, that of 'formal operations'.

## 1  Developmental background

Piaget's observations that it was not until 7 or 8 years of age that children could distinguish causes and effects in their speech have been the source of considerable research and experiment over the years. (See Morag Donaldson 1986; French and Nelson 1985; Hood, Fiess and Aron 1982, for reviews of research on the acquisition and use of causal connectives.) In much of this work, Piaget's classification of causal relationships into 'physical', 'psychological' and 'logical' types has also been adopted or adapted. These categories are exemplified in Table 6.1, using examples from Morag Donaldson (1986: 6), together with a gloss on the meaning of the categories.

**Table 6.1** Piagetian-based categories of cause

| Piagetian cause-type | Example | Meaning gloss |
|---|---|---|
| Physical | *The window broke because a ball hit it* | relation between observable events |
| Psychological | *Mary hit John because he pulled her hair* | attribution of motive for action |
| Logical | *Half 9 isn't 4 because 4 plus 4 is 8* | implication holding between two judgements |

Piaget's writings suggest that psychological cause will be expressed before physical or logical.

The few observational, rather than experimental, studies of children's use of causal relations have also found that physical causality is not prominent in the speech of very young children. Perhaps the most important observational studies are the republished accounts by Hood and Bloom (1991) and Bloom and Capatides (1991). These consider data from eight subjects between two and three-and-a-half years of age, collected in conversations between child and investigator or child and parent. Hood and Bloom (1991: 364) observe:

> The children in this study simply did not talk about causal events that occurred between physical objects in the world and rarely made reference to sequential actions in their causal statements.

In the later study by Bloom and Capatides (1991: 384–5), the data are coded according to whether causal connections were 'objective' (evident, 'fixed in the physical order of things'), exemplified by *I'm gonna pick this [=toy] up so it can't step on the cord,* or 'subjective' (not self-evident; social constructions), exemplified by *(we'll give him) nothing because not hungry.* The analysis thus distinguishes two examples of speaker intention on the grounds that the causal relations are somehow inherent in unconstrued reality in the first case but not in the second. (See Hood *et al.* 1982 for arguments against such a view.) A more relevant distinction made by Bloom and Capatides concerns the nature of the so-called 'objective' utterances from the 2-year-olds. The researchers found that when observable relations between things in 'the physical order of the world' were expressed, these

> were not the kinds of physical and mechanical causality between objects that depend on the detection of empirical regularities. Rather the concept of causality . . . involved the causes and consequences of their actions in everyday events. (Bloom and Capatides 1991: 389)

In other words, once again, the kind of physical causality valued by Piaget was found to be absent.

Hood and Bloom's study examines the 'content, use and forms of the causal utterances' (1991: 342). 'Negation', 'direction', 'intention' are examples of contents, while 'statement', 'question', 'response' are uses, and *because* and *so* are examples of forms. While this categorization is not entirely satisfactory since it treats a speech act like 'direction' (command) as more directly opposed to negation than to other speech acts like statement or question, the many examples provided are a very valuable source of data. Moreover, the data provide clear evidence that the expression of causality emerged first when expressing directives, intentions and negations.

French and Nelson (1985), however, argue that this finding may be an artefact of a data collection technique which relied on observations in a here-and-now 'free play' setting, since their own semi-naturalistic study (of children 2;11 and older) found causal relations expressed coherently in the children's verbalizations of everyday scripts[1] but also found that causality in directives, intentional or negative statements was hardly present. Their data did coincide with that of the other studies in the finding that young children did not talk about causal relationships between physical objects, but again French and Nelson (1985: 54) suggest that perhaps this 'has to do with the contexts in which the data in these two studies were collected and not with any lack of competence [in the children] to do so'.

Only the French and Nelson study, of those mentioned so far, deals with the expression of causality through the conditional relationship as well as that of 'reason' (*because, so, therefore*) or 'purpose' (*so that, (in order) to*). Their work, along with that of McCabe *et al.* (1983), includes an investigation of the children's use of utterances containing *if,* as well as reviewing earlier experimental research on this topic. Two points to emerge from their study are that conditionals were produced spontaneously only in the scripts of the children aged four and older, and that these children could also construe genuinely hypothetical meanings. McCabe and her colleagues, who observed siblings at play, found that even their youngest subject (aged 2;10) used a conditional link, and that the most frequent use was to offer bribes or issue threats.

From the literature, it is clear not only that children's linguistic and conceptual abilities appear much greater when observational rather than experimental data are considered, but that the context in which the observation occurs may favour particular forms or uses of language. The children in French and Nelson's study were responding to a request to explain what happens in various routine situations and therefore bribes and threats could be predicted to be less likely to occur than where siblings played together, and directives and negations would again be less likely than in a free play situation. It therefore remains an open question whether the lack of statements of physical causality and the apparently later emergence of the conditional relation are artefacts of the limited contexts in which children's speech has been observed, and whether the construal of reason and purpose relations will generally precede the expression of conditional ones. A parental diary study such as this one of Stephen can therefore usefully contribute to the data pool by admitting data from a much wider range of settings and contexts than can be achieved by more structured data collection methods.

## 2  Expressing causality in English

The cause–effect relations examined in language acquisition research generally involve the linking of two clauses into a clause-complex. When this is done, the two clauses may have an 'equal status' grammatically, as in *A rock hit the window so it broke,* or one clause can be constructed as dependent upon the other as in *Because a rock hit the window, it broke.* The first clause-complex, linked by *so,* is an example of a paratactic link, while the second, linked by *because,* is hypotactic (Halliday 1994: Chapter 7.2). The logical choice of parataxis or hypotaxis is therefore one relevant both to the area of projection discussed in the previous chapter and to all kinds of conjunctive relations, including that of cause.

Halliday (1994: 398) also points out that the relations expressed within the clause-complex 'recur throughout the semantic system of the language and are manifested in various other environments in the lexico-grammar'. Among the manifestations he cites for cause–effect relations are those shown in Table 6.2.

**Table 6.2**  Various grammatical realizations of causality in English

| Realization of cause | Example |
| --- | --- |
| Cohesive conjunction | *A rock hit the window.* **Therefore** *it broke.* |
| Clause complex | |
| hypotactic (finite) | *The window broke* **because** *a rock hit it.* |
| hypotactic (non-finite) | *It broke* **through** *being hit by a rock.* |
| paratactic | *A rock hit the window* **so** *it broke.* |
| Circumstance within clause | *The window rattled* **due to the storm.** |
| Attribute/circumstance within clause | *The vibrations were* **from the storm.** |
| Process within clause | *The storm* **caused** *the vibrations.* |

The relation expressed in these examples is that of 'reason' (or 'consequence' in Martin's (1992a) terminology (cf. Table 4.1 on p. 139). However, it needs to be noted that there is some difference in the possibilities for causal meaning available at different points in the language system, so no single set of cause options will be relevant in every grammatical environment. For example, the categories of cause recognized by Halliday as operating as circumstance choices are those of purpose, reason and behalf, while those constructing taxis or cohesive relations are purpose, reason and condition. See Table 6.3.

**Table 6.3** Categories of cause available for different grammatical contexts (after Halliday 1994)

|  | Reason | Purpose | Condition | Behalf |
|---|---|---|---|---|
| Circumstance | *due to the storm* | *for water* |  | *for Mary* |
| Interclausal | *because it rained* | *so that it rattled* | *if it rains* |  |

In this study it is the interclausal categories, particularly those of reason and condition, that will be given detailed examination in Stephen's language. Any within-clause construction of these relations will be noted also, since these are predicted to occur later on the grounds that they typically involve a degree of ideational grammatical metaphor.

One other distinction to be noted is that of an 'internal' causal link (see Halliday and Hasan 1976), exemplified by an utterance such as *He loves me because he gives me flowers*. This relation, discussed elsewhere in the case study, is also included in various other coding systems. For Morag Donaldson (1986: 6), it involves a 'deductive' mode of relating a 'logical' content, while French and Nelson (1985: 39) refer to the conditional link in *If you haven't been outside yet, the Christmas tree lights are on* as 'elliptical' in nature. The systemic framework does not construe these kinds of links as additional subtypes of reason or condition, but as involving an opposition which cross-classifies the three types of cause, as shown in Figure 6.1.

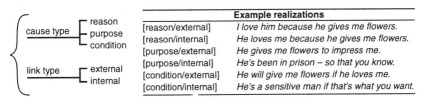

**Figure 6.1** Options for causal conjunctive links

The external/internal opposition (cf. Dijk's (1977) semantic/pragmatic connectives) is a more powerful one than Donaldson's 'deductive' mode of explanation or French and Nelson's 'elliptical' relation, in that it not only cross-classifies causal links but also other kinds of conjunctive relations, such as temporal ones, as shown in Table 6.4.

**Table 6.4** Examples of external and internal temporal conjunctive relations

| External | *First he polished his glasses, then he began his speech.* |
|---|---|
| Internal | *First he is a brilliant lawyer; secondly he has influential friends.* |

As discussed in Chapter 4, the nature of the internal/external opposition is that external conjunctive links are oriented to the field and relate activities within a sequence, or participants to activities, and so on, while internal conjunctive links are oriented to the text and the semantic organization of one part of the text to another. In written texts they may be used to organize the generic structure of the text, linking, for example, a conclusion to the body. In spoken texts, the environment is likely to be more local, linking parts of an exchange by different speakers or organizing two propositions by a single speaker. Because of their orientation to the semiosis rather than to the field being construed, internal conjunctive links can be 'experientialized' as a mental or verbal process, '*I am telling you this first, second*' (in the case of the above example) or '*I conclude, I know, I say this because . . .*' (in the case of the examples in Figure 6.1).

So far it has been suggested that causality can be considered in terms of the different grammatical environments in which it can occur (cohesively, between clauses, within a clause) and the type of causal relation (purpose, reason or condition) and the orientation to field or text (external, internal). In addition, to take up some of the issues raised in the literature, it is relevant to consider the nature of the meanings functioning as causes or effects; that is, the nature of the clauses being linked in a causal relation. This can be done in terms of their experiential nature as TRANSITIVITY structures and in terms of their interpersonal nature as speech interacts. This chapter will consider Stephen's development of a system of causal relations in terms of these various factors.

### 3  Stephen's language from 2;6 to 3;0 years

#### 3.1  Type of causal relation and typical expression

The types of causal relations and their expression found in Stephen's language up to 3 years are summarized in Table 6.5.

**Table 6.5**  Causal relations in Stephen's language, 2;6 to 3 years

| Cause type | Linkage | Within clause |
|---|---|---|
| Purpose | hypotaxis (*to . . .* ) | circumstance |
| Reason | hypotaxis (*because*) | *why?* as circumstance |
| (Condition) | cohesion (*then*) (one example) | |

Apart from Behalf circumstances, which will not be discussed here, only two types of causal meaning were well established in Stephen's language at the beginning of this study – those of purpose and reason. It is not possible to determine from this data set whether purpose or reason developed earliest,[2] but there was only a single recorded instance of a conditional relation. This was also the only cohesive causal link, one made to the addressee's proposition:

2;10;23   M:   It's time for your bath.
         S:   (cheekily) Give me some bath then.

Stephen could link two of his own clauses in a purpose or reason relation, but did not express the relation cohesively. Where causal links were made across utterances of the two interlocutors it was as a cooperative construction of a single clause complex, as in the following examples:

2;8;17    M:   Little boys can't drink wine.
         S:   (pause) 'Cause it makes sick.      (REASON)

or via ellipsis in the context of dialogue:

2;7;20    M:   Now don't touch it.
         S:   No, 'Cause it's too sticky.      (REASON)

2;10;30   M:   Why do you want it?
         S:   To draw.                    (PURPOSE)

Thus the favoured means of construing a cause–effect relation was by means of a hypotactic clause complex. Moreover on the basis of this study it can be confirmed that (apart from Behalf circumstances and *Why?* questions) the representation of cause within the transitivity structure is a later development than the linking via taxis of distinct clauses, since in the third year, only the purpose relation was observed in a circumstantial realization, and that only on one occasion:

2;7;8     S:   I want it for the blocks.

In sum, hypotaxis rather than parataxis, cohesion or circumstantial meaning was the initial form of realization for a causal relation, and purpose and reason relations were regularly construed while condition was not.

### 3.2 *Nature of constructions being linked: interpersonal*

In considering the adult linguistic system, the possibilities for linking clauses via taxis or cohesion are independent of the interpersonal status of the clauses being linked. However, this proves not to be the case early on in language development. Thus, although cause is a part of the ideational semantics with expression in the experiential system of transitivity and the logical one of taxis it is necessary to recognize that this ideational relation is initially developed within the interpersonal sphere.

There are two aspects to this, one being the nature of the speech functions which are the favoured utterance types for being extended by having a cause added. These prove to be those involved in the negotiation of goods and services rather than of information. The other aspect is that in those cases where it was information being exchanged, Stephen constructed himself into the role of participant within the transitivity structure, thus bringing the construal of experience within the personal domain.

Stephen's choices with respect to the kinds of speech acts that are elaborated by causal taxis will be illustrated shortly, based upon the fifty instances of *because* clauses recorded during this period. As an introduction to this description, the general outline of speech function options suggested by Halliday (1984) is described in Figure 6.2.

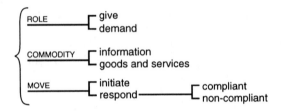

**Figure 6.2** Most general options for speech functions in English

Selections of features from this network can be given familiar speech function names as in Table 6.6.

No attempt will be made here to establish a more elaborate speech function network that would account for all possible utterances in this data. It will suffice to take Halliday's most general framework of options – all of which are in place by two-and-a-half years – and elaborate it only to the extent necessary to indicate the type of utterance Stephen chose to develop by adding a cause.

The initial network of Figure 6.2 could be expanded to include a simultaneous logical system for developing the initial message (see Figure 6.3). Doing this by explaining would of course only be one of the possibilities, although it is the only one which is being considered here.

**Table 6.6** Examples of basic speech functions in English

| Feature selection | Speech function | Example |
|---|---|---|
| give/info/initiate | Statement (S) | *John's here* |
| give/info/respond/compliant | Resp. Statement to Question (RSQ) | *Yes (John's here)* |
| non-compliant | Disclaimer | *I wouldn't know* |
| demand/info/initiate | Question (Q) | *Is John here?* |
| demand/info/respond/compliant | Acknowledge Statement (AS) | *Is he?* |
| non-compliant | Contradiction | *No, he isn't* |
| give/ g&s/initiate | Offer (O) | *Shall I lay the table?* |
| give/g&s/respond/compliant | Response Offer to Command (ROC) | *Okay (I'll do it)* |
| non-compliant | Refusal | *No (I won't)* |
| demand/g&s/initiate | Command (C) | *Lay the table* |
| demand/g&s/respond/compliant | Acknowledge Offer (AO) | *Yes, please do* |
| non-compliant | Rejection | *No, don't* |

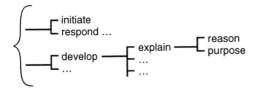

**Figure 6.3** Logical option available for expanding a move

However, in terms of Stephen's language in the third year, Figure 6.3 is misleading in its suggestion that every possible speech function could be developed by adding an explanatory cause. In fact the logical option was quite constrained with respect to speech function choice, as will be outlined below. In general it was in the negotiation of goods and services rather than information that causality was deployed in Stephen's early language. This was illustrated not only by his productive speech, but by his responses to the conditional relation which he was just coming to understand. In the parent's talk, there were models of both cohesive and hypotactic condition used in the negotiation of action. For example:

2;10;7   M: Did you hurt yourself?
        S: No.
        M: Well, don't cry then.

2;7;23   S: I don't need a bib.
        M: If you're very careful you don't need a bib.

These kinds of texts caused Stephen no difficulty, but in the following conversation when a hypothetical context (*if you see one*) was constructed by the parent in the course of giving advice, Stephen appeared to interpret it also as a here-and-now directive:

2;8;24    (M and S looking at picture of a large snake)
    S:    That's two snakes?
    M:    No, it's only one. He's wound round and round the branch.
        (tracing outline with finger) It's a big snake.
    (S touches snake's mouth)
    M:    You have to be careful of snakes. If you see one you don't
        touch it because they're dangerous.
    S:    Mm; this is a picture of a snake.

It was as if Stephen, at this stage, was so much oriented to the causal: conditional relation as a form of command that he could only construe a hypotactic conditional from the parent as a here-and-now directive, and so felt the need to remind her that they were actually looking at a picture, disregarding the hypotheticality of the context constructed by the parent. Thus in addition to Stephen's own production of causal utterances, his responses to other people's language suggest that causal meanings when they first emerged were closely identified with the negotiation of goods and services.

With respect to Stephen's productive language system, it was his own commands and responses to commands which were the principal sites for developing a dialogic move through the addition of justification – the link involved being one of reason. In the network in Figure 6.4 the grammatical realizations of the speech function choices are provided, together with examples of expanded forms where the options to [develop:explain: reason] have been taken up.

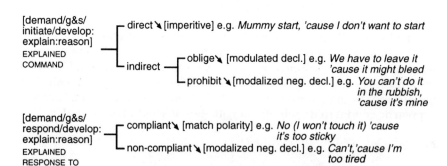

**Figure 6.4** Stephen's options for explaining commands and responses to commands, 2;6 to 3 years

A greater range of indirect commands were in fact explained by Stephen through a purpose choice, but this occurred only when negotiating a non-compliant response from the addressee:

[demand/g&s/initiate:indirect/ ↘ e.g.   *S: Can you come in the kitchen with me?*
develop:explain:purpose]                *H: What for?*
                                        *S: To bring the orange juice ...*

                                        *S: I want a pen .*
                                        *M: Why?*
                                        *S: To draw .*

In the exchange of goods and services, there were no examples of Stephen explaining one of his own offers [give goods and services], but he did occasionally develop his own rejections of adult offers, by adding a reason (see Figure 6.5).

[demand/g&s/respond/non-compliant: ↘
reject/develop:explain:reason]
EXPLAINED REJECTION OF OFFER        [1st p.neg.decl./ Mental:desire]
                                    e.g. *I don't want this 'cause it's cold*

**Figure 6.5** Explaining the rejection of an adult offer, 2;6 to 3 years

In sum, Stephen had clearly learned that while anything he might offer was likely to be accepted, his commands and his own responses to adult moves, especially if non-compliant, would be more effective if supported by a reason. In a context of negotiating goods and services in the home, Stephen was in a relation of unequal power to the other family members, but was learning verbal strategies for increasing his success in achieving his desires.

Although the majority of moves that were developed by being explained arose in the negotiation of action, there were also occasions when informative utterances were extended through hypotactic cause. Stephen's options here for the period 2;6 to 3 years are summarized in Figure 6.6.

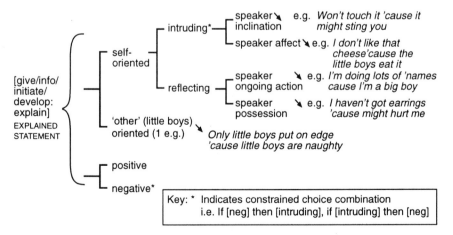

**Figure 6.6** Stephen's options for explaining statements, 2;6 to 3 years

Figure 6.6, taken in conjunction with Figures 6.4 and 6.5, shows that the main contexts motivating a specification of cause by Stephen were those involving the negotiation of action, since even where information was given it was often to specify intention or opinion – the [intruding] option above. These data thus support the findings of Hood and Bloom (1991: 342) that 2- to 3-year-olds' causal utterances 'made reference most often to actions or states that were either directions or intentions'. Since Stephen's language was tracked in a variety of contexts and not just a 'free play' situation, it would appear that the restriction on the deployment of causal language is not an artefact of the data collection process, but a genuinely developmental phenomenon.

Because it was preferences, intentions, prohibitions, commands and refusals that were being explained or justified by Stephen, these propositions were usually modalized. They were moreover often negative in polarity. Even among the information-giving kind, most of the propositions to which an explanation was added were negative, as if what needed explaining was the 'marked' situation or experience. Again, this finding is paralleled by Hood and Bloom's study where the directions and intentions expressed in causal statements were 'often with some negative aspect to the situation' (1991: 342). In the data from Stephen, the negation expressed in the primary clause constituting the command, refusal or statement can be compared with the explaining clauses themselves which, with only a single exception, were positive.

Thus, although hypotactic reason clauses were used frequently during this period, the system was constrained in a number of ways:  only particular kinds of dialogic moves were expanded through the addition of an explanation and within the realm of information-giving all but one occurrence involved Stephen himself as a participant. The exception was a 'preview' text explaining the behaviour of 'little boys', something of great affectual significance to Stephen personally.

An attempt to capture the systemic options available for a particular linguistic system has therefore revealed that the interpersonal negotiation of action and feeling is a source of expansion of the meaning options. On the one hand, the deictically centred negotiation of goods and services provided the principal impetus for developing this area of the grammar. On the other hand, when information was exchanged, it did not concern the 'objective' world of third parties, but was centred on the child's own current or contemplated engagement with that world, with the first move beyond this being a broadening of perspective to include 'little boys' in general.

*3.3 Seeking explanation*

At this early stage there was only a single instance of seeking confirmation of cause by means of a polar interrogative, and this was in response to an indirect command:

2;10     (S in bath)
         M:  It's not a good idea [to drink drips from the tap].
         S:  'Cause it's dirty?
         M:  No, it's not dirty but it might be hot.

By contrast, there were 58 recorded demands for explanation through the use of a *why?* interrogative. These do not require the child speaker to supplement his or her own dialogue move, but require that the addressee develop a circumstantial or hypotactic explanation to the speaker's proposition.

One reason for the prevalence of *why?* questions was undoubtedly Stephen's discovery that chaining of cause and effect can be continued indefinitely, and that asking *why?* is therefore a delightful way of coercing the addressee by perpetually assigning her/him the role of giver-of-information-in-response. Any dialogue could now be continued indefinitely, however absurdly, with the child controlling the initiating moves. Stephen became quite conscious of playing this game, and found it hilarious, while doubtless exploring in the course of it some important understandings about the nature of dialogue and of causality in English.

This was one context then for the seeking of explanation; one which was not much concerned with the content of the explanation, but rather with the control over the dialogue that the questioner achieved and with the general nature of a cause that, while functioning to explain an effect, it could simultaneously constitute an effect in need of explanation.

### 3.3.1 Intruding with *why?*

Apart from dialogic games where Stephen used *why?* to coerce the addressee into responding, the principal context for the seeking of explanation was again that of negotiating action. All the speech functions concerned with the exchange of goods and services for which Stephen gave explanations provided contexts for demanding explanation when produced by the addressee. In other words, having learned that commands in various guises as well as refusals needed to be justified to be taken seriously, he would also demand such justifications from the adult through challenging *why?* questions. Thus, as formalized in Figure 6.7, the [non-compliant] option within the speech function network for responses might be an outright refusal [refuse], or might be to stall or abort the exchange by some kind of challenge, including demanding a reason from the person giving the command [challenge:demand explanation].

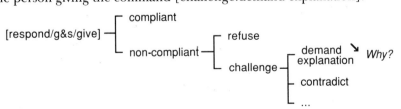

**Figure 6.7** Responding non-compliantly with *Why?*

Tables 6.7 and 6.8 exemplify the taking up of the [challenge] option. (For speech function abbreviations see Table 6.6.)

**Table 6.7** Examples of demanding an explanation to challenge a command, 2;6 to 3 years

| Age | Example | Speech function |
| --- | --- | --- |
| 2;7;8 | M: Oh, oh, Stevie!! Don't eat it like that!<br>S: Why? | M: C<br>S: challenge: demand explanation |
| 2;7;8 | (M and S playing with 'stacking' toy baskets)<br>M: Oh, not on there, no.<br>S: Why?<br>M: 'Cause it's not the biggest one. | <br>M: C<br>S: challenge: demand explanation<br>M: justify |
| 2;9;15 | (talking about playing with ball)<br>S: Why – why not in the house?<br>M: Because it bangs things, darling. | <br>S: challenge: demand explanation<br>M: justify |

**Table 6.8** Examples of demanding explanation to challenge a refusal, 2;6 to 3 years

| Age | Example | Speech function |
| --- | --- | --- |
| 2;7;7 | M: Would you like some salmon?<br>S: And peas too.<br>M: Peas? Peas have all gone, darling.<br>S: Why?<br>M: Because you ate them. | M: O<br>S: AO/C<br>M: refusal<br>S: challenge: demand explanation<br>M: justify |
| 2;10;7 | (earlier S requested salmon for tea)<br>S: Why we can't have chips?<br>M: You can't have chips every day.<br>S: Why we – why we can't have chips?<br>M: Because it's not good for you.<br>S: Yes it is.<br>M: Not every day.<br>S: Mm (contradictory tone).<br>M: Chips are good sometimes.<br>S: I like chips!<br>M: I know you do, darling.<br>S: (crying) I like chips.<br>M: Oh, don't be silly.<br>  You're having salmon, you said.<br>  I haven't got any chips.<br>S: Why?<br>  No, but at the chip shop.<br>M: I'm not going out to the chip shop.<br>S: Why?<br>M: I haven't got any money anyway. | S: Q/indirect C<br>M: RSQ/refusal<br>S: challenge:demand explanation<br>M:justify<br>S: challenge:contradict<br>M:challenge: contradict<br>S: challenge: contradict<br>M:S<br>S: S intrude/indirect C<br>M:AS<br>S: S intrude/indirect C<br>M:RSQ/refusal<br>S<br>S/indirect refusal<br>S: challenge: demand explanation<br>C<br>M: refusal<br>S: challenge: demand explanation<br>M:justify |

The last text in Table 6.8 (2;10;7), where Stephen insisted on chips for dinner, had his mother repeatedly on the defensive, responding to his challenges. It represents a contrast with earlier occasions before he had become experienced in these moves. For example, in a typical text from three months earlier (given as Table 6.9), Stephen's strategy for manipulating the addressee was simply to repeat his command (in the indirect form of an expression of affect), intensifying the phonological expression of affect and/or adding a politeness marker.

**Table 6.9** Example of early negotiation of goods and services

| Age | Example | | Speech function |
|-----|---------|---|---|
| 2;7;7 | (S watches M open cupboard) | | |
| | 1 | S: I want a vitamin. | S: C (indirect) |
| | 2 | (tearfully) I want a vitamin. | C |
| | 3 | M: No, no vitamins. | M: refusal |
| | 4 | S: I do want a vitamin. | S: C |
| | 5 | M: Yeah, I know you want a vitamin. | M: AS |
| | 6 | S: I want a <u>vitamin.</u> | S: C |
| | 7 | H: You don't have a vitamin. | H: refusal |
| | 8 | S: I <u>do</u> want a vitamin! | S: C |
| | 9 | M: I know we had it last night, but usually we have it in the morning. | M: S (implicit justification) |
| | 10 | H: We don't – (turns to M) he just wants a vitamin. He thinks he gets everything he wants, doesn't he? | |
| | 11 | M: Well, he seems to, yes. | |
| | 12 | S: I'm going to get a spoon (previously taken from him). | S: S |
| | 13 | M: You're <u>not</u>, Stevie. | M: C |
| | 14 | S: I am. | S: refusal |
| | 15 | M: I'm going to take them away again if you do. | M: S (threat) |
| | 16 | S: I <u>want</u> it. | S: C |
| | 17 | M: I don't want to listen to bang bang bang all through the meal, thank you. | M: refusal (implicit justification) |
| | 18 | S: I want it, please. | S: C |
| | 19 | M: Mm, afterwards. | M: ROC |

In fact, after three or four consecutive refusals, the parent did provide some unsolicited statements which served the function of justifying her refusals (e.g. 9, 17, Table 6.9), although these were not explicitly marked through causal links as explanations. More striking, though, is the sense of

Stephen's rhetorical powerlessness in this early text as he struggles to assert his wishes. All in all it does not seem surprising that, once having begun, the deployment of demands for explanation was such a frequent strategy for putting the addressee on the defensive in the negotiation of goods and services.

### 3.3.2 Reflecting with *why?*

During the period from 2;6 to 3 years, Stephen also sometimes demanded an explanation in the context of information exchange. However, information-seeking *why?* questions were not only much less frequent than challenging ones – only eight in number – but often appeared themselves to be a way of intruding into experience rather than simply reflecting upon it.

For example, when a *why?* question from Stephen followed an adult statement, this was often because that statement was in some way an unsatisfactory response to a previous demand for information:

2;8;15    (M has book and pen in hand)
        S:   What you gonna draw?
        M:   I'm not drawing, darling.
        S:   Why?

2;8;20    S:   Pocket in my trousers?
        M:   No.
        S:   Why?

In cases like these, the adult's response was not apparently the one Stephen was hoping for and thus the demand for explanation was verging on an indirect expression of affect, itself a 'metaphorical' way of giving commands. Thus these kinds of questions were perhaps still a way of intruding into the dialogue by challenging the addressee, rather than serving to reflect on states of affairs in the world. At the same time, the source of Stephen's dissatisfaction was some violation in what he had come to expect, rather than any control being exercised over him, and thus there was a genuine element of seeking to make sense of observed differences in activities and things he was learning about.

Later in the year, there were a few demands for explanation by Stephen which followed his own observations and statements, and these were again occasioned by some disruption to the predictable. For example:

2;8;7     (M is working using both a red and blue biro)
        S:   You doing two pens?

M:  Yes.
S:  Why?

2;10;7    (looking out of car window near park)
          S:  No garbage trucks today; no horsies! Why is there's no
              horsies?
          M:  I don't know, darling. Maybe they're having their tea.

2;10;7    (in car)
          S:  What – what – why not the drips are coming down?
          M:  'Cause it stopped raining a long time ago.
          S:  No, but but just a little bit (?rain) (indicating puddles on
              ground).

2;10;23   S:  He doesn't wear clothes (stroking cat).
          M:  No.
          S:  Why? Why he doesn't wear some clothes?
          M:  Well, animals don't wear clothes.
          S:  Why? Why they don't wear clothes?

As with the information-giving examples to which he developed causal
explanations himself (see the examples in Figure 6.6), these examples of
reflective enquiry sought to develop explanations for negative
propositions. In a study of the language of Halliday's subject, Phillips
(1985) shows that Nigel's early reflective negative propositions were used
to verbalize observed contrasts between things (*that soup; that not soup*,
etc.) or contrasts between actual and predicted events. It would seem that
the next step for an English-speaking child is to expect that such
differences should be explained. Thus early *why?* questions, unlike most
other interrogative forms, are more often negative in form. (In the earlier
case study of Hal's language, the first negative interrogative was a *why?*
question (*why it doesn't go round?*), commenting on the failure of a
clockwork toy to operate as predicted (Painter 1984: 257).)

### 3.4 Sequence and dependence of cause and effect

In the explicit linguistic construction of the cause–effect relationship,
effects preceded causes in every instance but one during this period up to
three years of age. That occasion (*It's a spider 'cause got to put it in the
dustbin*) saw Stephen incorrectly using the hypotactic linker *'cause*. Such
'incorrect' uses of *because* are generally treated in the psychological
literature as evidence of a cognitive confusion about what is cause and
what is effect. However, when viewed in the context of the child's other
causal utterances, as is possible in a longitudinal study, there may emerge
grounds for rejecting this interpretation.

    In Stephen's case, it should be first noted that he created cause–effect links correctly at all other times, but that the incorrect utterance was a little different from those other occasions. In other cases where a classification was causally linked to an action, the action being negotiated was at the forefront of attention (e.g. *you can't do it in the rubbish 'cause . . .* ; *I don't want this 'cause . . .*) whereas in the anomalous case Stephen was focusing on the object and deciding what it was. Having classified it *it's a spider*, he then wanted to retrospectively assign this proposition the status of cause in order to explain his proposed action – an action which only occurred to him after he had examined and classified the dead insect. Secondly, Stephen's system at this point had only the one causal conjunction, *(be)cause*. It can therefore be argued that the child was attempting to press into service his only reason linker, the hypotactic conjunction, to construe the semantic relation of causality. A third point in support of this interpretation is that there is evidence that 'overextending' current resources of wording when coping initially with a new meaning is a common strategy. This is discussed in the literature on lexical development, and examples have also been provided in this case study – for example Stephen's confusing use of *call* reported in Chapter 3, Section 4.1 (page 103).

The one anomalous example shows that Stephen would soon need to develop new realizations to enable a greater flexibility in the expression of cause and effect. But, leaving that example aside, the logical options for any speech function choice self-developed by explanation was as shown in Figure 6.8. This figure presents the earlier (boldface) choices from the perspective of later developments, after the model provided by Phillips (1985). From the perspective of the language in the third year itself, there were fewer systems, since the three options of [taxis:hypotaxis] and [effect initial] in fact constituted a single choice of linking by cause (ignoring the single conditional utterance here).

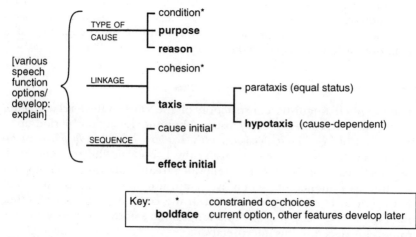

Figure 6.8 Stephen's options for causal links from 2;6 onwards

If the function of language were indeed to mirror prestructured reality, it would appear anomalous that the preferred construction of cause in English is as a hypotactic relation wherein the proposition constructing the reason is dependent on the one constructing the effect. Even odder perhaps would be the implication raised by these data that the unmarked case is for the cause to be sequenced to follow the effect. However, if one views language as developing as a tool for understanding and achieving in the world, then it seems reasonable that the earliest functional motivation for constructing cause-and-effect links might well be to negotiate action, and if this is the object, then both the sequencing and the dependency status appear predictable. One would expect both the starting point and the Head proposition of the utterance to be the specification of the action being negotiated, with the justification being added as a secondary development to enhance the initial dialogic move to make it more persuasive.

Moreover both the development of cause in the negotiation of action and the preferred sequencing can be traced to the models provided by the adult grammar. It is a well-described characteristic of middle-class parent–child talk (see e.g. Cloran 1989), that in contexts of control, specification of reasons can be expected from the adult. Indeed the parent may initially be the one to supply a reason on the child's behalf to justify the child's own non-compliant speech acts, as in the following example:

2;7;1    S:   I don't want this.
        M:   Aren't you hungry?

On other occasions, justifications for commands, refusals and rejections will be demanded by the adult, thereby teaching the child that the provision of explanation will be a necessary tool in the successful negotiation of goods and services. There are also innumerable examples in this data set of the parent justifying her own commands without prompting:

2;7;7    M:   Tell you what we're gonna do; we're gonna take those big heavy shoes off, 'cause-
        S:   I don't want to take shoes off!
        M:   Yes, because I haven't got shoes on and you might tread on me.

2;8;20    M:   Oh, leave the window, darling, 'cause it's raining now.

2;10;7    M:   Can we have this window up, because it's so noisy.

2;10;7    M:   Don't put your fingers in [fish tank] though, 'cause you might frighten the fish.

2;19;7    M:  Oh, don't play with that umbrella, darling; you'll make it all
open up.

The importance of adult models can also be seen in the 'odd one out'
in the types of causal link – the condition relation. This has already been
discussed as exceptional in that it developed later than the others and in
the first place only cohesively across speaker turns:

2;10;23   M:  It's time for your bath.
S:   (cheekily) Give me some bath then.

As this example shows, it was also an exception in that this (joint)
construction of causality involved the uttering of the cause (condition)
before that of the effect. In this, Stephen was simply mirroring many
examples where it was the parent who built on one of his utterances in
such a way as to show that certain consequences followed from his
statements, and not necessarily ones agreeable to him. For example:

2;7;7     S:   Don't want this.
M:   Well, eat the fish then.

2;10;7    S:   (not wanting a Band-aid removed) It might be bleeding.
M:   Well, then we put a new one on.

2;10;7    M:   Did you hurt yourself?
S:   No.
M:   Well, don't cry then.

Although the family members also provided models of hypotactic
condition, it was these kinds of dialogic texts which were first taken up by
Stephen. And it can be seen that he adopted the model very exactly in that
first recorded instance at 2;10;23, given above: the parent's indirect demand
for action by the child was transformed by the child's response into a
condition which required consequential (and possibly unwelcome) action
from the parent. So although in more structured contexts of data collection
the influence of adult modelling appears equivocal, when tracking a
particular grammatical system over time in a diary study, the importance of
the child's construal of jointly created texts can be seen more clearly.

### 3.5 Nature of constructions being linked: experiential

Some attention has now been given to the semantic and grammatical
nature of the causal links expressed (as hypotactic reason and purpose,
cohesive condition) and also to the speech functional status of the
propositions which might give rise to causal elaboration. And it has been
shown that the construal of the logical-semantic relation of cause was in

fact constrained by speech function choices from the interpersonal metafunction. A further question, which relates to the Piagetian issue of whether 'physical' or 'psychological' causality predominates, is to determine whether there were any constraints or tendencies with respect to the TRANSITIVITY status of the clauses functioning as causes and effects.

Given the pre-selection of a clause-complex structure, the possible TRANSITIVITY structures construed as effects and causes are exemplified in Table 6.10.

**Table 6.10** Examples of TRANSITIVITY selections for cause–effect links, 2;6 to 3 years

| Effect | Cause |
|---|---|
| **material** | **affect** |
| interactant action explained by affect of speaker: | |
| *Mummy start;* | *I don't want to start* |
| *I'm jumping* | *'cause I like jumping* |
| **material** | **material** |
| interactant action on object explained by possible action of object: | |
| *won't touch it* | *'cause it might sting you* |
| *we have to leave it* | *'cause it might bleed* |
| speaker action explained by previous unsuccessful action (one example): | |
| *I trying to put my arm in like that* | *'cause it wouldn't go* |
| **material** | **attributive** |
| (speaker) action explained by characteristic of Actor: | |
| *I'm doing lots of names* | *'cause I'm a big boy* |
| *only little boys put on edge* | *'cause little boys are naughty* |
| interactant action on object explained by characteristic of object: | |
| *?'cause got to put it in the dustbin* | *it's a spider* |
| *you can't do it in the rubbish* | *'cause it's mine* |
| **affect** | **material** |
| affect of speaker explained by action involving Phenomenon: | |
| *we don't want a big dog* | *'cause he would licks on my tongue* |
| *I don't like that cheese, no* | *'cause the little boys eat skin (? ) cheese* |
| **affect** | **attributive** |
| affect of speaker explained by characteristic of Phenomenon: | |
| *I don't like this* | *'cause make me sick* |
| *I don't want this* | *'cause it's cold* |
| **attributive/possessive** | **material** |
| speaker (non-)possession of object explained by purpose of object: | |
| *I've got a sword* | *for bang the fluff* |
| non-possession explained by hypothetical action of object: | |
| *I haven't got earrings* | *'cause might hurt me* |

Given the MOOD selection of [wh- interrogative], the effects queried were as shown in Table 6.11.

**Table 6.11** Examples of TRANSITIVITY selections for *Why?* interrogatives, 2;6 to 3 years

| Process type | Example *Why?* interrogative |
|---|---|
| material | |
|    interactant participants | *Why we can't have chips?* |
|    third-party participants | *Why not the drips are coming down?* |
| affect | *Why (do you like going this way)?* |
| existential | *Why is there's no horsies?* |
| attributive | *Why (isn't that one a pressing one)?* |

The variety of process types being explained via wh-interrogatives was partly due to the fact that most of these interrogatives occurred in response to adult utterances and depended on ellipsis (indicated by brackets in the examples of Table 6.11).

Overall, given that Stephen's system was almost certainly larger than the recorded text examples would allow, it would appear that material, mental:affect and relational attributive processes functioned relatively freely as cause or effect but with some restriction on participant realization, as summarized in Figure 6.9.

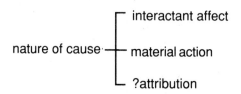

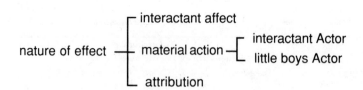

**Figure 6.9** Experiential options for clauses functioning as cause or effect, 2;6 to 3 years

This figure shows that there are both interpersonal and experiential influences on the kind of experience that could be construed as a cause or effect in Stephen's third year. In some cases the choice of process realizing the cause or effect element is in fact determined by the speech function choices discussed earlier. For example, mental:affect processes with speech role participants are a routine way of realizing a command or justifying a rejection, and it is noticeable that these are the only types of mental processes found as cause or effect in this first data set. Thus choices for experiential realizations of an ideational meaning (causality) would appear to be created in order to extend the speaker's interpersonal options.

Where there was no interpersonal impetus, mental processes did not figure in the data as causes or effects and nor did verbal symbolic processes. There was thus an experiential limitation on the construction of causality, since in his third year, Stephen neither gave nor demanded explanations for people's locutions, nor for their ideas. Moreover, when the tense realizations of the experiential structures are considered, it emerges that there was no linking of cause and effect in the recall of experience, nor across temporal domains (except for the single reflective example *I trying to put my arm in like that 'cause it wouldn't go*). This restriction can also be explained in terms of the embedding of causality in the ongoing negotiation of action.

From this data set, the Piagetian position that psychological cause develops earliest gains some credence, but needs modification. It is certainly not the case that this child was principally concerned with elucidating the motives and psychological states of others. Indeed that would be one of the things strikingly absent from these data, although it was present in the parent talk (mainly in talk over stories, explaining the characters' actions and reactions). On the other hand, the data are also striking in their lack of dispassionate 'uninvolved' observations of physical causality, just as was the case with Hood and Bloom's (1991: 364) data. It was the behaviour of the interlocutors and/or consequences to the self that gave rise to the linguistic expression of cause.

Thus when Stephen coded either cause or effect as a mental process of affect this was usually with a first-person Senser. And when he initially reflected on the causal relations between two physical events, two material processes, it was as a relation between an action and a possible consequence to himself, for example, *Won't touch it 'cause it might sting you* said as he peered at an insect. What was under attention in Stephen's utterance was the consequence of an action to the self, and the linguistic construction of this shows that it was the child's abstaining from action, the child's disinclination or self-prohibition, which was being accounted for rather than the relation between the physical actions (touching and stinging) themselves. Thus the effect action, stinging, is construed as the cause – the cause of the abstention/prohibition, the reason for not creating the condition for the second action, as shown in Example 6.1.

*Example 6.1*     *Won't touch it*          *'cause*     *(if did touch it)*     *it might sting you*

| neg. action [EFFECT] | | (IMPLICIT) | consequence to self [REASON] |
|---|---|---|---|
| action 1 (touch) [CAUSE] | | | action 2 (sting) [EFFECT] |

An example such as this, where Stephen monitored in language the predicted consequences of a proposed action, was one way that Stephen began to extend the use of causal expressions from the realm of negotiating action and intention to further interpreting and generalizing about experience. Another way this was done was to link an individual participant with a categorization, as with the utterance *I'm doing lots of names because I'm a big boy*. Being a big boy can only constitute an explanation if it is a characteristic of big boys that they do names. Thus the nature of the reason given, not an affectual one but a classification of the Actor, is a way of construing the generalization that *big boys do names*, although doing so in the familiar and specific context of monitoring his own ongoing action. Up to this point, any such generalizations were rare (see Chapter 4), but the deployment of cause was one way of achieving them.

The very rare genuinely information-seeking *why?* questions also allowed for a deeper reflection on experience. An enquiry such as *Why not the drips are coming down?* sought an antecedent reason for the observed and unexpected (non-)action, and showed what was taken for granted in the child's construction of experience. As discussed in Chapter 4, Stephen did not enquire why drips rolled downward because this was what always happened in his experience – too natural, too much 'the way things are known to be' – to require explanation. An exception to this was the enquiry about the family cat, *Why she doesn't wear clothes?*, where Stephen did step back and reflect quite explicitly on an already construed generalization. Perhaps the anomalous status of the pet as a family member and yet not a member of the human family, together with considerable experience of the anthropomorphism of children's picture-books, had made this an askable question.

### 3.6 Summary: 2;6 to 3;0 years

In the second half of the third year Stephen freely asked *why?* questions, used the logico-semantic relation of reason (as well as purpose) to link clauses into clause-complexes, and on a single occasion deployed a cohesive conditional conjunction. In all of this two things were apparent. One was close interrelation of interpersonal and ideational factors, while the other was the interrelation between models of language provided by adults and the child's own semantic explorations.

Potentially the cause for any event can be sought, it being possible to view each cause in turn as an effect of some antecedent causative action. In playing dialogic games asking *why?* children discover this as well as discovering a way to prolong any discourse indefinitely while staying in control of it. However, these data suggest that exploring and understanding such chains of events may not be the main goal in the service of which the linguistic expression of causality is deployed. For Stephen, it emerged not as a tool for dispassionate understanding and specification of the links between events, but as a tool for interpersonal negotiation, supporting commands and refusals and challenging non-compliant responses from the addressee. This interactional orientation also meant that the system of modality was heavily drawn upon.

Where cause–effect links were constructed more reflectively, they either were focused on explaining his own (negative) intention or were a means of generalizing by making reference to category membership or attributes as a cause for behaviour to or by an entity. Thus, even in more reflective uses, cause–effect relations between physical events were not fore-grounded at all – a finding which corroborates earlier naturalistic studies of this age group, also carried out on middle-class children.

Apart from verbal games and challenges to the addressee's moves, many *why?* questions actually constituted covert complaints, a way of wishing things to be different. However, there were also the beginnings of reflective explorations, where an expectation countered might give rise to true explanation seeking. Most of these questions, like the declarative clause complexes, included negative polarity, again confirming earlier findings in the literature.

The ordering of the clauses in the cause–effect relation – the fact that the clause construing the cause always followed that constructing the effect – needs to be understood in relation to the contexts in which the relation was instantiated. Stephen's attention was on the proposition construed as the effect, one which generally encoded a prohibited or desired action, and in some cases one cause would do as well as another as long as it made the speech act more effective. Even on more reflective occasions the effect–cause sequence is understandable. In such cases, the movement was predictably from the specific here-and-now observation as a starting point (*I haven't got earrings* said looking at M's earrings; *I'm doing lots of names* said while scribbling) to a hypothetical or general statement as a modifying comment (*'cause might hurt me*; *'cause I'm a big boy*). However, there was one recorded occasion when Stephen constructed a clause-complex with the alternate cause^effect ordering, suggesting that he would soon need to develop an appropriate grammatical form for this option.

The importance of adult models of the meanings he was creating was apparent in these data. The single conditional text was one in which Stephen adopted the role often taken by the dialogue partner in other texts, and the fact that middle-class households of this kind value the negotiation of action through talk, call for and model explanations of non-compliant action and offer unsolicited explanations of their own coercive behaviour has to be seen as a highly relevant one when interpreting the data. At the same time, children will only adopt those linguistic forms which are relevant to the meanings important to them at a particular stage. Stephen, for example, heard texts using hypotactic condition and using the reason relation to discuss other people's motives, or impersonal relation-ships, and he heard clause-complexes with a cause^effect ordering (using *so*), but did not adopt these options for himself at this stage. He took up initially only the meanings and realizations most relevant to his own discursive needs. While his development of meaning choices was guided by those he interacted with, he himself was an equal partner in the process.

Overall, these data confirm that the initial development of causality can be seen not as the initial understanding of pre-existent relations between material phenomena, but as arising from the child's social situation in which particular kinds of interacts become more effective if causally enhanced, in which the consequences of the child's own actions are continually brought to his attention linguistically and in which behaviours of and by particular categories of participants are seen as expectable (spiders are unwelcome, little boys do little boy things, etc.). In the third year of life for Stephen it was very clearly in engagement with the talk of others, rather than in private observation, that causality became a tool for achieving and potentially for learning.

## 4  Stephen's language from 3;0 to 4;0 years

In discussing the data for the fourth year, the main changes in the possibilities for realizing causality will be outlined, together with a consideration of the texts in which these were instantiated. Developments involved a general freeing-up of choice combinations between the logical, experiential and interpersonal metafunctions. Apart from this, the three most important changes to be discussed concern the emergence of paratactic clause-complexes of reason, the development of the conditional relation and the development of internal cause.

### 4.1  Type of causal relation and typical expression

By the end of the fourth year, a number of the 'holes' in the chart displaying the linguistic nature of the external causal relation were filled, as shown in Table 6.12, where new possibilities (arising from 3 to 4 years) are shown in bold.

**Table 6.12**  Causal relations in Stephen's language, 3 to 4 years

| Type | Linkage | | | Within clause |
|------|---------|---|---|---------------|
| Purpose | hypotaxis (*to ...; so*) | parataxis N/A | **cohesion** (*that's so*) | ?**participant**; circumstance |
| Reason | hypotaxis (*because*) | **parataxis** (*so*) | **cohesion** (*so; that's why/because*) | *Why?*; ?**participant** (embedded clause) |
| Condition | **hypotaxis** (*if*) | | **cohesion** (*then*) | N/A |

The table indicates that the two major areas of extension were in grammatical contexts for realizing the reason link and in the development of the conditional relation realized both hypotactically and cohesively.

## 4.1.1 Purpose

For the sake of economy, the purpose relation will not be pursued in this description. However, three new forms can be noted. For the first time an interrogative complex was produced (e.g. *What do you do to milk to make it turn into butter?*), for the first time *so (that)* was used to construe the relation and at 3;5 there was a single example of the cohesive and metaphorical form *That's so (that)* – (see discussion below under 'reason' links).

## 4.1.2 Reason: new paratactic and cohesive/metaphorical forms

The distribution of kinds of external reason links was as shown in Table 6.13.

**Table 6.13** External reason links recorded from 3 to 4 years

| Type of link | hypotaxis | parataxis | cohesion (*so*) | metaphor *That's why/because* |
|---|---|---|---|---|
| Number of examples | 153 | 12 | 4 | 20 |

This shows that new ways of constructing a reason relation emerged in the fourth year. Paratactic links were created for the first time, as in *I'm just a little boy so I do little blows,* and a very few occasions of *so* may be taken as cohesive, as in:

3;7;17     S:  Some big trucks; so let's look for more . . .

Another new possibility for constructing a reason relation was through REFERENCE and TRANSITIVITY in the production of *that's why*. This was first recorded at 3;5;6 a little before an attested example of the purpose relation using *that's so*. Initially, *that's why* developed as a way of linking to the addressee's utterance and may perhaps best be interpreted as a cohesive conjunction. The use of *that's why* is clearly comparable with a cohesive conjunction like *therefore* in that it allows for a causal link to be made across independent propositions outside the clause-complex structure. However, within the adult system a preferable analysis is to treat the expression of reason as a participant within a relational process:

*Example 6.2*     *That*     *is*     *[[why . . . ]]*          CAUSE AS PARTICIPANT

| Token | | Value |
|---|---|---|

This is to interpret *that's why* as an ideational grammatical metaphor and such an interpretation captures the proportionality between constructions such as the following:

|  |  |  |
|---|---|---|
| *That* | *is* | *why/because . . .* |
| *The reason/effect* | *is* | *that . . .* |
| *The fact that . . .* | *is* | *the reason that . . .* |

It also allows for the possibility of variation in the form of the process (e.g. *would be, might've been*).

At first *That's why* was used indiscriminately to construct the embedded *why?* clause as either cause or effect. On the first recorded occasion, Stephen actually double-coded as follows:

3;5;6    (S calls Hal to breakfast)
        H:  (protests) <u>You</u>'re not having breakfast yet.
        S:  That's why because you're not coming. Come on, have your porridge.

Thereafter, he simply used *that's why* without making it explicit as to which proposition served as cause and which as effect, as in the following examples:

3;5;12   M:  (to self, stuck in traffic jam) Oh, why didn't we move?
        S:  Oh, that's why there's red traffic lights.

3;6      S:  See, I call that a mudiot, 'cause it's a little bit small; that's why.
        M:  What are you talking about?
        S:  That's why I call it a little mudiot.

It was not till the end of this period that he developed *that's because* as an additional realization, allowing him to differentiate between an embedded clause functioning as cause and one functioning as effect.

3;10;7   S:  (making joke) Pegs stick on the washing line. That's because there's marmalade on the washing line and the pegs stick on.

Again, there seems no reason to assume that after such a long period of successfully construing cause–effect relations via hypotaxis, Stephen had suddenly become cognitively confused about the relation itself when he first used *that's why* inappropriately. It is rather that in the attempt to construct the relation in a new fashion, he had adopted a single expression form to make the causal link with the preceding utterance, concentrating at first on simply managing the link via cohesion. The addressees made the appropriate interpretations until the point where he was confident enough in using the embedding to expand the system to include an explicit coding of the embedded clause as either cause or effect.

### 4.1.3 Condition: hypotactic and cohesive links

In the earlier data set, there had been a single late example of a conditional relation in the form of a cohesive link to the addressee's utterance (using *then*). In the fourth year, condition became quite prominent, as shown in Table 6.14.

**Table 6.14** Conditional links recorded from 3 to 4 years

| Type of link | hypotaxis: <br> *if (then)*     *unless* | cohesion to addressee's speech: *then* |
|---|---|---|
| Number of examples | 55        2 | 7 |

Although there were several further examples of cohesive links across speaker turns, the great majority of conditionals were in the form of hypotactic clauses using *if*. The first was recorded at 3;3, as soon as intensive data collection resumed in the fourth year.

The only example of a paratactic conditional link was when Stephen 'took over' a frequently heard adult utterance when 'speaking for' the adult:

3;11;19   M: Shut the door.
          S:  Or the heat will go out.

The two recorded examples of *unless* were also immediate imitations of adult speech, so were probably not yet part of Stephen's own productive system.

*4.2 Sequencing and interdependence of cause and effect*

In addition to expansion of the options in terms of semantic type and inter-dependency relation, another freeing-up of the possibilities for expressing causality concerns the sequencing of cause and effect. Largely due to the new options for realizing causality, Stephen was no longer restricted to sequencing the effect before the cause. The possibilities in the earlier data set and the new possibilities at age three to four are summarized in Table 6.15.

**Table 6.15** Sequencing possibilities for cause–effect links, 2;7 to 4 years

| | Hypotactic link | | | | Paratactic/ cohesion | | Within clause | |
|---|---|---|---|---|---|---|---|---|
| | Effect initial | | Cause initial | | | | | |
| | 2;7–3 | 3–4 | 2;7–3 | 3–4 | 2;7–3 | 3–4 | 2;7–3 | 3–4 |
| purpose | √ | √ | x | x | N/A | N/A | 1 e.g. | √ |
| reason | √ | √ | x | x | 1 e.g.? | √ | x | √ |
| condition | x | √ (rare) | x | √ | 1 e.g. | √ | x | x |

When two clauses are linked through hypotaxis, the dependent clause will always construe the cause and the main clause the effect, but either clause may begin the clause-complex, as shown in Examples 6.3a–b:

*Example 6.3a*    *It broke because I dropped it.*    EFFECT FIRST

*Example 6.3b*    *Because I dropped it, it broke.*    CAUSE FIRST

Within systemic theory, the difference in ordering is interpreted as a textual choice, with Example 6.3a representing an unmarked ordering and Example 6.3b representing a 'Theme-marked' option. However, in Stephen's language during the fourth year, the possibility of varying the textual organization of the clause-complex was scarcely developed. All hypotactic complexes linked by reason took the unmarked, effect-first ordering (as was the case with all Hood and Bloom's subjects), while, with only three exceptions, all conditional complexes realized the alternative sequence with the condition preceding the effect.

### 4.2.1 Sequence within reason clause-complexes

Although there was no flexibility in the sequencing of hypotactic reason or purpose complexes at this stage, Stephen could now deploy a paratactic link to achieve a cause + effect ordering (as well as deploying grammatical metaphor). In making use of a different form of taxis to achieve a different ordering of cause and effect, Stephen was following the same pattern of development as Hood and Bloom's subjects.

One context for the use of paratactic reason (and its cause + effect sequencing) was the staging of a recount of experience. In a recount, the sequence of events is always foregrounded and thus the presentation of cause before effect is very natural:

3;10;2    (S considers a puzzling experience of coming home to an empty house, checking for H at the school and then returning home to find him there)
S:    Hal was at school and we couldn't see him and – and – and Hal was – and Hal <u>was</u> at school but we couldn't see him so – so – so we went back . . .

However, most examples of paratactic cause involved some kind of negotiation with the addressee. In the following examples, the relevant complex is in bold:

3;4;30    S:    (ineffectually dabbing at nose after much sniffing)
M:    Big blow (holding hanky to S's nose); big blow (S snuffles weakly); big blow! (wipes his nose)
S:    I can't always do a big blow; big boys, big boys, they do big blows. **I'm just a little boy so I do little blows.**

3;7;17    (S talking about friend at preschool)
          S:   And he could take my thing home and he will give it back to
               me tomorrow.
          M:   Which thing is that, my darling?
          S:   My blue – my blue thing that makes stamps; that make-
          M:   Blue thing that makes stamps?
          S:   Yeah.
          M:   Oh, I don't know that thing. Is that yours or does that
               belong to the kindy?
          S:   Um, belongs to kindy. But **I found it so I could take it home.**
          M:   It doesn't really make it yours.
          S:   <u>Yeah.</u> (contradictory tone) I found it, on the floor, at kindy.

The invariant effect + cause ordering of the *because* clause-complexes in
the previous year was explained by the fact that the cause was 'added' to a
speech act as a way of modifying it to make it more persuasive. These
examples too were concerned with the negotiation of action, but in a
more sophisticated way than by adding a reason to a command or refusal.
Stephen was now able to construct a more elaborate argument by
thematizing a piece of information which was to constitute the cause for
the action. Being a little boy or having found the toy stamp were facts that
could hardly be disputed, and thus constructing them as the causes of the
actions which were under dispute made the latter less assailable. And
although his mother demurred at this logic in the latter example, Stephen
did end up with the last word in such texts, testifying to their effectiveness.
   At this stage, therefore, Stephen could vary the sequencing of cause and
effect, but could not do so independently of the choice of taxis relation.
The further development of this area of causality therefore illustrates the
way a meaning system may grow by dissociating co-occurring variables,
which Halliday (1992) has suggested is a path of development both
phylogenetically and ontogenetically. The starting-point in this instance
was that Stephen's language by four years allowed for a choice of [reason]
to coexist with a system of TAXIS.

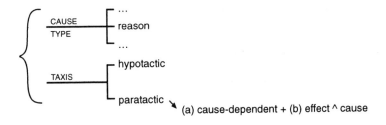

**Figure 6.10** Two aspects to the realization of [reason]/[hypotaxis]

As shown in Figure 6.10, the choice of [hypotaxis] was realized in a dual way, in the dependency of the clause construing the cause (a dependency signalled by *because*) together with the ordering of the effect before the cause in the clause-complex.

However, what can be predicted to happen at some future point is the occasional production of a text in which the (a) realization of dependent cause did not co-occur with the (b) realization of effect-before-cause ordering. These instances of text (together with adult texts being processed by the child) become a source of disturbance in the current system, initiating change.This will lead to a dissociating of the realizational variables so that having chosen [hypotaxis], different textual organizations would be an additional choice possible, as shown in Figure 6.11. (This had already begun to occur with the choices of [condition] and [hypotactic], as will be discussed later.)

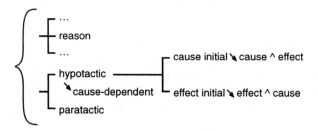

**Figure 6.11** Clause dependency as a distinct choice from textual ordering (adult system)

### 4.2.2 Sequence within hypotactic conditional complexes

In beginning a conditional clause-complex with the hypotactic *if* clause, Stephen was adopting the model most frequently used to him, where the cause-condition was 'thematic'. That is, the condition was construed as the local textual context providing the relevant orientation for the effect clause. Whether there was a genuine Theme choice in Stephen's speech at this stage is arguable, but the ordering of conditional clause as Theme does seem appropriate given the role of Stephen's conditional clause, which had the following principal functions:

(a) expressing the first event in a generalized sequence:
e.g.      *if you hit them, they scratch you;*
(b) providing a context (and therefore a Theme) within which a fact will be valid:
e.g.      *if you fall down bump, you might cry;*
(c) providing a non-here-and-now context for reflection on consequences:
e.g.      *if I grow up, I could sit there.*

That this was a genuine choice of ordering, realizing Theme, could be argued from the fact that there were three isolated recorded examples where the hypotactic conditional clause followed the effect. In these cases, the condition appeared to be added as an afterthought to the main proposition. For example:

3;5;23     S:    (referring to new bottle of milk) Yes, that's for later, for
                 porridge – if Daddy buys some more porridge.

3;11;2     (M admiring other children's artwork at pre-school. S never does
           any)
           M:   Why don't you do one for Mummy sometimes?
           S:   I could do one – I could do one at home; (pause) I could do
                one at home, if you buy some [=paints].

*4.3 Nature of constructions being linked: interpersonal*

One of the characteristics of the earlier period was that the representation of the logico-semantic relation could not be divorced from a specification of moves within the interpersonal metafunction. Up till age three, the actualization of the causal relation by Stephen had in fact occurred almost exclusively in relatively specific contexts. These were contexts of negotiating demands for goods and services, of monitoring his own behaviour in terms of consequences to himself or in terms of his own status (as a big boy). Because of this, the causality options had to be represented as dependent on particular speech function choices.

By four years of age, the picture is very different. In particular, speech function choices were no longer the major determinant of whether a proposition would be developed through the addition of a cause. Causal relations were now extensively used in the exchange of information as well as that of goods and services. In particular of course it was the class of information-giving utterances categorized in Figure 6.6 as [reflecting] that were expanded in this fourth year. Moreover, since the [intruding] group were no longer obligatorily negative, the opposition between these features need not be maintained for the purposes of describing Stephen's potential for developing an utterance through explanation. In effect, the metafunctional components had separated out and were available as genuinely simultaneous systems of speech function and causal ideation, as represented in Figure 6.12.

Thus where the choice of developing a move by explaining had previously been a sub-option available for particular speech functions, it was now an option combinable with any major speech function. This development of simultaneous systems for choices which had previously been available only as a more delicate option available for particular features constitutes another way in which a meaning system can expand.

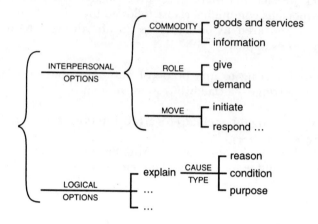

**Figure 6.12** Parallel simultaneous systems of speech function and causal ideation

### 4.4 Nature of constructions being linked: experiential

The experiential meanings being linked were similarly unconstrained by the end of the fourth year, as indicated by the summary chart of typical patterns given below. All but the 'other' category were attested by several examples and although the speech interactants still figured frequently as participants there now appeared to be very little restriction on what kind of process+participant configuration might be construed as a cause or effect. The only noticeable imbalance was that a mental:cognition process was constructed only once as a cause and once as an effect. Examples of clause-complexes are given in Table 6.16.

Given the MOOD selection of [wh-interrogative], the effects queried were also varied, as shown in Table 6.17.

The general point to be made from Tables 6.16 and 6.17 is that the earlier restrictions on process or participant selection in the construal of causes and effects no longer applied. It was no longer only the interactants who could be construed as participants in mental: affect clauses functioning as cause or effect, or material process clauses functioning as effects.

One remaining limitation was that verbal processes arose only in seeking explanation for the addressee's sayings or commanding the addressee not to say something and mental processes of cognition appeared only twice in a causal clause-complex. Thus, while the semiotic processes were more visible in causal utterances than in the previous year, mental processes of cognition in particular were far less so than any other domain of experience.

**Table 6.16** Examples of TRANSITIVITY selections for cause–effect links, 3 to 4 years

| Effect | Cause |
|---|---|
| **material** | **mental: affect** |
| interactant action explained in terms of speaker affect: | |
| *Don't take that one [=marble]* | *'cause I want it* |
| action explained by affect of Actor: | |
| *He's riding on his back* | *'cause he likes it* |
| **verbal** | **mental: affect** |
| addressee action explained in terms of speaker affect: | |
| *Don't say that* | *'cause I don't like laughing* |
| **material/behavioural** | **material/behavioural** |
| action of participant explained by previous action: | |
| *you go atishoo* | *Sometimes if you look at the sun like that* |
| unfavourable action conditional upon inappropriate action: | |
| *they scratch you* | *If you hit them* |
| (non-)action of participant explained by (in)ability: | |
| *She puts her foot round* | *'cause she can't open it* |
| action of participant explained by possible consequence to Goal: | |
| *M: Hold it carefully* | *S: Because it might drop* |
| **mental: perception** | **material** |
| action affects perception: | |
| *that's why you can't see* | *The sun is shining* |
| **material** | **attributive** |
| action explained by characteristic of Goal: | |
| *And then threw him over* | *because he was a baddy* |
| action explained in terms of attribute of Actor: | |
| *They could crash* | *'cause they got strong muscles* |
| *we could easily paddle in the water* | *If we had bare feet* |
| characteristic behaviour explained by classification of participant: | |
| *so I do little blows* | *I'm a little boy* |
| *Lions roar* | *'cause they're lions* |

| attributive | material |
|---|---|
| present state explained by past action of object: | |
| *It's got a hole in it* | *'cause Hal banged it* |

| mental: affect | attributive |
|---|---|
| affect explained by characteristic of Senser: | |
| *Snails like the rain* | *'cause they got shells* |
| speaker affect explained by characteristic of Phenomenon: | |
| *I don't like chops* | *'cause they get stuck in my teeth* |

**other various (occasional)**

| existential | attributive |
|---|---|
| *There's no one in my bed* | *'cause I'm in your bed* |
| **material** | **mental: cognition** |
| *Only animals bite people* | *because they don't know* |
| **verbal** | **attributive** |
| *Don't tell* | *'cause it's a word that you don't say* |
| **mental: cognition** | **verbal** |
| *M: What don't they know?* | *S: Because the teacher says 'you don't bite'* |

**Table 6.17** Examples of TRANSITIVITY selections for causal interrogatives, 3 to 4 years

| material | *Why does the door rattle?* |
|---|---|
| | *What happens if you touch it?* |
| **mental: affect** | *Why don't cats like dogs?* |
| **verbal (addressee Sayer)** | *Why say 'you stupid nong'?* |
| **existential** | *Why is there a hump?* |
| **attributive** | *Why is that one green?* |
| **identifying** | *Why is she called Dolly?* |

*4.5  The deployment of the reason relation*

Although the reason relation was now used to link a variety of speech functions and a variety of experiential contents, there were particular patterns of discourse which are worth commenting on, as developments from the previous year and/or as particularly favoured patterns of discourse.

4.5.1 Negotiating action

As described earlier, the use of causal links, particularly the hypotactic reason relation, developed initially as a strategy to strengthen challenges, 'justify' refusals of goods and make commands more persuasive. These continued throughout the fourth year but became more sophisticated by becoming less direct.

Perhaps the most direct way of supporting commands and refusals is through the simple expression of affect: *(don't) do it because I (don't) want you to/(don't) like it; I (don't) want because I (don't) like*, etc. However, as shown in the previous section, Stephen at two-and-a-half had already learned that likes and wants might be constructed more effectively if 'explained' in terms of some characteristic of the *object* (e.g. *I don't like this 'cause make me sick; I don't want this 'cause it's cold*).

By three-and-a-half he had found another way to support a demand, which was through an 'objective' expression of feeling; that is, by constructing the latter as an Attribute in a relational process as if it were an inherent characteristic of the object or event in question. For example:

3;5;13    M:   We might have fish and chips.
          S:   Oh goody, but I want Daddy to come 'cause it's not good with just Mummy.

Although there is an overt evaluation in the choice of lexical item, *good*, the grammatical choice with a third-person Subject creates the expression of what Stephen likes as if it were a fact, something that is the case, so that Stephen's personal preference emerged as a less personal generalization. In adopting this form, Stephen was taking up models heard in the parent talk addressed to the older child, when rules of behaviour were laid down as if they were universal givens: *it's not polite to attack your food; it's silly to lean back on your stool*, etc.

As well as this way of justifying a demand, Stephen had also developed ways of negotiating his behaviour without any direct reference to feelings or wishes. In the previous period, one of his more reflective strategies had been to monitor his action in terms of a possible undesirable consequence to himself (*it might sting you*). In the fourth year, there were also examples where the consequences of his action for the object, rather than for himself, were foregrounded. This is illustrated in the following joint construction:

3;6;3    M:   Now be careful of that dish-
         S:   Because it might smash.

This again shifts away from a self-orientation.

A third way of negotiating behaviour towards an entity without reference to personal inclination had appeared just twice in the previous data set. This was to refer to some classification of the thing acted upon (*it's a spider; it's mine*). This was a strategy much more in evidence in Stephen's fourth year and drew upon the knowledge of qualities and classifications he had been establishing over the previous year.

For example, in the following case, Stephen's justification for a non-compliant response depended on shared knowledge that wood is hard and strong and does not break if banged. Thus simply to state that his head is made of wood constituted a justification for treating it roughly:

3;5;13    S: My head's hollow (hits it).
          F: Don't hit it so hard.
          S: Yes [I can], 'cause it's wood (all laugh).

Of course once the link has been made in this way, it can be challenged by the addressee in terms of the classification itself or in terms of the assumed characteristics of such a class. And in playful examples such as this one, Stephen was probably as interested in trying out his descriptions ('hollow', 'wooden') as in practising argumentation.

Finally, although parataxis was not used with anything like the frequency of hypotaxis, it did provide the means of deploying a new argumentative strategy. This was to negotiate action through an appeal to some norm of typical behaviour of an implied or specified class. To do this, the 'norm' was set up first as the justifying cause and a paratactic link was deployed to 'oblige' the effect to follow. For example:

3;5;16    S: Mummy, we usually go on trains but we don't go on a train any more, so I want to go on (?two) trains.

Going on a train was not in fact the 'usual' behaviour, but Stephen has construed it as such in order to make the repetition of the action something inherently reasonable.

This strategy was also used without reference to feelings to explain his non-compliant behaviour. For example, when justifying his irritating behaviour towards his brother, he said:

3;10;16   S: He always says it to me so I always say it to him 'cause he always says it to me so I always say it to him.

This familiar justification only makes sense on the premise that one person 'naturally' behaves as equivalent others behave. And all the family talk which presented norms of behaviour and referred to the behaviour of others to exemplify such 'rules' contributed to building up this ideological position.

Examples of other members of the family demonstrating this strategy at this time are given below:

3;4;19    (H refuses to move out of S's bed)
          H: You sleep in my bed so I can sleep in your bed. You sleep in my bed so I can sleep in your bed.
          S: No! Daddy come here.

3;10;2  M:  Hal, if you're at the table you do not write.
        H:  <u>You</u> were writing.

3;10;21  (S crying at beach – wants to follow H up cliff; M prohibits)
        M:  Look at all those little children playing there – <u>they</u>'re all having a lovely time, none of them are crying.

On the other hand, of course, differences in the lives of the two brothers, four-and-a-half years apart in age, were explained in terms of their age grouping. Stephen could now use this as an additional tool for justifying his own behaviour by appealing to information about the way things are, with no reference to his feelings. Thus in the following example, already cited, Stephen did not justify his reluctance to comply with M's command on the basis that he 'doesn't want to' but said:

3;4;30  S:  (ineffectually dabbing at nose after much sniffing)
        M:  Big blow (holding hanky to S's nose); big blow (S snuffles weakly); big blow! (wipes his nose)
        S:  I can't always do a big blow; big boys, big boys, they do big blows. I'm just a little boy so I do little blows.

To sum up, many of the developments in Stephen's use of reason to negotiate action were associated with appealing to 'facts' and norms in order to persuade the addressee to do what he wanted or to justify his behaviour or his non-compliance with respect to the addressee's commands. Thus it would seem that as early as the fourth year of life a middle-class child such as Stephen has begun to learn the value of sounding 'reasonable' in order to be persuasive, in contexts where getting one's own way has to be achieved through language. To accept or justify an effect by appealing to an objectively presented evaluation (*it's not good*), a category (*it's wood*) or to a norm of behaviour for a category (*we usually go on trains; big boys do big blows*) as its cause can be effective because it appeals to information treated as shared objective knowledge. The information causing the effect then has to be challenged by the addressee before the child's demand or refusal can be countered.

## 4.5.2 Explaining reflectively

In the earlier data set, many of the information-giving utterances reflected directly or indirectly on Stephen's status as a 'big' or 'little' boy. During the fourth year, however, Stephen began building on this by explaining observed behaviour more generally by linking attributes of an entity to its participation in a process.

In the next two examples, the Actor in material processes is under attention:

3;7;5    S:    They could crash 'cause they got strong muscles.

3;7;5    S:    Yeah, we can go faster than sport cars. They can't go fast 'cause they're quite little cars.
M:    Oh they're little <u>cars</u> but they got big engines.

Such statements provide a way of revealing implicit understandings about the relationships between qualities and behaviours of entities. These utterances can only constitute explanations if it is known or inferred by the hearer that muscles contribute to strength in a person and size to speed power in a car. Thus the construction of such causal links makes available for validation (or contradiction) the implicit knowledge on which the relation depends, and so provides an additional means of learning through talk.

On other occasions it was the characteristics of the Goal that were relevant:

3;5;16    S:    The train shop can't be shut, 'cause, guess what? It doesn't have a door!

3;5;11    S:    Look! A red tow truck pulling a car, because its engine's broken.

By explaining his observations or assertions in terms of the nature of the participant, Stephen was adopting an 'outward' focus, away from interpersonal relations of speaker and addressee to explanatory construals of goings-on in the world.

This outward focus was also evident in a new exploration of causal relations linking physical processes, such that a presently observed attribute might be explained in terms of an antecedent action, thus making for the first time causal links across time:

3;5;1    S:    (examining bag) It's got a hole in it, 'cause Hal banged it.

In the above example Stephen had witnessed the causing action, while in the next one he made an inference on the basis of linguistically mediated past experience:

3;5;17    S:    My bottom-
M:    Sore is it?
S:    Yes, that's why the sun burned it.

Here Stephen can be seen making his best effort at interpreting a phenomenon on the basis of past experience. Having some months previously had sore shoulders – a state of affairs explained to him carefully as the result of being burned by the sun – he made the inference that this new instance of the effect of soreness had the same cause.

To summarize the use of the reason relation to interpret experience, it can be suggested that Stephen was no longer basically concerned with a self-orientation. In other words he was no longer using 'reflective' cause only as a means of explaining his own inclinations, intentions or status. He was now equally 'other-focused', linking category members to particular actions, linking qualities to a participant's capacity for action, interpreting single actions in terms of preceding ones or current states in terms of preceding actions.

### 4.5.3 Seeking explanation

Probably the most noticeable development in the use of the reason relation during the fourth year was the increase in *why?* questions. In the previous year, only a tiny minority had been 'reflective' in character, puzzling over some unfulfilled expectation as to what should be the case (*why is there's no horsies?* etc.). In the fourth year, however, almost 85 per cent of the 127 recorded *why?* questions were genuinely seeking an explanation in terms of reason or purpose, as in the following examples:

3;4;1   S:  (pointing at cars) Why they got those little things up? [=aerials]

3;4;6   S:  Why is that one [=spaceship in book] upside down?

3;5;11   S:  Why does the noise make that noise?
        M:  It's the door rattling.
        S:  Why does the door rattle?

Something different in the questioning was the disinterested exploration of the motives of others for their actions which began at this time. For example:

3;5;1   (S in back of car playing with a discarded party bag)
        S:  It's got a hole in it, 'cause Hal banged it. Why Hal banged the bag?
        M:  Well, it's fun to pop it, isn't it?
        S:  But you said, 'Never, never don't bang the bag in the car.'
        M:  Yes, because it's dangerous to make a loud noise when someone's driving.

3;5;7   (observing chimps at zoo)
        S:  He's got a little tiny baby thing on his tummy. Why has he?

3;5;12   (they observe someone pushing a car backwards across junction)
        S:  Why's he pushing the car, Mum?
        M:  I don't know, darling; engine must have broken.

3;5;23    S:   Why did you wipe the window, Mum?

3;9;1     S:   We were looking – Stephen and Hal were looking for the
               car, and it wasn't there!
          M:   No, it was down the road, wasn't it?
          S:   Why didn't you put it in front of our house?

          S:   Hal, why don't you like to be a darling?

Clearly these, like the negative questions of the previous period, depend on an understanding of what constitutes predictable behaviour. Indeed, Stephen's question about the bag (3;5;1)was puzzling at the time, but his elucidation of it suggests that he was really asking why Hal broke a rule, not yet finding this a routine matter.

As the examples illustrate, past action or the relation between past action and present state might now be the focus of enquiry as well as ongoing activity. And while the great majority of questions did arise from immediate perceptual observations of specific persons and objects, Stephen also explored generalizations about specific individuals, as in *Why don't you like to be a darling?* and about generic categories, with questions such as *Why don't cats like dogs?* and *Why don't buses come over here?*

### 4.6 The deployment of the conditional relation

In the talk addressed to Stephen during the third [i.e. previous] year, conditional clauses were not uncommon. As described in the previous section, the use of cohesive condition from the parent occurred in the negotiation of action, and served to make an action that was probably unpalatable to the addressee the likely obligatory conclusion of the addressee's own statement. For example:

2;10;7    M:   Did you hurt yourself?
          S:   No.
          M:   Well, don't cry then.

Stephen's sole conditional up to age 3 was constructed on this model.

During the fourth year, only seven further texts were recorded in which Stephen used cohesive condition in a dialogic context. They were interesting, though, in that four of these involved the negotiation of information rather than behaviour. For example:

3;0;3     (watching TV)
          S:   What's that?
          M:   Skeleton.
          S:   Then why does it move?
          M:   It's a magic skeleton.

Having begun as a means of obliging the addressee to do something they were reluctant to do, the relation came to be used by Stephen to 'hold' an addressee to a statement in the negotiation of information. There may still have been an element of negotiating power – by scoring rhetorical points rather than manipulating action – but there was no doubt that Stephen was also seriously interested in the explanation to be given in an example such as the following:

3;7;5     S:   Batman and Superman are nice.
          M:   Yes.
          S:   Why – then why do they punch holes through people?

This kind of discourse seems to be an important forerunner of 'logical' argumentation, where a conclusion is drawn on the basis of a premise whose validity derives from the talk rather than from observational experience, and which began in a small way in the following year.

Although cohesive conditional moves of this kind were very few, Stephen used hypotactic condition with much greater frequency and again it was in the exchange of information rather than goods and services. This was unexpected given the first uses of the reason relation and the fact that McCabe *et al.*'s (1983) study of spontaneously occurring conditionals in the speech of children from 2;10 to 7;3 found that offering bribes or issuing threats was the most frequent use. However, their data concerned siblings at play, whereas almost all examples recorded from Stephen were in speech to an adult. In fact, the earliest recorded examples of hypotactic condition from Stephen were similar to his early information-giving examples of hypotactic reason, where consequences to himself of an envisaged action were construed.

Using a condition relation to do this allowed for a greater explicitness regarding the causal relations between the material processes concerned. This can be illustrated by the following example, when Stephen approached M holding a long and unstable Lego construction which he was holding carefully balanced:

3;5;29    S:   You have to hold on tight (holding it up to M gingerly). If
               you hold it two hands close together it will crash, see?

He could, on the model of *Won't touch it 'cause it might sting you*, have said *I won't hold it two hands close together because it will crash* or *Don't hold it two hands close together because it will crash*. However, these formulations using *because* are different in two important respects. One is that the relation between the two material processes of holding and crashing is less explicit. The holding is expressed as a negative clause and it is the intention or instruction of not doing this first process which is constructed linguistically as an effect. Thus it is the negative polarity which is being explicitly explained rather than the cause–effect relation between the physical processes themselves. When the relation between the two processes is expressed explicitly in terms of condition, the clause-complex serves more readily to generalize experience from an 'observer' rather than an 'intruder' perspective, by foregrounding the experiential relation between the material processes.

A further example illustrates again the difference between the early hypotactic reason clauses of the third year and the early hypotactic conditionals of the fourth year:

3;5;13    (S talking about a cat he has noticed)
       S:    You're allowed to stroke stripey pussy cats, aren't you, Mum?
       M:    Oh yes.
       S:    They don't hurt you; if you hit them they scratch you.

This particular instance is very similar to the previous year's *Won't touch it 'cause it might sting you* but it was construed linguistically entirely as a general relation using generic second person throughout. It was thus much closer to a statement about the circumstances in which animals are dangerous than the earlier statement of (negative) intention.

Moreover, even when speech-role interactants were explicitly involved in the construal of experience by means of a conditional relation, it was not necessarily because the child had any emotional investment in the consequential action and its avoidance. Instead it was a more neutral reflection on the relations between events. For example:

3;6;13    S:    Can I reach up there? (looking at a crane)
       M:    No.
       S:    If I eat more porridge, one day I'll get fat and fat- (distracted)

3;9;25    (S sneezes during car ride)
       S:    Sometimes if you look at the sun you go atishoo.

3;10;2    (S observes cat sniffing at something M has left on counter)
       S:    Hey, if you put it there Katy will eat it.

These examples use the relation of condition to predict or generalize relations between events and/or states. The first example shows that, as with the reason relation, the experience being drawn on to formulate the prediction may be experience of other texts rather than material experience. The relation between eating and changing size or shape is hardly accessible to observation, and in reflecting on growing bigger Stephen appeared to be recalling other texts, some of which concerned getting fat from overeating, while others, deriving from the family context, had to do with the virtues of a good breakfast of porridge for growing big and strong, etc. The other two examples, which occurred in the second half of the year, illustrate a new tendency in the construal of specific incidents. These utterances were the child's interpretation of what was occurring in the immediate context of situation. What was typical of the fourth year, however, was that instead of simply 'monitoring' observed behaviour as a running commentary, Stephen chose to generalize the incident as a relation between two actions by these participants that would hold good beyond this particular context. (See Chapter 4.)

Hypotactic condition thus provided Stephen with a powerful tool for interpreting experience. It constituted a strategy for bringing past material and semiotic experience to bear in the formulation of a generalization. Once he controlled the relation, it also enabled him to interpret specific individual incidents in terms of an explicitly constructed general relation between events even when there was not a history of material or semiotic observations to draw on. His generalizations were not always correct in terms of the adult's understanding of cause and effect, but the strategy of interpreting sequences of actions in terms of obligatory and likely relationships was a move which allowed the interpretation of experience to be less concerned with the specific occasion and more concerned with relationships which hold across contexts.

All the examples discussed so far pertain to material processes very much part of the child's own experience (eating, holding Lego, tow trucks pulling, people looking, etc.), but a fundamental characteristic of a conditional clause is obviously that it allows for the construction of an event whose status is hypothetical. This makes it a powerful tool for the exploration of goings-on beyond those personally accessible. For example, Stephen at three-and-a-half had had a number of conversations in which he attempted to make sense of the information that he had bones inside him, but that nonetheless he was vulnerable to injury. Neither of these facts was accessible to verification through observation or personal experience. Examples of the conversations follow.

3;5;20     (M warns S that he will smash his head if he has accident on
           hard floor)
           S:   No, 'cause it's got bone in see? (taps head)
           M:   But bones can break.
           S:   No, it's hard.
           M:   Yes, but if you bang your head on the hard floor, it can still
                break, the bones can smash.

           (M pretends to eat S)
           S:   No, you can't eat me.
           M:   Yes, I can. (pretends) Yum.
           S:   No, 'cause I've got bones in.

To further explore this notion he began a later conversation as follows:

3;6;1      S:   If a dragon bites you your bones will go crunch; if you fall
                down-

> H:   (reviving a teasing episode of previous day) You will die.
> S:   You <u>won't</u>.
> M:   Keep out of it, Hal. (to S) What will happen if you fall down?
> S:   You'll just hurt yourself.

Stephen was presumably attempting to reconcile his own experience of having had many falls without serious damage, with parental warnings about the possibility of breaking a bone. To do this he constructed a hypothetical case sufficiently extreme for him to be able to envisage the proposition about the breaking of bones as having validity.

This strategy of supplying linguistically a pertinent context for a generalization was familiar in the parents' talk during this period, which had responded to Stephen's developing ability by extending the use of condition in speech they addressed to him to reflective contexts:

> 3;6;5   S:   Mum, could you cry; could you cry or not?
> M:   Yes, I could cry.
> S:   How?
> M:   What do you mean? If I hurt myself I might cry, same as you.
> S:   If you fell down bump really really hard.

In this example it was initially the parent who provided a linguistically constructed conditional context within which the generalization (*I could cry*) could hold good, and immediately Stephen built on this by elaborating it into a more specific possibility, constructed in the same way.

The possibility of directly enquiring about linguistically constructed rather than actually observed experience was also a powerful way for Stephen to extend his knowledge beyond his personal experience. In the second half of the year interrogatives constructed with a hypotactic conditional relation (e.g. *what happens if . . .?*) were occasionally formulated:

> 3;5;25   (M encourages S to clean his teeth)
> S:   What happens – what happens if you leave them all white?
> M:   Well, they don't stay white. If you don't clean them, they go all brown and smelly.
> H:   And people won't want to look at you.
> S:   If you don't clean them will you die?
> M:   No, you won't die, but your teeth will go bad.

Here, rather than resisting the command with respect to his own here-and-now behaviour by challenging with *why?*, Stephen reflected on the reason for the rule in a more distanced way by raising the hypothetical possibility of a person behaving differently.

Similarly, on other occasions, condition was not used to articulate a generalization, nor to create a semiotic context in which some important generalization could hold good, but simply to allow reflection on experience other than the current actual one:

3;6;29    (in car, S strapped into infant car seat)
          S:    If I grow up, I could sit there and Hal could sit there
                (pointing).

3;9;24    (on a walk, they all carefully skirt a large puddle in the path)
          S:    If we had bare feet, if we didn't have our socks on, we could
                easily paddle in the water.

These remarks were not veiled suggestions as to how the dialogue
interactants might act differently at the moment of speaking, but were
rather an imaginative projection of himself behaving differently. In a
similar way, the consequences of having very long hair were laughingly
imagined in the following conversation:

3;5;26    (discussing hair)
          S:    It's supposed to go right down to my neck (passing his hand
                from forehead to chin).
          M:    !!
          S:    If I want to talk to you, I go spit it out, spit it out, spit it out!
                (laughs)
          M:    You'd have to, wouldn't you?

These kinds of examples can be interpreted as attempts to shift
perspective, to consider the present circumstances in a future context, to
consider the possible actions if circumstances were different, or to consider
the consequences of things being other than they are. In this last example,
there is a sense in which Stephen is following through the 'logic' of his
previous utterance, and in this it was similar to the occasional use of
cohesive condition described earlier.

In sum, the development of hypotactic condition provided a valuable tool
for Stephen in the exploration of experience. First, it allowed for the
formulation of predictions and generalizations by specifying explicitly
obligatory relations between two processes (or a process and resultant state).
These processes might be ones he planned to engage in or to avoid (*if I eat
more porridge, one day I'll get fat; if you hit them they scratch you*). Secondly it
enabled the here-and-now instance to be interpreted as an exemplar of a
relationship which would hold across contexts. Specific participants might
be involved (*if you put it there Katy will eat it*) or specific incidents might be
further generalized (*sometimes if you look at the sun you go atishoo*). Thirdly it
allowed for the investigation of relationships between experiences not
observed but which could be construed as language. This could be done by
imaginatively constructing a context in which a generalization would apply
(*if you don't clean them . . .; If a dragon bites you . . .*). Finally it was used to
imaginatively place himself into an alternative experience to the present
actual one (*if I want to talk to you [with long hair]. . . ; if we didn't have shoes on*).

### 4.7 *Internal cause*

One final development in the deployment of causal relations in the fourth year was the first use of internal cause. No examples had been recorded up to age three, but during the fourth year there were 32 recorded occasions when *because* was used with an internal meaning (in addition to the external instances represented in Table 6.13) and a single instance of an internal conditional link. There were also two occasions when the internal reason relation was represented 'metaphorically', through the phrase *that means.*

Internal cause was a necessary tool for Stephen if he was to use language in order to reflect on the taxonomic and other understandings previously and currently being reached. By pressing the relation of causality into service he could articulate for himself and make available for verification by the addressee his 'grounds' for categorizations and he could hold his own in arguments about classification.

The earliest recorded example where an internal causal relation could be inferred was the following text:

3;5;1    (S indicates his tangled bedclothes)
        S:    Who did that?
        M:    (playfully, picking up soft toy) Rabbit.
        S:    It can't be rabbit; he's not alive. (?he's just a teddy.)

On this occasion the juxtaposition of the clauses in Stephen's speech allows the toy rabbit's inanimacy to be read as a justification for rejecting M's joking construction of it as the Actor. Thus the rabbit's qualities were construed as evidence for its possible behaviour.

Alternatively, the habitual or potential behaviour of an object could be construed as an 'explanation' of its correct classification:

3;7;5    (comparing Batman and Superman)
        S:    But you know Superman is stronger 'cause he – 'cause he could kill you.

3;7;8    S:    It wasn't a strange mouse 'cause strange mouses kill you.

On other occasions, an attribute of a participant rather than its behaviour provided the explicit rationale for categorizing it as a member or non-member of a named class:

3;5;7    (at zoo, M teasingly interprets the bear's growls)
        M:    I want boy, nice juicy boys!
        S:    We're not juicy boys 'cause we haven't got juice in.

3;7;24    H:    He's not a boy, he's a man.
        S:    He is a boy 'cause he's got a penis.

In the last example, 'justifying' his categorization through an internal causal link was a necessary rhetorical move to support Stephen's challenge to the addressee's classification. And in the previous year, there had been a few exceptional occasions when the addressee had pressed him for a justification of that kind:

2;7;1    (S names 'Snap the crocodile' as a clown)
         M:  Why's he like a clown?

On other rare occasions, the adult had modelled the internal relation when a classification was disputed:

2;10;7    M:  It's spray; it's water, a fountain.
          S:  No, it's steam.
          M:  Well, it looks like steam, yes. Steam comes when water's very hot.
          S:  Where?
          M:  Like out of the kettle; when it comes out of the kettle, that's steam, 'cause it's very very hot.
          S:  That's steam, 'cause that's cold.
          M:  That's cold, so that's just called spray.

Stephen's final move, using an internal link, was clearly modelled on the adult utterance at a point when an internal option was not part of his own system. In Vygotskyan terms, by participating in dialogic interaction, Stephen had been enabled to produce text that went beyond his current independent abilities but was in his zone of proximal development.

Occasions like this may have alerted Stephen to the importance of being able to 'explain' a position in order to hold his own in talk with older addressees. But when he began to use internal cause it was very often not to support a response to a challenge. The 'justification' was often given unrequested or was articulated to clarify matters for himself:

3;6;23    (S has previously been told that a queue is only a traffic jam when the car cannot move even when the traffic lights are green)
          S:  When it's green it's called a traffic jam, but this is not a traffic jam 'cause it's red; a green one is a traffic jam.

On three occasions cause and effect were construed using *that(s) mean(s)*:

3;5;6     S:  It's got a plate and that's mean it's tea.

3;6;12    S:  (checking book) There's words; that means it's a story.

3;9;21    S:    It's got two wings there and two wings there and that means it's a biplane.

These utterances, discussed in Chapter 3, Section 4.5, can conservatively be treated as examples of a cohesive conjunctive item construing an internal causal link (equivalent to *So (I know)*). Alternatively, they can be seen as an example of grammatical metaphor, whereby the internal causal relation is experientialized (constructed as content) by being construed as the relational process *mean*.

Whichever interpretation is preferred, the creation of an internal conjunctive link itself is of major importance. Martin (1992a: 416) argues that, like text reference which identifies facts rather than participants, internal conjunction is a metasemiotic resource. Links are made between messages, not to organize participants and activity sequences but to 'orchestrate' textual sequences.

In Stephen's language the development of an internal causal relation by means of conjunction (or metaphorically through a relational process) arose as a strategy for making explicit the criteria for classification, either to substantiate a contested categorization or simply to reflect on the classification, the better to understand it. This greater 'consciousness' about the basis for naming things amounts to a new ability to treat semiosis as an 'object' of reflection. The development of this internal, rhetorical form of causal link is thus a crucial aspect of bringing meaning to consciousness.

The development of the internal conjunctive option for causality can also serve to exemplify one of the ways in which a meaning system can expand. The first step is for a development in delicacy (subclassification) at a certain point in the network. In the case of the internal/external distinction, that development is initially dependent on the entry feature [reason], as shown in Figure 6.13. It develops through the processing of dialogic text embodying the option and through the child's own first attempts at the meaning modelled on the speech he is listening and responding to (cf. text 2;10;7 cited on p. 293 above).

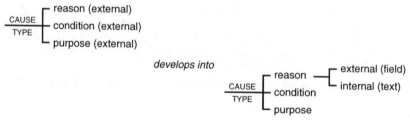

**Figure 6.13** A meaning system extends in delicacy

Once in place, the more delicate option may 'spread' by analogy to another feature in the system of which the entry feature is a term. This had begun to occur for Stephen by the end of the fourth year when he produced the following text embodying choices of [internal] and [condition]:

3;11;9    (S and M are arriving at preschool)
          S:   We're a little bit late [=early] if Frank's not here.

Figure 6.14 shows this next stage of development when the external/internal opposition is available also for the feature [condition]. However, since initially the probability of an internal choice being selected for this feature will be lower than for [reason], hypothetical probabilities have been added to the features on the figure.

**Figure 6.14** A meaning choice 'spreads' to another feature

Once internal condition has been deployed often enough so that the [internal]/[external] choice is equally freely available to [reason] and [condition], then the two sets of options have become simultaneous systems, as shown in Figure 6.15 (although in fact there may remain different probabilities on co-selection of features).

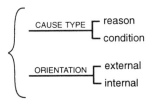

**Figure 6.15** Simultaneous systems of CAUSE TYPE and ORIENTATION

Thus the oppositional and probabilistic characteristics of the semiotic system allow for the *possibility* of changes of these kinds, while the contextualized mobilization of the system into text, achieved in dialogic interaction, provides the functional impetus which achieves the observed changes in the system itself.

*4.8 Summary: 3;0 to 4;0 years*

The main developments discussed in this section concern new functions and realizations for use of the reason relation, the emergence of a new causal relation – that of condition – and the appearance of internal cause. In considering these developments it has also been possible to make some generalizations about the way a meaning system may expand in ontogenesis.

To express the reason relation, Stephen developed new paratactic and cohesive forms. These enabled him to vary the ordering of cause and effect at a point before he could use Theme marking to vary the order within a hypotactic clause-complex. Paratactic reason (as with hypotactic reason in the previous year) was first used in the negotiation of behaviour. However, this was achieved by construing a piece of information as the cause which preceded and 'obliged' a particular behaviour on Stephen's part. Thus the negotiation was distanced from the realm of commands and refusals, 'dressed up' as an exchange of information.

This less overt kind of negotiation of action that emerged with paratactic cause was simply one manifestation of a common thread to many of the developments of the fourth year; namely the 'experientialization' of the causal relation. Even where hypotactic causality was used for the interpersonal negotiation of goods and services, Stephen could achieve a distancing of his personal involvement by construing facts and impersonal generalizations as causes. This might be done by representing his feelings as facts (*it's not good*), by focusing on the consequences to the other participant rather than himself (*it might smash*) or by categorizing the participant (*it's wood; it's a long one*). And the earlier restriction that the speech role interactant(s) themselves always figured in any material processes as effect, or any affect process construed as cause or effect, no longer applied.

The experiential focus was also evident in a new interest in preceding causes for observed or experienced states (e.g. *my bottom (is sore); that's why the sun burned it*), while at the same time the motives and behaviours of third parties were also now interpreted and enquired into, whether or not they impinged on himself (e.g. *Why Hal banged the bag?*).

Developments within the conditional relation also reflected the motif of experientialization. Cohesive condition had first emerged in the negotiation of action but now was also used in arguing about information by pointing out a logical inconsistency between a verified fact about a participant (*it's a skeleton; Superman is nice*) and some observation of its behaviour. Hypotactic condition was a new relation and was used far more frequently than the cohesive relation, again in reflective rather than active contexts. It enabled an explicit formulation of understandings (*if you hit them they scratch you*) which would earlier have been left implicit or construed only in terms of specific participants or specific occasions (cf. *I won't touch because it might sting*). The impetus to construct implicit understandings into language and to generalize specific experience thus appeared to motivate the development of the condition relation. The deployment of condition also provided a new tool for exploring experience beyond the here-and-now, there and then.

Finally the development of the internal causal conjunctive relation took place in the fourth year. The deployment of internal reason was an important strategy particularly for making available for reflection and validation Stephen's understandings about criteria for category membership which had hitherto been left implicit. Thus again the impetus to use language to reflect explicitly on linguistically construed understandings was apparent.

## 5  Stephen's language from 4;0 to 5;0 years

In the fifth year of life, Stephen's system of causality continued to expand, not only with new forms of realization, but with extended contexts of use for paratactic reason, hypotactic condition and internal cause, all of which were first used in the previous year.

### 5.1  Type of causal relation and typical expression

Table 6.18 displays the types of grammatical realization possible for external causal meanings by the end of the fifth year. Apart from a single example of paratactic condition, the main development was the increase in within-clause realizations for the reason relation. Included in this category are clauses beginning *That's why/because* . . . , which could now be more confidently coded as 'metaphorical' realizations. (See discussion below.)

**Table 6.18** Causal relations in Stephen's language, 4 to 5 years

| Type | Linkage | | | Within clause |
|------|---------|---|---|---------------|
| Purpose | hypotaxis (*to* . . . ; *so that*) | (parataxis N/A) | – | *What for?; Why (for)?;* circumstance; participant |
| Reason | hypotaxis (*because, in case*) | parataxis (*so*) | cohesion (*so*) | *Why?; How come?* Relational participant; circumstance (prep.phrase; embedded clause) |
| Condition | hypotaxis (*if* . . . (*then*); *when; unless*) | – | cohesion (*then*) | |

5.1.1 Expression of reason relation

The distribution of realizations of the external reason relation was as shown in Table 6.19.

**Table 6.19** External reason links from 4 to 5 years

| Type of link | hypotaxis | parataxis | cohesion (*so*) | metaphor |
|---|---|---|---|---|
| Number of examples | 112 | 34 | 6 | 8 |

Although the total number of causal utterances was less than the previous year, the number of paratactic links had increased almost threefold. The use of cohesive *so* remained marginal (and was difficult to determine unless a link was being made across speaker turns). Surprisingly, the recorded occurrence of *that's why/because* (attested twenty times in the previous year) had reduced to only three occasions. However, there were additionally two instances where the process was modalized, evidence that a relational process was being constructed rather than *that's why* functioning as a conjunction:

4;7;24    (looking at picture book. 'Wallace' the ape has got into a show-case in the museum)
M:  I don't see how he got inside the glass, do you?
S:  Oh, I see; that might be because it opens up at the top – at the bottom.

4;10;2    (discussing a friend)
M:  Apparently he's had a very bad sore throat.
S:  That could be why he didn't come – didn't come to Eric's party.

The analysis of the cause as a 'metaphorical' participant is given in Example 6.4.

*Example 6.4*

| That | could be | [[why he didn't come to Eric's party]] |
|---|---|---|
| Token | Relational | Value |
| text ref. (Fact as participant) | | embedded clause (Material process configuration as participant) |

Such an example shows there was no longer any ambiguity about Stephen's ability to construct a cause or effect as a participant using rankshift. But, as with the examples of rankshift cited in Chapter 3, the embedded clauses themselves construed perfectly 'concrete' meanings, although the associated use of text reference did constitute a move into abstraction.

In addition to these forms involving cohesive text reference, there were other examples of cause construed within the clause as a circumstance, realized either by a prepositional phrase or an embedded clause. The relevant utterance is in bold in the following examples:

4;3      S:  (knuckling his forehead) Mummy, Mummy, um – my head feels like a brick here.
         M:  (laughs)
         S:  (laughs) My head's full of brick.
         (M and F talking together)
         S:  Mum, my head's full of brick **because of the skeleton**; my head's full of brick **because of the skeleton.**
         M:  Yeah, do you know what the skeleton inside your head is?
         S:  What?
         M:  It's called 'skull'.
         S:  What's your tummy's one inside called?

4;5;7    (M points out some horses from the car)
         M:  They're coming out of the park over there.
         S:  Oh yeah, <u>one</u> horse; can't even see properly **with [[all those cars going past]]**.

4;5;1    S:  My finger's sore **from [[when we bumped in together with our skateboards]]**; and I didn't cry.
         M:  Didn't you?

The first example is interesting in that the nominalized cause *because of the skeleton* suited Stephen's purpose particularly well by allowing him to be inexplicit about exactly what role the skeleton played, something he was not clear about at that time. The other examples illustrate how Stephen now used rankshifted clauses very freely in his discourse, though not with the compacting, abstracting effect such embeddings take in mature written language.

5.1.2 Expression of condition relation

The distribution of realizations for the conditional relation is given in Table 6.20.

**Table 6.20** External condition links from 4 to 5 years

| Type of link | hypotaxis | | | parataxis | cohesion to addressee's speech |
| --- | --- | --- | --- | --- | --- |
| | *if (then)* | *unless* | *when* | *so* | *then* |
| Number of examples | 70 | 1 | 5 | 1 | 6 |

In the fifth year, hypotactic condition was very prominent, chiefly realized as before by the conjunction *if* (very occasionally by *if . . . then*). There were also a few occasions when *when* was chosen as the conditional conjunction. If cause is a way of modalizing the relation between processes (see Table 4.1, p. 139), with condition realizing probability, then *if* can be regarded as a low-value modal relation and *when* as a high-value one. (No mid-value realizations, such as *provided that*, were found in the data.)

There had, in the previous year, been some instances of *when* which could have been interpreted as conditional *or* as a generalized temporal 'whenever' (e.g. *It's still called bolognese when we eat it*). But in the fifth year there were occasions that were unequivocally conditional in meaning, for example *How come that bus is beating us when cars go faster than buses?* Thus the combination of the features [condition] and [hypotaxis] now provided an entry point for a small set of more delicate options, as shown in Figure 6.16.

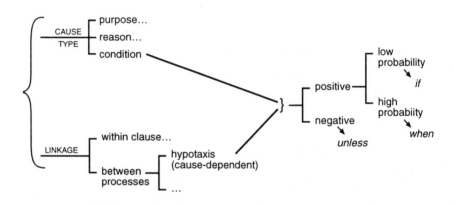

**Figure 6.16** The system of cause extends in delicacy

Cohesive links with *then* continued to be used occasionally. In all but one case it was to link Stephen's own utterance to that of the addressee. On the other occasion it was used in a monologue after a rhetorical question:

4;5;13    (in car. F picks a beetle off newly purchased plant and puts it out of window)
          S:    (plaintively) You wouldn't like it if someone put you out the window, would you, Daddy? **Then**, Daddy, don't put the beetle out the window; he might get squashed.

Although no negative cohesive realization was recorded from Stephen, he appeared to have no difficulty with understanding *otherwise*, when used to him. (The negative hypotactic conjunction *unless*, first used in the previous year, reappeared once in this data set.)

### 5.2 *Sequencing and interdependence of cause and effect*

When Table 6.15 is expanded, as Table 6.21, to include the data from the fifth year it shows two changes. One is a single occurrence for the first time of a hypotactic clause-complex of reason where the cause precedes the effect. The other is that hypotactic clause-complexes of condition with the effect preceding the cause were no longer marginal, but clearly a distinct option within the system.

**Table 6.21** Sequencing possibilities for cause–effect links, 2;7 to 5 years

| | Hypotactic link | | | | | | Paratactic/cohesion | | | Within clause | | |
|---|---|---|---|---|---|---|---|---|---|---|---|---|
| | Effect initial | | | Cause initial | | | | | | | | |
| | 2;7-3 | 3-4 | 4-5 | 2;7-3 | 3-4 | 4-5 | 2;7-3 | 3-4 | 4-5 | 2;7-3 | 3-4 | 4-5 |
| Purpose | √ | √ | √ | x | x | x | N/A | N/A | N/A | 1 e.g. | √ | √ |
| Reason | √ | √ | √ | x | x | 1 e.g. | 1 e.g.? | √ | √ | x | √ | √ |
| Condition | x | √ (rare) | √ | x | √ | √ | 1 e.g. | √ | √ | x | x | x |

### 5.2.1 Sequence within reason clause-complexes

As noted above, there was a single text where the *because* clause preceded the primary clause in the complex:

4;5;7    (S in rear of car fiddling with card with glued-on decorations)
   S: (?I found) sticky tape; now where's the star? Mum, because you're going too fast, the star's gone.

Whether or not Stephen had a textual option for varying the ordering of cause and effect in a reason clause cannot be determined from a single recorded example, but his having tried it out very appropriately on at least one occasion will be an important move towards developing a systemic opposition.

Given that there was not one single example of a Theme-initial *because* clause from any speaker recorded in conversation with Stephen, it can be suggested that this patterning is one which rarely arises in casual conversation and is likely to be developed ontogenetically in written language texts under the pressure of organizing and staging monologic material.

### 5.2.2 Sequence in condition clause-complexes

With conditional clause-complexes the evidence is unequivocal that the thematic organization of the complex could be systematically varied. Of the 71 hypotactic complexes, 17 took the less preferred ordering of effect before cause. (In the speech addressed to Stephen, the proportion was higher: 25 out of 40 instances.) The following text illustrates Stephen using both orderings.

4;2;30   (S sobbing over hurt toe)
       S:   (?Will) <u>you</u> be crying very much if you hurt your little toe like that?
       M:   Yes, I'm sure I would cry; it's very painful when you hurt your toe.
       S:   Would you be crying longer – longer and – and louder than usually you do?
       M:   Mm, probably, darling.
       S:   If you would be me, it would sting.

For two or three months, one favourite kind of text which deployed the effect^cause ordering was when Stephen admonished the addressee to empathize with others. For example:

4;6;16   (F shouts at cat)
       S:   Daddy, <u>you</u> wouldn't like it if someone shouted at you.

However, it was not only in the setting up of a comparison between speaker and addressee or addressee and Goal that this textual patterning occurred. It continued to be used in occasional interrogatives of the form *What happens if . . .* where the interrogative process is naturally enough thematized. And it was also used in declarative complexes when the course of dialogue made the primary clause an appropriate starting-point, thematizing a previous piece of information:

4;5;26   (in the car waiting at red light at intersection)
       S:   Does green mean stop?
       M:   No, green means go – those cars (pointing at cross-traffic) have a green light so they can go.
       S:   Does green mean stop for the people?
       F:   It's always red for stop.
       M:   Oh, no, when it says green for the cars, the light for the people is red.
       S:   The people can't go if the cars are going.

4;10   (at breakfast of cereal and rhubarb S twirls his empty spoon around)
       M:   Steve, not at the table; you know you shouldn't be doing that.
       S:   (seriously) Oh, I wouldn't do it if there was rhubarb on it; the rhubarb would go all over the wall!

### 5.3 Nature of constructions causally linked

It was during the fourth year that the initial restrictions on the major speech functions which might be construed as a causal clause-complex disappeared. And it was also in the fourth year that most combinations of process types appeared in such clause-complexes, with both interactant and third-person participants. However, at that time, it did appear very rare for a cognition process to be construed as a cause or effect. This limitation in the texts created by Stephen was no longer apparent between 4 and 5 years. For example, during the fifth year, a cognition process might constitute the cause of an action. This occurred when Stephen made an interpretation that how people act and are acted on was determined by their own or others' mental abilities. For example:

4;4;10    S:   I know how to do an 's' now; I can do it lots of times 'cause I know.

4;2;4    S:   And Hal will have to point to the giant slide 'cause I don't know which one it is.

4;3    S:   I didn't ask him because he – he – he doesn't understand.

Examples where a mental:cognition process was construed as an effect show Stephen reflecting on the causal relationships involved in learning itself. Here he explicitly talked about knowing as an effect caused by sensing or being verbally informed (see discussion in Chapter 5, Section 6.3).

4;2;4    S:   I haven't tasted it before so I don't know what it's like.

4;7;28    S:   I know [it's only eight sleeps] 'cause Hal told me.

### 5.4 Deployment of the reason relation

In the fifth year, the most important new pattern observable in the deployment of reason arose in the use of parataxis to construe and negotiate information. In the previous period, paratactic links enabling a cause^effect sequencing had developed as a way of negotiating action by making the desired effect the reasonable outcome of the preceding fact or norm. Within the realm of genuine information exchange, such links were observed in narrating events. Both these uses of parataxis continued, but there was in addition a new use of paratactic reason links in the construal of information.

On some occasions, Stephen drew a conclusion from an observation – a conclusion that would only make sense on the basis of some unstated premise. For example:

4;1;28    S:    Stacey's [skateboard] looks like yours, so his must be the
                 same as yours.

The implicit premise here is that only the same brand of skateboards will
look similar.

In the next example, the unstated premise is that at a traffic
intersection, when the cross-traffic stops, the other stream starts moving:

4;6;8    (car stationary at lights)
         S:    Their cars – those cars are stopping so we must be able to go.

These examples are analogous to the 'he does it to me so I do it to him'
reasoning of the previous year (which made sense on the premise that one
is entitled to 'tit for tat'), but they differ in being removed from any
attempt to negotiate behaviour.

There were also just a few occasions when a premise for a conclusion
introduced with *so* was more explicit. In the following example the
conclusion drawn depends on information received in the course of this
conversation together with information received from any number of
disparate earlier texts. This latter information (that M is not a millionaire)
is explicitly stated as his premise for the conclusion that he draws
concerning her intentions. The relevant clause-complex is in bold.

4;7;18    (discussing prices)
          S:    How about a house! A thousand [dollars]!
          M:    More than that.
          S:    A million!!
          M:    Sometimes. Some houses cost that much.
          S:    **You haven't got that much, so you don't get another –
                 another thing – another house**, but if you did you could get a
                 good house.

In the following text Stephen uses linguistic reasoning to address the
problem he was interested in exploring. Again it involves constructing a
premise (*vans go faster than cars*) on the basis of previous texts, but in this
case it is as a means of addressing an explicitly formulated problem (*what
about vans?*), and for this reason is perhaps a clearer example of thinking
through language:

4;5;9    S:    Mum, can bikes go faster than cars? Can bikes go faster than
                cars?
         M:    You're always asking me that.
         S:    I can't remember.
         M:    They go the same.
         S:    What about vans? (ponders) **Vans go faster than cars so vans
                should go faster than motorbikes.**

Thus, whereas paratactic reason originated in the previous year in an attempt to make requests and refusals the obligatory effect of certain factual causes, it was now being deployed to make factual generalizations the obligatory conclusion of known facts.

In doing this, Stephen was taking up the forms of reasoning which were increasingly being modelled for him, as in the following example:

4;11;16   S:   I keep thinking that the earth goes round the sun instead of
               the sun goes round the earth.
          M:   The earth does go round the sun!
          S:   (pleased) Oh! How come you can't feel it go round?
          M:   Yeah, it's funny that you can't feel it . . . (further talk)
          S:   Are the houses going round?
          M:   They're on the earth so they have to go round, don't they?

In a final example, Stephen can be seen using a similar text pattern to lay out linguistically the basis for drawing a conclusion, one that becomes problematic because it does not square with experience.

4;6;25    (S and M observing and talking about some birds overhead)
          S:   We got hands to fly and birds have wings to fly; so how come
               we can't fly?

In all these texts the meaning of the reason relation as setting up an obligatory relation between the first clause and the conclusion which follows, or 'should' follow, is readily seen.

## 5.4.1 Seeking explanation through reason

During the fifth year, there were 89 recorded *why?* questions and, in the last quarter of the year, 15 *how come?* enquiries. These latter were particularly favoured when formulating a question that itself required a clause-complex to be stated, though *why?* questions were also multi-clausal on occasion. For example:

4;0       (M tells S to put dirty clothes in the washbasket)
          S:   Why, when you wear them, do you have to put them in the
               wash?

4;10;12   S:   How come Hal got bigger before I did?

4;10;13   S:   How come it's a bigger day when it's summer?

4;10;24   S:   How come, when birds get sick, they die?

It can be seen how the combination of temporal and causal meaning within a single complex enabled Stephen on his own to formulate more complex kinds of enquiries than simply questioning a participant's motive or seeking clarification of an unexpected event.

On one occasion the queried clause-complex was linked by an implicit counter-expectancy relation ('and yet'):

5;0;5    S:    How come I'm five and I still can't read?

This enquiry, which occurred a few days after Stephen's birthday, shows that Stephen had construed an inferential link between category membership and the behaviour of a category member, a link which had not proved to hold good. In a similar way, just after his fourth birthday, he had begun asking repeatedly and earnestly *Can I swim yet?* This had seemed very puzzling at the time since he was regularly at the pool and beach and knew perfectly well what it was to be able to swim and that he couldn't swim. But his confusion is actually quite understandable, given that he had spent the previous year drawing cause–effect links between categories and their members' potential for action (cf. *I'm just a little boy so I do little blows; they can't go fast 'cause they're quite little cars; they could crash 'cause they got strong muscles*). The reason for doing or being able to do something in such cases was construed in terms of the attribution of parts, qualities or class membership. So when he asked *Can I swim yet?* he was checking whether changing his age category from 3 to 4 would have enabled him to engage in the 'big boy' behaviour of swimming. Similarly, on turning 5 he was again disappointed to realize that this in itself did not entail a change in his potential for behaviour. What is interesting here is that even where his own potentiality was concerned, his semiotically constituted knowledge was as relevant to him as his 'concrete' lived experience.

### 5.5 Deployment of condition clause-complexes

Perhaps the most striking development in the fifth year was the prominent deployment of the conditional relation. It was used to switch point of view – or request such a switch in order to manipulate the addressee – to further reflect on unobserved experience and to arrive at a conclusion drawn from a linguistically established premise.

### 5.5.1 Condition to switch perspective for negotiating

Switching perspective was a feature of Stephen's use of the conditional from the very beginning of the fifth year, when he began to adopt and adapt the disguised manner of giving advice that he was frequently exposed to, namely *if I were you*.

4;1;22    (M concerned about petrol level in car)
          S:    If I was you – if I was you – if I was you – if I was you I would
                get some of Daddy's money and buy the petrol.

4;6;8     (stuck in a traffic jam)
          S:    The car in front is lucky 'cause then he gets to go – 'cause
                then he gets to do anything. If I was in that car I would just –
                I would just keep on going fast.

He also repeatedly invited the addressee to take on the perspective of
his own self to better empathize with him. For example:

4;1;22    (M attempts to stop S complaining about heat)
          S:    If you were me you'd feel how sweaty it was, if you were me,
                if you were me.

4;2;30    S:    I don't care if I'm all wet; would you care if you were me?

On one occasion he even invited himself to take on the perspective of
his better self:

4;2;31    (S finds he has made bathroom awash, genuinely regretful)
          S:    I didn't mean to. (attempts to mop it up) I wouldn't do that
                if I was me. (delightedly) I am me!!

As discussed earlier, he also frequently admonished the addressee to
take on the perspective of a third party with whom he but not they were
empathizing:

4;5;13    (in car, F picks a beetle off newly purchased plant and puts it out
          of window)
          S:    (plaintively) You wouldn't like it if someone put you out the
                window, would you, Daddy? Then, Daddy, don't put the
                beetle out the window; he might get squashed.
          F:    Beetles can fly away.

4;5;18    (H enters whining with hurt knee. M ignores)
          S:    (indignantly) Mummy, how would you feel if your knee
                hurted? How would you feel if your knee hurted?

In a final example, Stephen can be seen to strategically distance his
indignation by constructing an actual past situation as a hypothetical one
involving other people and putting this to M for her reflection:

4;3;4     (several days previously S – against advice – held his soft toy up at
          window of car; he accidentally dropped it. M was furious at

having to stop illegally on a very busy road to retrieve it)
S:   If some other boy dropped his teddy out the window, I bet
the other Mummy wouldn't shout at him.

In all these negotiations Stephen compared one being with another. This
he had learned was an appropriate strategy in negotiating action (see
discussion at end of Section 4.5.1 on pp. 282–3). He further invited the
addressee to empathize with another being, namely the one they were acting
on or the one whose problems they were ignoring. This again was an
approach modelled for him in the talk of others and was effective for two
reasons. One is that he was exemplifying a moral stance valued by the
addressees (treat others as you would like to be treated yourself) and the other
was that he was adopting an indirect means of telling others what they should
do or chastizing them for what they had done. He was not in a social position
to tell adults what to do directly and be heeded, but by 'reasoning' with them
through these strategies he could be quite successful in gaining a voice.

5.5.2  Condition to reflect on imagined situations

Counter-factual condition also continued to be a prominent tool with which
to construe imagined situations, including fantasy ones explored for fun:

4;10;13   S:   Imagine Mummy's head on me and mine on Mummy's!
          M:   I'd look good with your face.
          S:   With a dress on!!! If I had your head I'd frighten everyone.
          M:   Thank you!

Using the conditional relation in an enquiry was also a serious means of
working though activity sequences beyond Stephen's experience that he
was trying to understand:

4;1       (F and H talking about new item on 'stomach-stapling'
          operations for slimmers. S listening intently)
          S:   What if you cut a bit of yourself off, and then let all the food
          come out and then (pause) put your body back in?

In the following text, Stephen was trying to understand M's statement
that baby birds might die by falling out of the nest. (He had probably
never been told that new chicks cannot fly.)

4;10;3    (discussing how birds can die)
          M:   Baby birds sometimes die when they fall out the nest, or – in
          the winter – if you were in a cold place birds might die
          because they can't get enough food.
          S:   But what happens if one bird falls out and then – and then –
          and when it's just about at the ground, it flies?

M: Yes, well if it's big enough to fly it'll be all right.

As in the conversations given earlier involving paratactic reason, Stephen can be seen attempting to reconcile the information given him in this conversation (birds die when they fall out of the nest) with his current knowledge (that birds can fly). Here he used hypotactic condition to reformulate the information he had just been given to suggest an example situation to which he could then relate his previous knowledge.

### 5.5.3 Condition for logical argument

Finally, further examples illustrate again the new tendency to consider a premise and then construct it as a necessary condition for a conclusion, sometimes a surprising one. The following text is one from the end of the previous year, although more typical of talk after age 4.

3;11;10   (at service station F explains that he is putting air in the tyres)
          S:   Why?
          F:   Otherwise the tyre might go flat.
          S:   (pause) If all of the tyres be flat, the car will walk!!

Here Stephen was given a piece of information, namely that car tyres can 'go flat', which he then reformulated as a condition that would entail a surprising consequence.
    In the next text, Stephen took the verified information that trees grow and drew the conclusion that they will therefore end up endlessly high:

4;0;20   S:   Trees can grow can't they?
        M:   Yes, they certainly can.
        S:   They can grow and grow and grow.
        M:   Mm.
        S:   If they grow and grow they will (?    ) right up – right up in the sky.
        M:   They are up in the sky.
        S:   Incept that one (peering at bush in garden).
        M:   (?    )
        S:   Some of them finish growing before the others; (pause) that one's finished.

In some final examples, Stephen can be seen using the conditional relation to formulate a problem by finding some inconsistency between two pieces of information received or between information and observation. For example, in the following conversation, Stephen established that ghosts have no existence (and therefore no appearance) but that nonetheless their appearance can be imitated. He found this illogical:

4;3;17   S:   Is there such thing as a wolf and a fox?
          M:   Oh yes.
          S:   Is there such thing as ghosts?
          M:   No.
          S:   But a person can dress up as a ghost.
          M:   Yes . . .
          S:   How can you be dressed up as a ghost if there's no such thing as a ghost?

The next enquiries stem from Stephen's attempt to reconcile the mobility of people with the learned information that people are made of hard bones, two facts which evidently appeared contradictory to Stephen.

4;3;6   S:   Mummy, how can you move when something's hard inside you?

4;3;13   S:   How can something move your bones when – when – when – when your bones so hard and you can't kick it?

In the following text, Stephen took the premise that cars can go faster than buses and drew the conclusion that a particular bus should not therefore go faster than a particular car. Experience did not match this understanding so Stephen challenged the information on which his conclusion had been based:

4;5;13   S:   How come that bus is beating us when cars can go faster than buses?

This text can be compared with one cited from the previous year:

3;7;5   S:   Batman and Superman are nice.
       M:   Yes.
       S:   Why – then why do they punch holes through people?

The logical relations are the same, but the difference is that in the fifth year Stephen could use hypotactic condition to formulate the problem monologically.

All these examples illustrate the importance, in learning from talk in the fifth year, of being able to follow through the implications of a statement to a logical conclusion, and of problematizing occasions when different pieces of information conflict. Construing a conditional link between what is accepted information and what necessarily 'follows' from it was an important strategy in achieving this.

## 5.6 Internal cause

Finally, it can be noted that internal causal links continued to be made as a means of building relationships in the text (see Table 6.22).

**Table 6.22** Instances of internal cause, 4 to 5 years

| Link | hypotactic reason | paratactic reason | metaphor: *That means* |
|---|---|---|---|
| Number of examples | 24 | 4 | 1 |

Two developments in the use of the internal reason relation were firstly that the links were made in a wider variety of situations and secondly that paratactic links were recorded for the first time. Metaphorical uses remained rare and there were no recorded instances of internal condition despite its appearance in the previous year.

Internal reason had developed in the previous year principally as a means of making explicit the grounds for classification. In the fifth year it was still used prominently in this way but was also deployed much more generally to make explicit the evidence for Stephen's assertions:

4;5;26   S:   Jason's friend's cat bites.
         M:   Does it?
         S:   Yeah, 'cause he was just stroking him or her and he bit him.

Thus, as with the use of external cause and condition, this resource was used initially to construe links within a particular domain, and gradually became extended to wider uses. And as well as being extended within the reflective sphere, internal cause was increasingly used in the fifth year to support a variety of speech functions other than information-giving. In the following case, it was used to support an offer:

4;5;17   S:   Would you like some grapes or something 'cause I'm having grapes?

More often it was a ploy for supporting a request, as in:

4;2;12   S:   Can I have a biscuit 'cause there's some in there.

For the first time, too, paratactic internal links were made:

3;7;4   (in earlier discussions F had explained that a sports car was unsuitable for them because it has no rear seating)
        S:   Before I saw a sports car so you <u>can</u> have a sports car; you <u>can</u> buy a sports car.
        M:   Yes.
        S:   It <u>has</u> got a back seat.

The development of paratactic internal cause illustrates once again the dissociation of co-occurring features to create simultaneous choices. That is, the constraint that the feature [internal] could only be selected in conjunction with the feature [hypotaxis] no longer applied. Instead the ORIENTATION system of [internal] or [external] had become simultaneous with the TAXIS system of [hypotaxis] or [parataxis] (though at first this simultaneity would only be available for the reason relation).

### 5.7 Summary: 4;0 to 5;0 years

One characteristic of the expression of causality in the fifth year was a greater textual flexibility in its realizations. For the reason relation, there were participant and circumstance forms possible in addition to the hypotactic and paratactic links between processes. For the condition relation, different thematic orderings were regularly taken up as appropriate to manage the discourse.

This greater flexibility contributed to the characteristic new ways of using causality in the fifth year. For both the reason and condition relations there were new moves towards the kind of reasoning that construes acceptance of one fact as entailing also acceptance of some conclusion that 'follows' from the first. Stephen used causal taxis both to work through a problem and to formulate a problem to pose to the addressee, when a conclusion arrived at textually caused some conflict.

In addition, conditional links were used to switch point of view, both as a rhetorical strategy for manipulating the addressee and as a way of placing himself into a different activity sequence (*if I was in that car. . .*). It also continued to be an important means of exploring situations outside his lived experience.

### 6  Overview: the development of cause–effect relations from 2;6 to 5;0 years

This chapter has taken the single semantic domain of cause–effect relations and tracked aspects of its developments over the period from 2;6 to 5;0 years. The goal has been to illustrate some of the ways in which a meaning system can grow, and to provide an account of the development of the cognitive, i.e. semantic, strategy of reasoning.

With respect to the growth of the general meaning system, one finding was that not all grammatical environments for its expression emerge at the same time. The first explicit expression of reason occurred with hypotactic linking of two processes, followed by paratactic/cohesive, followed by metaphorical within-clause expressions. For condition, the pattern was different. The first recorded occasion involved cohesion across speaker turns, to be followed by hypotactic links within a turn, which later became the dominant form. (There are of course other aspects to causal meaning, such as the expression of Agency in a transitivity structure, and/or the use of causative verbs within the verbal group, as in *the coach made the team work hard*, which were not included in this discussion.)

Focusing on cause as an example of a meaning area that was growing during this period, the following ways for a system to expand were illustrated:

(i) the 'loosening' of interdependencies between metafunctional components;
(ii) the dissociation of linked variables;
(iii) an extension in delicacy of choices leading to a new sub-system which 'spreads' to other features.

(i) Loosening interdependencies between metafunctional components

Language is theorized by Halliday to consist of three metafunctional components, comprising sets of options which are simultaneously available. Many and close interrelations between systems and sub-systems are expected within a metafunction, but choices within one metafunction are relatively independent of choices from within another. However, with the development of the logico-semantic relation of cause in the third year, it was found that the possibility of taking up the ideational option of causal hypotaxis was initially constrained by choices from the interpersonal systems of SPEECH FUNCTION, PERSON and POLARITY. Then, as more and more speech functions could constitute meanings to be developed through a causal modification, and as third-person and non-negative forms were construed as causes and effects, the logical and interpersonal systems gradually became 'simultaneously' available.

(ii) Dissociation of linked variables

A system may also grow when co-occurring realizational variables are dissociated and simultaneous systems of meaning choices eventuate. This was illustrated when sequencing of cause and effect in Stephen's language became distinct from the choice of hypotactic linkage. That is, initially the choice of hypotaxis was realized both by the dependence of the cause clause and its sequencing *vis-à-vis* the main clause. Then – at least in conjunction with a choice of [condition] – the grammatical dependence of the causal relation became in time a separate realization from the sequencing of cause and effect. At that point sequencing had developed into a textual choice that was simultaneously available with the ideational one.

(iii) Increase in delicacy, leading to creation of simultaneous choices

A final illustration of system growth can be seen when a system increases in delicacy, allowing for sub-meanings within a general category, as when Stephen's option of [reason] opened up to a further choice of [internal] or [external] ORIENTATION. This in itself clearly constitutes an increase in the meaning potential, but in some cases such an additional, more delicate systemic choice may in turn become available for other features in the original system (in this case the system of CAUSE TYPE). Eventually the more delicate system may become simultaneous with the original one, extending the options for meaning even further.

During Stephen's fourth year all these kinds of developments either took place or were set in train, made possible not only by the probabilistic, paradigmatic nature of the system's organization but by its permeability through instances of text. That is, the changes discussed above occurred not as a predetermined flowering of meaning options, but as the result of the child mobilizing this particular semantic relation to act on and in the world, materially and intellectually.

Turning then to an examination of how causality was actualized in text, the general patterns in the development of meanings are summarized in Figures 6.17 and 6.18. Figure 6.17 provides an overview of the deployment of the reason relation, and Figure 6.18 summarizes that of the condition relation.

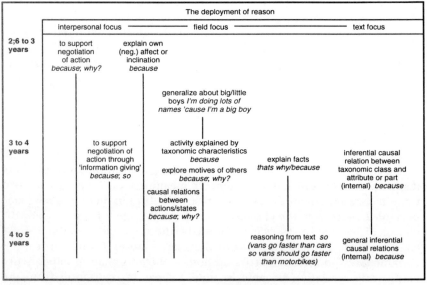

**Figure 6.17** Developments in the deployment of the cause:reason relation, 2;6 to 5 years

The summaries given in Figures 6.17 and 6.18 illustrate three major themes in the development and use of the relations of reason and condition. One is that for Stephen this ideational semantic domain was initially developed and exploited for interpersonal ends, a finding in keeping with Hood and Bloom's earlier naturalistic study of children aged up to three years. Since data for the present study were collected in a far greater variety of situations than in the earlier research, it is significant that the pattern of use in the different studies was broadly similar for this period (i.e. up till age three). This finding of 'interpersonal first' also echoes the earlier finding of this case study concerning the origins of mental process projection. And, as with the development of generalizations (see Chapter 4), the emotionally charged topic of 'big boys' was the one in which Stephen previewed new experientially oriented developments, another sense in which the (inter)personal leads the changes.

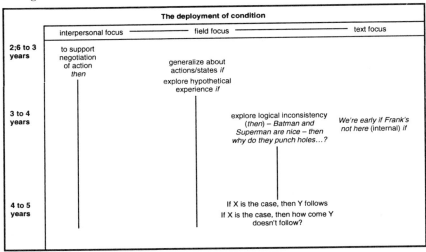

**Figure 6.18** Developments in the deployment of the cause:condition relation, 2;6 to 5 years

A second point about the use of causality summarized above is that it illustrates two aspects of development in mode. That is, there was a move from dialogically to monologically created text and this in turn was related to a new rhetorical organization of text. The move from dialogic to monologic construal of meaning was evident initially in the shared creation of a reason clause-complex with a more reflective orientation, when Stephen supplied an explanation for a warning or prohibition being made by the adult. For example:

2;8;17    M:    Little boys can't drink wine-
          S:    'cause it makes sick.

The shift to monologic expression was most strikingly evident in the use of the condition relation which initially was only construed as a cohesive link across speaker turns. In the fourth year, this cohesive link could be used to problematize the relation between one piece of information and another, the 'argument' being built up in successive dialogue moves:

3;7;5     S:   Batman and Superman are nice.
          M:   Yes.
          S:   Why – then why do they punch holes through people?

By the fifth year, a problem arising from an inconsistency between two
pieces of related knowledge could be construed entirely monologically:
*How come that bus is beating us when cars go faster than buses?*

Martin (1992a) points out that in addition to being concerned with the
semiotic space between action and reflection (as discussed in Chapters 3
and 4), mode is also concerned, along the interpersonal dimension, with
the semiotic space between monologue and dialogue:

> Mode refers to the role language is playing in realising social action . . . and . . .
> [it] is realised primarily through the textual metafunction in language . . . As
> with textual meaning in general, mode is concerned with symbolic reality – with
> texture. Since symbolic reality (i.e. text/process) has the function of construct-
> ing social reality, mode is oriented to both interpersonal and experiential
> meaning . . . Interpersonally, mode mediates the semiotic space between
> monologue and dialogue. (508–9)

The end result of this development from dialogue to monologue was a
new ability to reason from text. On the one hand an orientation towards
reflection on textual meaning is evident in the development of the
internal causal relation. When Stephen used external reason, saying *He
can crash 'cause he's got strong muscles* or *It's got a hole in it 'cause Hal banged it*,
he was construing understandings of field. That is, he was explaining the
relation between a participant's attributes and the activity sequences in
which it took part, or explaining the relation between one activity and
another in a sequence. With the internal relation, Stephen was doing
something a little different. An utterance like *He's not a strange mouse 'cause
strange mouses bite you* involves verbalizing the semiotic basis for an
inference. This is indicated on the figures as an orientation to text rather
than to field, because the speaker is reflecting not on the field directly but
on its semiotic construal.

In addition to the internal use of the conjunction, the other
development which was a part of this orientation to the text was the
beginning ability to engage in proto-syllogistic forms of reasoning. That is,
by the fifth year, Stephen had occasionally construed new information in
the course of a dialogue by following one piece of information through to
its logical conclusion. Here, two conditional texts can be compared:

(a) *If you hold it two hands close together, it will break.*
(b) *If all the tyres be flat, the car will walk.*

The earlier text, (a), constitutes a generalizing from lived experience,
but text (b) is different in kind. It takes up a newly received piece of
information (tyres can go flat) of which Stephen had no observational

experience and construes it as a condition that will necessarily lead to a conclusion (also outside his experience).

And in a similar way, paratactic reason could eventually be used to set up information as a cause that entailed an effect which itself constituted new knowledge (*Vans go faster than cars so vans should go faster than motorbikes*).

Thus in the experientialization of the meaning over time, the move from dialogic to monologic texts in the construal of problems and observations, the new orientations to internal or 'rhetorical' causality and the eventual attempts to construe new knowledge which was neither observed directly, induced from comparable observed instances nor directly told to him, Stephen was developing and deploying the semantic strategy of reasoning as a way of creating text in order to construe new understandings.

## Notes

1 See Chapter 4 for a brief description of this research.
2 In the Hood and Bloom (1991) studies *so (that)* and *because* appear to be used at about the same time.

# 7   Learning through language

This book has described and interpreted changes in one child's language between the ages of two-and-a-half and five years, as he used this resource to build knowledge of the world around him and of his own means of learning. The goal has been to document these changes so as to understand better both general characteristics of language development and the way these particular developments might 'ready' the child for school learning.

In drawing conclusions, it needs to be said at the outset that this research is very limited in that only one child's development has been studied. However, taking the theoretical perspective that language is a social and not an individual or even simply inter-individual process, it can be predicted that the broad patterns of Stephen's language use are likely to be similar to those of other middle-class children learning English as their mother tongue. And whenever naturalistic data have been available from other studies with respect to particular aspects of development, it has been apparent that Stephen's language does indeed conform to that of other children of his social group. So although the generalizability of the findings cannot be taken for granted, there are good reasons for supposing that Stephen's experience is typical of those children who are likely to be successful in the transition to institutionalized learning.

On that basis, this final chapter will offer some generalizations about the nature of learning through language. Firstly the case study will be used to focus on the 'how' of learning, illustrating some general principles of the process when viewed from a linguistic perspective. Then the general character of 'what' has been learned in the pre-school period will be reviewed and related to the question of how this semiotic experience constitutes a preparation for learning uncommonsense knowledge.

## 1   Developing the system through use

A key aspect of explaining how the systemic resources of a language are able to be built up is the relation between the system and the text, discussed in Chapter 2. As explained there, systemic theory pays equal attention to language as a map of resources and language as an ongoing process of text, with each text seen as an instance of the system and also as a source of data for readjusting the system. A case study such as the one presented in this book provides various examples of the way using language (i.e. creating text) builds new meaning possibilities, in a spiralling process whereby the current achievements in text step the learner up to new developments (cf. Vygotsky 1978).

Three perspectives on the system–process relationship will be offered here. First the flexible nature of the system itself will be considered as contributing to its own development. Then the importance of the learner's creation of text in order to manifest comparison and contrast relations will be considered as a means of developing the system further. Finally, interpersonal dimensions of the manifestation of language in text will be briefly reviewed as another dimension to the relationship between the resource and its development through use.

*1.1 System and process: the flexibility of the resource*

The case study of Stephen has shown the great flexibility of language as a resource for meaning and how that contributes to an expansion of the resource. For example, the system's potential for multiple construals of 'the same' reality can be exploited to increase meaning possibilities. In other words, there are points within a single metafunction where two different systems converge to construe the same semantic domain, creating a 'topological' overlap. This in turn can result in text realizations which blend the two meanings in a way which ultimately provides the learner with access to new meaning possibilities.

An example of such a blended meaning was provided in Chapter 5 where 'saying' as a relationship of identification was seen to overlap semantically with 'saying' as a more active process of verbalizing and projecting speech. By age two-and-a-half, Stephen had developed both meanings, as exemplified by utterances such as *that says Peter Rabbit* (identifying relationship) and *I can say 'accident'* (verbal process), the former involving a non-human symbol in the Token role and the latter a human symbolizer in the Sayer role. For an interim period these meanings were blended in the speech of child and adult (*the bag says 'shop'; the sign says 'Bronte over there'*), a phenomenon which facilitated Stephen's extension of verbal process options to include non-human symbol sources (*the book tells us that . . .* ) on the model of non-human symbols as Token. It would seem then that the permeability of meaning boundaries allowing for topological overlap can facilitate the construal of new meaning possibilities where that semantic overlap has been manifested in the text.

A different kind of flexibility in the system is exhibited by grammatical metaphor, and this too can provide an exemplification of the way the use of the system leads to new options. Unlike a blend, a grammatical metaphor allows two distinct meanings to be represented by a single lexico-grammatical structure. These meanings may derive from different metafunctions, as when mental processes (e.g. *I think; do you know?*) are used to construe additional MODALITY or MOOD options, a case also discussed in Chapter 5. It was argued there that what appeared to be a construal of cognition processes initially served in fact to provide additional interpersonal choices within the system. However, it was also suggested that using the language in this way enabled the child a better access to the experiential meanings represented by the structure, since these too became available for negotiation with the addressee and might be taken up as the proposition under focus. Thus the exploitation of stratal non-congruence through grammatical metaphor both allows for and facilitates the development of new meanings.

A third example of the flexible nature of the system and its role in development concerns the 'self-reflexivity' of language – its ability to turn back on itself and serve as its own metalanguage, thus contributing to its own expansion. For example, the use of lexis and relational processes to name the things and processes of experience created semantic taxonomies which were in place by age two-and-a-half. Relational transitivity could then be used to reflect on the taxonomies themselves, as well as directly on the aspects of experience. Attempts to do this led to the development of a new [identifying] option realized by *mean*, allowing linguistic meanings to be related. Clearly, asking *What does drown mean?* on hearing the word in an unfamiliar setting, or offering definitions such as *Flood means windy* or *Any person who's riding a horse who's got a round hat on is a cowboy*, can provide a short-cut to further developing language by providing opportunities for responses that can be used for rapid revision of the meaning system. The ability to exploit the metasemiotic character of language in fact changes fundamentally the child's potential for developing language further.

All three exemplifications of the system/process relation outlined above have been discussed here in linguistic terms, as extensions to the linguistic potential achieved through its manifestation as text. But, as argued in Chapter 2, any development to the linguistic meaning potential is by definition a development of the child's cognitive potential, if looked at in such terms. Viewed in this light, the ability to interpret an inanimate object as a symbolizer can be characterized as an important conceptual development underpinning the learning of the written medium of language, while the ability to represent the cognitions of oneself and others can be seen as fundamental, not only for monitoring one's own learning, but for reflecting on the world of ideas and beliefs generally. Similarly, the ability to make use of paraphrase and definitions is a crucial 'cognitive' development enabling the child to learn from talk which is not embedded in personal observation, and to renovate the system of knowledge from just a single text experience. Developing a linguistic system means developing a resource for thinking.

### 1.2 System and process: the use of comparison and contrast

Systemic theory suggests that semiotic systems are modelled as paradigmatic resources organized in terms of value relations. Given this, a fundamental strategy for building them will be to engage in comparison and contrast – to compare like meanings and forms with some point of difference between them and to contrast different meanings and forms against a background of similarity between them. This is not only the stock in trade of the linguist but also that of the child as the builder of a semiotic system. The notion of the child as 'little linguist' is a longstanding one in language acquisition studies and one which recognizes that the task of construing a meaning system is common to the researcher construing a 'linguistics' and the language learner construing the language itself together with the semiotic systems it realizes. This child as systemic linguist thus engages in 'the use of likeness as a mode of meaning' exploiting 'a fundamental semiotic strategy' (Halliday 1975: 138).

This case study of Stephen provides additional evidence to that detailed in Phillips (1985) that the realization of comparison and contrast relations pervades the development of the entire linguistic system. These meaning relations were at the heart of the deployment of language for learning, leading to an expansion of the linguistic and non-linguistic meaning potential, as can be seen from the examples given in Table 7.1.

**Table 7.1** Examples of Stephen's use of comparison and contrast as a learning strategy

| Object of learning | Relation | Example |
|---|---|---|
| Interpret graphic representation | Similarity | *looks like a koala* |
| Recognize possibility of misconstrual | Similarity Contrast | *that looks like fireworks but it's not* |
| Construe taxonomic relations: | | |
|   interpret variability of states of feeling | Contrast | *I'm not grumpy; I'm happy* |
|   relate unfamiliar abstract to known concrete | Similarity | *100 is big like Daddy* |
|   explore criterial features of category | Sameness | *That one's got a knob too* |
| | | *All parks . . . haven't got a gate* |
|   explore non-criterial variation in features of category | Contrast | *Not all trees grow bark;* |
| | | *Some are scruffy and some are beautiful* |
|   discriminate categories | Contrast | *Snakes and worms don't have legs but lizards do* |
|   construe superordinate thing category | Sameness | *Hal has and you have and Daddy has; grown-ups have* |
| | Contrast | *Crocodiles die . . . cars break* |
|   construe superordinate quality category | Sameness | *They go the same fast* |
| Construe personal identity | Contrast | *Hal can, I can't;* |
| | | *I don't like that cheese no, 'cause the little boys eat cheese (?) skin* |
| Construe typicality of participant behaviour | Similarity | *Would you do that when you were three?* |
| | Contrast | *Only little boys put on edge* |
| Construe potential participant and process configurations | Sameness | *Crocodiles die, ants die . . .* |
| | Contrast | *cars break* |
| Construe the predictable/'marked' | Contrast | *There wasn't any soap . . . and it made it clean!* |
| | | *Why not the drips are coming down?* |
| Negotiate alternate action | Contrast | *But we could park it somewhere* |
| Problematize general/specific; semiotic/observed relation | Contrast | *F: They go fast . . . S: But that doesn't go faster than us* |
| Explore 'deceit' | Contrast | *(I want) Vegemite . . . I'm tricking you, I really want marmalade* |
| Explore alternative reality | Contrast | *If some other boy dropped his teddy out the window, I bet the other Mummy wouldn't shout at him* |

Even a skeletal summary such as Table 7.1 provides can serve to illustrate both the variety of aspects of experience interpreted through comparing and contrasting and also the variety of ways the relations of sameness, similarity and difference might be realized grammatically. For example, at group rank, the realization might be in the Post-Deictic (*the same*, *the other*) or Qualifier (*like Daddy*), at clause rank a Comparison circumstance (*like a koala*), a modal Finite or Adjunct (*supposed to*, *really*) or through successive choices of POLARITY. Options from the discourse-semantics stratum were also deployed, such as CONJUNCTION, REFERENCE and LEXICAL COHESION, while the phonological stratum was implicated in choices of tone realizing KEY and INFORMATION. This list is not exhaustive but it shows how the text actualization of this learning strategy might involve realizations at any rank and within any metafunction, so funda-mental is it to the process of building meaning.

Since every option within the meaning resources is constituted by its relations of likeness and unlikeness to other choices, the manifestation of these relations in text provides an indispensable means of creating the systemic resources – not only those options which themselves construct comparison and contrast, but the systems of language and field as a whole. And while educators certainly confirm the importance of comparing and contrasting as cognitive skills necessary for learning in school, its foundational nature and the extent to which every child will already be oriented to and experienced in making use of this strategy long before beginning formal education is less well recognized.

### *1.3  System and process: interpersonal dimensions*

In talking about the use of comparison and contrast, it may appear that the actualization of system in text is primarily a matter of an individual learner using his or her meaning system in the effort to make sense of the world. However, systemic theory has always emphasized the social-interactional aspects of language and the importance of recognizing that language functions not only to represent the world but to act in it. Although this research was focused on representation – on how things, processes and relations were interpreted and represented linguistically – the fact that the representation took place in dialogue (or multilogue) with other persons was always in evidence. In particular, it was apparent in the development of ideational systems in contexts of interpersonal negotiation, in the need for systems of the interpersonal metafunction to facilitate ideational reflection, and in the use of jointly produced text as a source of change for the child's developing system.

### 1.3.1  Interpersonal origins of ideational choices

Language is an instrument for learning with, but it is one that is used in concert with other persons. Because of this, a system that is significant in the representation of reality may first be tried out in the service of interpersonal negotiation and action rather than in the reflective interpretation of the 'third-person' world. For example, as discussed in Chapters 4 and 6, the development of both temporal and causal hypotaxis may typically evolve to negotiate with the addressee the carrying out of desired activities, rather than to interpret dispassionately the way the world is. Development of mental processes provides another example. As discussed in Chapter 5, the representation of cognition processes first arises as a means of negotiating roles and intruding assessments, while Stephen's further exploration of the relation between seeing and knowing also took place initially via interpersonal games, exploring the dialogue partner's construals and reactions to the speaker's representations, rather than representing the rest of the world as thinking, knowing beings. A final example of the 'interpersonal first' principle concerns the importance of trying out new meanings (such as causality or generalization) with respect to an interpersonally salient topic. In Stephen's case this involved one central to his self-identity, arising from his position vis-à-vis other persons at home and at childcare – that of *little boys* versus *big boys*.

As suggested in Chapter 6, these findings run counter to the notion that development entails a movement from the egocentric basis of the asocial individual. Instead, the child's development needs to be understood as a 'moving out' or extension of meaning-making from the deictic centre of interpersonal negotiation. The implications for educational theory are not only that language is an interpersonal process, but that the you–me, here-and-now centre of interpersonal exchange is the most accessible starting place for the learning of new things. This in turn means that the ability to use a meaning system in situations of dialogic negotiation and personal intrusion need not necessarily imply a current capacity to deploy the relevant system in a more distanced, reflective mode in relation to 'objective' content.

## 1.3.2 Interpersonal metafunction facilitates ideational reflection

The fact that language as an interpersonal process is a crucial aspect of the development of language as system is also evident in the fact that the construal of what is 'out there' develops not only ideational but interpersonal systems. An ideational resource is needed for representing field but an interpersonal resource is also needed because that interpretation is being developed with other persons.

The most obvious aspect to this is the learner's use of questions – mapping an interrogative structure onto experiential representations in demands for information (*Is this a traffic jam? Can shoes break?*) or coding such demands metaphorically (*Tell me about . . .*). Inevitably in the process of learning through language any child will be aware of older persons as having greater knowledge, and, in families like Stephen's, will indeed construe information-giving as an integral part of the care-giving role (cf. *You have to tell something to me* from Chapter 5). Again, contrary to the models of educational learning influenced by Piagetian theory, learning by 'being told' is not at all at odds with many children's previous experience, and nor is the learner thereby rendered 'passive', as so often suggested. The challenge of engaging the child in learning within the educational context is not therefore to be met by devaluing the role of talk, but by working to enable relevant linguistic interaction to take place.

However, it is not only through direct information-seeking that the interpersonal metafunction is involved in the construal of field. Equally, when giving information, the interpersonal metafunction comes into play because the interpretation of experience involves the creation of text in which the learner's assessments are manifested for validation or negotiation. This was apparent in the construal of knowledge detailed in Chapter 4, where the move to reflect on the potential for particular processes to configure with particular participants required the exploitation of the systems of USUALITY and PROBABILITY. Using these systems, a negotiable assessment was overlaid on an experiential representation when the latter went beyond the interpretation of the observable. By being put forward as negotiable, the interpretation could be tried out and if necessary adjusted in the light of the addressee's response, as in:

2;7;5    S:   Babies go in the prams sometimes.
         M:   Yes they do.

3;10;2   S:   The falling-down car is gone . . . maybe it's gone under the
              garage.
         M:   Yeah, maybe it's gone right inside.

In this way the interpersonal metafunction was valuably deployed in the construal of experience through dialogue.

Another intrusion of attitude that necessarily arises in the interpretation of experience as text is the expression of counter-expectation, which – manifested in the text phonologically through choices of KEY – can be responded to in a way which furthers ideational understandings. Chapter 4 illustrated the way developing a sense of the predictable patterning to experience gave rise to the expression of surprise on occasions when expectations were not met. In dialogue this expression would be responded to in a way which clarified the validity of the current assessment and/or which directed the child to construe an event as having a preceding cause:

2;10;13   S:   Daddy smashing the biscuits!
          F:   I didn't smash them, I dropped them, 'cause my hands are
               cold.

Thus quite apart from the direct seeking of information using the interpersonal option of [interrogative], the manifestation in the text of

the interpersonal metafunction in other ways was able to facilitate the
further development of ideational understandings precisely because the
instantiation of the meaning systems occurs in a dialogic exchange.

1.3.3  Use of jointly produced text as a source of change

One final aspect of the interpersonal dimension of the system–text
relation concerns the importance of the text as the instantiation of the
adult's meaning system alongside the child's, so that in construing the
jointly created process into system, the child has the opportunity to learn
new forms and meanings.

At the level of lexico-grammar, learning from adult models is apparent
where the child imitates or adapts an adult utterance as an aid to
construing a meaning not yet part of the child's own system, as with the
temporal relation realized by *till* in the following example from Chapter 4:

2;8;21    S:   Mummy can I have that?
          M:   Not till you've finished your muffin.
          S:   Not till finished y- my muffin.

Alternatively the adult may be able to supply for the child a form which
the latter recognizes as realizing the appropriate meaning. The shared
text provides the opportunity for the child to extend his/her own
resources to include the new term:

4;8;30    F:   This car can't go as fast as ours.
          S:   I thought – I thought all cars could – all cars could go the
               same – all cars could go the same (pause) fast.
          M:   The same speed.
          S:   Yes, same speed.

Comparable examples can be found throughout the 'social-interactive'
language development literature discussed in Chapter 1, where the adult's
contribution to learning language is explored and theorized. From a
systemic perspective, it is important to recognize that it is not only the
lexico-grammatical forms that are being learned, but the knowledge (the
aspects of field) that those forms realize. Thus when the adult and child
already share the lexico-grammatical systems being deployed, the child may
still re-express the adult meaning as a means of learning. This can be seen
in the deployment of conditionals in the following texts, cited in Chapter 6:

3;6;30    S:   But that doesn't go faster than us. See? We will go faster.
          F:   He's not trying; if he was really trying he could go much
               faster than us.
          S:   If he goes very fast he can – if he goes very fast he can beat us.

3;6;5   S:   Mum, could you cry; could you cry or not?
       M:   Yes, I could cry.
       S:   How?
       M:   What do you mean? If I hurt myself I might cry, same as you.
       S:   If you fell down bump really really hard.

In such cases the adult's contribution is interpreted by the child, who then activates his own system to produce a comparable meaning as a way of verifying his understanding and trying out the new knowledge construed. The lexico-grammatical options involved were already available to the child, but the particular meaning being construed – the condition on which the validity of the generalization holds – was a new piece of knowledge being arrived at through the course of the text.

Further than this, the child – in reworking the adult meaning for himself – was adopting not just the specific knowledge it realized but the more general rhetorical strategy embodied by the move. In the above case this involves the strategy of limiting generalizations and thus reconciling them with specific observations by means of constraining 'scenarios' or conditions. Another example of the adoption by the child of such habits of meaning would be the provision of causes for observed unexpected goings-on, discussed in Chapter 4. Texts manifesting this rhetorical move were created jointly when the child expressed surprise and the adult explained – and it is reasonable to suggest that this can lead to the child evolving the semiotic habit of seeking and finding causes for 'marked' events. In a similar way, the seeking and provision of counter-evidence to generalizations can be initiated by the parent in response to the child's over-generalizations, allowing the child to take on the same strategy in other dialogues, as illustrated again in Chapter 4. And as a final example of the importance of the dialogue as a means of scaffolding later development, Stephen's use of language to explore problems 'syllogistically' can be cited. Initially he formulated a problem in stages, by checking first on the validity of a premise (e.g. *Trees can grow, can't they?; Batman and Superman are nice*). The problem could then be constructed as a challenge linked cohesively to the adult's move (*then why do they punch holes through people?*). Later the whole problem could be formulated as a clause-complex without the collaboration of the adult.

Clearly Vygotsky's ideas on the significance of collaborative effort between the novice and a more expert party within the child's zone of proximal development can be understood and accepted very readily within the systemic theory of the relationship between system and process. Since the systems of language and knowledge are construed from their instantiations in text, then in interpreting a text accessible to him because he participated in its construction, but more complete than he could have produced from his own meaning resources, the child has the ideal opportunity to increase the meaning potential itself at all levels.

## 2  Developments in mode from 2;6 to 5;0 years

The various aspects of the relation between system and process help to explain how it is that language is learnable, while the other crucial dimension in such an explanation concerns the relation between context and text. This was foregrounded in the story of the move from protolanguage into the mother tongue, detailed in Halliday (1975) and Painter (1990), where the child's development of a metafunctionally organized grammar was shown to depend on coming to construe a context for speech as having both a field and a tenor component.

The construal of context as a semiotic construct accompanies the construal of language as a metafunctionally organized system because of the realizational relationship between the two. And it is this relationship which helps to explain how the language is learned:

> It is this that enables, and disposes, the child to learn the lexicogrammar: since the system is organized along functional lines, it relates closely to what the child can see language doing as he observes it going on around him. (Halliday 1975: 128)

With the very first move into lexis, a child's speech is freed from 'dependence' on the context in the sense that non-visible things and processes can be referred to, something not possible with protolanguage. However, this case study suggests that inexperienced mother tongue speakers will at first make meanings that are relevant to a context that can be construed with the minimum of linguistic work. This does not mean that only things in view can be talked about, but it does mean that only specific actions, things and qualities are referred to and that language itself is only called upon to 'constitute' the field and tenor in a limited way. With respect to field, even when the activity or content referred to in the text is not simply ancillary to the text, it may well be accessible primarily through shared observation, shared memory or joint participation in the process.

Many of the developments from 2;6 to 5 years have been interpreted in this book in terms of a change in this relationship, a change described in terms of developments in mode, developments which could also be seen as constituting new textual strategies in learning. One such development was a move into generalization in the fourth year; that is, the use of language to construe meanings which have relevance beyond the immediate context of situation. Another development was the bringing of semiosis to consciousness in the attempt to understand the world of meaning being created in this way, while the possibility of abstract and grammatically metaphorical meaning was something new which resulted from these two moves. Finally, a different aspect of mode development involved the monologic constitution of meanings that initially required a joint construction in dialogue, something already touched on in discussing system and process.

## 2.1 *Distancing language from the immediate context of situation*

A move towards generalizing was apparent in Stephen's language of the fourth year in comparison with that of the third, and was detailed in Chapters 3 and 4. In learning about things, generalizing required taxonomizing the categories that make up the meaning potential rather than simply classifying the things that make up the observed actuality (e.g. *dogs are animals* as opposed to *that's a dog*). In learning about happenings it meant representing processes, participants and circumstances as potential configurations rather than interpretations of actual specific events (*plates can break* as opposed to *that plate broke*). It also meant generalizing the temporal succession between specific events by construing this in terms of causal relations (*you went the wrong way; that's why it broke* as opposed to *you went the wrong way and then it broke*).

Once the child was generalizing experience in this way, the linguistic representation of contextual information was also called for, using thematic temporal or conditional clauses to specify the scope of the generalization being construed (*when we eat it, it's still called bolognese; if you look at the sun you go tishoo*). And attempts to construe experience more distant from the current context also took the form of representing 'autobiographical' events distant in time. This placed greater responsibility for achieving a successful outcome onto the language, rather than on shared participation or shared prior experience. To manage this, time was construed 'statically', as a location for an activity or sequence, rather than simply a relation between them (e.g. *one day; when I was a little boy*).

A different manner of distancing was described in Chapter 5, involving Stephen's reflection on the speech of others. While children are alert to the speech addressed to them from the outset, and recall, quote and report speech they have heard, Stephen was shown to develop his use of projection over the period to achieve a distance between his current meaning base and other representations. As early as the third year, he used projection to represent 'at one remove' (as a representation of a representation) an interpretation he was now abandoning (*I thought . . .* ) and by the fifth year, he would reintroduce problematic texts into a new context for exploration, distancing them from his own meaning system by explicitly projecting them as the wordings and meanings of others.

Thus the various respects in which the language was distanced from the specific or local context of situation was a striking aspect of development over this period. The period between three and four years was most crucial here in the construal of things and events, while the fifth year was most important in the construal of semiosis.

## 2.2 *Bringing semiosis to consciousness*

If Stephen is typical, then the period from two-and-a-half to five years is one in which there will be a new orientation to language as an object of attention, involving language both as system and as process. This occurred in a number of ways, as outlined below.

### 2.2.1 Reflecting on meaning, wording and spelling/sounding

The use of *mean* as a relational process in the fourth year enabled the exploration of relationships at the interface of semantics and lexico-grammar. Stephen tried out different ways to word the same meaning (*X means Y*) and checked up on the addressee's use of unfamiliar terms, or words used in unfamiliar contexts (e.g. *What does drown mean?*). At the same time the use of *say* as a relational process manifested an awareness of relationships between lexico-grammar and graphology (*That says Daddy*), while graphology and phonology were also related in various ways (*Handbag has got 'b'*; *Ireland starts with I*). In addition, speech interacts were named (*joke, question*) and exemplified from the fourth year onwards (see Chapter 4). Thus, all levels of the linguistic system were attended to and both spoken and written realizations.

### 2.2.2 Explication of criteria for categorizing in the fourth year

Chapter 3 also showed how Stephen used an internal (or textual) causal relation to link a category and its defining characteristics (*He's a boy 'cause he's got a penis*). In doing this Stephen was reflecting on the nature of the categories and the interrelationships between taxonomies of qualities, parts and things and so on. At the same time, the mobilization of language as text in order to engage in this reflection involved the organization of aspects of field knowledge into a clause-complex structured textually with an internal conjunctive link. Thus the meaning potential as system was oriented to and also the organization of its instantiation as text.

### 2.2.3 Countering the dialogue partner's move

The reason relation was not the only internal conjunction developed during the fourth year. As shown in Chapter 4, the exploration of generalizations in dialogue led to challenges to parental statements (*F: They go fast . . . S: But that one doesn't go faster than us*). Familiarity with activity sequences also allowed for counter-proposals for action (*M: (We can't go on the train) 'cause we're in the car S: But we could park it*). These countering moves extended the dialogue through an internal textual link rather than by simply representing sequences iconic to the field and provide another illustration of a textual strategy developed during this period.

### 2.2.4 Representing information exchange

In addition to the ways of orienting to system and text which have been summarized so far, language was treated as an 'object' of reflection during this period in the talk about talking and about giving and receiving information, which was discussed in Chapter 5. Verbalizing as the production of sound was commented upon in the third year (*I can say 'accident'*) but from the fourth year onwards there was a new focus on language as an exchange of meaning. The process of dialogue was repeatedly represented in the ideational grammar (*Tell me, do you know?*, etc.) as Stephen brought to consciousness his understanding of language as an exchange of information. By the fifth year he represented this understanding even more explicitly by construing language received as the source of his knowledge (*I know that because X told me*).

The period from 2;6 to 5 years can therefore fairly be described as one when, in a variety of ways, language came to the fore as an object of reflection, and Stephen gained experience in exploiting different aspects of its metasemiotic capability, which Vygotsky regarded as so important for the understanding of scientific concepts.

### 2.3  Abstract and metaphorical meanings

The attempts to construe meanings with general relevance and to reflect on language itself in turn gave rise to another strand of development – the first representations of non-thing meanings as participants, moves already summarized in Figure 3.8 (p. 134).

For example, in the construction of definitions, described above as an aspect of orienting to language as system, it was frequently necessary to organize meanings into a single Theme-Rheme structure by construing events as participants in identifying clauses (e.g. *drown is [[go down to the bottom and be dead]]*). This textual organization for ideational ends thus enabled a dual construction of the meaning as both activity and thing.

Another example of the textual metafunction being called upon to facilitate the construal of field arose in the production of causal meanings. In the creation of external causal links as a means of generalizing, and in the creation of internal causal links as a means of reflecting on the meaning system, Stephen also developed 'text' reference to construe a previous utterance as a fact, so as to constitute it as the Token role in an identifying clause (e.g. *That means it's a biplane, That's why there's red traffic lights*). Here then, something more abstract than either a thing *or* an event was construed as a participant, while the reason relation was represented metaphorically either as a process (*mean*) or as a participant (*[[why there's red traffic lights]]*). These developments occurred as a means of organizing appropriate textual structures to achieve the new mode options of the fourth and fifth years.

Moreover, the new orientation to language in the use of synonymy and definition to learn new meanings also led to the representation of time as a measurable thing (*a week is seven sleeps*), while the reflection on the language system at all levels necessitated the construal of names for symbolic forms of various kinds, as touched on above. Thus many related small moves into abstraction and ideational metaphor occurred as a result of the mode developments which took place after age 3.

### 2.4 The monologic representation of meaning

Finally, one further development in mode was represented by the child's ability, by the end of this period, to use clause-complexing to build a context for posing a question or arriving at a conclusion. Before this, the context for an enquiry was provided by shared attention and observation, or else was built up through the dynamics of dialogue, as in the example already cited from Chapter 6:

3;7;5    S:   Batman and Superman are nice.
         M:  Yes.
         S:   Why – then why do they punch holes through people?

In the fifth year, problems of this type could be posed in a single clause-complex (e.g. *How come that bus is beating us when cars can go faster than buses?*) which meant the direct engagement with the dialogue partner was no longer necessary to construct the problem. This greater facility with linguistic reasoning can additionally facilitate the solving of a problem without the to-and-fro of face-to-face interaction (e.g. *Vans go faster than cars so vans should go faster than motorbikes*). As discussed earlier, arriving at this point builds on experience in dialogue. But what results from this experience is a new potential for using one's own linguistic resources to build new knowledge, a move towards learning in a more monologic mode.

## 3 Semiotic preparation for school learning

The findings of this study can be related to the initial question of why children are ready for learning new things and learning them in a new institutional setting only after some years of experience with their mother tongue. To consider this, the distinction between commonsense and educational knowledge discussed in the introductory chapters can provide a starting-point. Table 7.2 lists some of the ways in which everyday community knowledge and the more specialized knowledge that is learned in school and other formal settings tend to be different.

There will always be debate as to the degree to which the learning of commonsense knowledge and educational knowledge should be polarized, and clearly different models of institutional learning exist – especially with regard to the degree of discretion allowed the learner in determining the pace and content of what is to be learned ('framing' in Bernstein's (1975) terminology), the rigidity of the boundaries maintained between areas of knowledge ('classification') and the continuing relevance of personal experience. Whatever position is taken on these issues, however, there is no question that there will inevitably be a significant degree of difference between the two, deriving from differences in the nature of what is being learned, which in turn makes different demands of the learning process.

**Table 7.2** Some characteristics of commonsense and educational knowledge

| Commonsense knowledge | Educational knowledge |
| --- | --- |
| Built up slowly and gradually with pace of learning at discretion of learner | Built up rapidly with pace of learning largely at discretion of teacher |
| Built up in a piecemeal, fragmented way | Systematic, logically sequenced |
| Relevant to specific context | Universalistic in orientation |
| Based on personal/shared experience, language-mediated observation and participation | Distant from personal experience; based on semiotic representation |
| Concrete, non-technical meanings | Abstract and technical meanings |
| Non-compartmentalized | Boundaries between disciplines |
| Negotiated in spoken language | Constituted in written language |
| Built up unconsciously | Built up consciously |

It can be seen that the points listed in Table 7.2 as characteristic of the building of commonsense knowledge accurately reflect Stephen's learning experience at the beginning of this study, in the second half of the third year. However, by age 5, without any of these having been abandoned, new ways of learning were additionally becoming established – ways which relate to the characteristics of educational knowledge. Table 7.3 summarizes the relevance of Stephen's pre-school experience for school learning.

Although the systematicity of educational knowledge, its abstraction and its written mode will all provide a significant challenge, it can be seen that Stephen's linguistic experience between 2;6 and 5 years has provided an important semiotic preparation for the next phase of his education, his first experience with 'formal' teaching and learning.

Formal education will be at a far greater distance from their pre-school experience for many children, but all will have had some relevant experience on which the school can build. Successfully guiding children towards using their meaning potential and developing it further in ways relevant to the learning of educational knowledge will depend upon a recognition of the different linguistic demands of commonsense and educational learning and an appreciation that teaching is a matter of 'intervening in what are indisputably linguistic processes' (Halliday 1988b: 2). Unless it can be shown that the kinds of knowledge to be accessed in formal education are to change radically from their traditional form, then a successful apprenticeship into these forms of knowledge will necessarily involve a radical shifting in mode and a thoroughgoing exploitation of the metasemiotic potential of language. At the same time, the interpersonal dimensions of the system–process relation need to be reflected upon in building pedagogies that can best ensure a successful transition into educational learning for all children.

**Table 7.3** Stephen's linguistic preparation for learning uncommonsense knowledge

| Educational knowledge | Semiotic preparation |
| --- | --- |
| Built up rapidly | Experience in learning through definitions. Revision of knowledge from a single text possible |
| Universalistic in orientation | Generalizations; definitions; causal relations |
| Systematic | Criteria for concepts can be articulated |
| Logically sequenced | Overall, sequencing at discretion of learner, but at very local level. Some experience in building logical argument and relating information logically |
| Distant from personal experience | Hypothetical meaning; extension of various meaning systems (e.g. cause, projection) to 'objective realm' of 'third party' |
| Based on linguistic representation | Some experience with constitutive text |
| Abstract and technical meanings | Names for symbols, superordinate qualities |
| Constituted in written language | Extension of resources for spoken monologue/constitutive text; construal of written text objects as Sayers; some experience in reflecting on text |
| Built up consciously | Experience in reflecting on meaning system and text realizations |

This description of Stephen's experience in learning through language in his pre-school years has aimed at the most general level to illustrate significant aspects of the nature of language as a semiotic in which the content of learning is constructed and through which it is mediated. More particularly, the case study has been used to support an argument that for at least some children, their linguistic experience involves developing an orientation to those ways of learning that are best tuned to the demands of educational knowledge. In pursuing this argument, the description of Stephen's developing language in use illustrates the general theoretical position that learning is a linguistic process. More specifically it demonstrates how a study of the texts in which a child manifests the language in the process of developing it can fruitfully be read as a study of the child's intellectual development.

# References

Adlam, D. (1977) *Code in Context*. London: Routledge and Kegan Paul.

Aitchison, J. (1996) *The Seeds of Speech: Language Origin and Evolution*. Cambridge: Cambridge University Press.

Anglin, J.M. (1977) *Word, Object, and Conceptual Development*. New York: Norton.

Anglin, J.M. (1983) 'Extensional aspects of preschool child's word concepts'. In T.B. Seiler and W. Wannenmacher (eds) *Concept Development and the Development of Word Meaning*. Berlin: Springer, 247–66.

Applebee, A.N. and Langer, J.A. (1983) 'Instructional scaffolding'. *Language Arts* 60, 168–75.

Astington, J.W. (1994) *The Child's Discovery of the Mind*. London: Fontana.

Astington, J.W. and Gopnik, A. (1991) 'Theoretical explanations of children's understanding of the mind'. *British Journal of Developmental Psychology* 9, 7–31.

Atkinson, M. (1992) *Children's Syntax: An Introduction to Principles and Parameters Theory*. Oxford: Blackwell.

Baker, C.L. and McCarthy, J.J. (eds) (1981) *The Logical Problem of Language Acquisition*. Cambridge, MA: MIT Press.

Bakhtin, M. (1986) *Speech Genres and Other Late Essays*, C. Emerson and M. Holquist (eds). Manchester: Manchester University Press.

Barrett, M.D. (1978) 'Lexical development and overextension in child language'. *Journal of Child Language* 5, 205–15.

Barrett, M.D. (1983) 'The early acquisition and development of the meanings of action-related words'. In T.B. Seiler and W. Wannenmacher (eds) *Concept Development and the Development of Word Meaning*. Berlin: Springer, 191–209.

Barrett, M.D. (1986) 'Early semantic representations and early word-usage'. In S.A. Kuczaj and M.D. Barrett (eds) *The Development of Word Meaning: Progress in Cognitive Development Research*. New York: Springer, 39–67.

Barthes, R. (1977) 'Introduction to the structural analysis of narratives'. In his *Image-music-text*. London: Fontana, pp. 79–124. First published in *Communications* 8 (1966).

Bartsch, K. and Wellman, H.M. (1995) *Children Talk about the Mind*. New York: Oxford University Press.

Bates, E. (1976) *Language and Context: The Acquisition of Pragmatics*. New York: Academic Press.

Bates, E., Benigni, L. *et al.* (1979) *The Emergence of Symbols: Cognition and Communication in Infancy*. New York: Academic.

Bates, E. and MacWhinney, B. (1979) 'A functionalist approach to the acquisition of grammar'. In E. Ochs and B.B. Schieffelin (eds) *Developmental Pragmatics*. New York: Academic, 167–211.

Bateson, G. (1978) *Mind and Nature*. New York: Dutton.

Bateson, M.C. (1971) 'The interpersonal context of infant vocalization'. In *Quarterly Progress Report of the Research Laboratory of Electronics, MIT* 100. 170–6.

Behrend, Douglas A. (1990) 'Constraints and development: a reply to Nelson (1988)'. *Cognitive Development* 5, 313–30.

Bernstein, B. (1962a) 'Linguistic codes, hesitation phenomena and intelligence'. *Language and Speech* 5, 31–46.

Bernstein, B. (1962b) 'Social class, linguistic codes and grammatical elements'. *Language and Speech* 5, 221–40.

Bernstein, B. (1965) 'A socio-linguistic approach to social learning'. In J. Gould (ed.) *Penguin Survey of the Social Sciences*. Harmondsworth: Penguin.

Bernstein, B. (1971) *Class, Codes and Control*, vol. 1: *Theoretical Studies towards a Sociology of Language*. London: Routledge and Kegan Paul.

Bernstein, B. (ed.) (1973) *Class, Codes and Control*, vol. 2: *Applied Studies towards a Sociology of Language*. London: Routledge and Kegan Paul.

Bernstein, B. (1975) *Class, Codes and Control*, vol. 3: *Towards a Theory of Educational Transmission*. London: Routledge and Kegan Paul.

Bernstein, B. (1982) 'Codes, modalities and the process of cultural reproduction: a model'. In M.W. Apple (ed.) *Cultural and Economic Reproduction in Education*. London: Routledge and Kegan Paul, 304–55.

Bernstein, B. (1987) 'Elaborated and restricted codes: an overview 1958–85'. In U. Ammon, N. Dittmar and K.J. Mattheier (eds) *Sociolinguistics: An International Handbook of the Science of Society*, vol. 1. Berlin: De Gruyter.

Bernstein, B. (1990) *The Structuring of Pedagogic Discourse: Class, Codes and Control*, vol. 4. London: Routledge.

Berry, M. (1981) 'Systemic linguistics and discourse analysis: a multi-layered approach to exchange structure'. In M. Coulthard and M. Montgomery (eds) *Studies in Discourse Analysis*. London: Routledge and Kegan Paul, 120–45.

Bickerton, D. (1982) 'Learning without experience the creole way'. In L. Menn and L. K. Obler (eds) *Exceptional Language and Linguistics*. New York: Academic, 15–29.

Bickerton, D. (1984) 'The language bioprogram hypothesis'. *Behavioural and Brain Sciences* 7, 173–88.

Bickerton, D. (1990) *Language and Species*. Chicago: University of Chicago Press.

Blank, M., Rose, S.A. and Berlin, L.J. (1978) *The Language of Learning: The Preschool Years*. New York: Grune and Stratton.

Bloom, K., Russell, A. and Wassenberg, K. (1987) 'Turn-taking affects the quality of infant vocalisations'. *Journal of Child Language* 14, 211–27.

Bloom, L. (1973) *One Word at a Time*. The Hague: Mouton.

Bloom, L. (1993) *The Transition from Infancy to Language: Acquiring the Power of Expression*. Cambridge: Cambridge University Press.

Bloom, L. and Capatides, J.B. (1991) 'Sources of meaning in the acquisition of complex syntax: the sample case of causality'. In L. Bloom *et al.*, *Language Development from Two to Three*. New York: Cambridge University Press, 377–93. First published in *Journal of Experimental Child Psychology* 43 (1987), 112–28.

Borke, H. (1975) 'Piaget's mountain revisited: changes in the egocentric landscape'. *Developmental Psychology* 11, 240–3.

Bourdieu, P. (1991) *Language and Symbolic Power*, J.B. Thomson (ed.). Cambridge: Polity.

Bowerman, M. (1985) 'What shapes children's grammars?'. In D.I. Slobin (ed.) *The Crosslinguistic Study of Language Acquisition*, vol. 2: *Theoretical Issues*. Hillsdale, NJ: L. Erlbaum Assoc., 1257–1319.

Bowerman, M. (1993) 'Learning a semantic system: what role do cognitive predispositions play?'. In P. Bloom (ed.) *Language Acquisition: Core Readings*. Cambridge, MA: MIT Press, 329–63. First published in R.L. Schiefelbusch and M.L. Rice (eds) *The Teachability of Language*. Paul H. Brookes Publishing Co. (1989).

Brazelton, T.B. and Tronick, E. (1980) 'Preverbal communication between mother and infant'. In D.R. Olson (ed.) *The Social Foundations of Language and Thought*. New York: Norton, 299–315.

Bretherton, I., McNew, S. and Beeghly-Smith, M. (1981) 'Early person knowledge as expressed in gestural and verbal communication: when do infants acquire a "theory of mind"?'. In M.E. Lamb and L.R. Sherod (eds) *Infant Social Cognition: Empirical and Theoretical Considerations*. Hillsdale, NJ: Erlbaum, 333–73.

Brown, R. (1973) *A First Language*. London: Allen and Unwin.

Brown, R. (1977) 'Introduction'. In C. Snow and C. Ferguson (eds) *Talking to Children: Language Input and Acquisition*. New York: Academic.

Brown, R. (1980) 'The maintenance of conversation'. In D. Olson (ed.) *The Social Foundations of Language and Thought*. New York: Norton, 187–210.

Brown, R. and Bellugi, U. (1964) 'Three processes in the acquisition of syntax'. *Harvard Educational Review* 34, 133–51.

Bruner, J.S. (1975) 'The ontogenesis of speech acts'. *Journal of Child Language* 2, 1–19.

Bruner, J.S. (1978) 'The role of dialogue'. In A. Sinclair, R.J. Jarvella and W.J.M. Levelt (eds) *The Child's Conception of Language*. Berlin: Springer, 241–56.

Bruner, J.S. (1986) *Actual Minds, Possible Worlds*. Cambridge, MA: Harvard University Press.

Bryant, P. and Trabasso, T. (1971) 'Transitive inference and memory in young children'. *Nature* 232, 456–8.

Bullowa, M. (ed.) (1979) *Before Speech: The Beginning of Interpersonal Communication*. Cambridge: Cambridge University Press.

Butt, D. (1989) 'The object of language'. In R. Hasan and J.R. Martin (eds) *Language Development: Learning Language, Learning Culture. Meaning and Choice in Language: Studies in Honour of Michael Halliday* (Advances in Discourse Processes 27). Norwood, NJ: Ablex, 66–110.

Butterworth, G. (1992) 'Context and cognition in models of cognitive growth'. In P. Light and G. Butterworth (eds) *Context and Cognition: Ways of Learning and Knowing*. Hemel Hempstead: Harvester Wheatsheaf, 1–13.

Carter, A.L. (1978) 'The development of systematic vocalizations prior to words: a case study'. In N. Waterson and C. Snow (eds) *The Development of Communication*. Chichester: Wiley, 127–38.

Carter, A.L. (1979) 'Prespeech meaning relations'. In P. Fletcher and M. Garman (eds) *Language Acquisition*. Cambridge: Cambridge University Press, 71–92.

Cazden, C. (1965) *Environmental Assistance to the Child's Acquisition of Grammar*. Doctoral dissertation, Harvard University.

Chomsky, N. (1976) *Reflections on Language*. London: Temple Smith in association with Fontana Books.

Chomsky, N. (1986) *Knowledge of Language: Its Nature, Origin, and Use.* New York: Praeger.

Christie, F., Gray, B., Gray, P., Macken, M., Martin, J.R. and Rothery, J. (1992) *Exploring Explanations: Teacher's Book (Levels 1–4)* (HBJ Language: A Resource for Meaning). Sydney: Harcourt, Brace, Jovanovich.

Clark, E.V. (1973) 'What's in a word? On the child's acquisition of semantics in his first language'. In T.E. Moore (ed.) *Cognitive Development and the Development of Language.* New York: Academic, 65–110.

Clark, E.V. (1975) 'Knowledge, context, and strategy in the acquisition of meaning'. In D. Plato (ed.) *Georgetown University Round Table on Languages and Linguistics, 1975.* Washington: Georgetown University Press.

Clark, E.V. (1978) 'Awareness of language: some evidence from what children say and do'. In A. Sinclair, R.J. Jarvella and W.J.M. Levelt (eds) *The Child's Conception of Language.* New York: Springer, 17–43.

Clark, E.V. (1991) 'Acquisitional principles in lexical development'. In S.A. Gelman and J.P. Byrnes (eds) *Perspectives on Language and Thought: Interrelations in Development.* Cambridge: Cambridge University Press, 31–71.

Cloran, C. (1989) 'Learning through language'. In R. Hasan and J.R. Martin (eds) *Language Development: Learning Language, Learning Culture. Meaning and Choice in Language: Studies in Honour of Michael Halliday* (Advances in Discourse Processes 27). Norwood, NJ: Ablex, 111–51.

Cloran, C. (1999) 'Instruction at home and at school'. In F. Christie (ed.) *Pedagogy and the Shaping of Consciousness.* London: Cassell, 31–65.

Cohen, D. (1983) *Piaget: Critique and Reassessment.* London: Croom Helm.

Condon, W. (1974) 'Speech makes babies move'. *New Scientist* 62, 624–7.

Cook, V.J. and Newson, M. (1996) *Chomsky's Universal Grammar: An Introduction.* 2nd edn. Oxford: Blackwell.

Cope, W. and Kalantzis, M. (eds) (1993) *The Powers of Literacy: A Genre Approach to Teaching Literacy.* London: Falmer (Critical Perspectives on Literacy and Education); Pittsburgh: University of Pittsburgh Press (Pittsburgh Series in Composition, Literacy and Culture).

Crain, S. (1993) 'Language acquisition in the absence of experience'. In P. Bloom (ed.) *Language Acquisition: Core Readings.* Cambridge, MA: MIT Press, 364–409. Originally published in *Behavioural and Brain Sciences* 14.

Cross, T. (1977) 'Mothers' speech adjustments: the contribution of selected child listener variables'. In C. Snow and C.A. Ferguson (eds) *Talking to Children: Language Input and Acquisition.* Cambridge: Cambridge University Press, 151–88.

Cross, T. (1978) 'Mothers' speech and its association with rate of linguistic development in young children'. In N. Waterson and C. Snow (eds) *The Development of Communication.* Chichester: Wiley, 199–216.

Danes, F. (ed.) (1974) *Papers on Functional Sentence Perspective.* Prague: Academia.

Day, J.D., French, L.A. and Hall, L.K. (1985) 'Social influences on cognitive development'. In D.L. Forrest-Pressley, G.E. MacKinnon and T.G. Waller (eds) *Metacognition, Cognition and Human Performance,* vol. 1: *Theoretical Perspectives.* New York: Academic Press, 33–56.

Demopoulos, W. and Marras, A. (eds) (1986) *Language Learning and Concept Acquisition: Foundational Issues.* Norwood, NJ: Ablex.

Dickson, W.P. (ed.) (1981) *Children's Oral Communication Skills.* New York: Academic Press.

Dijk, T.A. van (1977) *Text and Context: Explorations in the Semantics and Pragmatics of*

*Discourse.* London: Longman.

Dockrell, J. and Campbell, R. (1986) 'Lexical acquisition strategies in the preschool child'. In S.A. Kuczaj and M.D. Barrett (eds) *The Development of Word Meaning: Progress in Cognitive Development Research.* New York: Springer, 121–54.

Donaldson, Margaret (1978) *Children's Minds.* London: Fontana.

Donaldson, Morag L. (1986) *Children's Explanations: A Psycholinguistic Study.* Cambridge: Cambridge University Press.

Dore, J. (1975) 'Holophrases, speech acts and language universals'. *Journal of Child Language* 2, 21–40.

Dore, J. (1978) 'Conditions for the acquisition of speech acts'. In I. Markova (ed.) *The Social Context of Language.* Chichester: Wiley, 87–111.

Dore, J., Franklin, M., Miller, R. and Ramer, A. (1976) 'Transitional phenomena in early language acquisition'. *Journal of Child Language* 3, 13–28.

Dromi, E. (1987) *Early Lexical Development.* Cambridge: Cambridge University Press.

Dromi, E. (ed.) (1993a) *Language and Cognition: A Developmental Perspective* (Human Development, vol. 5). Norwood, NJ: Ablex.

Dromi, E. (1993b) 'The mysteries of early lexical development: underlying cognitive and linguistic processes in meaning acquisition'. In *Language and Cognition: A Developmental Perspective* (Human Development, vol. 5). Norwood, NJ: Ablex, 32–60.

Edelman, G.M. (1992) *Bright Air, Brilliant Fire: On the Matter of the Mind.* New York: Basic Books.

Eggins, S., Wignell, P. and Martin, J.R. (1987) *Writing Project Report* (Working Papers in Linguistics, no. 5). Sydney: Linguistics Department, University of Sydney.

Ellis, J.M. (1993) *Language, Thought and Logic.* Evanston, IL: Northwestern University Press.

Ervin, S. (1964) 'Imitation and structural change in children's language'. In E. Lenneberg (ed.) *New Directions in the Study of Language.* Cambridge, MA: MIT Press.

Ferguson, C.A. (1977) 'Baby talk as a simplified register'. In C.E. Snow and C.A. Ferguson (eds) *Talking to Children: Language Input and Acquisition.* Cambridge: Cambridge University Press, 219–35.

Field, T.M. and Fox, N. (eds) (1985) *Social Perception in Infants.* Norwood, NJ: Ablex.

Firth, J.R. (1957) *Papers in Linguistics 1934–1951.* London: Oxford University Press.

Foley, W.A. (1984) 'Nature versus nurture: the genesis of language: a review article'. *Comparative Studies in Society and History* 26, 335–44.

Foucault, M. (1972) *The Archaeology of Knowledge.* New York: Random House.

Foucault, M. (1978) *A History of Sexuality.* New York: Random House.

French, L.A. and Nelson, K. (1985) *Young Children's Knowledge of Relational Terms: Some Ifs, Ors, and Buts.* New York: Springer.

Furrow, D., Nelson, K. and Benedict, H. (1979) 'Mothers' speech to children and syntactic development: some simple relationships'. *Journal of Child Language* 6, 432–42.

Gallaway, C. and Richards, B.J. (eds) (1994) *Input and Interaction in Language Acquisition.* Cambridge: Cambridge University Press.

Garnica, O.K. (1977) 'Some prosodic and paralinguistic features of speech to young children'. In C.E. Snow and C.A. Ferguson (eds) *Talking to Children:*

*Language Input and Acquisition.* Cambridge: Cambridge University Press, 63–88.

Gelman, S.A. and Coley, J.D. (1991) 'Language and categorization: the acquisition of natural kind terms'. In S.A. Gelman and J.P. Byrnes (eds) *Perspectives on Language and Thought.* Cambridge: Cambridge University Press, 146–96.

Gleitman, L. (1986) 'Biological dispositions to learn language'. In W. Demopolous and A. Marras (eds) *Language Learning and Concept Acquisition.* Norwood, NJ: Ablex, 3–28. Reprinted in M.B. Franklin and S.S. Barten (eds) *Child Language: A Reader.* New York: Oxford University Press (1988), 158–75.

Gleitman, L.R., Gleitman, H. and Shipley, E.S. (1972) 'The emergence of the child as a grammarian'. *Cognition* 1, 137–64.

Goodman, M. (1984) 'Are creole structures innate?' *Behavioral and Brain Sciences* 7, 193–4.

Gopnik, A. and Meltzoff, A.N. (1986) 'Words, plans, things and locations: interactions between semantic and cognitive development in the one-word stage'. In S.A. Kuczaj and M.D. Barrett (eds) *The Development of Word Meaning: Progress in Cognitive Development Research.* New York: Springer, 199–219.

Gray, B. (1986) 'Creating a context for the negotiation of written text'. Keynote Address to the Twelfth Australian Reading Association Conference, Perth.

Greenfield, P.M. (1978) 'Structural parallels between language and action in development'. In A. Lock (ed.) *Action, Gesture and Symbol: The Emergence of Language.* London: Academic, 415–45.

Greenfield, P.M. and Smith, J.H. (1976) *The Structure of Communication in Early Language Development.* New York: Academic.

Hakes, D. T. (in collaboration with J.S. Evans and W.E. Tunmer) (1980) *The Development of Metalinguistic Abilities in Children.* Berlin: Springer.

Halford, G. (1982) *The Development of Thought.* Hillsdale, NJ: Erlbaum.

Halliday, M.A.K. (1975) *Learning How to Mean: Explorations in the Development of Language.* London: Arnold.

Halliday, M.A.K. (1978a) *Language as Social Semiotic: The Social Interpretation of Language and Meaning.* London: Arnold.

Halliday, M.A.K. (1978b) 'Meaning and the construction of reality in early childhood'. In H.L. Pick and E. Saltzman (eds) *Modes of Perceiving and Processing of Information.* Hillsdale, NJ: Erlbaum, 67–96.

Halliday, M.A.K. (1979a) 'One child's protolanguage'. In M. Bullowa (ed.) *Before Speech: The Beginning of Interpersonal Communication.* Cambridge: Cambridge University Press, 171–90.

Halliday, M.A.K. (1979b) 'The development of texture in child language'. In T. Myers (ed.) *The Development of Conversation and Discourse.* Edinburgh: Edinburgh University Press.

Halliday, M.A.K. (1980) 'Three aspects of children's language development: learning language, learning through language, learning about language'. In Y.M. Goodman, M.M. Haussler and D.S. Strickland (eds) *Oral and Written Language Development: Impact on Schools* (Proceedings from the 1979–1980 Impact conferences). International Reading Association and National Council of Teachers of English, 7–19.

Halliday, M.A.K. (1984a) 'Language as code and language as behaviour: a systemic-functional interpretation of the nature and ontogenesis of dialogue'. In R. Fawcett *et al.* (eds) *The Semiotics of Culture and Language*, vol. 1. London: Pinter, 3–35.

Halliday, M.A.K. (1984b) *Listening to Nigel: Conversations with a Very Small Child.*

Sydney: University of Sydney, mimeo.

Halliday, M.A.K. (1985) *Introduction to Functional Grammar.* London: Arnold.

Halliday, M.A.K. (1987) 'Language and the order of nature'. In N. Fabb, D. Attridge, A. Durant and C. MacCabe (eds) *The Linguistics of Writing.* Manchester: Manchester University Press, 135–54.

Halliday, M.A.K. (1988a) 'Language and socialisation: home and school'. In L. Gerot, J. Oldenburg and T. Van Leeuwen (eds) *Language and Socialisation: Home and School: Proceedings from the Working Conference on Language in Education, Macquarie University 17–21 November 1986*, 1–12.

Halliday, M.A.K. (1988b) 'Language and the enhancement of learning'. Paper presented at the Language in Learning Symposium held at Brisbane College of Advanced Education, Brisbane.

Halliday, M.A.K. (1989) *Spoken and Written Language.* London: Oxford University Press.

Halliday, M.A.K. (1991a) 'Linguistic perspectives on literacy: a systemic-functional approach'. In F. Christie (ed.) *Literacy in Social Processes: Papers from the Inaugural Australian Systemic Linguistics Conference, Held at Deakin University, Jan. 1990.* Darwin: Centre for Studies of Language in Education, Northern Territory University, 1–22.

Halliday, M.A.K. (1991b) 'The notion of "context" in language education'. In T. Le and M. McCausland (eds) *Language Education: Interaction and Development. Proceedings of the International Conference, Vietnam, 1991.* Launceston: University of Tasmania, 1–26.

Halliday, M.A.K. (1991c) 'The place of dialogue in children's construction of meaning'. In S. Stati, E. Weigand and F. Hundsnurscher (eds) *Dialoganalyse III: Referate der 3. Arbeitstagung, Bologna 1990* (Beitrage zur Dialogforschung, Bd 1). Tübingen: Niemeyer, 417–30.

Halliday, M.A.K. (1992) 'How do you mean?' In M. Davies and L. Ravelli (eds) *Advances in Systemic Linguistics: Recent Theory and Practice.* London: Pinter, 20–35.

Halliday, M.A.K. (1993a) 'The act of meaning'. In J.E. Alatis (ed.) *Language, Communication and Social Meaning. Proceedings of the 1992 Georgetown University Round Table Meeting on Linguistics and Language Study.* Washington, D.C.: Georgetown University Press, 7–21.

Halliday, M.A.K. (1993b) 'Towards a language-based theory of learning'. *Linguistics and Education* 5: 93–116.

Halliday, M.A.K. (1994) *An Introduction to Functional Grammar*, 2nd edn. London: Edward Arnold.

Halliday, M.A.K. (1996) 'Literacy and linguistics: a functional perspective'. In R. Hasan and G. Williams (eds) *Literacy in Society.* London: Longman, 339–76.

Halliday, M.A.K. (forthcoming) *The Language of Learning.*

Halliday, M.A.K. and Hasan, R. (1976) *Cohesion in English.* London: Longman.

Halliday, M.A.K. and Hasan, R. (1989) *Language, Context and Text: Aspects of Language in a Social-Semiotic Perspective.* London: Oxford University Press.

Halliday, M.A.K. and Martin, J.R. (1993) *Writing Science: Literacy and Discursive Power.* London: Falmer Press.

Harre, R. and Gillett, G. (1994) *The Discursive Mind.* Thousand Oaks, CA: Sage.

Hasan, R. (1985) 'Meaning, context and text – fifty years after Malinowski'. In J.D. Benson and W.S. Greaves (eds) *Systemic Perspectives on Discourse, vol. 1: Selected Theoretical Papers from the 9th International Systemic Workshop.* Norwood, NJ: Ablex, 16–49.

Hasan, R. (1988) 'Language in the processes of socialisation: home and school'. In

L. Gerot, J. Oldenburg and T. Van Leeuwen (eds) *Language and Socialisation: Home and School: Proceedings from the Working Conference on Language in Education, Macquarie University 17–21 November 1986*, 36–96.

Hasan, R. (1989) 'Semantic variation and sociolinguistics'. *Australian Journal of Linguistics* 9; 221–76.

Hasan, R. (1991) 'Questions as a mode of learning in everyday talk'. In T. Le and M. McCausland (eds) *Language Education: Interaction and Development.* Launceston: University of Tasmania, 70–119.

Hasan, R. (1992) 'Rationality in everyday talk: from process to system'. In J. Svartik (ed.) *Directions in Corpus Linguistics: Proceedings of Nobel Symposium 82, Stockholm 4–8 August 1991.* Berlin: De Gruyter, 257–307.

Hasan, R. (1995) 'On social conditions for semiotic mediation: the genesis of mind in society'. In A.R. Sadovnik (ed.) *Knowledge and Pedagogy: The Sociology of Basil Bernstein.* NJ: Ablex, 171–96.

Hasan, R. (1999) 'Society, language and the mind'. In F. Christie (ed.) *Pedagogy and the Shaping of Consciousness.* London: Cassell, 10–30.

Hasan, R. and Cloran, C. (1990) 'A sociolinguistic interpretation of everyday talk between mothers and children'. In M.A.K. Halliday, J. Gibbons and H. Nicholas (eds) *Learning, Keeping and Using Language, vol. 1: Selected Papers from the 8th World Congress of Applied Linguistics, 1987.* Amsterdam: Benjamins, 67–100.

Heath, S.B. (1983) *Ways with Words.* Cambridge: Cambridge University Press.

Hickmann, M. (ed.) (1987) *Social and Functional Approaches to Language and Thought.* New York: Academic.

Hirst, P. H. (1974) 'Language and thought'. In *Knowledge and the Curriculum: A Collection of Philosophical Papers.* London: Routledge and Kegan Paul.

Hjelmslev, L. (1961) *Prolegomena to a Theory of Language.* Madison: University of Wisconsin Press.

Hood, L. and Bloom, L. (1991) 'What, when, and how about why: a longitudinal study of early expressions of causality'. In L. Bloom *et al., Language Development from Two to Three.* New York: Cambridge University Press, 335–73. First published as *Monograph of the Society for Research in Child Development*, serial no. 181, vol. 44. Chicago: Society for Research in Child Development (1979).

Hood, L., Fiess, K. and Aron, J. (1982) 'Growing up explained: Vygotskians look at the language of causality'. In C.J. Brainerd and M. Pressley (eds) *Verbal Processes in Children.* New York: Springer, 265–85.

Hornstein, N. and Lightfoot, D. (eds) (1981) *Explanation in Linguistics: The Logical Problem of Language Acquisition.* New York: Longman.

Howe, C. (1981) *Acquiring Language in a Conversational Context.* New York: Academic Press.

Hyams, N. (1986) *Language Acquisition and the Theory of Parameters.* Dordrecht: Reidel.

Hymes, D. (1971) 'Competence and performance in linguistic theory'. In R. Huxley and E. Ingram (eds) *Language Acquisition: Models and Methods.* London: Academic, 3–28.

Ingram, D. (1989) *First Language Acquisition: Method, Description, and Explanation.* Cambridge: Cambridge University Press.

Inhelder, B. and Piaget, J. (1964) *The Early Growth of Logic in the Child.* London: Routledge and Kegan Paul.

Johnston, J.R. (1985) 'Cognitive prerequisites: the evidence from children learning English'. In D.I. Slobin (ed.) *The Crosslinguistic Study of Language*

*Acquisition*, vol. 2: *Theoretical Issues*. Hillsdale, NJ: Erlbaum, 961–1004.

Kaye, K. and Charney, R. (1980) 'How mothers maintain "dialogue" with two-year-olds'. In D. Olson (ed.) *The Social Foundations of Language and Thought*. New York: Norton, 211–30.

Labov, W. (1969) *Language in the Inner City: Studies in the Black English Vernacular*. Philadelphia: University of Pennsylvania Press.

Lee, B. (1987) 'Recontextualizing Vygotsky'. In M. Hickmann (ed.) *Social and Functional Approaches to Language and Thought*. New York: Academic Press, 87–104.

Lehr, F. (1985) 'ERIC/RCS report: Instructional scaffolding'. *Language Arts* 62, 667–72.

Lemke, J.L. (1990) *Talking Science: Language, Learning, and Values*. Norwood, NJ: Ablex.

Leopold, W. (1949) *Speech Development of a Bilingual Child*, vol. 3: *Grammar and General Problems in the First Two Years*; vol. 4: *Diary from Age Two*. Evanston, IL: Northwestern University Press.

Levinson, S.C. (1983) *Pragmatics*. Cambridge: Cambridge University Press.

Lieven, E.V.M. (1978) 'Conversations between mothers and young children: individual differences and their possible implications for the study of language learning'. In N. Waterson and C. Snow (eds) *The Development of Communication*. New York: Wiley.

Lightfoot, D. (1991) *How to Set Parameters: Arguments from Language Change*. Cambridge, MA: MIT Press.

Limber, J. (1973) 'The genesis of complex sentences'. In T.E. Moore (ed.) *Cognitive Development and the Acquisition of Language*. New York: Academic, 169–85.

Lock, A. (ed.) (1978) *Action, Gesture and Symbol: The Emergence of Language*. London: Academic Press.

Lock, A. (1980) *The Guided Reinvention of Language*. London: Academic Press.

Lyons, J. (1977) *Semantic Theory*. Cambridge: Cambridge University Press.

McCabe, A., Evely, S., Abramovitch, R., Corter, C. and Pepler, D. (1983) 'Conditional statements in young children's spontaneous speech'. *Journal of Child Language* 10, 253–8.

McGarrigle, J. and Donaldson, M. (1974) 'Conservation accidents'. *Cognition* 3, 341–50.

Macken, M. (1989) *A Genre Based Approach to Teaching Writing Years 3–6*, 4 vols. Sydney: LERN, NSW Dept of Education.

Macken-Horarik, M. (1996) 'Literacy and learning across the curriculum: towards a model of register for secondary school teachers'. In R. Hasan and G. Williams (eds) *Literacy in Society*. London: Longman, 232–78.

Macnamara, J. (1982) *Names for Things: A Study of Human Learning*. Cambridge, MA: MIT Press.

McTear, Michael (1985) *Children's Conversation*. Oxford: Blackwell.

Malinowski, Bronislaw (1923) 'The problem of meaning in primitive languages'. Supplement I to C.K. Ogden and I.A. Richards, *The Meaning of Meaning*. London: Kegan Paul, Trench, Trubner, 451–510.

Malinowski, B. (1935) *Coral Gardens and Their Magic*, vol. 2. London: Allen and Unwin.

Markman, E. (1989) *Categorisation and Naming in Children: Problems of Induction*. Cambridge, MA: MIT Press.

Martin, J.R. (1985) 'Process and text: two aspects of semiosis'. In J.D. Benson and

W.S. Greaves (eds) *Systemic Perspectives on Discourse*, vol. 1: *Selected Theoretical Papers from the 9th International Systemic Workshop*. Norwood, NJ: Ablex, 248–74.

Martin, J.R. (1987) 'Language turned back on itself: a stratal conspiracy in English'. Paper presented at the 14th International Systemic Workshop, Sydney.

Martin, J.R. (1992a) *English Text: System and Structure*. Amsterdam: Benjamins.

Martin, J.R. (1992b) 'Macroproposals: meaning by degree'. In W.C. Mann and S.A. Thompson (eds) *Discourse Description: Diverse Linguistic Analyses of a Fundraising Text*. Amsterdam: Benjamins, 359–95.

Martin, J.R. and Matthiessen, C. (1991) 'Systemic typology and topology'. In F. Christie (ed.) *Literacy in Social Processes: Papers from the Inaugural Australian Systemic Linguistics Conference held at Deakin University, January 1990*. Darwin: Centre for Studies of Language in Education, 345–83.

Martin, J.R. and Rothery, J. (1981) 'Writing Project Report 1981', Working Papers in Linguistics no. 2, Linguistics Dept, University of Sydney.

Matthiessen, C. (1991) 'Language on language'. *Social Semiotics* vol. 1, no. 2, 69–111.

Menn, L. (1978) *Pattern, Control and Contrast in Beginning Speech*. Bloomington: Indiana University Linguistics Club.

Merriman, W.E. (1986) 'How children learn the reference of concrete nouns: a critique of current hypotheses'. In S.A. Kuczaj and M.D. Barrett (eds) *The Development of Word Meaning: Progress in Cognitive Development Research*. New York: Springer, 1–38.

Messer, D.J. (1994) *The Development of Communication: From Social Interaction to Language*. Chichester: Wiley.

Michaels, S. (1981) '"Sharing time": children's narrative styles and differential access to literacy'. *Language in Society* 10, 423–42.

Morgan, J.L. (1986) *From Simple Input to Complex Grammar*. Cambridge, MA: MIT Press.

Mundy, P., Kasari, C. and Sigman, M. (1992) 'Nonverbal communication, affective sharing and intersubjectivity'. *Infant Behavior and Development* 15, 377–81.

Murray, L. and Trevarthen, C. (1985) 'Emotional regulation of interactions between two-month-olds and their mothers'. In T.M. Field and N.A. Fox (eds) *Social Perception in Infants*. NJ: Ablex, 177–97.

Nelson, K. (1973) *Structure and Strategy in Learning How to Talk* (Monograph no. 149 of the Society for Research in Child Development). Chicago: Society for Research in Child Development.

Nelson, K. (1974) 'Concept, word and sentence: interrelations in acquisition and development'. *Psychological Review* 81, 267–85.

Nelson, K. (1978) 'How young children represent knowledge of their world in and out of language'. In R.S. Siegler (ed.) *Children's Thinking: What Develops?* Hillsdale, NJ: Erlbaum, 255–73.

Nelson, K. (1979) 'Explorations in the development of a functional semantic system'. In W.A. Collins (ed.) *Children's Language and Communication*. Hillsdale, NJ: Erlbaum, 47–81.

Nelson, K. (1983) 'The conceptual basis for language'. In T.B. Seiler and W. Wannenmacher (eds) *Concept Development and the Development of Word Meaning*. Berlin: Springer, 173–88.

Nelson, K. (1991a) 'Concept development in the perspective of the recent history of developmental psychology'. In F.S. Kessel, M.H. Bornstein and J.S. Arnold (eds) *Contemporary Constructions of the Child: Essays in Honor of William Kessen*.

Hillsdale, NJ: Erlbaum, 93–109.

Nelson, K. (1991b) 'The matter of time: interdependencies between language and thought in development'. In S.A. Gelman and J.P. Byrnes (eds) *Perspectives on Language and Thought: Interrelations in Development.* Cambridge: Cambridge University Press, 278–318.

Nelson, K. and Gruendel, J.M. (1979) 'At morning it's lunchtime: a scriptal view of children's dialogues'. *Discourse Processes*, 2, 73–94.

Nelson, K. and Lucariello, J. (1985) 'The development of meaning in first words'. In M. Barrett (ed.) *Children's Single Word Speech.* New York: Wiley, 59–86.

Nelson, K. and Seidman, S. (1984) 'Playing with scripts'. In I. Bretherton (ed.) *Symbolic Play: The Development of Social Understanding.* Orlando: Academic Press, 45–71.

Nelson, K.E., Carskaddon, G. and Bonvillian, J. (1973) 'Syntax acquisition: impact of experimental variation in adult verbal interaction with the child'. *Child Development* 44, 497–504.

Newport, E.L., Gleitman, H. and Gleitman, L.R. (1977) 'Mother, I'd rather do it myself: some effects and non-effects of maternal speech style'. In C.E. Snow and C.A. Ferguson (eds) *Talking to Children: Language Input and Acquisition.* Cambridge: Cambridge University Press, 109–49.

Newson, J. (1978) 'Dialogue and development'. In A. Lock (ed.) *Action, Gesture and Symbol.* London: Academic Press, 31–42.

Ninio, A. and Bruner, J.S. (1978) 'The achievements and antecedents of labelling'. *Journal of Child Language* 5, 1–15.

Ochs, E. (1990) 'Indexicality and socialisation'. In J.W. Stigler, R.A. Shweder and G. Herdt (eds) *Cultural Psychology: Essays on Comparative Human Development.* New York: Cambridge University Press, 287–308.

Ochs, E. and Schieffelin, B.B. (1984) 'Language acquisition and socialization: three developmental stories and their implications'. In R.A. Shweder and R.A. LeVine (eds) *Culture Theory: Essays on Mind, Self, and Emotion.* Cambridge: Cambridge University Press, 276–320.

Ochs Keenan, E. and Schieffelin, B.B. (1983) 'Topic as a discourse notion: a study of topic in the conversations of children and adults'. In *Acquiring Conversational Competence.* London: Routledge and Kegan Paul, 66–113.

Oldenburg, J. (1987) *From Child Tongue to Mother Tongue: A Case Study of Language Development in the First Two-and-a-Half Years.* PhD thesis, University of Sydney.

Oldenburg, J. (1990) 'Learning the language and learning through language in early childhood'. In M.A.K. Halliday, J. Gibbons and H. Nicholas (eds) *Learning, Keeping and Using Language: Selected Papers from the Eighth World Congress of Applied Linguistics.* Amsterdam: Benjamins, 27–38.

Painter, C. (1984) *Into the Mother Tongue.* London: Pinter.

Painter, C. (1986) 'The role of interaction in learning to speak and learning to write'. In C. Painter and J.R. Martin (eds) *Writing to mean: teaching genres across the curriculum.* Applied Linguistics Association of Australia (Occasional papers no. 9), 62–97.

Painter, C. (1989) 'Learning language: a functional view of language development'. In R. Hasan and J.R. Martin (eds) *Language Development: Learning Language, Learning Culture. Meaning and Choice in Language: Studies in Honour of Michael Halliday* (Advances in Discourse Processes 27). Norwood, NJ: Ablex, 18–65.

Painter, C. (1990) *Learning the Mother Tongue,* 2nd edn. Geelong: Deakin University

Press.

Peters, A. (1983) *The Units of Language Acquisition*. Cambridge: Cambridge University Press.

Phillips, J. (1985) *The Development of Comparisons and Contrasts in Young Children's Language*. Master's Honours thesis, University of Sydney.

Piaget, J. (1955) *Language and Thought of the Child*. Cleveland: World Publishing.

Piaget, J. (1972) 'Problems of equilibration'. In C. Nodine, J. Gallagher and R. Humphrey (eds) *Piaget and Inhelder on Equilibration*. Philadelphia: Jean Piaget Society.

Piaget, J. (1976) *Judgement and Reasoning in the Child*, M. Warden (trans). Totowa, NJ: Littlefield Adams.

Piaget, J. (1977) *The Essential Piaget*, H.E. Gruber and J.J. Vonèche (eds). London: Routledge and Kegan Paul.

Piaget, J. and Inhelder, B. (1964) *The Early Growth of Logic in the Child: Classification and Seriation*, E.A. Lunzer and D. Papert (trans.). London: Routledge and Kegan Paul.

Piatelli-Palmerini, M. (ed.) (1980) *Language and Learning: The Debate between Jean Piaget and Noam Chomsky*. London: Routledge and Kegan Paul.

Pine, J.M. (1994) 'The language of primary caregivers'. In C. Gallaway and B.I. Richards (eds) *Input and Interaction in Language Acquisition*. Cambridge: Cambridge University Press, 15–37.

Pinker, S. (1984) *Language Learnability and Language Development*. Cambridge, MA: Harvard University Press.

Pinker, S. (1986) 'Productivity and conservatism in language acquisition'. In W. Demopoulous and A. Marras (eds), *Language Learning and Concept Acquisition: Foundational Issues*. Norwood, NJ: Ablex, 54–79.

Poynton, C. (1989) *Language and Gender: Making the Difference*. London: Oxford University Press.

Pratt, C., Tunmer, W.E. and Bowey, J.A. (1984) 'Children's capacity to correct grammatical violations in sentences'. *Journal of Child Language* 11, 129–41.

Qiu, S. (1985) *Early Language Development in Chinese Children*. Master's thesis, Dept of Linguistics, University of Sydney.

Reddy, M.J. (1979) 'The conduit metaphor: a case of frame conflict in our language about language'. In A. Ortony (ed.) *Metaphor and Thought*. Cambridge: Cambridge University Press, 284–324.

Rescorla, L. (1980) 'Overextension in early language development'. *Journal of Child Language* 7, 321–35.

Rogoff, B. (1990) *Apprenticeship in Thinking: Cognitive Development in Social Context*. New York: Oxford University Press.

Rommetveit, R. (1978) 'On the relationship between children's mastery of Piagetian cognitive operations and their semantic competence'. In R.N. Campbell and P.T. Smith (eds) *Recent Advances in the Psychology of Language*. New York: Plenum, 25–36.

Rommetveit, R. (1985) 'Language acquisition as increasing linguistic structuring of experience and symbolic behaviour control'. In J.V. Wertsch (ed.) *Culture, Communication and Cognition: Vygotskian Perspectives*. New York: Cambridge University Press, 183–203.

Rosch, E.H. (1973) 'On the internal structure of perceptual and semantic categories'. In T.E. Moore (ed.) *Cognitive Development and the Acquisition of Language*. New York: Academic, 111–44.

Rosch, E. (1977) 'Human categorization'. In N. Warren (ed.) *Studies in Cross-Cultural Psychology*. London: Academic Press, 3–49.

Rosch, E., Mervis, C.B., Gray, W., Johnson, D. and Boyes-Braem, P. (1976) 'Basic objects in natural categories'. *Cognitive Psychology* 8, 382–439.

Rothery, J. (1989) 'Learning about language'. In R. Hasan and J.R. Martin (eds) *Language Development: Learning Language, Learning Culture. Meaning and Choice in Language: Studies in Honour of Michael Halliday* (Advances in Discourse Processes 27). Norwood, NJ: Ablex, 199–256.

Rothery, J. (1993) *Exploring Literacy in School English*. Erskineville, NSW: Metropolitan East Disadvantaged Schools Program.

Rothery, J. (1996) 'Making changes: developing an educational linguistics'. In R. Hasan and G. Williams (eds) *Literacy in Society*. London: Longman 86–123.

Sachs, J.S., Brown, R. and Salerno, R. (1976) 'Adults' speech to children'. In W. Von Raffler-Engel and Y. Lebrun (eds) *Baby Talk and Infant Speech*. Lisse, Netherlands: Swets and Zeitlinger, 240–5.

Saleemi, A. P. (1992) *Universal Grammar and Language Learnability*. Cambridge: Cambridge University Press.

Samarin, W. (1984) 'Socioprogrammed linguistics'. *Behavioral and Brain Sciences* 7, 206–7.

Samuel, J. and Bryant, P.E. (1984) 'Asking only one question in the conservation experiment'. *Journal of Child Psychology and Psychiatry* 25, 315–18.

Sapir, E. (1949) *Language: An Introduction to the Study of Speech*. New York: Harcourt Brace.

Saussure, F. de (1978) *Course in General Linguistics*, C. Bally and S. Sechehaye (eds), in collaboration with A. Riedlinger. Glasgow: Fontana/Collins.

Scaife, M. and Bruner, J.S. (1975) 'The capacity for joint visual attention in the infant'. *Nature* 253, 5789, 265–6.

Schachter, F.F. *et al.* (1979) *Everyday Mother Talk to Toddlers: Early Intervention*. New York: Academic.

Schaffer, H.R. (ed.) (1977) *Studies in Mother–Infant Interaction*. New York: Academic Press.

Schank, R.C. and Abelson, R.P. (1977) *Scripts, Plans, Goals, and Understanding*. Hillsdale, NJ: Lawrence Erlbaum.

Schieffelin, B.B. and Ochs, E. (1986) *Language Socialization across Cultures*. Cambridge: Cambridge University Press.

Schlesinger, I.M. (1977) 'The role of cognitive development and linguistic input in language acquisition'. *Journal of Child Language* 4, 153–69.

Schwebel, M. and Raph, J. (1974) 'Before and beyond the Three R's'. In M. Schwebel and J. Raph (eds) *Piaget in the Classroom*. London: Routledge and Kegan Paul, 3–31.

Scollon, R. (1976) *Conversations with a One Year Old*. Honolulu: University of Hawaii Press.

Scollon, R. (1979) 'A real early stage: an unzippered condensation of a dissertation on child language'. In E. Ochs and B.B. Schieffelin (eds) *Developmental Pragmatics*. New York: Academic Press, 215–27.

Scollon, R. and Scollon, S. (1981) *Narrative, Literacy and Face in Interethnic Communication*. Norwood, NJ: Ablex.

Searle, J.R. (1969) *Speech Acts: An Essay in the Philosophy of Language*. Cambridge: Cambridge University Press.

Seuren, P. (1984) 'The bioprogram hypothesis: facts and fancy'. *Behavioral and*

*Brain Sciences* 7, 208–9.

Shatz, M., Wellman, H.M. and Silber, S. (1983) 'The acquisition of mental verbs: a systematic investigation of the first reference to mental state'. *Cognition* 14, 301–21.

Shotter, J. (1978) 'The cultural context of communication studies'. In A. Lock (ed.) *Action, Gesture and Symbol.* London: Academic Press, 43–78.

Shweder, R.A. (1990) 'Cultural psychology: What is it?' In J.W. Stigler, R.A. Shweder and G. Herdt (eds) *Cultural Psychology: Essays on Comparative Human Development.* Cambridge: Cambridge University Press, 1–43.

Siegel, L.S. (1978) 'The relationship of language and thought in the preoperational child: a reconsideration of nonverbal alternatives to Piagetian tasks'. In L.S. Siegel and C.J. Brainerd (eds) *Alternatives to Piaget: Critical Essays on the Theory.* New York: Academic Press, 43–67.

Sinclair, A., Jarvella, R.J. and Levelt, W.J.M. (eds) (1978) *The Child's Conception of Language*. New York: Springer.

Sinclair, H. (1974) 'Recent Piagetian research in learning studies'. In M. Schwebel and J. Raph (eds) *Piaget in the Classroom.* London: Routledge and Kegan Paul, 57–72.

Sinclair de Zwart, H.S. (1967) *Acquisition du langage et développement de la pensée: sous-systèmes linguistiques et opérations concrètes.* Paris: Dunod.

Skinner, B.F. (1957) *Verbal Behavior.* New York: Appleton-Century-Crofts.

Slobin, D.I. (1973) 'Cognitive prerequisites for the development of grammar'. In C.A. Ferguson and D.I. Slobin (eds) *Studies of Child Language Development.* New York: Holt, Rinehart and Winston, 175–208.

Slobin, D. I. (1982) 'Universal and particular in the acquisition of language'. In L.R. Gleitman and E. Wanner (eds) *Language Acquisition: The State of the Art.* New York: Cambridge University Press, 128–70.

Smedslund, J. (1964) *Concrete Reasoning: A Study of Intellectual Development.* (Monograph no. 29 of the Society for Research in Child Development, Serial no. 93). Chicago: Society for Research in Child Development.

Snow, C.E. (1972) 'Mothers' speech to children learning language'. *Child Development* 43, 549–65.

Snow, C.E. (1977) 'Mothers' speech research: from input to interaction'. In C.E. Snow and C.A. Ferguson (eds) *Talking to Children: Language Input and Acquisition.* Cambridge: Cambridge University Press, 31–49.

Snow, C.E. (1979)'The role of social interaction in language acquisition'. In W.A. Collins (ed.) *Children's Language and Communication.* Hillsdale, NJ: Erlsbaum, 157–82.

Sugarman, S. (1987) *Piaget's Construction of the Child's Reality.* Cambridge: Cambridge University Press.

Sugarman, S. (1993) 'Piaget on the origins of mind: a problem in accounting for the development of mental capacities'. In E. Dromi (ed.) *Language and Cognition: A Developmental Perspective.* Norwood, NJ: Ablex (*Human Development*, vol. 5), 18–31.

Tizard, B. and Hughes, M. (1984) *Young Children Learning.* London: Fontana.

Torr, J. (1998) *From Child Tongue to Mother Tongue: Language Development in the First Two and a Half Years. Monographs in Systemic Linguistics.* Nottingham: Nottingham University.

Trevarthen, C. (1974) 'Conversations with a two-month-old'. *New Scientist* 62, 230–4.

Trevarthen, C. (1975) 'Early attempts at speech'. In R. Lewin (ed.) *Child Alive.* London: Temple-Smith, 62–80.

Trevarthen, C. (1980) 'The foundations of intersubjectivity: development of interpersonal and cooperative understanding in infants'. In D. Olson (ed.) *The Social Foundations of Language and Thought.* New York: Norton, 316–42.

Trevarthen, C. (1987) 'Sharing makes sense'. In R. Steele and T. Threadgold (eds) *Language Topics: Essays in Honour of Michael Halliday,* vol. 1. Amsterdam: Benjamins, 177–99.

Trevarthen, C. and Hubley, P. (1978) 'Secondary intersubjectivity: confidence, confiding and acts of meaning in the first year'. In A. Lock (ed.) *Action, Gesture and Symbol.* London: Academic Press, 183–229.

Tversky, B. (1990) 'Where taxonomies and partonomies meet'. In S.L. Tsohatzidis (ed.) *Meanings and Prototypes.* New York: Routledge.

Urwin, C. (1984) 'Power relations and the emergence of language'. In J. Henriques *et al., Changing the Subject: Psychology, Social Regulation and Subjectivity.* London: Methuen, 264–322.

Vygotsky, L.S. (1962) *Thought and Language,* E. Hanfmann and G. Vakar (eds and trs). New York: Wiley.

Vygotsky, L.S. (1978) *Mind in Society: The Development of Higher Psychological Processes,* M. Cole, V. John-Steiner, S. Scribner and E. Souberman (eds). Cambridge, MA: Harvard University Press.

Vygotsky, L.S. (1981a) 'The development of higher forms of attention in childhood'. In J.V. Wertsch (tr. and ed.) *The Concept of Activity in Soviet Psychology.* New York: M.E. Sharpe, 189–240.

Vygotsky, L.S. (1981b) 'The genesis of higher mental functions'. In J.V. Wertsch (tr. and ed.) *The Concept of Activity in Soviet Psychology.* New York: M.E. Sharpe.

Vygotsky, L.S. (1987) *Collected Works,* vol. 1, *Problems of General Psychology,* N. Minick (tr.), R.W. Rieber and A.S. Carton (eds). New York: Plenum.

Walkerdine, V. (1984) 'Developmental psychology and the child-centred pedagogy: the insertion of Piaget into early education'. In J. Henriques *et al., Changing the Subject: Psychology, Social Regulation and Subjectivity.* London: Methuen, 153–202.

Walkerdine, V. and Lucey, H. (1989) *Democracy in the Kitchen: Regulating Mothers and Socialising Daughters.* London: Virago.

Waterson, N. and Snow, C. (eds) (1978) *The Development of Communication.* New York: Wiley.

Waxman, S.R. (1990) 'Linguistic biases and conceptual hierarchies'. *Cognitive Development* 5, 123–50.

Wellman, H.M. and Bartsch, K. (1988) 'Young children's reasoning about beliefs'. *Cognition* 30, 239–77.

Wells, C.G. (1980) 'Adjustments in adult-child conversation: some effects of interaction'. In H. Giles, W.P. Robinson and P.M. Sith (eds) *Language: Social Psychological Perspectives.* Oxford: Pergamon, 41–8.

Wells, C.G. and Robinson, W.P. (1982) 'The role of adult speech in language development'. In C. Fraser and K.R. Scherer (eds) *Advances in the Social Psychology of Language.* Cambridge: Cambridge University Press.

Wells, G. (1986) *The Meaning Makers: Children Learning Language and Using Language to Learn.* London: Hodder and Stoughton.

Wells, G. and Gutfreund, M. (1987) 'The development of conversation'. In G. Steele and T. Threadgold (eds) *Language Topics: Essays in Honour of Michael*

*Halliday*, vol. 1. Amsterdam: Benjamins, 201–25.

Wertsch, J.V. (ed.) (1984) *Culture, Communication and Cognition: Vygotskian Perspectives*. Cambridge: Cambridge University Press.

Wertsch, J.V. (1991) *Voices of the Mind: A Sociocultural Approach to Mediated Action*. Cambridge, MA: Harvard University Press.

Wexler, K. (1982) 'A principle theory for language acquisition'. In E. Wanner and L.R. Gleitman (eds) *Language Acquisition: The State of the Art*. Cambridge: Cambridge University Press, 288–315.

Whitehurst, G. and Vasta, R. (1975) 'Is language acquired through imitation?' *Journal of Psycholinguistic Research* 4, 37–59.

Whorf, B.L. (1956) *Language, Thought and Reality: Selected Essays*, J.B. Carroll (ed.). Cambridge, MA: MIT Press.

Williams, E. (1987) 'Introduction'. In T. Roeper and E. Williams (eds) *Parameter Setting*. Dordrecht: Reidel, vii–xix.

Williams, G. (1995) *Joint Book-Reading and Literacy Pedagogy: A Socio-Semantic Examination*, vol. 1, CORE 19(3) Fiche 2 B01–Fiche 6 B01.

Williams, G. (1996) *Joint Book-Reading and Literacy Pedagogy: A Socio-Semantic Examination*, vol. 2, CORE 20(1) Fiche 3 B01–Fiche 8 E10.

Wood, D. (1988) *How Children Think and Learn: The Social Contexts of Cognitive Development*. Oxford: Blackwell.

# Index